Eugene Field,

Collection children's poetry

In this book:
Love-Songs of Childhood
A Little Book of Western Verse
Songs and Other Verse
Second Book of Verse
Hoosier Lyrics
Christmas Tales and Christmas Verse
The Mouse and The Moonbeam

Eugene Field, Sr. (1850 – 1895) was an American writer, best known for his children's poetry and humorous essays. Field first started publishing poetry in 1879, when his poem "Christmas Treasures" appeared in A Little Book of Western Verse. Over a dozen volumes of poetry followed and he became well known for his light-hearted poems for children, among the most famous of which are "Wynken, Blynken, and Nod" and "The Duel" (which is perhaps better known as "The Gingham Dog and the Calico Cat"). Field also published a number of short stories, including "The Holy Cross" and "Daniel and the Devil."

In this book:
Love-Songs of Childhood…………………..Pag. 3
A Little Book of Western Verse…………..Pag. 25
Songs and Other Verse……………………Pag. 65
Second Book of Verse……………………..Pag. 106
Hoosier Lyrics……………………………..Pag. 160
Christmas Tales and Christmas Verse….Pag. 196
The Mouse and The Moonbeam………....Pag. 210

Love-Songs of Childhood

THE ROCK-A-BY LADY

The Rock-a-By Lady from Hushaby
  street
Comes stealing; comes creeping;
The poppies they hang from her
  head to her feet,
And each hath a dream that is tiny
  and fleet—
She bringeth her poppies to you, my
  sweet,
  When she findeth you sleeping!

There is one little dream of a
  beautiful drum—
  "Rub-a-dub!" it goeth;
There is one little dream of a big
  sugar-plum,
And lo! thick and fast the other
  dreams come
Of popguns that bang, and tin tops
  that hum,
  And a trumpet that bloweth!

And dollies peep out of those wee
  little dreams
  With laughter and singing;
And boats go a-floating on silvery
  streams,
And the stars peek-a-boo with their
  own misty gleams,
And up, up, and up, where the
  Mother Moon beams,
  The fairies go winging!

Would you dream all these dreams
  that are tiny and fleet?
  They'll come to you sleeping;
So shut the two eyes that are weary,
  my sweet,
For the Rock-a-By Lady from
  Hushaby street,
With poppies that hang from her
  head to her feet,
  Comes stealing; comes creeping.

"BOOH!"

On afternoons, when baby boy has
  had a splendid nap,
And sits, like any monarch on his
  throne, in nurse's lap,
In some such wise my handkerchief
  I hold before my face,
And cautiously and quietly I move
  about the place;
Then, with a cry, I suddenly expose
  my face to view,
And you should hear him laugh and
  crow when I say "Booh"!

Sometimes the rascal tries to make
  believe that he is scared,
And really, when I first began, he
  stared, and stared, and stared;
And then his under lip came out and
  farther out it came,
Till mamma and the nurse agreed it
  was a "cruel shame"—
But now what does that same wee,
  toddling, lisping baby do
But laugh and kick his little heels
  when I say "Booh!"

He laughs and kicks his little heels
  in rapturous glee, and then
In shrill, despotic treble bids me "do
  it all aden!"
And I—of course I do it; for, as his
  progenitor,
It is such pretty, pleasant play as this
  that I am for!
And it is, oh, such fun I and sure that
  we shall rue
The time when we are both too old
  to play the game "Booh!"

GARDEN AND CRADLE

When our babe he goeth walking in
  his garden,
  Around his tinkling feet the
  sunbeams play;
The posies they are good to him,
And bow them as they should to
  him,
As fareth he upon his kingly way;
And birdlings of the wood to him
Make music, gentle music, all the
  day,
When our babe he goeth walking in
  his garden.

When our babe he goeth swinging in
  his cradle,

Then the night it looketh ever
    sweetly down;
The little stars are kind to him,
The moon she hath a mind to him
And layeth on his head a golden
    crown;
And singeth then the wind to him
A song, the gentle song of Bethlem-
    town,
When our babe he goeth swinging in
    his cradle.

THE NIGHT WIND
Have you ever heard the wind go
    "Yooooo"?
'T is a pitiful sound to hear!
It seems to chill you through and
    through
With a strange and speechless fear.
'T is the voice of the night that
    broods outside
When folk should be asleep,
And many and many's the time I've
    cried
To the darkness brooding far and
    wide
Over the land and the deep:
"Whom do you want, O lonely
    night,
That you wail the long hours
    through?"
And the night would say in its
    ghostly way:
        "Yoooooooo!
        Yoooooooo!
        Yoooooooo!"

My mother told me long ago
    (When I was a little tad)
That when the night went wailing
    so,
    Somebody had been bad;
And then, when I was snug in bed,
    Whither I had been sent,
With the blankets pulled up round
    my head,
I'd think of what my mother'd said,
And wonder what boy she meant!
And "Who's been bad to-day?" I'd
    ask
Of the wind that hoarsely blew,
And the voice would say in its
    meaningful way:
        "Yoooooooo!
        Yoooooooo!
        Yoooooooo!"

That this was true I must allow—
    You'll not believe it, though!
Yes, though I'm quite a model now,
    I was not always so.
And if you doubt what things I say,
    Suppose you make the test;
Suppose, when you've been bad
    some day
And up to bed are sent away
From mother and the rest—
Suppose you ask, "Who has been
    bad?"
And then you'll hear what's true;
For the wind will moan in its
    ruefulest tone:
        "Yoooooooo!
        Yoooooooo!
        Yoooooooo!"

KISSING TIME
'T is when the lark goes soaring
    And the bee is at the bud,
When lightly dancing zephyrs
    Sing over field and flood;
When all sweet things in nature
    Seem joyfully achime—
'T is then I wake my darling,
    For it is kissing time!

Go, pretty lark, a-soaring,
    And suck your sweets, O bee;
Sing, O ye winds of summer,
    Your songs to mine and me;
For with your song and rapture
    Cometh the moment when
It's half-past kissing time
    And time to kiss again!

So—so the days go fleeting
    Like golden fancies free,
And every day that cometh
    Is full of sweets for me;
And sweetest are those moments
    My darling comes to climb
Into my lap to mind me
    That it is kissing time.

Sometimes, maybe, he wanders
    A heedless, aimless way—
Sometimes, maybe, he loiters
    In pretty, prattling play;

But presently bethinks him
And hastens to me then,
For it's half-past kissing time
And time to kiss again!

JEST 'FORE CHRISTMAS

Father calls me William, sister calls me Will,
Mother calls me Willie, but the fellers call me Bill!
Mighty glad I ain't a girl—ruther be a boy,
Without them sashes, curls, an' things that's worn by Fauntleroy!
Love to chawnk green apples an' go swimmin' in the lake—
Hate to take the castor-ile they give for bellyache!
'Most all the time, the whole year round, there ain't no flies on me,
But jest 'fore Christmas I'm as good as I kin be!

Got a yeller dog named Sport, sick him on the cat;
First thing she knows she doesn't know where she is at!
Got a clipper sled, an' when us kids goes out to slide,
'Long comes the grocery cart, an' we all hook a ride!
But sometimes when the grocery man is worrited an' cross,
He reaches at us with his whip, an' larrups up his hoss,
An' then I laff an' holler, "Oh, ye never teched me!"
But jest 'fore Christmas I'm as good as I kin be!

Gran'ma says she hopes that when I git to be a man,
I'll be a missionarer like her oldest brother, Dan,
As was et up by the cannibuls that lives in Ceylon's Isle,
Where every prospeck pleases, an' only man is vile!
But gran'ma she has never been to see a Wild West show,
Nor read the Life of Daniel Boone, or else I guess she'd know
That Buff'lo Bill an' cow-boys is good enough for me!
Excep' jest 'fore Christmas, when I'm good as I kin be!

And then old Sport he hangs around, so solemn-like an' still,
His eyes they seem a-sayin': "What's the matter, little Bill?"
The old cat sneaks down off her perch an' wonders what's become
Of them two enemies of hern that used to make things hum!
But I am so perlite an' 'tend so earnestly to biz,
That mother says to father: "How improved our Willie is!"
But father, havin' been a boy hisself, suspicions me
When, jest 'fore Christmas, I'm as good as I kin be!

For Christmas, with its lots an' lots of candies, cakes, an' toys,
Was made, they say, for proper kids an' not for naughty boys;
So wash yer face an' bresh yer hair, an' mind yer p's and q's,
An' don't bust out yer pantaloons, and don't wear out yer shoes;
Say "Yessum" to the ladies, an' "Yessur" to the men,
An' when they's company, don't pass yer plate for pie again;
But, thinkin' of the things yer'd like to see upon that tree,
Jest 'fore Christmas be as good as yer kin be!

BEARD AND BABY

I say, as one who never feared
The wrath of a subscriber's bullet,
I pity him who has a beard
But has no little girl to pull it!

When wife and I have finished tea,
Our baby woos me with her prattle,
And, perching proudly on my knee,
She gives my petted whiskers battle.

With both her hands she tugs away,
While scolding at me kind o' spiteful;
You'll not believe me when I say
I find the torture quite delightful!

No other would presume, I ween,
To trifle with this hirsute wonder,
Else would I rise in vengeful mien
And rend his vandal frame asunder!

But when her baby fingers pull
This glossy, sleek, and silky treasure,
My cup of happiness is full—
I fairly glow with pride and pleasure!

And, sweeter still, through all the day
I seem to hear her winsome prattle—
I seem to feel her hands at play,
As though they gave me sportive battle.

Yes, heavenly music seems to steal
Where thought of her forever lingers,
And round my heart I always feel
The twining of her dimpled fingers!

THE DINKEY BIRD
In an ocean, 'way out yonder
(As all sapient people know),
Is the land of Wonder-Wander,
Whither children love to go;
It's their playing, romping, swinging,
That give great joy to me
While the Dinkey-Bird goes singing
In the amfalula tree!

There the gum-drops grow like cherries,
And taffy's thick as peas—
Caramels you pick like berries
When, and where, and how you please;
Big red sugar-plums are clinging
To the cliffs beside that sea
Where the Dinkey-Bird is singing
In the amfalula tree.

So when children shout and scamper
And make merry all the day,
When there's naught to put a damper
To the ardor of their play;
When I hear their laughter ringing,
Then I'm sure as sure can be
That the Dinkey-Bird is singing
In the amfalula tree.

For the Dinkey-Bird's bravuras
And staccatos are so sweet—
His roulades, appoggiaturas,
And robustos so complete,
That the youth of every nation—
Be they near or far away—
Have especial delectation
In that gladsome roundelay.

Their eyes grow bright and brighter,
Their lungs begin to crow,
Their hearts get light and lighter,
And their cheeks are all aglow;
For an echo cometh bringing
The news to all and me,
That the Dinkey-Bird is singing
In the amfalula tree.

I'm sure you like to go there
To see your feathered friend—
And so many goodies grow there
You would like to comprehend!
Speed, little dreams, your winging
To that land across the sea
Where the Dinkey-Bird is singing
In the amfalula tree!

THE DRUM
I'm a beautiful red, red drum,
And I train with the soldier boys;
As up the street we come,
Wonderful is our noise!
There's Tom, and Jim, and Phil,
And Dick, and Nat, and Fred,
While Widow Cutler's Bill
And I march on ahead,
With a r-r-rat-tat-tat
And a tum-titty-um-tum-tum—
Oh, there's bushels of fun in that
For boys with a little red drum!

The Injuns came last night
While the soldiers were abed,
And they gobbled a Chinese kite
And off to the woods they fled!
The woods are the cherry-trees
Down in the orchard lot,
And the soldiers are marching to seize
The booty the Injuns got.
With tum-titty-um-tum-tum,

And r-r-rat-tat-tat,
When soldiers marching come
Injuns had better scat!

Step up there, little Fred,
And, Charley, have a mind!
Jim is as far ahead
As you two are behind!
Ready with gun and sword
Your valorous work to do—
Yonder the Injun horde
Are lying in wait for you.
And their hearts go pitapat
When they hear the soldiers come
With a r-r-rat-tat-tat
And a tum-titty-um-tum-tum!

Course it's all in play!
The skulking Injun crew
That hustled the kite away
Are little white boys, like you!
But "honest" or "just in fun,"
It is all the same to me;
And, when the battle is won,
Home once again march we
With a r-r-rat-tat-tat
And tum-titty-um-tum-tum;
And there's glory enough in that
For the boys with their little red drum!

THE DEAD BABE

Last night, as my dear babe lay dead,
In agony I knelt and said:
"O God! what have I done,
Or in what wise offended Thee,
That Thou should'st take away from me
My little son?

"Upon the thousand useless lives,
Upon the guilt that vaunting thrives,
Thy wrath were better spent!
Why should'st Thou take my little son—
Why should'st Thou vent Thy wrath upon
This innocent?"

Last night, as my dear babe lay dead,
Before mine eyes the vision spread
Of things that might have been:

Licentious riot, cruel strife,
Forgotten prayers, a wasted life
Dark red with sin!

Then, with sweet music in the air,
I saw another vision there:
A Shepherd in whose keep
A little lamb—my little child!
Of worldly wisdom undefiled,
Lay fast asleep!

Last night, as my dear babe lay dead,
In those two messages I read
A wisdom manifest;
And though my arms be childless now,
I am content—to Him I bow
Who knoweth best.

THE HAPPY HOUSEHOLD

It's when the birds go piping and the daylight slowly breaks,
That, clamoring for his dinner, our precious baby wakes;
Then it's sleep no more for baby, and it's sleep no more for me,
For, when he wants his dinner, why it's dinner it must be!
And of that lacteal fluid he partakes with great ado,
While gran'ma laughs,
And gran'pa laughs,
And wife, she laughs,
And I—well, I laugh, too!

You'd think, to see us carrying on about that little tad,
That, like as not, that baby was the first we'd ever had;
But, sakes alive! he isn't, yet we people make a fuss
As if the only baby in the world had come to us!
And, morning, noon, and night-time, whatever he may do,
Gran'ma, she laughs,
Gran'pa, he laughs,
Wife, she laughs,
And I, of course, laugh, too!

But once—a likely spell ago—when that poor little chick

From teething or from some such ill
of infancy fell sick,
You wouldn't know us people as the
same that went about
A-feelin' good all over, just to hear
him crow and shout;
And, though the doctor poohed our
fears and said he'd pull him through,
Old gran'ma cried,
And gran'pa cried,
And wife, she cried,
And I—yes, I cried, too!

It makes us all feel good to have a
baby on the place,
With his everlastin' crowing and his
dimpling, dumpling face;
The patter of his pinky feet makes
music everywhere,
And when he shakes those fists of
his, good-by to every care!
No matter what our trouble is, when
he begins to coo,
Old gran'ma laughs,
And gran'pa laughs,
Wife, she laughs,
And I—you bet, I laugh, too!

SO, SO, ROCK-A-BY SO!
So, so, rock-a-by so!
Off to the garden where dreamikins
grow;
And here is a kiss on your
winkyblink eyes,
And here is a kiss on your
dimpledown cheek
And here is a kiss for the treasure
that lies
In the beautiful garden way up in the
skies
Which you seek.
Now mind these three kisses
wherever you go—
So, so, rock-a-by so!

There's one little fumfay who lives
there, I know,
For he dances all night where the
dreamikins grow;
I send him this kiss on your
droopydrop eyes,
I send him this kiss on your rosyred
cheek.

And here is a kiss for the dream that
shall rise
When the fumfay shall dance in
those far-away skies
Which you seek.
Be sure that you pay those three
kisses you owe—
So, so, rock-a-by so!

And, by-low, as you rock-a-by go,
Don't forget mother who loveth you
so!
And here is her kiss on your
weepydeep eyes,
And here is her kiss on your
peachypink cheek,
And here is her kiss for the
dreamland that lies
Like a babe on the breast of those
far-away skies
Which you seek—
The blinkywink garden where
dreamikins grow—
So, so, rock-a-by so!

THE SONG OF LUDDY-DUD
A sunbeam comes a-creeping
Into my dear one's nest,
And sings to our babe a-sleeping
The song that I love the best:
"'T is little Luddy-Dud in the
morning—
'T is little Luddy-Dud at night;
And all day long
'T is the same sweet song
Of that waddling, toddling, coddling
little mite,
Luddy-Dud."

The bird to the tossing clover,
The bee to the swaying bud,
Keep singing that sweet song over
Of wee little Luddy-Dud.
"'T is little Luddy-Dud in the
morning—
'T is little Luddy-Dud at night;
And all day long
'T is the same dear song
Of that growing, crowing, knowing
little sprite,
Luddy-Dud."

Luddy-Dud's cradle is swinging
Where softly the night winds blow,

And Luddy-Dud's mother is singing
A song that is sweet and low:
"'T is little Luddy-Dud in the morning—
'T is little Luddy-Dud at night;
And all day long
'T is the same sweet song
Of my nearest and my dearest heart's delight,
Luddy-Dud!"

THE DUEL

The gingham dog and the calico cat
Side by side on the table sat;
'T was half-past twelve, and (what do you think!)
Nor one nor t' other had slept a wink!
The old Dutch clock and the Chinese plate
Appeared to know as sure as fate
There was going to be a terrible spat.
(I wasn't there; I simply state
What was told to me by the Chinese plate!)

The gingham dog went "bow-wow-wow!"
And the calico cat replied "mee-ow!"
The air was littered, an hour or so,
With bits of gingham and calico,
While the old Dutch clock in the chimney place
Up with its hands before its face,
For it always dreaded a family row!
(Now mind: I'm only telling you
What the old Dutch clock declares is true!)

The Chinese plate looked very blue,
And wailed, "Oh, dear! what shall we do!"
But the gingham dog and the calico cat
Wallowed this way and tumbled that,
Employing every tooth and claw
In the awfullest way you ever saw—
And, oh! how the gingham and calico flew!
(Don't fancy I exaggerate—
I got my news from the Chinese plate!)

Next morning, where the two had sat
They found no trace of dog or cat;
And some folks think unto this day
That burglars stole that pair away!
But the truth about the cat and pup
Is this: they ate each other up!
Now what do you really think of that!
(The old Dutch clock it told me so,
And that is how I came to know.)

GOOD-CHILDREN STREET

There's a dear little home in Good-Children street—
My heart turneth fondly to-day
Where tinkle of tongues and patter of feet
Make sweetest of music at play;
Where the sunshine of love illumines each face
And warms every heart in that old-fashioned place.

For dear little children go romping about
With dollies and tin tops and drums,
And, my! how they frolic and scamper and shout
Till bedtime too speedily comes!
Oh, days they are golden and days they are fleet
With little folk living in Good-Children street.

See, here comes an army with guns painted red,
And swords, caps, and plumes of all sorts;
The captain rides gaily and proudly ahead
On a stick-horse that prances and snorts!
Oh, legions of soldiers you're certain to meet—
Nice make-believe soldiers—in Good-Children street.

And yonder Odette wheels her dolly about—
Poor dolly! I'm sure she is ill,

9

For one of her blue china eyes has
dropped out
And her voice is asthmatic'ly shrill.
Then, too, I observe she is minus her
feet,
Which causes much sorrow in
Good-Children street.

'T is so the dear children go romping
about
With dollies and banners and drums,
And I venture to say they are sadly
put out
When an end to their jubilee comes:
Oh, days they are golden and days
they are fleet
With little folk living in Good-
Children street!

But when falleth night over river
and town,
Those little folk vanish from sight,
And an angel all white from the sky
cometh down
And guardeth the babes through the
night,
And singeth her lullabies tender and
sweet
To the dear little people in Good-
Children Street.

Though elsewhere the world be
o'erburdened with care,
Though poverty fall to my lot,
Though toil and vexation be always
my share,
What care I—they trouble me not!
This thought maketh life ever joyous
and Sweet:
There's a dear little home in Good-
Children street.

THE DELECTABLE BALLAD OF THE WALLER LOT

Up yonder in Buena Park
There is a famous spot,
In legend and in history
Yclept the Waller Lot.

There children play in daytime
And lovers stroll by dark,
For 't is the goodliest trysting-place
In all Buena Park.

Once on a time that beauteous maid,
Sweet little Sissy Knott,
Took out her pretty doll to walk
Within the Waller Lot.

While thus she fared, from
Ravenswood
Came Injuns o'er the plain,
And seized upon that beauteous
maid
And rent her doll in twain.

Oh, 't was a piteous thing to hear
Her lamentations wild;
She tore her golden curls and cried:
"My child! My child! My child!"

Alas, what cared those Injun chiefs
How bitterly wailed she?
They never had been mothers,
And they could not hope to be!

"Have done with tears," they rudely
quoth,
And then they bound her hands;
For they proposed to take her off
To distant border lands.

But, joy! from Mr. Eddy's barn
Doth Willie Clow behold
The sight that makes his hair rise up
And all his blood run cold.

He put his fingers in his mouth
And whistled long and clear,
And presently a goodly horde
Of cow-boys did appear.

Cried Willie Clow: "My comrades
bold,
Haste to the Waller Lot,
And rescue from that Injun band
Our charming Sissy Knott!"

"Spare neither Injun buck nor
squaw,
But smite them hide and hair!
Spare neither sex nor age nor size,
And no condition spare!"

Then sped that cow-boy band away,
Full of revengeful wrath,
And Kendall Evans rode ahead
Upon a hickory lath.

And next came gallant Dady Field
And Willie's brother Kent,
The Eddy boys and Robbie James,
On murderous purpose bent.

For they were much beholden to
That maid—in sooth, the lot
Were very, very much in love
With charming Sissy Knott.

What wonder? She was beauty's queen,
And good beyond compare;
Moreover, it was known she was
Her wealthy father's heir!

Now when the Injuns saw that band
They trembled with affright,
And yet they thought the cheapest thing
To do was stay and fight.

So sturdily they stood their ground,
Nor would their prisoner yield,
Despite the wrath of Willie Clow
And gallant Dady Field.

Oh, never fiercer battle raged
Upon the Waller Lot,
And never blood more freely flowed
Than flowed for Sissy Knott!

An Injun chief of monstrous size
Got Kendall Evans down,
And Robbie James was soon o'erthrown
By one of great renown.

And Dady Field was sorely done,
And Willie Clow was hurt,
And all that gallant cow-boy band
Lay wallowing in the dirt.

But still they strove with might and main
Till all the Waller Lot
Was strewn with hair and gouts of gore—
All, all for Sissy Knott!

Then cried the maiden in despair:
"Alas, I sadly fear
The battle and my hopes are lost,
Unless some help appear!"

Lo, as she spoke, she saw afar
The rescuer looming up—
The pride of all Buena Park,
Clow's famous yellow pup!

"Now, sick'em, Don," the maiden cried,
"Now, sick'em, Don!" cried she;
Obedient Don at once complied—
As ordered, so did he.

He sicked'em all so passing well
That, overcome by fright,
The Indian horde gave up the fray
And safety sought in flight.

They ran and ran and ran and ran
O'er valley, plain, and hill;
And if they are not walking now,
Why, then, they're running still.

The cow-boys rose up from the dust
With faces black and blue;
"Remember, beauteous maid," said they,
"We've bled and died for you!"

"And though we suffer grievously,
We gladly hail the lot
That brings us toils and pains and wounds
For charming Sissy Knott!"

But Sissy Knott still wailed and wept,
And still her fate reviled;
For who could patch her dolly up—
Who, who could mend her child?

Then out her doting mother came,
And soothed her daughter then;
"Grieve not, my darling, I will sew
Your dolly up again!"

Joy soon succeeded unto grief,
And tears were soon dried up,
And dignities were heaped upon
Clow's noble yellow pup.

Him all that goodly company
Did as deliverer hail—
They tied a ribbon round his neck,
Another round his tail.

And every anniversary day

Upon the Waller Lot
They celebrate the victory won
For charming Sissy Knott.

And I, the poet of these folk,
Am ordered to compile
This truly famous history
In good old ballad style.

Which having done as to have earned
The sweet rewards of fame,
In what same style I did begin
I now shall end the same.

So let us sing: Long live the King,
Long live the Queen and Jack,
Long live the ten-spot and the ace,
And also all the pack.

THE STORK

Last night the Stork came stalking,
And, Stork, beneath your wing
Lay, lapped in dreamless slumber,
The tiniest little thing!
From Babyland, out yonder
Beside a silver sea,
You brought a priceless treasure
As gift to mine and me!

Last night my dear one listened—
And, wife, you knew the cry—
The dear old Stork has sought our home
A many times gone by!
And in your gentle bosom
I found the pretty thing
That from the realm out yonder
Our friend the Stork did bring.

Last night a babe awakened,
And, babe, how strange and new
Must seem the home and people
The Stork has brought you to;
And yet methinks you like them—
You neither stare nor weep,
But closer to my dear one
You cuddle, and you sleep!

Last night my heart grew fonder—
O happy heart of mine,
Sing of the inspirations
That round my pathway shine!
And sing your sweetest love-song
To this dear nestling wee
The Stork from 'Way-Out-Yonder
Hath brought to mine and me!

THE BOTTLE TREE

A bottle tree bloometh in Winkyway land—
Heigh-ho for a bottle, I say!
A snug little berth in that ship I demand
That rocketh the Bottle-Tree babies away
Where the Bottle Tree bloometh by night and by day
And reacheth its fruit to each wee, dimpled hand;
You take of that fruit as much as you list,
For colic's a nuisance that doesn't exist!
So cuddle me and cuddle me fast,
And cuddle me snug in my cradle away,
For I hunger and thirst for that precious repast—
Heigh-ho for a bottle, I say!

The Bottle Tree bloometh by night and by day!
Heigh-ho for Winkyway land!
And Bottle-Tree fruit (as I've heard people say)
Makes bellies of Bottle-Tree babies expand—
And that is a trick I would fain understand!
Heigh-ho for a bottle to-day!
And heigh-ho for a bottle to-night—
A bottle of milk that is creamy and white!
So cuddle me close, and cuddle me fast,
And cuddle me snug in my cradle away,
For I hunger and thirst for that precious repast—
Heigh-ho for a bottle, I say!

GOOGLY-GOO

Of mornings, bright and early,
When the lark is on the wing
And the robin in the maple
Hops from her nest to sing,

From yonder cheery chamber
Cometh a mellow coo—
'T is the sweet, persuasive treble
Of my little Googly-Goo!

The sunbeams hear his music,
And they seek his little bed,
And they dance their prettiest
dances
Round his golden curly head:
Schottisches, galops, minuets,
Gavottes and waltzes, too,
Dance they unto the music
Of my googling Googly-Goo.

My heart—my heart it leapeth
To hear that treble tone;
What music like thy music,
My darling and mine own!
And patiently—yes, cheerfully
I toil the long day through—
My labor seemeth lightened
By the song of Googly-Goo!

I may not see his antics,
Nor kiss his dimpled cheek:
I may not smooth the tresses
The sunbeams love to seek;
It mattereth not—the echo
Of his sweet, persuasive coo
Recurreth to remind me
Of my little Googly-Goo.

And when I come at evening,
I stand without the door
And patiently I listen
For that dear sound once more;
And oftentimes I wonder,
"Oh, God! what should I do
If any ill should happen
To my little Googly-Goo!"

Then in affright I call him—
I hear his gleeful shouts!
Begone, ye dread forebodings—
Begone, ye killing doubts!
For, with my arms about him,
My heart warms through and
through
With the oogling and the googling
Of my little Googly-Goo!

THE BENCH-LEGGED FYCE

Speakin' of dorgs, my bench-legged
fyce
Hed most o' the virtues, an' nary a
vice.
Some folks called him Sooner, a
name that arose
From his predisposition to chronic
repose;
But, rouse his ambition, he couldn't
be beat—
Yer bet yer he got thar on all his
four feet!

Mos' dorgs hez some forte—like
huntin' an' such,
But the sports o' the field didn't
bother him much;
Wuz just a plain dorg, an' contented
to be
On peaceable terms with the
neighbors an' me;
Used to fiddle an' squirm, and grunt
"Oh, how nice!"
When I tickled the back of that
bench-legged fyce!

He wuz long in the bar'l, like a fyce
oughter be;
His color wuz yaller as ever you see;
His tail, curlin' upward, wuz long,
loose, an' slim—
When he didn't wag it, why, the tail
it wagged him!
His legs wuz so crooked, my bench-
legged pup
Wuz as tall settin' down as he wuz
standin' up!

He'd lie by the stove of a night an'
regret
The various vittles an' things he had
et;
When a stranger, most likely a
tramp, come along,
He'd lift up his voice in significant
song—
You wondered, by gum! how there
ever wuz space
In that bosom o' his'n to hold so
much bass!

Of daytimes he'd sneak to the road
an' lie down,
An' tackle the country dorgs comin'
to town;

By common consent he wuz boss in St. Joe,
For what he took hold of he never let go!
An' a dude that come courtin' our girl left a slice
Of his white flannel suit with our bench-legged fyce!

He wuz good to us kids—when we pulled at his fur
Or twisted his tail he would never demur;
He seemed to enjoy all our play an' our chaff,
For his tongue 'u'd hang out an' he'd laff an' he'd laff;
An' once, when the Hobart boy fell through the ice,
He wuz drug clean ashore by that bench-legged fyce!

We all hev our choice, an' you, like the rest,
Allow that the dorg which you've got is the best;
I wouldn't give much for the boy 'at grows up
With no friendship subsistin' 'tween him an' a pup!
When a fellow gits old—I tell you it's nice
To think of his youth and his bench-legged fyce!

To think of the springtime 'way back in St. Joe—
Of the peach-trees abloom an' the daisies ablow;
To think of the play in the medder an' grove,
When little legs wrassled an' little han's strove;
To think of the loyalty, valor, an' truth
Of the friendships that hallow the season of youth!

LITTLE MISS BRAG

Little Miss Brag has much to say
To the rich little lady from over the way
And the rich little lady puts out a lip
As she looks at her own white, dainty slip,
And wishes that she could wear a gown
As pretty as gingham of faded brown!
For little Miss Brag she lays much stress
On the privileges of a gingham dress—
"Aha,
Oho!"

The rich little lady from over the way
Has beautiful dolls in vast array;
Yet she envies the raggedy home-made doll
She hears our little Miss Brag extol.
For the raggedy doll can fear no hurt
From wet, or heat, or tumble, or dirt!
Her nose is inked, and her mouth is, too,
And one eye's black and the other's blue—
"Aha,
Oho!"

The rich little lady goes out to ride
With footmen standing up outside,
Yet wishes that, sometimes, after dark
Her father would trundle her in the park;—
That, sometimes, her mother would sing the things
Little Miss Brag says her mother sings
When through the attic window streams
The moonlight full of golden dreams—
"Aha,
Oho!"

Yes, little Miss Brag has much to say
To the rich little lady from over the way;
And yet who knows but from her heart
Often the bitter sighs upstart—
Uprise to lose their burn and sting
In the grace of the tongue that loves to sing

Praise of the treasures all its own!
So I've come to love that treble tone—
"Aha,
Oho!"

THE HUMMING TOP

The top it hummeth a sweet, sweet song
To my dear little boy at play—
Merrily singeth all day long,
As it spinneth and spinneth away.
And my dear little boy
He laugheth with joy
When he heareth the monotone
Of that busy thing
That loveth to sing
The song that is all its own.

Hold fast the string and wind it tight,
That the song be loud and clear;
Now hurl the top with all your might
Upon the banquette here;
And straight from the string
The joyous thing
Boundeth and spinneth along,
And it whirrs and it chirrs
And it birrs and it purrs
Ever its pretty song.

Will ever my dear little boy grow old,
As some have grown before?
Will ever his heart feel faint and cold,
When he heareth the songs of yore?
Will ever this toy
Of my dear little boy,
When the years have worn away,
Sing sad and low
Of the long ago,
As it singeth to me to-day?

LADY BUTTON-EYES

When the busy day is done,
And my weary little one
Rocketh gently to and fro;
When the night winds softly blow,
And the crickets in the glen
Chirp and chirp and chirp again;
When upon the haunted green
Fairies dance around their queen—
Then from yonder misty skies
Cometh Lady Button-Eyes.

Through the murk and mist and gloam
To our quiet, cozy home,
Where to singing, sweet and low,
Rocks a cradle to and fro;
Where the clock's dull monotone
Telleth of the day that's done;
Where the moonbeams hover o'er
Playthings sleeping on the floor—
Where my weary wee one lies
Cometh Lady Button-Eyes.

Cometh like a fleeting ghost
From some distant eerie coast;
Never footfall can you hear
As that spirit fareth near—
Never whisper, never word
From that shadow-queen is heard.
In ethereal raiment dight,
From the realm of fay and sprite
In the depth of yonder skies
Cometh Lady Button-Eyes.

Layeth she her hands upon
My dear weary little one,
And those white hands overspread
Like a veil the curly head,
Seem to fondle and caress
Every little silken tress;
Then she smooths the eyelids down
Over those two eyes of brown—
In such soothing, tender wise
Cometh Lady Button-Eyes.

Dearest, feel upon your brow
That caressing magic now;
For the crickets in the glen
Chirp and chirp and chirp again,
While upon the haunted green
Fairies dance around their queen,
And the moonbeams hover o'er
Playthings sleeping on the floor—
Hush, my sweet! from yonder skies
Cometh Lady Button-Eyes!

THE RIDE TO BUMPVILLE

Play that my knee was a calico mare
Saddled and bridled for Bumpville;
Leap to the back of this steed, if you dare,

And gallop away to Bumpville!
I hope you'll be sure to sit fast in your seat,
For this calico mare is prodigiously fleet,
And many adventures you're likely to meet
As you journey along to Bumpville.

This calico mare both gallops and trots
While whisking you off to Bumpville;
She paces, she shies, and she stumbles, in spots,
In the tortuous road to Bumpville;
And sometimes this strangely mercurial steed
Will suddenly stop and refuse to proceed,
Which, all will admit, is vexatious indeed,
When one is en route to Bumpville!

She's scared of the cars when the engine goes "Toot!"
Down by the crossing at Bumpville;
You'd better look out for that treacherous brute
Bearing you off to Bumpville!
With a snort she rears up on her hindermost heels,
And executes jigs and Virginia reels—
Words fail to explain how embarrassed one feels
Dancing so wildly to Bumpville!

It's bumpytybump and it's jiggytyjog,
Journeying on to Bumpville
It's over the hilltop and down through the bog
You ride on your way to Bumpville;
It's rattletybang over boulder and stump,
There are rivers to ford, there are fences to jump,
And the corduroy road it goes bumpytybump,
Mile after mile to bumpville!

Perhaps you'll observe it's no easy thing
Making the journey to Bumpville,
So I think, on the whole, it were prudent to bring
An end to this ride to Bumpville;
For, though she has uttered no protest or plaint,
The calico mare must be blowing and faint—
What's more to the point, I'm blowed if I ain't!
So play we have got to Bumpville!

THE BROOK
I looked in the brook and saw a face—
Heigh-ho, but a child was I!
There were rushes and willows in that place,
And they clutched at the brook as the brook ran by;
And the brook it ran its own sweet way,
As a child doth run in heedless play,
And as it ran I heard it say:
"Hasten with me
To the roistering sea
That is wroth with the flame of the morning sky!"

I look in the brook and see a face—
Heigh-ho, but the years go by!
The rushes are dead in the old-time place,
And the willows I knew when a child was I.
And the brook it seemeth to me to say,
As ever it stealeth on its way—
Solemnly now, and not in play:
"Oh, come with me
To the slumbrous sea
That is gray with the peace of the evening sky!"

Heigh-ho, but the years go by—
I would to God that a child were I!

PICNIC-TIME
It's June ag'in, an' in my soul I feel the fillin' joy
That's sure to come this time o' year to every little boy;
For, every June, the Sunday-schools at picnics may be seen,

Where "fields beyont the swellin'
floods stand dressed in livin' green";
Where little girls are skeered to
death with spiders, bugs, and ants,
An' little boys get grass-stains on
their go-to meetin' pants.
It's June ag'in, an' with it all what
happiness is mine—
There's goin' to be a picnic, an' I'm
goin' to jine!

One year I jined the Baptists, an'
goodness! how it rained!
(But grampa says that's the way
"baptizo" is explained.)
And once I jined the 'Piscopils an'
had a heap o' fun—
But the boss of all the picnics was
the Presbyteriun!
They had so many puddin's, sallids,
sandwidges, an' pies,
That a feller wisht his stummick was
as hungry as his eyes!
Oh, yes, the eatin' Presbyteriuns
give yer is so fine
That when they have a picnic, you
bet I'm goin' to jine!

But at this time the Methodists have
special claims on me,
For they're goin' to give a picnic on
the 21st, D. V.;
Why should a liberal universalist
like me object
To share the joys of fellowship with
every friendly sect?
However het'rodox their articles of
faith elsewise may be,
Their doctrine of fried chick'n is a
savin' grace to me!
So on the 21st of June, the weather
bein' fine,
They're goin' to give a picnic, and
I'm goin' to jine!

SHUFFLE-SHOON AND AMBER-LOCKS
Shuffle-shoon and Amber-Locks
Sit together, building blocks;
Shuffle-Shoon is old and gray,
Amber-Locks a little child,
But together at their play
Age and Youth are reconciled,
And with sympathetic glee
Build their castles fair to see.

"When I grow to be a man"
(So the wee one's prattle ran),
"I shall build a castle so—
With a gateway broad and grand;
Here a pretty vine shall grow,
There a soldier guard shall stand;
And the tower shall be so high,
Folks will wonder, by and by!"

Shuffle-Shoon quoth: "Yes, I know;
Thus I builded long ago!
Here a gate and there a wall,
Here a window, there a door;
Here a steeple wondrous tall
Riseth ever more and more!
But the years have leveled low
What I builded long ago!"

So they gossip at their play,
Heedless of the fleeting day;
One speaks of the Long Ago
Where his dead hopes buried lie;
One with chubby cheeks aglow
Prattleth of the By and By;
Side by side, they build their
blocks—
Shuffle-Shoon and Amber-Locks.

THE SHUT-EYE TRAIN
Come, my little one, with me!
There are wondrous sights to see
As the evening shadows fall;
In your pretty cap and gown,
Don't detain
The Shut-Eye train—
"Ting-a-ling!" the bell it goeth,
"Toot-toot!" the whistle bloweth,
And we hear the warning call:
"All aboard for Shut-Eye Town!"

Over hill and over plain
Soon will speed the Shut-Eye train!
Through the blue where bloom the
stars
And the Mother Moon looks down
We'll away
To land of Fay—
Oh, the sights that we shall see
there!
Come, my little one, with me
there—
'T is a goodly train of cars—

All aboard for Shut-Eye Town!

Swifter than a wild bird's flight,
Through the realms of fleecy light
We shall speed and speed away!
Let the Night in envy frown—
What care we
How wroth she be!
To the Balow-land above us,
To the Balow-folk who love us,
Let us hasten while we may—
All aboard for Shut-Eye Town!

Shut-Eye Town is passing fair—
Golden dreams await us there;
We shall dream those dreams, my dear,
Till the Mother Moon goes down—
See unfold
Delights untold!
And in those mysterious places
We shall see beloved faces
And beloved voices hear
In the grace of Shut-Eye Town.

Heavy are your eyes, my sweet,
Weary are your little feet—
Nestle closer up to me
In your pretty cap and gown;
Don't detain
The Shut-Eye train!
"Ting-a-ling!" the bell it goeth,
"Toot-toot!" the whistle bloweth
Oh, the sights that we shall see!
All aboard for Shut-Eye Town!

LITTLE-OH DEAR

See, what a wonderful garden is here,
Planted and trimmed for my Little-Oh-Dear!
Posies so gaudy and grass of such brown—
Search ye the country and hunt ye the town
And never ye'll meet with a garden so queer
As this one I've made for my Little-Oh-Dear!

Marigolds white and buttercups blue,
Lilies all dabbled with honey and dew,
The cactus that trails over trellis and wall,
Roses and pansies and violets—all
Make proper obeisance and reverent cheer
When into her garden steps Little-Oh-Dear.
And up at the top of that lavender-tree
A silver-bird singeth as only can she;
For, ever and only, she singeth the song
"I love you—I love you!" the happy day long;—
Then the echo—the echo that smiteth me here!
"I love you, I love you," my Little-Oh-Dear!

The garden may wither, the silver-bird fly—
But what careth my little precious, or I?
From her pathway of flowers that in spring time upstart
She walketh the tenderer way in my heart
And, oh, it is always the summer-time here
With that song of "I love you," my Little-Oh-Dear!

THE FLY-AWAY HORSE

Oh, a wonderful horse is the Fly-Away Horse—
Perhaps you have seen him before;
Perhaps, while you slept, his shadow has swept
Through the moonlight that floats on the floor.
For it's only at night, when the stars twinkle bright,
That the Fly-Away Horse, with a neigh
And a pull at his rein and a toss of his mane,
Is up on his heels and away!
The Moon in the sky,
As he gallopeth by,
Cries: "Oh! what a marvelous sight!"
And the Stars in dismay
Hide their faces away
In the lap of old Grandmother Night.

It is yonder, out yonder, the Fly-Away Horse
Speedeth ever and ever away—
Over meadows and lanes, over mountains and plains,
Over streamlets that sing at their play;
And over the sea like a ghost sweepeth he,
While the ships they go sailing below,
And he speedeth so fast that the men at the mast
Adjudge him some portent of woe.
"What ho there!" they cry,
As he flourishes by
With a whisk of his beautiful tail;
And the fish in the sea
Are as scared as can be,
From the nautilus up to the whale!

And the Fly-Away Horse seeks those faraway lands
You little folk dream of at night—
Where candy-trees grow, and honey-brooks flow,
And corn-fields with popcorn are white;
And the beasts in the wood are ever so good
To children who visit them there—
What glory astride of a lion to ride,
Or to wrestle around with a bear!
The monkeys, they say:
"Come on, let us play,"
And they frisk in the cocoanut-trees:
While the parrots, that cling
To the peanut-vines, sing
Or converse with comparative ease!

Off! scamper to bed—you shall ride him tonight!
For, as soon as you've fallen asleep,
With a jubilant neigh he shall bear you away
Over forest and hillside and deep!
But tell us, my dear, all you see and you hear
In those beautiful lands over there,
Where the Fly-Away Horse wings his faraway course
With the wee one consigned to his care.
Then grandma will cry
In amazement: "Oh, my!"
And she'll think it could never be so;
And only we two
Shall know it is true—
You and I, little precious! shall know!

SWING HIGH AND SWING LOW
Swing high and swing low
While the breezes they blow—
It's off for a sailor thy father would go;
And it's here in the harbor, in sight of the sea,
He hath left his wee babe with my song and with me:
"Swing high and swing low
While the breezes they blow!"

Swing high and swing low
While the breezes they blow—
It's oh for the waiting as weary days go!
And it's oh for the heartache that smiteth me when
I sing my song over and over again:
"Swing high and swing low
While the breezes they blow!"

"Swing high and swing low "—
The sea singeth so,
And it waileth anon in its ebb and its flow;
And a sleeper sleeps on to that song of the sea
Nor recketh he ever of mine or of me!
"Swing high and swing low
While the breezes they blow—
'T was off for a sailor thy father would go!"

WHEN I WAS A BOY
Up in the attic where I slept
When I was a boy, a little boy,
In through the lattice the moonlight crept,
Bringing a tide of dreams that swept
Over the low, red trundle-bed,
Bathing the tangled curly head,
While moonbeams played at hide-and-seek

With the dimples on the sun-
brownéd cheek—
When I was a boy, a little boy!

And, oh! the dreams—the dreams I
dreamed!
When I was a boy, a little boy!
For the grace that through the lattice
streamed
Over my folded eyelids seemed
To have the gift of prophecy,
And to bring me glimpses of times
to be
When manhood's clarion seemed to
call—
Ah! that was the sweetest dream of
all,
When I was a boy, a little boy!

I'd like to sleep where I used to sleep
When I was a boy, a little boy!
For in at the lattice the moon would
peep,
Bringing her tide of dreams to
sweep
The crosses and griefs of the years
away
From the heart that is weary and
faint to-day;
And those dreams should give me
back again
A peace I have never known since
then—
When I was a boy, a little boy!

AT PLAY

Play that you are mother dear,
And play that papa is your beau;
Play that we sit in the corner here,
Just as we used to, long ago.
Playing so, we lovers two
Are just as happy as we can be,
And I'll say "I love you" to you,
And you say "I love you" to me!
"I love you" we both shall say,
All in earnest and all in play.

Or, play that you are that other one
That some time came, and went
away;
And play that the light of years
agone
Stole into my heart again to-day!
Playing that you are the one I knew

In the days that never again may be,
I'll say "I love you" to you,"
And you say "I love you" to me!
"I love you!" my heart shall say
To the ghost of the past come back
to-day!

Or, play that you sought this
nestling-place
For your own sweet self, with that
dual guise
Of your pretty mother in your face
And the look of that other in your
eyes!
So the dear old loves shall live anew
As I hold my darling on my knee,
And I'll say "I love you" to you,
And you say "I love you" to me!
Oh, many a strange, true thing we
say
And do when we pretend to play!

A VALENTINE

Go, Cupid, and my sweetheart tell
I love her well.
Yes, though she tramples on my
heart
And rends that bleeding thing apart;
And though she rolls a scornful eye
On doting me when I go by;
And though she scouts at everything
As tribute unto her I bring—
Apple, banana, caramel—
Haste, Cupid, to my love and tell,
In spite of all, I love her well!

And further say I have a sled
Cushioned in blue and painted red!
The groceryman has promised I
Can "hitch" whenever he goes by—
Go, tell her that, and, furthermore,
Apprise my sweetheart that a score
Of other little girls implore
The boon of riding on that sled
Painted and hitched, as aforesaid;—
And tell her, Cupid, only she
Shall ride upon that sled with me!
Tell her this all, and further tell
I love her well.

LITTLE ALL-ALONEY

Little All-Aloney's feet
Pitter-patter in the hall,

And his mother runs to meet
And to kiss her toddling sweet,
  Ere perchance he fall.
He is, oh, so weak and small!
Yet what danger shall he fear
When his mother hovereth near,
And he hears her cheering call:
  "All-Aloney"?

Little All-Aloney's face
It is all aglow with glee,
As around that romping-place
At a terrifying pace
  Lungeth, plungeth he!
And that hero seems to be
All unconscious of our cheers—
Only one dear voice he hears
Calling reassuringly:
  "All-Aloney!"

Though his legs bend with their load,
Though his feet they seem so small
That you cannot help forebode
Some disastrous episode
  In that noisy hall,
Neither threatening bump nor fall
Little All-Aloney fears,
But with sweet bravado steers
Whither comes that cheery call:
  "All-Aloney!"

Ah, that in the years to come,
When he shares of Sorrow's store,—
When his feet are chill and numb,
When his cross is burdensome,
  And his heart is sore:
Would that he could hear once more
The gentle voice he used to hear—
Divine with mother love and cheer—
Calling from yonder spirit shore:
  "All, all alone!"

SEEIN' THINGS

I ain't afeard uv snakes, or toads, or bugs, or worms, or mice,
An' things 'at girls are skeered uv I think are awful nice!
I'm pretty brave, I guess; an' yet I hate to go to bed,
For, when I'm tucked up warm an' snug an' when my prayers are said,
Mother tells me "Happy dreams!" and takes away the light,
An' leaves me lyin' all alone an' seein' things at night!

Sometimes they're in the corner, sometimes they're by the door,
Sometimes they're all a-standin' in the middle uv the floor;
Sometimes they are a-sittin' down, sometimes they're walkin' round
So softly an' so creepylike they never make a sound!
Sometimes they are as black as ink, an' other times they're white—
But the color ain't no difference when you see things at night!

Once, when I licked a feller 'at had just moved on our street,
An' father sent me up to bed without a bite to eat,
I woke up in the dark an' saw things standin' in a row,
A-lookin' at me cross-eyed an' p'intin' at me—so!
Oh, my! I wuz so skeered that time I never slep' a mite—
It's almost alluz when I'm bad I see things at night!

Lucky thing I ain't a girl, or I'd be skeered to death!
Bein' I'm a boy, I duck my head an' hold my breath;
An' I am, oh! so sorry I'm a naughty boy, an' then
I promise to be better an' I say my prayers again!
Gran'ma tells me that's the only way to make it right
When a feller has been wicked an' sees things at night!
An' so, when other naughty boys would coax me into sin,
I try to skwush the Tempter's voice 'at urges me within;
An' when they's pie for supper, or cakes 'at 's big an' nice,
I want to—but I do not pass my plate f'r them things twice!
No, ruther let Starvation wipe me slowly out o' sight
Than I should keep a-livin' on an' seein' things at night!

THE CUNNIN' LITTLE THING

When baby wakes of mornings,
Then it's wake, ye people all!
For another day
Of song and play
Has come at our darling's call!
And, till she gets her dinner,
She makes the welkin ring,
And she won't keep still till she's had her fill—
The cunnin' little thing!

When baby goes a-walking,
Oh, how her paddies fly!
For that's the way
The babies say
To other folk "by-by";
The trees bend down to kiss her,
And the birds in rapture sing,
As there she stands and waves her hands—
The cunnin' little thing!

When baby goes a-rocking
In her bed at close of day,
At hide-and-seek
On her dainty cheek
The dreams and the dimples play;
Then it's sleep in the tender kisses
The guardian angels bring
From the Far Above to my sweetest love—
You cunnin' little thing!

THE DOLL'S WOOING

The little French doll was a dear little doll
Tricked out in the sweetest of dresses;
Her eyes were of hue
A most delicate blue
And dark as the night were her tresses;
Her dear little mouth was fluted and red,
And this little French doll was so very well bred
That whenever accosted her little mouth said
"Mamma! mamma!"

The stockinet doll, with one arm and one leg,
Had once been a handsome young fellow;
But now he appeared
Rather frowzy and bleared
In his torn regimentals of yellow;
Yet his heart gave a curious thump as he lay
In the little toy cart near the window one day
And heard the sweet voice of that French dolly say:
"Mamma! mamma!"

He listened so long and he listened so hard
That anon he grew ever so tender,
For it's everywhere known
That the feminine tone
Gets away with all masculine gender!
He up and he wooed her with soldierly zest
But all she'd reply to the love he professed
Were these plaintive words (which perhaps you have guessed):
"Mamma! mamma!"

Her mother—a sweet little lady of five—
Vouchsafed her parental protection,
And although stockinet
Wasn't blue-blooded, yet
She really could make no objection!
So soldier and dolly were wedded one day,
And a moment ago, as I journeyed that way,
I'm sure that I heard a wee baby voice say:
"Mamma! mamma!"

INSCRIPTION FOR MY LITTLE SON'S SILVER PLATE

When thou dost eat from off this plate,
I charge thee be thou temperate;
Unto thine elders at the board
Do thou sweet reverence accord;
And, though to dignity inclined,
Unto the serving-folk be kind;
Be ever mindful of the poor,

Nor turn them hungry from the door;
And unto God, for health and food
And all that in thy life is good,
Give thou thy heart in gratitude.

FISHERMAN JIM'S KIDS

Fisherman Jim lived on the hill
With his bonnie wife an' his little boys;
'T wuz "Blow, ye winds, as blow ye will—
Naught we reck of your cold and noise!"
For happy and warm were he an' his,
And he dandled his kids upon his knee
To the song of the sea.

Fisherman Jim would sail all day,
But, when come night, upon the sands
His little kids ran from their play,
Callin' to him an' wavin' their hands;
Though the wind was fresh and the sea was high,
He'd hear'em—you bet—above the roar
Of the waves on the shore!

Once Fisherman Jim sailed into the bay
As the sun went down in a cloudy sky,
And never a kid saw he at play,
And he listened in vain for the welcoming cry.
In his little house he learned it all,
And he clinched his hands and he bowed his head—
"The fever!" they said.

'T wuz a pitiful time for Fisherman Jim,
With them darlin's a-dyin' afore his eyes,
A-stretchin' their wee hands out to him
An' a-breakin' his heart with the old-time cries
He had heerd so often upon the sands;
For they thought they wuz helpin' his boat ashore—
Till they spoke no more.

But Fisherman Jim lived on and on,
Castin' his nets an' sailin' the sea;
As a man will live when his heart is gone,
Fisherman Jim lived hopelessly,
Till once in those years they come an' said:
"Old Fisherman Jim is powerful sick—
Go to him, quick!"

Then Fisherman Jim says he to me:
"It's a long, long cruise-you understand—
But over beyont the ragin' sea
I kin see my boys on the shinin' sand
Waitin' to help this ol' hulk ashore,
Just as they used to—ah, mate, you know!—
In the long ago."

No, sir! he wuzn't afeard to die;
For all night long he seemed to see
His little boys of the days gone by,
An' to hear sweet voices forgot by me!
An' just as the mornin' sun come up—
"They're holdin' me by the hands!" he cried,
An' so he died.

"FIDDLE-DEE-DEE"

There once was a bird that lived up in a tree,
And all he could whistle was "Fiddle-dee-dee"—
A very provoking, unmusical song
For one to be whistling the summer day long!
Yet always contented and busy was he
With that vocal recurrence of "Fiddle-dee-dee."

Hard by lived a brave little soldier of four,
That weird iteration repented him sore;
"I prithee, Dear-Mother-Mine! fetch me my gun,

For, by our St. Didy! the deed must be done
That shall presently rid all creation and me
Of that ominous bird and his 'Fiddle-dee-dee'!"

Then out came Dear-Mother-Mine, bringing her son
His awfully truculent little red gun;
The stock was of pine and the barrel of tin,
The "bang" it came out where the bullet went in—
The right kind of weapon I think you'll agree
For slaying all fowl that go "Fiddle-dee-dee"!

The brave little soldier quoth never a word,
But he up and he drew a straight bead on that bird;
And, while that vain creature provokingly sang,
The gun it went off with a terrible bang!
Then loud laughed the youth—"By my Bottle," cried he,
"I've put a quietus on 'Fiddle-dee-dee'!"
Out came then Dear-Mother-Mine, saying: "My son,
Right well have you wrought with your little red gun!
Hereafter no evil at all need I fear,
With such a brave soldier as You-My-Love here!"
She kissed the dear boy.
(The bird in the tree
Continued to whistle his "Fiddle-dee-dee")

OVER THE HILLS AND FAR AWAY

Over the hills and far away,
A little boy steals from his morning play
And under the blossoming apple-tree
He lies and he dreams of the things to be:
Of battles fought and of victories won,
Of wrongs o'erthrown and of great deeds done—
Of the valor that he shall prove some day,
Over the hills and far away—
Over the hills, and far away!

Over the hills and far away
It's, oh, for the toil the livelong day!
But it mattereth not to the soul aflame
With a love for riches and power and fame!
On, O man! while the sun is high—
On to the certain joys that lie
Yonder where blazeth the noon of day,
Over the hills and far away—
Over the hills, and far away!

Over the hills and far away,
An old man lingers at close of day;
Now that his journey is almost done,
His battles fought and his victories won—
The old-time honesty and truth,
The trustfulness and the friends of youth,
Home and mother-where are they?
Over the hills and far away—
Over the years, and far away!

24

A Little Book of Western Verse

CASEY'S TABLE D'HÔTE

Oh, them days on Red Hoss
Mountain, when the skies wuz fair 'nd
blue,
When the money flowed like likker,
'nd the folks wuz brave 'nd true!
When the nights wuz crisp 'nd
balmy, 'nd the camp wuz all astir,
With the joints all throwed wide
open 'nd no sheriff to demur!
Oh, them times on Red Hoss
Mountain in the Rockies fur away,—
There's no sich place nor times like
them as I kin find to-day!
What though the camp hez busted? I
seem to see it still
A-lyin', like it loved it, on that big
'nd warty hill;
And I feel a sort of yearnin' 'nd a
chokin' in my throat
When I think of Red Hoss Mountain
'nd of Casey's tabble dote!
Wal, yes; it's true I struck it rich, but
that don't cut a show
When one is old 'nd feeble 'nd it's
nigh his time to go;
The money that he's got in bonds or
carries to invest
Don't figger with a codger who has
lived a life out West;
Us old chaps like to set around,
away from folks 'nd noise,
'Nd think about the sights we seen
and things we done when boys;
The which is why I love to set 'nd
think of them old days
When all us Western fellers got the
Colorado craze,—
And that is why I love to set around
all day 'nd gloat
On thoughts of Red Hoss Mountain
'nd of Casey's tabble dote.
This Casey wuz an Irishman,—
you'd know it by his name
And by the facial features
appertainin' to the same.
He'd lived in many places 'nd had
done a thousand things,
From the noble art of actin' to the
work of dealin' kings,
But, somehow, hadn't caught on; so,
driftin' with the rest,
He drifted for a fortune to the
undeveloped West,
And he come to Red Hoss Mountain
when the little camp wuz new,
When the money flowed like likker,
'nd the folks wuz brave 'nd true;
And, havin' been a stewart on a
Mississippi boat,
He opened up a caffy 'nd he run a
tabble dote.
The bar wuz long 'nd rangy, with a
mirrer on the shelf,
'Nd a pistol, so that Casey, when
required, could help himself;
Down underneath there wuz a row
of bottled beer 'nd wine,
'Nd a kag of Burbun whiskey of the
run of '59;
Upon the walls wuz pictures of
hosses 'nd of girls,—
Not much on dress, perhaps, but
strong on records 'nd on curls!
The which had been identified with
Casey in the past,—
The hosses 'nd the girls, I mean,—
and both wuz mighty fast!
But all these fine attractions wuz of
precious little note
By the side of what wuz offered at
Casey's tabble dote.
There wuz half-a-dozen tables
altogether in the place,
And the tax you had to pay upon
your vittles wuz a case;
The boardin'-houses in the camp
protested 't wuz a shame
To patronize a robber, which this
Casey wuz the same!
They said a case was robbery to tax
for ary meal;
But Casey tended strictly to his biz,
'nd let 'em squeal;
And presently the boardin'-houses
all began to bust,
While Casey kept on sawin' wood
'nd layin' in the dust;
And oncet a tray'lin' editor from
Denver City wrote
A piece back to his paper, puffin'
Casey's tabble dote.

A tabble dote is different from orderin' aller cart:
In one case you git all there is, in t' other, only part!
And Casey's tabble dote began in French,—as all begin,—
And Casey's ended with the same, which is to say, with "vin;"
But in between wuz every kind of reptile, bird, 'nd beast,
The same like you can git in high-toned restauraws down east;
'Nd windin' up wuz cake or pie, with coffee demy tass,
Or, sometimes, floatin' Ireland in a soothin' kind of sass
That left a sort of pleasant ticklin' in a feller's throat,
'Nd made him hanker after more of Casey's tabble dote.
The very recollection of them puddin's 'nd them pies
Brings a yearnin' to my buzzum 'nd the water to my eyes;
'Nd seems like cookin' nowadays ain't what it used to be
In camp on Red Hoss Mountain in that year of '63;
But, maybe, it is better, 'nd, maybe, I'm to blame—
I'd like to be a-livin' in the mountains jest the same—
I'd like to live that life again when skies wuz fair 'nd blue,
When things wuz run wide open 'nd men wuz brave 'nd true;
When brawny arms the flinty ribs of Red Hoss Mountain smote
For wherewithal to pay the price of Casey's tabble dote.
And you, O cherished brother, a-sleepin' 'way out west,
With Red Hoss Mountain huggin' you close to its lovin' breast,—
Oh, do you dream in your last sleep of how we used to do,
Of how we worked our little claims together, me 'nd you?
Why, when I saw you last a smile wuz restin' on your face,
Like you wuz glad to sleep forever in that lonely place;
And so you wuz, 'nd I 'd be, too, if I wuz sleepin' so.
But, bein' how a brother's love ain't for the world to know,
Whenever I've this heartache 'nd this chokin' in my throat,
I lay it all to thinkin' of Casey's tabble dote.

LITTLE BOY BLUE
The little toy dog is covered with dust,
But sturdy and stanch he stands;
And the little toy soldier is red with rust,
And his musket molds in his hands.
Time was when the little toy dog was new
And the soldier was passing fair,
And that was the time when our Little Boy Blue
Kissed them and put them there.
"Now, don't you go till I come," he said,
"And don't you make any noise!"
So toddling off to his trundle-bed
He dreamed of the pretty toys.
And as he was dreaming, an angel song
Awakened our Little Boy Blue,—
Oh, the years are many, the years are long,
But the little toy friends are true.
Ay, faithful to Little Boy Blue they stand,
Each in the same old place,
Awaiting the touch of a little hand,
The smile of a little face.
And they wonder, as waiting these long years through,
In the dust of that little chair,
What has become of our Little Boy Blue
Since he kissed them and put them there.

MADGE: YE HOYDEN
At Madge, ye hoyden, gossips scofft,
Ffor that a romping wench was shee—
"Now marke this rede," they bade her oft,
"Forsooken sholde your folly bee!"
But Madge, ye hoyden, laught & cried,
"Oho, oho," in girlish glee,

And noe thing mo replied.

II

No griffe she had nor knew no care,
But gayly rompit all daies long,
And, like ye brooke that everywhere
Goes jinking with a gladsome song,
Shee danct and songe from morn till night,—
Her gentil harte did know no wrong,
Nor did she none despight.

III

Sir Tomas from his noblesse halle
Did trend his path a somer's daye,
And to ye hoyden he did call
And these ffull evill words did say:
"O wolde you weare a silken gown
And binde your haire with ribands gay?
Then come with me to town!"

IV

But Madge, ye hoyden, shoke her head,—
"I'le be no lemman unto thee
For all your golde and gownes," shee said,
"ffor Robin hath bespoken mee."
Then ben Sir Tomas sore despight,
And back unto his hall went hee
With face as ashen white.

V

"O Robin, wilt thou wed this girl,
Whenas she is so vaine a sprite?"
So spak ffull many an envious churle
Unto that curteyse countrie wight.
But Robin did not pay no heede;
And they ben wed a somer night
& danct upon ye meade.

VI

Then scarse ben past a yeare & daye
Whan Robin toke unto his bed,
And long, long time therein he lay,
Nor colde not work to earn his bread; in soche an houre, whan times ben sore,
Sr. Tomas came with haughtie tread & knockit at ye doore.

VII

Saies: "Madge, ye hoyden, do you know how that you once despighted me? But He forgiff an you will go my swete harte lady ffor to bee!" But Madge, ye hoyden, heard noe more,— straightway upon her heele turnt shee, & shote ye cottage doore.

VIII

Soe Madge, ye hoyden, did her parte whiles that ye years did come and go; 't was somer allwais in her harte, tho' winter strewed her head with snowe. She toilt and span thro' all those years nor bid repine that it ben soe, nor never shad noe teares.

IX

Whiles Robin lay within his bed,
A divell came and whispered lowe,—
"Giff you will doe my will," he said,
"None more of sickness you shall knowe!"
Ye which gave joy to Robin's soul—
Saies Robin: "Divell, be it soe,
an that you make me whoale!"

X

That day, upp rising ffrom his bed,
Quoth Robin: "I am well again!"
& backe he came as from ye dead,
& he ben mickle blithe as when
he wooed his doxy long ago;
& Madge did make ado & then
Her teares ffor joy did flowe.

XI

Then came that hell-born cloven thing— Saies: "Robin, I do claim your life, and I hencefoorth shall be your king, and you shall do my evil strife. Look round about and you shall see sr. Tomas' young and ffoolish wiffe— a comely dame is shee!"

XII

Ye divell had him in his power, and not colde Robin say thereto: Soe Robin from that very houre did what that divell bade him do; He wooed and dipt, and on a daye Sr. Tomas' wife and Robin flewe a many leagues away.

XIII

Sir Tomas ben wood wroth and swore,
And sometime strode thro' leaf & brake
and knockit at ye cottage door
and thus to Madge, ye hoyden, spake:
Saies, "I wolde have you ffor mine own,
So come with mee & bee my make,
syn tother birds ben flown."

XIV

But Madge, ye hoyden, bade him noe; Saies: "Robin is my swete harte

still, And, tho' he doth despight me soe,
I mean to do him good for ill. So goe,
Sir Tomas, goe your way; ffor whiles I
bee on live I will ffor Robin's coming
pray!"

XV

Soe Madge, ye hoyden, kneelt &
prayed that Godde sholde send her
Robin backe. And tho' ye folke vast
scoffing made, and tho' ye worlde ben
colde and blacke, And tho', as moneths
dragged away, ye hoyden's harte ben
like to crack With griff, she still did
praye.

XVI

Sicke of that divell's damnèd
charmes, Aback did Robin come at last,
And Madge, ye hoyden, sprad her arms
and gave a cry and held him fast; And
as she clong to him and cried, her
patient harte with joy did brast, &
Madge, ye hoyden, died.

OLD ENGLISH LULLABY

Hush, bonnie, dinna greit;
Moder will rocke her sweete,—
Balow, my boy!
When that his toile ben done,
Daddie will come anone,—
Hush thee, my lyttel one;
Balow, my boy!

Gin thou dost sleepe, perchaunce
Fayries will come to daunce,—
Balow, my boy!
Oft hath thy moder seene
Moonlight and mirkland queene
Daunce on thy slumbering een,—
Balow, my boy!

Then droned a bomblebee
Saftly this songe to thee:
"Balow, my boy!"
And a wee heather bell,
Pluckt from a fayry dell,
Chimed thee this rune hersell:
"Balow, my boy!"

Soe, bonnie, dinna greit;
Moder doth rock her sweete,—
Balow, my boy!
Give mee thy lyttel hand,
Moder will hold it and
Lead thee to balow land,—
Balow, my boy!

THE BIBLIOMANIAC'S PRAYER

Keep me, I pray, in wisdom's way
That I may truths eternal seek;
I need protecting care to-day,—
My purse is light, my flesh is weak.
So banish from my erring heart
All baleful appetites and hints
Of Satan's fascinating art,
Of first editions, and of prints.
Direct me in some godly walk
Which leads away from bookish strife,
That I with pious deed and talk
May extra-illustrate my life.

But if, O Lord, it pleaseth Thee
To keep me in temptation's way,
I humbly ask that I may be
Most notably beset to-day;
Let my temptation be a book,
Which I shall purchase, hold, and keep,
Whereon when other men shall look,
They'll wail to know I got it cheap.
Oh, let it such a volume be
As in rare copperplates abounds,
Large paper, clean, and fair to see,
Uncut, unique, unknown to Lowndes.

THE LYTTEL BOY

Sometime there ben a lyttel boy
That wolde not renne and play,
And helpless like that little tyke
Ben allwais in the way.
"Goe, make you merrie with the rest,"
His weary moder cried;
But with a frown he catcht her gown
And hong untill her side.
That boy did love his moder well,
Which spake him faire, I ween;
He loved to stand and hold her hand
And ken her with his een;
His cosset bleated in the croft,
His toys unheeded lay,—
He wolde not goe, but, tarrying soe,
Ben allwais in the way.

Godde loveth children and doth gird
His throne with soche as these,
And He doth smile in plaisaunce while
They cluster at His knees;
And sometime, when He looked on earth
And watched the bairns at play,

He kenned with joy a lyttel boy
Ben allwais in the way.
And then a moder felt her heart
How that it ben to-torne,—
She kissed eche day till she ben gray
The shoon he used to worn;
No bairn let hold untill her gown,
Nor played upon the floore,—
Godde's was the joy; a lyttel boy
Ben in the way no more!

THE TRUTH ABOUT HORACE

It is very aggravating
To hear the solemn prating
Of the fossils who are stating
That old Horace was a prude;
When we know that with the ladies
He was always raising Hades,
And with many an escapade his
Best productions are imbued.
There's really not much harm in a
Large number of his carmina,
But these people find alarm in a
Few records of his acts;
So they'd squelch the muse caloric,
And to students sophomoric
They d present as metaphoric
What old Horace meant for facts.
We have always thought 'em lazy;
Now we adjudge 'em crazy!
Why, Horace was a daisy
That was very much alive!
And the wisest of us know him
As his Lydia verses show him,—
Go, read that virile poem,—
It is No. 25.
He was a very owl, sir,
And starting out to prowl, sir,
You bet he made Rome howl, sir,
Until he filled his date;
With a massic-laden ditty
And a classic maiden pretty
He painted up the city,
And Maecenas paid the freight!

THE DEATH OF ROBIN HOOD

"Give me my bow," said Robin Hood,
"An arrow give to me;
And where 't is shot mark thou that spot,
For there my grave shall be."
Then Little John did make no sign,
And not a word he spake;
But he smiled, altho' with mickle woe
His heart was like to break.
He raised his master in his arms,
And set him on his knee;
And Robin's eyes beheld the skies,
The shaws, the greenwood tree.
The brook was babbling as of old,
The birds sang full and clear,
And the wild-flowers gay like a carpet lay
In the path of the timid deer.
"O Little John," said Robin Hood,
"Meseemeth now to be
Standing with you so stanch and true
Under the greenwood tree.
"And all around I hear the sound
Of Sherwood long ago,
And my merry men come back again,—
You know, sweet friend, you know!
"Now mark this arrow; where it falls,
When I am dead dig deep,
And bury me there in the greenwood where
I would forever sleep."
He twanged his bow. Upon its course
The clothyard arrow sped,
And when it fell in yonder dell,
Brave Robin Hood was dead.
The sheriff sleeps in a marble vault,
The king in a shroud of gold;
And upon the air with a chanted pray'r
Mingles the mock of mould.
But the deer draw to the shady pool,
The birds sing blithe and free,
And the wild-flow'rs bloom o'er a hidden tomb
Under the greenwood tree.

"LOLLYBY, LOLLY, LOLLYBY"

Last night, whiles that the curfew bell ben ringing,
I heard a moder to her dearie singing
"Lollyby, lolly, lollyby."
And presently that chylde did cease hys weeping,
And on his moder's breast did fall a-sleeping,
To "lolly, lolly, lollyby."

Faire ben the chylde unto his moder clinging,
But fairer yet the moder's gentle singing,—
"Lollyby, lolly, lollyby."
And angels came and kisst the dearie smiling
In dreems while him hys moder ben beguiling
With "lolly, lolly, lollyby!"
Then to my harte saies I, "Oh, that thy beating
Colde be assuaged by some swete voice repeating
'Lollyby, lolly, lollyby;'
That like this lyttel chylde I, too, ben sleeping
With plaisaunt phantasies about me creeping,
To 'lolly, lolly, lollyby!'"
Sometime—mayhap when curfew bells are ringing—
A weary harte shall heare straunge voices singing,
"Lollyby, lolly, lollyby;"
Sometime, mayhap, with Chrysts love round me streaming,
I shall be lulled into eternal dreeming
With "lolly, lolly, lollyby."

HORACE AND LYDIA RECONCILED

HORACE

When you were mine in auld lang syne,
And when none else your charms might ogle,
I'll not deny,
Fair nymph, that I
Was happier than a Persian mogul.

LYDIA

Before she came—that rival flame!—
(Was ever female creature sillier?)
In those good times,
Bepraised in rhymes,
I was more famed than Mother Ilia!

HORACE

Chloe of Thrace! With what a grace
Does she at song or harp employ her!
I'd gladly die
If only I
Might live forever to enjoy her!

LYDIA

My Sybaris so noble is
That, by the gods! I love him madly—
That I might save
Him from the grave
I'd give my life, and give it gladly!

HORACE

What if ma belle from favor fell,
And I made up my mind to shake her,
Would Lydia, then,
Come back again
And to her quondam flame betake her?

LYDIA

My other beau should surely go,
And you alone should find me gracious;
For no one slings
Such odes and things
As does the lauriger Horatius!

OUR TWO OPINIONS

Us two wuz boys when we fell out,—
Nigh to the age uv my youngest now;
Don't rec'lect what't wuz about,
Some small deeff'rence, I'll allow.
Lived next neighbors twenty years,
A-hatin' each other, me 'nd Jim,—
He havin' his opinyin uv me,
'Nd I havin' my opinyin uv him.
Grew up together 'nd would n't speak,
Courted sisters, 'nd marr'd 'em, too;
Tended same meetin'-house oncet a week,
A-hatin' each other through 'nd through!
But when Abe Linkern asked the West
F'r soldiers, we answered,—me 'nd Jim,—
He havin' his opinyin uv me,
'Nd I havin' my opinyin uv him.
But down in Tennessee one night
Ther' wuz sound uv firin' fur away,

'Nd the sergeant allowed ther' 'd be a fight
With the Johnnie Rebs some time nex' day;
'Nd as I wuz thinkin' uv Lizzie 'nd home
Jim stood afore me, long 'nd slim,—
He havin' his opinyin uv me,
'Nd I havin' my opinyin uv him.
Seemed like we knew there wuz goin' to be
Serious trouble f'r me 'nd him;
Us two shuck hands, did Jim 'nd me,
But never a word from me or Jim!
He went his way 'nd I went mine,
'Nd into the battle's roar went we,—
I havin' my opinyin uv Jim,
'Nd he havin' his opinyin uv me.
Jim never come back from the war again,
But I ha' n't forgot that last, last night
When, waitin' f'r orders, us two men
Made up 'nd shuck hands, afore the fight.
'Nd, after it all, it's soothin' to know
That here I be 'nd yonder's Jim,—
He havin' his opinyin uv me,
'Nd I havin' my opinyin uv him.

MOTHER AND CHILD
One night a tiny dewdrop fell
Into the bosom of a rose,—
"Dear little one, I love thee well,
Be ever here thy sweet repose!"
Seeing the rose with love bedight,
The envious sky frowned dark, and then
Sent forth a messenger of light
And caught the dewdrop up again.
"Oh, give me back my heavenly child,—
My love!" the rose in anguish cried;
Alas! the sky triumphant smiled,
And so the flower, heart-broken, died.

ORKNEY LULLABY
A moonbeam floateth from the skies,
Whispering, "Heigho, my dearie!
I would spin a web before your eyes,—
A beautiful web of silver light,
Wherein is many a wondrous sight
Of a radiant garden leagues away,
Where the softly tinkling lilies sway,
And the snow-white lambkins are at play,—
Heigho, my dearie!"
A brownie stealeth from the vine
Singing, "Heigho, my dearie!
And will you hear this song of mine,—
A song of the land of murk and mist
Where bideth the bud the dew hath kist?
Then let the moonbeam's web of light
Be spun before thee silvery white,
And I shall sing the livelong night,—
Heigho, my dearie!"
The night wind speedeth from the sea,
Murmuring, "Heigho, my dearie!
I bring a mariner's prayer for thee;
So let the moonbeam veil thine eyes,
And the brownie sing thee lullabies;
But I shall rock thee to and fro,
Kissing the brow he loveth so,
And the prayer shall guard thy bed, I trow,—
Heigho, my dearie!"

LITTLE MACK
This talk about the journalists that run the East is bosh,
We've got a Western editor that's little, but, O gosh!
He lives here in Mizzoora where the people are so set
In ante-bellum notions that they vote for Jackson yet;
But the paper he is running makes the rusty fossils swear,—
The smartest, likeliest paper that is printed anywhere!
And, best of all, the paragraphs are pointed as a tack,
And that's because they emanate From little Mack.
In architecture he is what you'd call a chunky man,
As if he'd been constructed on the summer cottage plan;
He has a nose like Bonaparte; and round his mobile mouth
Lies all the sensuous languor of the children of the South;

His dealings with reporters who affect a weekly bust
Have given to his violet eyes a shadow of distrust;
In glorious abandon his brown hair wanders back
From the grand Websterian forehead
Of little Mack.
No matter what the item is, if there's an item in it,
You bet your life he's on to it and nips it in a minute!
From multifarious nations, countries, monarchies, and lands,
From Afric's sunny fountains and India's coral strands,
From Greenland's icy mountains and Siloam's shady rills,
He gathers in his telegrams, and Houser pays the bills;
What though there be a dearth of news, he has a happy knack
Of scraping up a lot of scoops,
Does little Mack.
And learning? Well he knows the folks of every tribe and age
That ever played a part upon this fleeting human stage;
His intellectual system's so extensive and so greedy
That, when it comes to records, he's a walkin' cyclopedy;
For having studied (and digested) all the books a-goin',
It stands to reason he must know about all's worth a-knowin'!
So when a politician with a record's on the track,
We're apt to hear some history
From little Mack.
And when a fellow-journalist is broke and needs a twenty,
Who's allus ready to whack up a portion of his plenty?
Who's allus got a wallet that's as full of sordid gain
As his heart is full of kindness and his head is full of brain?
Whose bowels of compassion will in-va-ri-a-bly move
Their owner to those courtesies which plainly, surely prove
That he's the kind of person that never does go back
On a fellow that's in trouble?

Why, little Mack!
I've heard 'em tell of Dana, and of Bonner, and of Reid,
Of Johnnie Cockerill, who, I'll own, is very smart indeed;
Yet I don't care what their renown or influence may be,
One metropolitan exchange is quite enough for me!
So keep your Danas, Bonners, Reids, your Cockerills, and the rest,
The woods is full of better men all through this woolly West;
For all that sleek, pretentious, Eastern editorial pack
We wouldn't swap the shadow of
Our little Mack!

TO ROBIN GOODFELLOW

I see you, Maister Bawsy-brown,
Through yonder lattice creepin';
You come for cream and to gar me dream,
But you dinna find me sleepin'.
The moonbeam, that upon the floor
Wi' crickets ben a-jinkin',
Now steals away fra' her bonnie play—
Wi' a rosier blie, I'm thinkin'.
I saw you, Maister Bawsy-brown,
When the blue bells went a-ringin'
For the merrie fays o' the banks an' braes,
And I kenned your bonnie singin';
The gowans gave you honey sweets,
And the posies on the heather
Dript draughts o' dew for the faery crew
That danct and sang together.
But posie-bloom an' simmer-dew
And ither sweets o' faery
C'u'd na gae down wi' Bawsy-brown,
Sae nigh to Maggie's dairy!
My pantry shelves, sae clean and white,
Are set wi' cream and cheeses,—
Gae, gin you will, an' take your fill
Of whatsoever pleases.
Then wave your wand aboon my een
Until they close awearie,
And the night be past sae sweet and fast
Wi' dreamings o' my dearie.

But pinch the wench in yonder room,
For she's na gude nor bonnie,—
Her shelves be dust and her pans be rust,
And she winkit at my Johnnie!

APPLE-PIE AND CHEESE

Full many a sinful notion
Conceived of foreign powers
Has come across the ocean
To harm this land of ours;
And heresies called fashions
Have modesty effaced,
And baleful, morbid passions
Corrupt our native taste.
O tempora! O mores!
What profanations these
That seek to dim the glories
Of apple-pie and cheese!

I'm glad my education
Enables me to stand
Against the vile temptation
Held out on every hand;
Eschewing all the tittles
With vanity replete,
I'm loyal to the victuals
Our grandsires used to eat!
I'm glad I've got three willing boys
To hang around and tease
Their mother for the filling joys
Of apple-pie and cheese!

Your flavored creams and ices
And your dainty angel-food
Are mighty fine devices
To regale the dainty dude;
Your terrapin and oysters,
With wine to wash 'em down,
Are just the thing for roisters
When painting of the town;
No flippant, sugared notion
Shall my appetite appease,
Or bate my soul's devotion
To apple-pie and cheese!

The pie my Julia makes me
(God bless her Yankee ways!)
On memory's pinions takes me
To dear Green Mountain days;
And seems like I see Mother
Lean on the window-sill,
A-handin' me and brother
What she knows 'll keep us still;
And these feelings are so grateful,
Says I, "Julia, if you please,
I'll take another plateful
Of that apple-pie and cheese!"

And cheese! No alien it, sir,
That's brought across the sea,—
No Dutch antique, nor Switzer,
Nor glutinous de Brie;
There's nothing I abhor so
As mawmets of this ilk—
Give me the harmless morceau
That's made of true-blue milk!
No matter what conditions
Dyspeptic come to feaze,
The best of all physicians
Is apple-pie and cheese!

Though ribalds may decry 'em,
For these twin boons we stand,
Partaking thrice per diem
Of their fulness out of hand;
No enervating fashion
Shall cheat us of our right
To gratify our passion
With a mouthful at a bite!
We'll cut it square or bias,
Or any way we please,
And faith shall justify us
When we carve our pie and cheese!

De gustibus, 't is stated,
Non disputandum est.
Which meaneth, when translated,
That all is for the best.
So let the foolish choose 'em
The vapid sweets of sin,
I will not disabuse 'em
Of the heresy they're in;
But I, when I undress me
Each night, upon my knees
Will ask the Lord to bless me
With apple-pie and cheese!

KRINKEN

Krinken was a little child,—
It was summer when he smiled.
Oft the hoary sea and grim
Stretched its white arms out to him,
Calling, "Sun-child, come to me;
Let me warm my heart with thee!"
But the child heard not the sea,
Calling, yearning evermore
For the summer on the shore.
Krinken on the beach one day
Saw a maiden Nis at play;
On the pebbly beach she played
In the summer Krinken made.
Fair, and very fair, was she,
Just a little child was he.
"Krinken," said the maiden Nis,
"Let me have a little kiss,

Just a kiss, and go with me
To the summer-lands that be
Down within the silver sea."
Krinken was a little child—
By the maiden Nis beguiled,
Hand in hand with her went he,
And 'twas summer in the sea.
And the hoary sea and grim
To its bosom folded him—
Clasped and kissed the little form,
And the ocean's heart was warm.
Now the sea calls out no more;
It is winter on the shore,—
Winter where that little child
Made sweet summer when he smiled;
Though 'tis summer on the sea
Where with maiden Nis went he,—
Summer, summer evermore,—
It is winter on the shore,
Winter, winter evermore.
Of the summer on the deep
Come sweet visions in my sleep:
His fair face lifts from the sea,
His dear voice calls out to me,—
These my dreams of summer be.
Krinken was a little child,
By the maiden Nis beguiled;
Oft the hoary sea and grim
Reached its longing arms to him,
Crying, "Sun-child, come to me;
Let me warm my heart with thee!"
But the sea calls out no more;
It is winter on the shore,—
Winter, cold and dark and wild;
Krinken was a little child,—
It was summer when he smiled;
Down he went into the sea,
And the winter bides with me.
Just a little child was he.

BÉRANGER'S "BROKEN FIDDLE"

I
There, there, poor dog, my faithful friend,
Pay you no heed unto my sorrow:
But feast to-day while yet you may,—
Who knows but we shall starve to-morrow!

II
"Give us a tune," the foemen cried,
In one of their profane caprices;
I bade them "No"—they frowned, and, lo!
They dashed this innocent in pieces!

III
This fiddle was the village pride—
The mirth of every fête enhancing;
Its wizard art set every heart
As well as every foot to dancing.

IV
How well the bridegroom knew its voice,
As from its strings its song went gushing!
Nor long delayed the promised maid
Equipped for bridal, coy and blushing.

V
Why, it discoursed so merrily,
It quickly banished all dejection;
And yet, when pressed, our priest confessed
I played with pious circumspection.

VI
And though, in patriotic song,
It was our guide, compatriot, teacher,
I never thought the foe had wrought
His fury on the helpless creature!

VII
But there, poor dog, my faithful friend,
Pay you no heed unto my sorrow;
I prithee take this paltry cake,—
Who knows but we shall starve to-morrow!

VIII
Ah, who shall lead the Sunday choir
As this old fiddle used to do it?
Can vintage come, with this voice dumb
That used to bid a welcome to it?

IX
It soothed the weary hours of toil,
It brought forgetfulness to debtors;
Time and again from wretched men
It struck oppression's galling fetters.

X
No man could hear its voice, and hate;
It stayed the teardrop at its portal;
With that dear thing I was a king
As never yet was monarch mortal!

XI
Now has the foe—the vandal foe—

Struck from my hands their pride and glory;
There let it lie! In vengeance, I
Shall wield another weapon, gory!
XII
And if, O countrymen, I fall,
Beside our grave let this be spoken:
"No foe of France shall ever dance
Above the heart and fiddle, broken!"
XIII
So come, poor dog, my faithful friend,
I prithee do not heed my sorrow,
But feast to-day while yet you may,
For we are like to starve to-morrow.

THE LITTLE PEACH

A little peach in the orchard grew,—
A little peach of emerald hue;
Warmed by the sun and wet by the dew,
It grew.
One day, passing that orchard through,
That little peach dawned on the view
Of Johnny Jones and his sister Sue—
Them two.
Up at that peach a club they threw—
Down from the stem on which it grew
Fell that peach of emerald hue.
Mon Dieu!
John took a bite and Sue a chew,
And then the trouble began to brew,—
Trouble the doctor couldn't subdue.
Too true!
Under the turf where the daisies grew
They planted John and his sister Sue,
And their little souls to the angels flew,—
Boo hoo!
What of that peach of the emerald hue,
Warmed by the sun, and wet by the dew?
Ah, well, its mission on earth is through.
Adieu!
1880.

HORACE III. 13

O fountain of Bandusia,
Whence crystal waters flow,
With garlands gay and wine I'll pay
The sacrifice I owe;
A sportive kid with budding horns
I have, whose crimson blood
Anon shall dye and sanctify
Thy cool and babbling flood.
O fountain of Bandusia,
The dog-star's hateful spell
No evil brings unto the springs
That from thy bosom well;
Here oxen, wearied by the plough,
The roving cattle here,
Hasten in quest of certain rest
And quaff thy gracious cheer.
O fountain of Bandusia,
Ennobled shalt thou be,
For I shall sing the joys that spring
Beneath yon ilex-tree;
Yes, fountain of Bandusia,
Posterity shall know
The cooling brooks that from thy nooks
Singing and dancing go!

THE DIVINE LULLABY

I hear Thy voice, dear Lord;
I hear it by the stormy sea
When winter nights are black and wild,
And when, affright, I call to Thee;
It calms my fears and whispers me,
"Sleep well, my child."
I hear Thy voice, dear Lord,
In singing winds, in falling snow,
The curfew chimes, the midnight bell.
"Sleep well, my child," it murmurs low;
"The guardian angels come and go,—
O child, sleep well!"
I hear Thy voice, dear Lord,
Ay, though the singing winds be stilled,
Though hushed the tumult of the deep,
My fainting heart with anguish chilled
By Thy assuring tone is thrilled,—
"Fear not, and sleep!"
Speak on—speak on, dear Lord!
And when the last dread night is near,

With doubts and fears and terrors wild,
Oh, let my soul expiring hear
Only these words of heavenly cheer,
"Sleep well, my child!"

IN THE FIRELIGHT

The fire upon the hearth is low,
And there is stillness everywhere,
While like winged spirits, here and there,
The firelight shadows fluttering go.
And as the shadows round me creep,
A childish treble breaks the gloom,
And softly from a further room
Comes, "Now I lay me down to sleep."
And somehow, with that little prayer
And that sweet treble in my ears,
My thoughts go back to distant years
And linger with a loved one there;
And as I hear my child's amen,
My mother's faith comes back to me,—
Crouched at her side I seem to be,
And Mother holds my hands again.
Oh, for an hour in that dear place!
Oh, for the peace of that dear time!
Oh, for that childish trust sublime!
Oh, for a glimpse of Mother's face!
Yet, as the shadows round me creep,
I do not seem to be alone,—
Sweet magic of that treble tone,
And "Now I lay me down to sleep."
1885.

HEINE'S "WIDOW OR DAUGHTER?"

Shall I woo the one or other?
Both attract me—more's the pity!
Pretty is the widowed mother,
And the daughter, too, is pretty.
When I see that maiden shrinking,
By the gods I swear I'll get 'er!
But anon I fall to thinking
That the mother 'll suit me better!
So, like any idiot ass
Hungry for the fragrant fodder,
Placed between two bales of grass,
Lo, I doubt, delay, and dodder!

CHRISTMAS TREASURES

I count my treasures o'er with care.—
The little toy my darling knew,
A little sock of faded hue,
A little lock of golden hair.
Long years ago this holy time,
My little one—my all to me—
Sat robed in white upon my knee
And heard the merry Christmas chime.
"Tell me, my little golden-head,
If Santa Claus should come to-night,
What shall he bring my baby bright,—
What treasure for my boy?" I said.
And then he named this little toy,
While in his round and mournful eyes
There came a look of sweet surprise,
That spake his quiet, trustful joy.
And as he lisped his evening prayer
He asked the boon with childish grace;
Then, toddling to the chimney-place,
He hung this little stocking there.
That night, while lengthening shadows crept,
I saw the white-winged angels come
With singing to our lowly home
And kiss my darling as he slept.
They must have heard his little prayer,
For in the morn, with rapturous face,
He toddled to the chimney-place,
And found this little treasure there.
They came again one Christmas-tide,—
That angel host, so fair and white!
And singing all that glorious night,
They lured my darling from my side.
A little sock, a little toy,
A little lock of golden hair,
The Christmas music on the air,
A watching for my baby boy!
But if again that angel train
And golden-head come back for me,
To bear me to Eternity,
My watching will not be in vain!
1879.

DE AMICITIIS

Though care and strife
Elsewhere be rife,
Upon my word I do not heed 'em;
In bed I lie
With books hard by,
And with increasing zest I read 'em.

36

Propped up in bed,
So much I've read
Of musty tomes that I've a headful
Of tales and rhymes
Of ancient times,
Which, wife declares, are "simply dreadful!"
They give me joy
Without alloy;
And isn't that what books are made for?
And yet—and yet—
(Ah, vain regret!)
I would to God they all were paid for!
No festooned cup
Filled foaming up
Can lure me elsewhere to confound me;
Sweeter than wine
This love of mine
For these old books I see around me!
A plague, I say,
On maidens gay;
I'll weave no compliments to tell 'em!
Vain fool I were,
Did I prefer
Those dolls to these old friends in vellum!
At dead of night
My chamber's bright
Not only with the gas that's burning,
But with the glow
Of long ago,—
Of beauty back from eld returning.
Fair women's looks
I see in books,
I see them, and I hear their laughter,—
Proud, high-born maids,
Unlike the jades
Which men-folk now go chasing after!
Herein again
Speak valiant men
Of all nativities and ages;
I hear and smile
With rapture while
I turn these musty, magic pages.
The sword, the lance,
The morris dance,
The highland song, the greenwood ditty,
Of these I read,
Or, when the need,
My Miller grinds me grist that's gritty!
When of such stuff
We've had enough,
Why, there be other friends to greet us;
We'll moralize
In solemn wise
With Plato or with Epictetus.
Sneer as you may,
I'm proud to say
That I, for one, am very grateful
To Heaven, that sends
These genial friends
To banish other friendships hateful!
And when I'm done,
I'd have no son
Pounce on these treasures like a vulture;
Nay, give them half
My epitaph,
And let them share in my sepulture.
Then, when the crack
Of doom rolls back
The marble and the earth that hide me,
I'll smuggle home
Each precious tome,
Without a fear my wife shall chide me!

OUR LADY OF THE MINE

The Blue Horizon wuz a mine us fellers all thought well uv,
And there befell the episode I now perpose to tell uv;
'T wuz in the year uv sixty-nine,—somewhere along in summer,—
There hove in sight one afternoon a new and curious comer;
His name wuz Silas Pettibone,—a' artist by perfession,—
With a kit of tools and a big mustache and a pipe in his possession.
He told us, by our leave, he 'd kind uv like to make some sketches
Uv the snowy peaks, 'nd the foamin' crick, 'nd the distant mountain stretches;
"You're welkim, sir," sez we, although this scenery dodge seemed to us

A waste uv time where scenery wuz already sooper-floo-us.
All through the summer Pettibone kep' busy at his sketchin',—
At daybreak off for Eagle Pass, and home at nightfall, fetchin'
That everlastin' book uv his with spider-lines all through it;
Three-Fingered Hoover used to say there warn't no meanin' to it.
"Gol durn a man," sez he to him, "whose shif'less hand is sot at
A-drawin' hills that's full uv quartz that's pinin' to be got at!"
"Go on," sez Pettibone, "go on, if joshin' gratifies ye;
But one uv these fine times I'll show ye sumthin' will surprise ye!"
The which remark led us to think—although he didn't say it—
That Pettibone wuz owin' us a gredge 'nd meant to pay it.
One evenin' as we sat around the Restauraw de Casey,
A-singin' songs 'nd tellin' yarns the which wuz sumwhat racy,
In come that feller Pettibone, 'nd sez, "With your permission,
I'd like to put a picture I have made on exhibition."
He sot the picture on the bar 'nd drew aside its curtain,
Sayin', "I reckon you'll allow as how that's art, f'r certain!"
And then we looked, with jaws agape, but nary word wuz spoken,
And f'r a likely spell the charm uv silence wuz unbroken—
Till presently, as in a dream, remarked Three-Fingered Hoover:
"Onless I am mistaken, this is Pettibone's shef doover!"
It wuz a face—a human face—a woman's, fair 'nd tender—
Sot gracefully upon a neck white as a swan's, and slender;
The hair wuz kind uv sunny, 'nd the eyes wuz sort uv dreamy,
The mouth wuz half a-smilin', 'nd the cheeks wuz soft 'nd creamy;
It seemed like she wuz lookin' off into the west out yonder,
And seemed like, while she looked, we saw her eyes grow softer, fonder,—
Like, lookin' off into the west, where mountain mists wuz fallin',
She saw the face she longed to see and heerd his voice a-callin';
"Hooray!" we cried,—"a woman in the camp uv Blue Horizon!
Step right up, Colonel Pettibone, 'nd nominate your pizen!"
A curious situation,—one deservin' uv your pity,—
No human, livin', female thing this side of Denver City!
But jest a lot uv husky men that lived on sand 'nd bitters,—
Do you wonder that that woman's face consoled the lonesome critters?
And not a one but what it served in some way to remind him
Of a mother or a sister or a sweetheart left behind him;
And some looked back on happier days, and saw the old-time faces
And heerd the dear familiar sounds in old familiar places,—
A gracious touch of home. "Look here," sez Hoover, "ever'body
Quit thinkin' 'nd perceed at oncet to name his favorite toddy!"
It wuzn't long afore the news had spread the country over,
And miners come a-flockin' in like honey-bees to clover;
It kind uv did 'em good, they said, to feast their hungry eyes on
That picture uv Our Lady in the camp uv Blue Horizon.
But one mean cuss from Nigger Crick passed criticisms on 'er,—
Leastwise we overheerd him call her Pettibone's madonner,
The which we did not take to be respectful to a lady,
So we hung him in a quiet spot that wuz cool 'nd dry 'nd shady;
Which same might not have been good law, but it wuz the right manoeuvre
To give the critics due respect for Pettibone's shef doover.
Gone is the camp,—yes, years ago the Blue Horizon busted,
And every mother's son uv us got up one day 'nd dusted,
While Pettibone perceeded East with wealth in his possession,

And went to Yurrup, as I heerd, to
study his perfession;
So, like as not, you'll find him now
a-paintin' heads 'nd faces
At Venus, Billy Florence, and the
like I-talyun places.
But no sech face he'll paint again as
at old Blue Horizon,
For I'll allow no sweeter face no
human soul sot eyes on;
And when the critics talk so grand
uv Paris 'nd the Loover,
I say, "Oh, but you orter seen the
Pettibone shef doover!"

THE WANDERER
Upon a mountain height, far from
the sea,
I found a shell,
And to my listening ear the lonely
thing
Ever a song of ocean seemed to
sing,
Ever a tale of ocean seemed to tell.
How came the shell upon that
mountain height?
Ah, who can say
Whether there dropped by some too
careless hand,
Or whether there cast when Ocean
swept the Land,
Ere the Eternal had ordained the
Day?
Strange, was it not? Far from its
native deep,
One song it sang,—
Sang of the awful mysteries of the
tide,
Sang of the misty sea, profound and
wide,—
Ever with echoes of the ocean rang.
And as the shell upon the mountain
height
Sings of the sea,
So do I ever, leagues and leagues
away,—
So do I ever, wandering where I
may,—
Sing, O my home! sing, O my
home! of thee.
1883.

TO A USURPER
Aha! a traitor in the camp,
A rebel strangely bold,—
A lisping, laughing, toddling scamp,
Not more than four years old!
To think that I, who've ruled alone
So proudly in the past,
Should be ejected from my throne
By my own son at last!
He trots his treason to and fro,
As only babies can,
And says he'll be his mamma's beau
When he's a "gweat, big man"!
You stingy boy! you've always had
A share in mamma's heart;
Would you begrudge your poor old
dad
The tiniest little part?
That mamma, I regret to see,
Inclines to take your part,—
As if a dual monarchy
Should rule her gentle heart!
But when the years of youth have
sped,
The bearded man, I trow,
Will quite forget he ever said
He'd be his mamma's beau.
Renounce your treason, little son,
Leave mamma's heart to me;
For there will come another one
To claim your loyalty.
And when that other comes to you,
God grant her love may shine
Through all your life, as fair and
true
As mamma's does through mine!
1885.

LULLABY; BY THE SEA
Fair is the castle up on the hill—
Hushaby, sweet my own!
The night is fair, and the waves are
still,
And the wind is singing to you and
to me
In this lowly home beside the sea—
Hushaby, sweet my own!
On yonder hill is store of wealth—
Hushaby, sweet my own!
And revellers drink to a little one's
health;
But you and I bide night and day
For the other love that has sailed
away—
Hushaby, sweet my own!
See not, dear eyes, the forms that
creep
Ghostlike, O my own!

Out of the mists of the murmuring
    deep;
Oh, see them not and make no cry
    Till the angels of death have passed
    us by—
    Hushaby, sweet my own!
Ah, little they reck of you and me—
    Hushaby, sweet my own!
In our lonely home beside the sea;
They seek the castle up on the hill,
And there they will do their ghostly
    will—
    Hushaby, O my own!
Here by the sea a mother croons
    "Hushaby, sweet my own!"
In yonder castle a mother swoons
While the angels go down to the
    misty deep,
Bearing a little one fast asleep—
    Hushaby, sweet my own!

SOLDIER, MAIDEN, AND FLOWER

"Sweetheart, take this," a soldier
    said,
    "And bid me brave good-by;
It may befall we ne'er shall wed,
    But love can never die.
Be steadfast in thy troth to me,
    And then, whate'er my lot,
'My soul to God, my heart to
    thee,'—
    Sweetheart, forget me not!"
The maiden took the tiny flower
    And nursed it with her tears:
Lo! he who left her in that hour
    Came not in after years.
Unto a hero's death he rode
    'Mid shower of fire and shot;
But in the maiden's heart abode
    The flower, forget-me-not.
And when he came not with the rest
    From out the years of blood,
Closely unto her widowed breast
    She pressed a faded bud;
Oh, there is love and there is pain,
    And there is peace, God wot,—
And these dear three do live again
    In sweet forget-me-not.
'T is to an unmarked grave to-day
    That I should love to go,—
Whether he wore the blue or gray,
    What need that we should know?
"He loved a woman," let us say,
    And on that sacred spot,
To woman's love, that lives for aye,
    We'll strew forget-me-not.
    1887.

HORACE TO MELPOMENE

Lofty and enduring is the monument
    I've reared,—
    Come, tempests, with your
    bitterness assailing;
And thou, corrosive blasts of time,
    by all things mortal feared,
    Thy buffets and thy rage are
    unavailing!
I shall not altogether die; by far my
    greater part
    Shall mock man's common fate in
    realms infernal;
My works shall live as tributes to
    my genius and my art,—
My works shall be my monument
    eternal!
While this great Roman empire
stands and gods protect our fanes,
    Mankind with grateful hearts shall
    tell the story,
How one most lowly born upon the
    parched Apulian plains
    First raised the native lyric muse to
    glory.
Assume, revered Melpomene, the
    proud estate I've won,
    And, with thine own dear hand the
    meed supplying,
Bind thou about the forehead of thy
    celebrated son
    The Delphic laurel-wreath of fame
    undying!

AILSIE, MY BAIRN

Lie in my arms, Ailsie, my bairn,—
    Lie in my arms and dinna greit;
Long time been past syn I kenned
    you last,
But my harte been allwais the same,
    my swete.
    Ailsie, I colde not say you ill,
For out of the mist of your bitter
    tears,
And the prayers that rise from your
    bonnie eyes
    Cometh a promise of oder yeres.
I mind the time when we lost our
    bairn,—
Do you ken that time? A wambling
    tot,

You wandered away ane simmer day,
And we hunted and called, and found you not.
I promised God, if He'd send you back,
Alwaies to keepe and to love you, childe;
And I'm thinking again of that promise when
I see you creep out of the storm sae wild.
You came back then as you come back now,—
Your kirtle torn and your face all white;
And you stood outside and knockit and cried,
Just as you, dearie, did to-night.
Oh, never a word of the cruel wrang,
That has faded your cheek and dimmed your ee;
And never a word of the fause, fause lord,—
Only a smile and a kiss for me.
Lie in my arms, as long, long syne,
And sleepe on my bosom, deere wounded thing,—
I'm nae sae glee as I used to be,
Or I'd sing you the songs I used to sing.
But Ile kemb my fingers thro' y'r haire,
And nane shall know, but you and I,
Of the love and the faith that came to us baith
When Ailsie, my bairn, came home to die.

CORNISH LULLABY

Out on the mountain over the town,
All night long, all night long,
The trolls go up and the trolls go down,
Bearing their packs and crooning a song;
And this is the song the hill-folk croon,
As they trudge in the light of the misty moon,—
This is ever their dolorous tune:
"Gold, gold! ever more gold,—
Bright red gold for dearie!"
Deep in the hill the yeoman delves
All night long, all night long;
None but the peering, furtive elves
See his toil and hear his song;
Merrily ever the cavern rings
As merrily ever his pick he swings,
And merrily ever this song he sings:
"Gold, gold! ever more gold,—
Bright red gold for dearie!"
Mother is rocking thy lowly bed
All night long, all night long,
Happy to smooth thy curly head
And to hold thy hand and to sing her song;
'T is not of the hill-folk, dwarfed and old,
Nor the song of the yeoman, stanch and bold,
And the burden it beareth is not of gold;
But it's "Love, love!—nothing but love,—
Mother's love for dearie!"

UHLAND'S "THREE CAVALIERS"

There were three cavaliers that went over the Rhine,
And gayly they called to the hostess for wine.
"And where is thy daughter? We would she were here,—
Go fetch us that maiden to gladden our cheer!"
"I'll fetch thee thy goblets full foaming," she said,
"But in yon darkened chamber the maiden lies dead."
And lo! as they stood in the doorway, the white
Of a shroud and a dead shrunken face met their sight.
Then the first cavalier breathed a pitiful sigh,
And the throb of his heart seemed to melt in his eye,
And he cried, "Hadst thou lived, O my pretty white rose,
I ween I had loved thee and wed thee—who knows?"
The next cavalier drew aside a small space,
And stood to the wall with his hands to his face;
And this was the heart-cry that came with his tears:

"I loved her, I loved her these many long years!"
But the third cavalier kneeled him down in that place,
And, as it were holy, he kissed that dead face:
"I loved thee long years, and I love thee to-day,
And I'll love thee, dear maiden, forever and aye!"

A CHAUCERIAN PARAPHRASE OF HORACE

Syn that you, Chloe, to your moder sticken,
Maketh all ye yonge bacheloures full sicken;
Like as a lyttel deere you ben y-hiding
Whenas come lovers with theyre pityse chiding;
Sothly it ben faire to give up your moder
For to beare swete company with some oder;
Your moder ben well enow so farre shee goeth,
But that ben not farre enow, God knoweth;
Wherefore it ben sayed that foolysh ladyes
That marrye not shall leade an aype in Hadys;
But all that do with gode men wed full quickylye
When that they be on dead go to ye seints full sickerly.

NORSE LULLABY

The sky is dark and the hills are white
As the storm-king speeds from the north to-night,
And this is the song the storm-king sings,
As over the world his cloak he flings:
"Sleep, sleep, little one, sleep;"
He rustles his wings and gruffly sings:
"Sleep, little one, sleep."
On yonder mountain-side a vine
Clings at the foot of a mother pine;
The tree bends over the trembling thing,
And only the vine can hear her sing:
"Sleep, sleep, little one, sleep;
What shall you fear when I am here?
Sleep, little one, sleep."
The king may sing in his bitter flight,
The tree may croon to the vine to-night,
But the little snowflake at my breast
Liketh the song I sing the best,—
Sleep, sleep, little one, sleep;
Weary thou art, anext my heart
Sleep, little one, sleep.

BÉRANGER'S "MY LAST SONG PERHAPS" JANUARY, 181

When, to despoil my native France,
With flaming torch and cruel sword
And boisterous drums her foeman comes,
I curse him and his vandal horde!
Yet, what avail accrues to her,
If we assume the garb of woe?
Let's merry be,—in laughter we
May rescue somewhat from the foe!
Ah, many a brave man trembles now.
I (coward!) show no sign of fear;
When Bacchus sends his blessing, friends,
I drown my panic in his cheer.
Come, gather round my humble board,
And let the sparkling wassail flow,—
Chuckling to think, the while you drink,
"This much we rescue from the foe!"
My creditors beset me so
And so environed my abode,
That I agreed, despite my need,
To settle up the debts I owed;
When suddenly there came the news
Of this invasion, as you know;
I'll pay no score; pray, lend me more,—
I—I will keep it from the foe!
Now here's my mistress,—pretty dear!—
Feigns terror at this martial noise,
And yet, methinks, the artful minx
Would like to meet those soldier boys!
I tell her that they're coarse and rude,

Yet feel she don't believe 'em so,—
Well, never mind; so she be kind,
That much I rescue from the foe!
If, brothers, hope shall have in store
For us and ours no friendly glance,
Let's rather die than raise a cry
Of welcome to the foes of France!
But, like the swan that dying sings,
Let us, O Frenchmen, singing go,—
Then shall our cheer, when death is near,
Be so much rescued from the foe!

MR. DANA, OF THE NEW YORK SUN

Thar showed up out'n Denver in the spring uv '81
A man who'd worked with Dana on the Noo York Sun.
His name wuz Cantell Whoppers, 'nd he wuz a sight ter view
Ez he walked inter the orfice 'nd inquired fer work ter do.
Thar warn't no places vacant then,— fer be it understood,
That wuz the time when talent flourished at that altitood;
But thar the stranger lingered, tellin' Raymond 'nd the rest
Uv what perdigious wonders he could do when at his best,
Till finally he stated (quite by chance) that he hed done
A heap uv work with Dana on the Noo York Sun.

Wall, that wuz quite another thing; we owned that ary cuss
Who'd worked f'r Mr. Dana must be good enough fer us!
And so we tuk the stranger's word 'nd nipped him while we could,
For if we didn't take him we knew John Arkins would;
And Cooper, too, wuz mouzin' round fer enterprise 'nd brains,
Whenever them commodities blew in across the plains.
At any rate we nailed him, which made ol' Cooper swear
And Arkins tear out handfuls uv his copious curly hair;
But we set back and cackled, 'nd bed a power uv fun
With our man who'd worked with Dana on the Noo York Sun.

It made our eyes hang on our cheeks 'nd lower jaws ter drop,
Ter hear that feller tellin' how ol' Dana run his shop:
It seems that Dana wuz the biggest man you ever saw,—
He lived on human bein's, 'nd preferred to eat 'em raw!
If he hed Democratic drugs ter take, before he took 'em,
As good old allopathic laws prescribe, he allus shook 'em.
The man that could set down 'nd write like Dany never grew,
And the sum of human knowledge wuzn't half what Dana knew;
The consequence appeared to be that nearly every one
Concurred with Mr. Dana of the Noo York Sun.

This feller, Cantell Whoppers, never brought an item in,—
He spent his time at Perrin's shakin' poker dice f'r gin.
Whatever the assignment, he wuz allus sure to shirk,
He wuz very long on likker and all-fired short on work!
If any other cuss had played the tricks he dared ter play,
The daisies would be bloomin' over his remains to-day;
But somehow folks respected him and stood him to the last,
Considerin' his superior connections in the past.
So, when he bilked at poker, not a sucker drew a gun
On the man who 'd worked with Dana on the Noo York Sun.

Wall, Dana came ter Denver in the fall uv '83.
A very different party from the man we thought ter see,—
A nice 'nd clean old gentleman, so dignerfied 'nd calm,
You bet yer life he never did no human bein' harm!
A certain hearty manner 'nd a fulness uv the vest
Betokened that his sperrits 'nd his victuals wuz the best;
His face wuz so benevolent, his smile so sweet 'nd kind,

That they seemed to be the reflex uv
an honest, healthy mind;
And God had set upon his head a
crown uv silver hair
In promise uv the golden crown He
meaneth him to wear.
So, uv us boys that met him out'n
Denver, there wuz none
But fell in love with Dana uv the
Noo York Sun.

But when he came to Denver in that
fall uv '83,
His old friend Cantell Whoppers
disappeared upon a spree;
The very thought uv seein' Dana
worked upon him so
(They hadn't been together fer a year
or two, you know),
That he borrered all the stuff he
could and started on a bat,
And, strange as it may seem, we
didn't see him after that.
So, when ol' Dana hove in sight, we
couldn't understand
Why he didn't seem to notice that
his crony wa'n't on hand;
No casual allusion, not a question,
no, not one,
For the man who'd "worked with
Dana on the Noo York Sun!"

We broke it gently to him, but he
didn't seem surprised,
Thar wuz no big burst uv passion as
we fellers had surmised.
He said that Whoppers wuz a man
he 'd never heerd about,
But he mought have carried papers
on a Jarsey City route;
And then he recollected hearin' Mr.
Laffan say
That he'd fired a man named
Whoppers fur bein' drunk one day,
Which, with more likker underneath
than money in his vest,
Had started on a freight-train fur the
great 'nd boundin' West,
But further information or statistics
he had none
Uv the man who'd "worked with
Dana on the Noo York Sun."

We dropped the matter quietly 'nd
never made no fuss,—
When we get played for suckers,
why, that's a horse on us!—
But every now 'nd then we Denver
fellers have to laff
To hear some other paper boast uv
havin' on its staff
A man who's "worked with Dana,"
'nd then we fellers wink
And pull our hats down on our eyes
'nd set around 'nd think.
It seems like Dana couldn't be as
smart as people say,
If he educates so many folks 'nd lets
'em get away;
And, as for us, in future we'll be
very apt to shun
The man who "worked with Dana
on the Noo York Sun."

But bless ye, Mr. Dana! may you
live a thousan' years,
To sort o' keep things lively in this
vale of human tears;
An' may I live a thousan', too,—a
thousan' less a day,
For I shouldn't like to be on earth to
hear you'd passed away.
And when it comes your time to go
you'll need no Latin chaff
Nor biographic data put in your
epitaph;
But one straight line of English and
of truth will let folks know
The homage 'nd the gratitude 'nd
reverence they owe;
You'll need no epitaph but this:
"Here sleeps the man who run
That best 'nd brightest paper, the
Noo York Sun."

SICILIAN LULLABY

Hush, little one, and fold your
hands;
The sun hath set, the moon is high;
The sea is singing to the sands,
And wakeful posies are beguiled
By many a fairy lullaby:
Hush, little child, my little child!
Dream, little one, and in your
dreams
Float upward from this lowly
place,—
Float out on mellow, misty streams
To lands where bideth Mary mild,
And let her kiss thy little face,
You little child, my little child!
Sleep, little one, and take thy rest,
With angels bending over thee,—

Sleep sweetly on that Father's breast
Whom our dear Christ hath reconciled;
But stay not there,—come back to me,
O little child, my little child!

HORACE TO PYRRHA

What perfumed, posie-dizened sirrah,
With smiles for diet,
Clasps you, O fair but faithless Pyrrha,
On the quiet?
For whom do you bind up your tresses,
As spun-gold yellow,—
Meshes that go, with your caresses,
To snare a fellow?
How will he rail at fate capricious,
And curse you duly!
Yet now he deems your wiles delicious,
You perfect, truly!
Pyrrha, your love's a treacherous ocean;
He'll soon fall in there!
Then shall I gloat on his commotion,
For I have been there!

THE TWENTY-THIRD PSALM

My Shepherd is the Lord my God,—
There is no want I know;
His flock He leads in verdant meads,
Where tranquil waters flow.
He doth restore my fainting soul
With His divine caress,
And, when I stray, He points the way
To paths of righteousness.
Yea, though I walk the vale of death,
What evil shall I fear?
Thy staff and rod are mine, O God,
And Thou, my Shepherd, near!
Mine enemies behold the feast
Which my dear Lord hath spread;
And, lo! my cup He filleth up,
With oil anoints my head!
Goodness and mercy shall be mine
Unto my dying day;
Then will I bide at His dear side
Forever and for aye!

THE BIBLIOMANIAC'S BRIDE

The women-folk are like to books,—
Most pleasing to the eye,
Whereon if anybody looks
He feels disposed to buy.
I hear that many are for sale,—
Those that record no dates,
And such editions as regale
The view with colored plates.
Of every quality and grade
And size they may be found,—
Quite often beautifully made,
As often poorly bound.
Now, as for me, had I my choice,
I'd choose no folio tall,
But some octavo to rejoice
My sight and heart withal,—
As plump and pudgy as a snipe;
Well worth her weight in gold;
Of honest, clean, conspicuous type,
And just the size to hold!
With such a volume for my wife
How should I keep and con!
How like a dream should run my life
Unto its colophon!
Her frontispiece should be more fair
Than any colored plate;
Blooming with health, she would not care
To extra-illustrate.
And in her pages there should be
A wealth of prose and verse,
With now and then a jeu d'esprit,—
But nothing ever worse!
Prose for me when I wished for prose,
Verse when to verse inclined,—
Forever bringing sweet repose
To body, heart, and mind.
Oh, I should bind this priceless prize
In bindings full and fine,
And keep her where no human eyes
Should see her charms, but mine!
With such a fair unique as this
What happiness abounds!
Who—who could paint my rapturous bliss,
My joy unknown to Lowndes!

CHRISTMAS HYMN

Sing, Christmas bells!
Say to the earth this is the morn
Whereon our Saviour-King is born;
Sing to all men,—the bond, the free,
The rich, the poor, the high, the low,

The little child that sports in glee,
The aged folk that tottering go,—
Proclaim the morn
That Christ is born,
That saveth them and saveth me!
Sing, angel host!
Sing of the star that God has placed
Above the manger in the east;
Sing of the glories of the night,
The virgin's sweet humility,
The Babe with kingly robes bedight,
Sing to all men where'er they be
This Christmas morn;
For Christ is born,
That saveth them and saveth me!
Sing, sons of earth!
O ransomed seed of Adam, sing!
God liveth, and we have a king!
The curse is gone, the bond are free,—
By Bethlehem's star that brightly beamed,
By all the heavenly signs that be,
We know that Israel is redeemed;
That on this morn
The Christ is born
That saveth you and saveth me!
Sing, O my heart!
Sing thou in rapture this dear morn
Whereon the blessed Prince is born!
And as thy songs shall be of love,
So let my deeds be charity,—
By the dear Lord that reigns above,
By Him that died upon the tree,
By this fair morn
Whereon is born
The Christ that saveth all and me!

JAPANESE LULLABY

Sleep, little pigeon, and fold your wings,—
Little blue pigeon with velvet eyes;
Sleep to the singing of mother-bird swinging—
Swinging the nest where her little one lies.
Away out yonder I see a star,—
Silvery star with a tinkling song;
To the soft dew falling I hear it calling—
Calling and tinkling the night along.
In through the window a moonbeam comes,—
Little gold moonbeam with misty wings;
All silently creeping, it asks, "Is he sleeping—
Sleeping and dreaming while mother sings?"
Up from the sea there floats the sob
Of the waves that are breaking upon the shore,
As though they were groaning in anguish, and moaning—
Bemoaning the ship that shall come no more.
But sleep, little pigeon, and fold your wings,—
Little blue pigeon with mournful eyes;
Am I not singing?—see, I am swinging—
Swinging the nest where my darling lies.

"GOOD-BY—GOD BLESS YOU!"

I like the Anglo-Saxon speech
With its direct revealings;
It takes a hold, and seems to reach
'Way down into your feelings;
That some folk deem it rude, I know,
And therefore they abuse it;
But I have never found it so,—
Before all else I choose it.
I don't object that men should air
The Gallic they have paid for,
With "Au revoir," "Adieu, ma chère,"
For that's what French was made for.
But when a crony takes your hand
At parting, to address you,
He drops all foreign lingo and
He says, "Good-by—God bless you!"
This seems to me a sacred phrase,
With reverence impassioned,—
A thing come down from righteous days,
Quaintly but nobly fashioned;
It well becomes an honest face,
A voice that's round and cheerful;
It stays the sturdy in his place,
And soothes the weak and fearful.
Into the porches of the ears
It steals with subtle unction,
And in your heart of hearts appears
To work its gracious function;

And all day long with pleasing song
　　It lingers to caress you,—
I'm sure no human heart goes wrong
　　That's told "Good-by—God bless you!"
I love the words,—perhaps because,
　　When I was leaving Mother,
Standing at last in solemn pause
　　We looked at one another,
And I—I saw in Mother's eyes
　　The love she could not tell me,—
A love eternal as the skies,
　　Whatever fate befell me;
She put her arms about my neck
　　And soothed the pain of leaving,
And though her heart was like to break,
　　She spoke no word of grieving;
She let no tear bedim her eye,
　　For fear that might distress me,
But, kissing me, she said good-by,
　　And asked our God to bless me.

HORACE TO PHYLLIS

Come, Phyllis, I've a cask of wine
　　That fairly reeks with precious juices,
And in your tresses you shall twine
　　The loveliest flowers this vale produces.
My cottage wears a gracious smile,—
　　The altar, decked in floral glory,
Yearns for the lamb which bleats the while
　　As though it pined for honors gory.
Hither our neighbors nimbly fare,—
　　The boys agog, the maidens snickering;
And savory smells possess the air
　　As skyward kitchen flames are flickering.
You ask what means this grand display,
　　This festive throng, and goodly diet?
Well, since you're bound to have your way,
　　I don't mind telling, on the quiet.
'Tis April 13, as you know,—
　　A day and month devote to Venus,
Whereon was born, some years ago,
　　My very worthy friend Maecenas.
Nay, pay no heed to Telephus,—
　　Your friends agree he doesn't love you;
The way he flirts convinces us
　　He really is not worthy of you!
Aurora's son, unhappy lad!
　　You know the fate that overtook him?
And Pegasus a rider had—
　　I say he had before he shook him!
Haec docet (as you must agree):
　　'T is meet that Phyllis should discover
A wisdom in preferring me
　　And mittening every other lover.
So come, O Phyllis, last and best
　　Of loves with which this heart's been smitten,—
Come, sing my jealous fears to rest,
　　And let your songs be those I've written.

CHRYSTMASSE OF OLDE

God rest you, Chrysten gentil men,
　　Wherever you may be,—
God rest you all in fielde or hall,
　　Or on ye stormy sea;
For on this morn oure Chryst is born
　　That saveth you and me.
Last night ye shepherds in ye east
　　Saw many a wondrous thing;
Ye sky last night flamed passing bright
　　Whiles that ye stars did sing,
And angels came to bless ye name
　　Of Jesus Chryst, oure Kyng.
God rest you, Chrysten gentil men,
　　Faring where'er you may;
In noblesse court do thou no sport,
　　In tournament no playe,
In paynim lands hold thou thy hands
　　From bloudy works this daye.
But thinking on ye gentil Lord
　　That died upon ye tree,
Let troublings cease and deeds of peace
　　Abound in Chrystantie;
For on this morn ye Chryst is born
　　That saveth you and me.

AT THE DOOR

I thought myself indeed secure,
　　So fast the door, so firm the lock;
But, lo! he toddling comes to lure
　　My parent ear with timorous knock.
My heart were stone could it withstand
　　The sweetness of my baby's plea,—
That timorous, baby knocking and

47

"Please let me in,—it's only me."
I threw aside the unfinished book,
Regardless of its tempting charms,
And opening wide the door, I took
My laughing darling in my arms.
Who knows but in Eternity,
I, like a truant child, shall wait
The glories of a life to be,
Beyond the Heavenly Father's gate?
And will that Heavenly Father heed
The truant's supplicating cry,
As at the outer door I plead,
"'T is I, O Father! only I"?
1886.

HI-SPY

Strange that the city thoroughfare,
Noisy and bustling all the day,
Should with the night renounce its care,
And lend itself to children's play!
Oh, girls are girls, and boys are boys,
And have been so since Abel's birth,
And shall be so till dolls and toys
Are with the children swept from earth.
The self-same sport that crowns the day
Of many a Syrian shepherd's son,
Beguiles the little lads at play
By night in stately Babylon.
I hear their voices in the street,
Yet 't is so different now from then!
Come, brother! from your winding-sheet,
And let us two be boys again!
1886.

LITTLE CROODLIN DOO

Ho, pretty bee, did you see my croodlin doo?
Ho, little lamb, is she jinkin' on the lea?
Ho, bonnie fairy, bring my dearie back to me—
Got a lump o' sugar an' a posie for you,
Only bring back my wee, wee croodlin doo!
Why, here you are, my little croodlin doo!
Looked in er cradle, but didn't find you there,
Looked f'r my wee, wee croodlin doo ever'where;
Ben kind lonesome all er day withouten you;
Where you ben, my little wee, wee croodlin doo?
Now you go balow, my little croodlin doo;
Now you go rockaby ever so far,—
Rockaby, rockaby, up to the star
That's winkin' an' blinkin' an' singin' to you
As you go balow, my wee, wee croodlin doo!

THE "HAPPY ISLES" OF HORACE

Oh, come with me to the Happy Isles
In the golden haze off yonder,
Where the song of the sun-kissed breeze beguiles,
And the ocean loves to wander.
Fragrant the vines that mantle those hills,
Proudly the fig rejoices;
Merrily dance the virgin rills,
Blending their myriad voices.
Our herds shall fear no evil there,
But peacefully feed and rest them;
Neither shall serpent nor prowling bear
Ever come there to molest them.
Neither shall Eurus, wanton bold,
Nor feverish drouth distress us,
But he that compasseth heat and cold
Shall temper them both to bless us.
There no vandal foot has trod,
And the pirate hosts that wander
Shall never profane the sacred sod
Of those beautiful Isles out yonder.
Never a spell shall blight our vines,
Nor Sirius blaze above us,
But you and I shall drink our wines
And sing to the loved that love us.
So come with me where Fortune smiles
And the gods invite devotion,—
Oh, come with me to the Happy Isles
In the haze of that far-off ocean!

DUTCH LULLABY

Wynken, Blynken, and Nod one night
Sailed off in a wooden shoe,—
Sailed on a river of misty light

Into a sea of dew.
"Where are you going, and what do you wish?"
The old moon asked the three.
"We have come to fish for the herring-fish
That live in this beautiful sea;
Nets of silver and gold have we,"
Said Wynken,
Blynken,
And Nod.
The old moon laughed and sung a song,
As they rocked in the wooden shoe;
And the wind that sped them all night long
Ruffled the waves of dew;
The little stars were the herring-fish
That lived in the beautiful sea.
"Now cast your nets wherever you wish,
But never afeard are we!"
So cried the stars to the fishermen three,
Wynken,
Blynken,
And Nod.
All night long their nets they threw
For the fish in the twinkling foam,
Then down from the sky came the wooden shoe,
Bringing the fishermen home;
'T was all so pretty a sail, it seemed
As if it could not be;
And some folk thought 't was a dream they'd dreamed
Of sailing that beautiful sea;
But I shall name you the fishermen three:
Wynken,
Blynken,
And Nod.
Wynken and Blynken are two little eyes,
And Nod is a little head,
And the wooden shoe that sailed the skies
Is a wee one's trundle-bed;
So shut your eyes while Mother sings
Of wonderful sights that be,
And you shall see the beautiful things
As you rock on the misty sea
Where the old shoe rocked the fishermen three,—
Wynken,
Blynken,
And Nod.

HUGO'S "FLOWER TO BUTTERFLY"

Sweet, bide with me and let my love
Be an enduring tether;
Oh, wanton not from spot to spot,
But let us dwell together.
You've come each morn to sip the sweets
With which you found me dripping,
Yet never knew it was not dew
But tears that you were sipping.
You gambol over honey meads
Where siren bees are humming;
But mine the fate to watch and wait
For my beloved's coming.
The sunshine that delights you now
Shall fade to darkness gloomy;
You should not fear if, biding here,
You nestled closer to me.
So rest you, love, and be my love,
That my enraptured blooming
May fill your sight with tender light,
Your wings with sweet perfuming.
Or, if you will not bide with me
Upon this quiet heather,
Oh, give me wing, thou beauteous thing,
That we may soar together.

A PROPER TREWE IDYLL OF CAMELOT

Whenas ye plaisaunt Aperille shoures have washed and purged awaye
Ye poysons and ye rheums of earth to make a merrie May,
Ye shraddy boscage of ye woods ben full of birds that syng
Right merrilie a madrigal unto ye waking spring,
Ye whiles that when ye face of earth ben washed and wiped ycleane
Her peeping posies blink and stare like they had ben her een;
Then, wit ye well, ye harte of man ben turned to thoughts of love,
And, tho' it ben a lyon erst, it now ben like a dove!
And many a goodly damosel in innocence beguiles

Her owne trewe love with sweet discourse and divers plaisaunt wiles.
In soche a time ye noblesse liege that ben Kyng Arthure hight
Let cry a joust and tournament for evereche errant knyght,
And, lo! from distant Joyous-garde and eche adjacent spot
A company of noblesse lords fared unto Camelot,
Wherein were mighty feastings and passing merrie cheere,
And eke a deale of dismal dole, as you shall quickly heare.
It so befell upon a daye when jousts ben had and while
Sir Launcelot did ramp around ye ring in gallaunt style,
There came an horseman shriking sore and rashing wildly home,—
A mediaeval horseman with ye usual flecks of foame;
And he did brast into ye ring, wherein his horse did drop,
Upon ye which ye rider did with like abruptness stop,
And with fatigue and fearfulness continued in a swound
Ye space of half an hour or more before a leech was founde.
"Now tell me straight," quod Launcelot, "what varlet knyght you be,
Ere that I chine you with my sworde and cleave your harte in three!"
Then rolled that knyght his bloudy een, and answered with a groane,—
"By worthy God that hath me made and shope ye sun and mone,
There fareth hence an evil thing whose like ben never seene,
And tho' he sayeth nony worde, he bode the ill, I ween.
So take your parting, evereche one, and gird you for ye fraye,
By all that's pure, ye Divell sure doth trend his path this way!"
Ye which he quoth and fell again into a deadly swound,
And on that spot, perchance (God wot), his bones mought yet be founde.
Then evereche knight girt on his sworde and shield and hied him straight
To meet ye straunger sarasen hard by ye city gate;

Full sorely moaned ye damosels and tore their beautyse haire
For that they feared an hippogriff wolde come to eate them there;
But as they moaned and swounded there too numerous to relate,
Kyng Arthure and Sir Launcelot stode at ye city gate,
And at eche side and round about stode many a noblesse knyght
With helm and speare and sworde and shield and mickle valor dight.
Anon there came a straunger, but not a gyaunt grim,
Nor yet a draggon,—but a person gangling, long, and slim;
Yclad he was in guise that ill-beseemed those knyghtly days,
And there ben nony etiquette in his uplandish ways;
His raiment was of dusty gray, and perched above his lugs
There ben the very latest style of blacke and shiny pluggs;
His nose ben like a vulture beake, his blie ben swart of hue,
And curly ben ye whiskers through ye which ye zephyrs blewe;
Of all ye een that ben yseene in countries far or nigh,
None nonywhere colde hold compare unto that straunger's eye;
It was an eye of soche a kind as never ben on sleepe,
Nor did it gleam with kindly beame, nor did not use to weepe;
But soche an eye ye widdow hath,— an hongrey eye and wan,
That spyeth for an oder chaunce whereby she may catch on;
An eye that winketh of itself, and sayeth by that winke
Ye which a maiden sholde not knowe nor never even thinke;
Which winke ben more exceeding swift nor human thought ben thunk,
And leaveth doubting if so be that winke ben really wunke;
And soch an eye ye catte-fysshe hath when that he ben on dead
And boyled a goodly time and served with capers on his head;
A rayless eye, a bead-like eye, whose famisht aspect shows

50

It hungereth for ye verdant banks
whereon ye wild time grows;
An eye that hawketh up and down
for evereche kind of game,
And, when he doth espy ye which,
he tumbleth to ye same.
Now when he kenned Sir Launcelot
in armor clad, he quod,
"Another put-a-nickel-in-and-see-
me-work, be god!"
But when that he was ware a man
ben standing in that suit,
Ye straunger threw up both his
hands, and asked him not to shoote.
Then spake Kyng Arthure: "If soe
be you mind to do no ill,
Come, enter into Camelot, and eat
and drink your fill;
But say me first what you are hight,
and what mought be your quest."
Ye straunger quod, "I'm five feet
ten, and fare me from ye West!"
"Sir Fivefeetten," Kyng Arthure
said, "I bid you welcome here;
So make you merrie as you list with
plaisaunt wine and cheere;
This very night shall be a feast soche
like ben never seene,
And you shall be ye honored guest
of Arthure and his queene.
Now take him, good sir
Maligraunce, and entertain him well
Until soche time as he becomes our
guest, as I you tell."
That night Kyng Arthure's table
round with mighty care ben spread,
Ye oder knyghts sate all about, and
Arthure at ye heade:
Oh, 't was a goodly spectacle to ken
that noblesse liege
Dispensing hospitality from his
commanding siege!
Ye pheasant and ye meate of boare,
ye haunch of velvet doe,
Ye canvass hamme he them did
serve, and many good things moe.
Until at last Kyng Arthure cried:
"Let bring my wassail cup,
And let ye sound of joy go round,—
I'm going to set 'em up!
I've pipes of Malmsey, May-wine,
sack, metheglon, mead, and sherry,
Canary, Malvoisie, and Port, swete
Muscadelle and perry;

Rochelle, Osey, and Romenay,
Tyre, Rhenish, posset too,
With kags and pails of foaming ales
of brown October brew.
To wine and beer and other cheere I
pray you now despatch ye,
And for ensample, wit ye well,
sweet sirs, I'm looking at ye!"
Unto which toast of their liege lord
ye oders in ye party
Did lout them low in humble wise
and bid ye same drink hearty.
So then ben merrisome discourse
and passing plaisaunt cheere,
And Arthure's tales of hippogriffs
ben mervaillous to heare;
But stranger far than any tale told of
those knyghts of old
Ben those facetious narratives ye
Western straunger told.
He told them of a country many
leagues beyond ye sea
Where evereche forraine nuisance
but ye Chinese man ben free,
And whiles he span his monstrous
yarns, ye ladies of ye court
Did deem ye listening thereunto to
be right plaisaunt sport;
And whiles they listened, often he
did squeeze a lily hande,
Ye which proceeding ne'er before
ben done in Arthure's lande;
And often wank a sidelong wink
with either roving eye,
Whereat ye ladies laughen so that
they had like to die.
But of ye damosels that sat around
Kyng Arthure's table
He liked not her that sometime ben
ron over by ye cable,
Ye which full evil hap had harmed
and marked her person so
That in a passing wittie jest he
dubbeth her ye crow.
But all ye oders of ye girls did
please him passing well
And they did own him for to be a
proper seeming swell;
And in especial Guinevere esteemed
him wondrous faire,
Which had made Arthure and his
friend, Sir Launcelot, to sware
But that they both ben so far gone
with posset, wine, and beer,

51

They colde not see ye carrying-on,
nor neither colde not heare;
For of eche liquor Arthure quafft,
and so did all ye rest,
Save only and excepting that smooth
straunger from the West.
When as these oders drank a toast,
he let them have their fun
With divers godless mixings, but he
stock to willow run,
Ye which (and all that reade these
words sholde profit by ye warning)
Doth never make ye head to feel like
it ben swelled next morning.
Now, wit ye well, it so befell that
when the night grew dim,
Ye Kyng was carried from ye hall
with a howling jag on him,
Whiles Launcelot and all ye rest that
to his highness toadied
Withdrew them from ye banquet-
hall and sought their couches loaded.
Now, lithe and listen, lordings all,
whiles I do call it shame
That, making cheer with wine and
beer, men do abuse ye same;
Though eche be well enow alone, ye
mixing of ye two
Ben soche a piece of foolishness as
only ejiots do.
Ye wine is plaisaunt bibbing whenas
ye gentles dine,
And beer will do if one hath not ye
wherewithal for wine,
But in ye drinking of ye same ye
wise are never floored
By taking what ye tipplers call too
big a jag on board.
Right hejeous is it for to see soche
dronkonness of wine
Whereby some men are used to
make themselves to be like swine;
And sorely it repenteth them, for
when they wake next day
Ye fearful paynes they suffer ben
soche as none mought say,
And soche ye brenning in ye throat
and brasting of ye head
And soche ye taste within ye mouth
like one had been on dead,—Soche
be ye foul conditions that these
unhappy men
Sware they will never drink no drop
of nony drinke again.

Yet all so frail and vain a thing and
weak withal is man
That he goeth on an oder tear
whenever that he can.
And like ye evil quatern or ye hills
that skirt ye skies,
Ye jag is reproductive and jags on
jags arise.
Whenas Aurora from ye east in
dewy splendor hied
King Arthure dreemed he saw a
snaix and ben on fire inside,
And waking from this hejeous
dreeme he sate him up in bed,—
"What, ho! an absynthe cocktail,
knave! and make it strong!" he said;
Then, looking down beside him, lo!
his lady was not there—
He called, he searched, but, Goddis
wounds! he found her nonywhere;
And whiles he searched, Sir
Maligraunce rashed in, wood wroth,
and cried,
"Methinketh that ye straunger
knyght hath snuck away my bride!"
And whiles he spake a motley score
of other knyghts brast in
And filled ye royall chamber with a
mickle fearfull din,
For evereche one had lost his wiffe
nor colde not spye ye same,
Nor colde not spye ye straunger
knyght, Sir Fivefeetten of name.
Oh, then and there was grevious
lamentation all arounde,
For nony dame nor damosel in
Camelot ben found,—
Gone, like ye forest leaves that
speed afore ye autumn wind.
Of all ye ladies of that court not one
ben left behind
Save only that same damosel ye
straunger called ye crow,
And she allowed with moche regret
she ben too lame to go;
And when that she had wept full
sore, to Arthure she confess'd
That Guinevere had left this word
for Arthure and ye rest:
"Tell them," she quod, "we shall
return to them whenas we've made
This little deal we have with ye
Chicago Bourde of Trade."

BÉRANGER'S

"MA VOCATION"

Misery is my lot,
Poverty and pain;
Ill was I begot,
Ill must I remain;
Yet the wretched days
One sweet comfort bring,
When God whispering says,
"Sing, O singer, sing!"
Chariots rumble by,
Splashing me with mud;
Insolence see I
Fawn to royal blood;
Solace have I then
From each galling sting
In that voice again,—
"Sing, O singer, sing!"
Cowardly at heart,
I am forced to play
A degraded part
For its paltry pay;
Freedom is a prize
For no starving thing;
Yet that small voice cries,
"Sing, O singer, sing!"
I was young, but now,
When I'm old and gray,
Love—I know not how
Or why—hath sped away;
Still, in winter days
As in hours of spring,
Still a whisper says,
"Sing, O singer, sing!"
Ah, too well I know
Song's my only friend!
Patiently I'll go
Singing to the end;
Comrades, to your wine!
Let your glasses ring!
Lo, that voice divine
Whispers, "Sing, oh, sing!"

CHILD AND MOTHER

O mother-my-love, if you'll give me your hand,
And go where I ask you to wander,
I will lead you away to a beautiful land,—
The Dreamland that's waiting out yonder.
We'll walk in a sweet posie-garden out there,
Where moonlight and starlight are streaming,
And the flowers and the birds are filling the air
With the fragrance and music of dreaming.
There'll be no little tired-out boy to undress,
No questions or cares to perplex you,
There'll be no little bruises or bumps to caress,
Nor patching of stockings to vex you;
For I'll rock you away on a silver-dew stream
And sing you asleep when you're weary,
And no one shall know of our beautiful dream
But you and your own little dearie.
And when I am tired I'll nestle my head
In the bosom that's soothed me so often,
And the wide-awake stars shall sing, in my stead,
A song which our dreaming shall soften.
So, Mother-my-Love, let me take your dear hand,
And away through the starlight we'll wander,—
Away through the mist to the beautiful land,—
The Dreamland that's waiting out yonder.

THE CONVERSAZZHYONY

What conversazzhyonies wuz I really did not know,
For that, you must remember, wuz a powerful spell ago;
The camp wuz new 'nd noisy, 'nd only modrit sized,
So fashionable sossiety wuz hardly crystallized.
There hadn't been no grand events to interest the men,
But a lynchin', or a inquest, or a jackpot now an' then.
The wimmin-folks wuz mighty scarce, for wimmin, ez a rool,
Don't go to Colorado much, excep' for teachin' school,
An' bein' scarce an' chipper and pretty (like as not),

The bachelors perpose, 'nd air
accepted on the spot.
Now Sorry Tom wuz owner uv the
Gosh-all-Hemlock mine,
The wich allowed his better haff to
dress all-fired fine;
For Sorry Tom wuz mighty proud
uv her, an' she uv him,
Though she wuz short an' tacky, an'
he wuz tall an' slim,
An' she wuz edjicated, an' Sorry
Tom wuz not,
Yet, for her sake, he'd whack up
every cussid cent he'd got!
Waal, jest by way uv celebratin'
matrimonial joys,
She thought she'd give a
conversazzhyony to the boys,—
A peert an' likely lady, 'nd ez full uv
'cute idees
'Nd uv etiquettish notions ez a fyste
is full uv fleas.
Three-fingered Hoover kind uv
kicked, an' said they might be durned
So far ez any conversazzhyony was
concerned;
He'd come to Red Hoss Mountain to
tunnel for the ore,
An' not to go to parties,—quite
another kind uv bore!
But, bein' he wuz candidate for
marshal uv the camp,
I rayther had the upper holts in
arguin' with the scamp;
Sez I, "Three-fingered Hoover, can't
ye see it is yer game
To go for all the votes ye kin an'
collar uv the same?"
The wich perceivin', Hoover sez,
"Waal, ef I must, I must;
So I'll frequent that
conversazzhyony, ef I bust!"
Three-fingered Hoover wuz a
trump! Ez fine a man wuz he
Ez ever caused an inquest or
blossomed on a tree!—
A big, broad man, whose face
bespoke a honest heart within,—
With a bunch uv yaller whiskers
appertainin' to his chin,
'Nd a fierce mustache turnt up so fur
that both his ears wuz hid,
Like the picture that you always see
in the "Life uv Cap'n Kidd."

His hair wuz long an' wavy an' fine
as Southdown fleece,—
Oh, it shone an' smelt like Eden
when he slicked it down with grease!
I'll bet there wuzn't anywhere a man,
all round, ez fine
Ez wuz Three-fingered Hoover in
the spring uv '69!
The conversazzhyony wuz a notable
affair,
The bong tong deckolett 'nd en
regaly bein' there;
The ranch where Sorry Tom hung
out wuz fitted up immense,—
The Denver papers called it a
"palashal residence."
There wuz mountain pines an' fern
an' flowers a-hangin' on the walls,
An' cheers an' hoss-hair sofies wuz
a-settin' in the halls;
An' there wuz heaps uv pictures uv
folks that lived down East,
Sech ez poets an' perfessers, an' last,
but not the least,
Wuz a chromo uv old Fremont,—
we liked that best, you bet,
For there's lots uv us old miners that
is votin' for him yet!
When Sorry Tom received the gang
perlitely at the door,
He said that keerds would be
allowed upon the second floor;
And then he asked us would we like
a drop uv ody vee.
Connivin' at his meanin', we
responded promptly, "Wee."
A conversazzhyony is a thing where
people speak
The langwidge in the which they air
partickulerly weak:
"I see," sez Sorry Tom, "you grasp
what that 'ere lingo means."
"You bet yer boots," sez Hoover;
"I've lived at Noo Orleens,
An', though I ain't no Frenchie, nor
kin unto the same,
I kin parly voo, an' git there, too,
like Eli, toot lee mame!"
As speakin' French wuz not my
forte,—not even oovry poo,—
I stuck to keerds ez played by them
ez did not parly voo,
An' bein' how that poker wuz my
most perficient game,

54

I poneyed up for 20 blues an' set into the same.
Three-fingered Hoover stayed behind an' parly-vood so well
That all the kramy delly krame allowed he wuz the belle.
The other candidate for marshal didn't have a show;
For, while Three-fingered Hoover parlyed, ez they said, tray bow,
Bill Goslin didn't know enough uv French to git along,
'Nd I reckon that he had what folks might call a movy tong.
From Denver they had freighted up a real pianny-fort
Uv the warty-leg and pearl-around-the-keys-an'-kivver sort,
An', later in the evenin', Perfesser Vere de Blaw
Performed on that pianny, with considerble eclaw,
Sech high-toned opry airs ez one is apt to hear, you know,
When he rounds up down to Denver at a Emmy Abbitt show;
An' Barber Jim (a talented but ornery galoot)
Discoursed a obligatter, conny mory, on the floot,
'Till we, ez sot up-stairs indulgin' in a quiet game,
Conveyed to Barber Jim our wish to compromise the same.
The maynoo that wuz spread that night wuz mighty hard to beat,—
Though somewhat awkward to pernounce, it was not so to eat:
There wuz puddin's, pies, an' sandwidges, an' forty kinds uv sass,
An' floatin' Irelands, custards, tarts, an' patty dee foy grass;
An' millions uv cove oysters wuz a-settin' round in pans,
'Nd other native fruits an' things that grow out West in cans.
But I wuz all kufflummuxed when Hoover said he'd choose
"Oon peety morso, see voo play, de la cette Charlotte Rooze;"
I'd knowed Three-fingered Hoover for fifteen years or more,
'Nd I'd never heern him speak so light uv wimmin folks before!

Bill Goslin heern him say it, 'nd uv course he spread the news
Uv how Three-fingered Hoover had insulted Charlotte Rooze
At the conversazzhyony down at Sorry Tom's that night,
An' when they asked me, I allowed that Bill for once wuz right;
Although it broke my heart to see my friend go up the fluke,
We all opined his treatment uv the girl deserved rebuke.
It warn't no use for Sorry Tom to nail it for a lie,—
When it come to sassin' wimmin, there wuz blood in every eye;
The boom for Charlotte Rooze swep' on an' took the polls by storm,
An' so Three-fingered Hoover fell a martyr to reform!
Three-fingered Hoover said it was a terrible mistake,
An' when the votes wuz in, he cried ez if his heart would break.
We never knew who Charlotte wuz, but Goslin's brother Dick
Allowed she wuz the teacher from the camp on Roarin' Crick,
That had come to pass some foreign tongue with them uv our alite
Ez wuz at the high-toned party down at Sorry Tom's that night.
We let it drop—this matter uv the lady—there an' then,
An' we never heerd, nor wanted to, of Charlotte Rooze again,
An' the Colorado wimmin-folks, ez like ez not, don't know
How we vindicated all their sex a twenty year ago.
For in these wondrous twenty years has come a mighty change,
An' most of them old pioneers have gone acrosst the range,
Way out into the silver land beyond the peaks uv snow,—
The land uv rest an' sunshine, where all good miners go.
I reckon that they love to look, from out the silver haze,
Upon that God's own country where they spent sech happy days;
Upon the noble cities that have risen since they went;

Upon the camps an' ranches that are prosperous and content;
An' best uv all, upon those hills that reach into the air,
Ez if to clasp the loved ones that are waitin' over there.

PROF. VERE DE BLAW

Achievin' sech distinction with his moddel tabble dote
Ez to make his Red Hoss Mountain restauraw a place uv note,
Our old friend Casey innovated somewhat round the place,
In hopes he would ameliorate the sufferin's uv the race;
'Nd uv the many features Casey managed to import
The most important wuz a Steenway gran' pianny-fort,
An' bein' there wuz nobody could play upon the same,
He telegraffed to Denver, 'nd a real perfesser came,—
The last an' crownin' glory uv the Casey restauraw
Wuz that tenderfoot musicianer, Perfesser Vere de Blaw!

His hair wuz long an' dishybill, an' he had a yaller skin,
An' the absence uv a collar made his neck look powerful thin:
A sorry man he wuz to see, az mebby you'd surmise,
But the fire uv inspiration wuz a-blazin' in his eyes!
His name wuz Blanc, wich same is Blaw (for that's what Casey said,
An' Casey passed the French ez well ez any Frenchie bred);
But no one ever reckoned that it really wuz his name,
An' no one ever asked him how or why or whence he came,—
Your ancient history is a thing the Coloradan hates,
An' no one asks another what his name wuz in the States!

At evenin', when the work wuz done, an' the miners rounded up
At Casey's, to indulge in keerds or linger with the cup,
Or dally with the tabble dote in all its native glory,
Perfessor Vere de Blaw discoursed his music repertory
Upon the Steenway gran' piannyfort, the wich wuz sot
In the hallway near the kitchen (a warm but quiet spot),
An' when De Blaw's environments induced the proper pride,—
Wich gen'rally wuz whiskey straight, with seltzer on the side,—
He throwed his soulful bein' into opry airs 'nd things
Wich bounded to the ceilin' like he'd mesmerized the strings.

Oh, you that live in cities where the gran' piannies grow,
An' primy donnies round up, it's little that you know
Uv the hungerin' an' the yearnin' wich us miners an' the rest
Feel for the songs we used to hear before we moved out West.
Yes, memory is a pleasant thing, but it weakens mighty quick;
It kind uv dries an' withers, like the windin' mountain crick,
That, beautiful, an' singin' songs, goes dancin' to the plains,
So long ez it is fed by snows an' watered by the rains;
But, uv that grace uv lovin' rains 'nd mountain snows bereft,
Its bleachin' rocks, like dummy ghosts, is all its memory left.

The toons wich the perfesser would perform with sech eclaw
Would melt the toughest mountain gentleman I ever saw,—
Sech touchin' opry music ez the Trovytory sort,
The sollum "Mizer Reery," an' the thrillin' "Keely Mort;"
Or, sometimes, from "Lee Grond Dooshess" a trifle he would play,
Or morsoze from a' opry boof, to drive dull care away;
Or, feelin' kind uv serious, he'd discourse somewhat in C,—
The wich he called a' opus (whatever that may be);
But the toons that fetched the likker from the critics in the crowd
Wuz not the high-toned ones, Perfesser Vere de Blaw allowed.

'T wuz "Dearest May," an' "Bonnie Doon," an' the ballard uv "Ben Bolt,"
Ez wuz regarded by all odds ez Vere de Blaw's best holt;
Then there wuz "Darlin' Nellie Gray," an' "Settin' on the Stile,"
An' "Seein' Nellie Home," an' "Nancy Lee," 'nd "Annie Lisle,"
An' "Silver Threads among the Gold," an' "The Gal that Winked at Me,"
An' "Gentle Annie," "Nancy Till," an' "The Cot beside the Sea."
Your opry airs is good enough for them ez likes to pay
Their money for the truck ez can't be got no other way;
But opry to a miner is a thin an' holler thing,—The
music that he pines for is the songs he used to sing.
One evenin' down at Casey's De Blaw wuz at his best,
With four-fingers uv old Wilier-run concealed beneath his vest;
The boys wuz settin' all around, discussin' folks an' things,
'Nd I had drawed the necessary keerds to fill on kings;
Three-fingered Hoover kind uv leaned acrosst the bar to say
If Casey'd liquidate right off, he'd liquidate next day;
A sperrit uv contentment wuz a-broodin' all around
(Onlike the other sperrits wich in restauraws abound),
When, suddenly, we heerd from yonder kitchen-entry rise
A toon each ornery galoot appeared to recognize.
Perfesser Vere de Blaw for once eschewed his opry ways,
An' the remnants uv his mind went back to earlier, happier days,
An' grappled like an' wrassled with a' old familiar air
The wich we all uv us had heern, ez you have, everywhere!
Stock still we stopped,—some in their talk uv politics an' things,
I in my unobtrusive attempt to fill on kings,
'Nd Hoover leanin' on the bar, an' Casey at the till,—

We all stopped short an' held our breaths (ez a feller sometimes will),
An' sot there more like bumps on logs than healthy, husky men,
Ez the memories uv that old, old toon come sneakin' back again.
You've guessed it? No, you hav n't; for it wuzn't that there song
Uv the home we'd been away from an' had hankered for so long,—
No, sir; it wuzn't "Home, Sweet Home," though it's always heard around
Sech neighborhoods in wich the home that is "sweet home" is found.
And, ez for me, I seemed to see the past come back again,
And hear the deep-drawed sigh my sister Lucy uttered when
Her mother asked her if she'd practised her two hours that day,
Wich, if she hadn't, she must go an' do it right away!
The homestead in the States 'nd all its memories seemed to come
A-floatin' round about me with that magic lumty-tum.
And then uprose a stranger wich had struck the camp that night;
His eyes wuz sot an' fireless, 'nd his face wuz spookish white,
'Nd he sez: "Oh, how I suffer there is nobody kin say,
Onless, like me, he's wrenched himself from home an' friends away
To seek surcease from sorrer in a fur, seclooded spot,
Only to find—alars, too late!—the wich surcease is not!
Only to find that there air things that, somehow, seem to live
For nothin' in the world but jest the misery they give!
I've travelled eighteen hundred miles, but that toon has got here first;
I'm done,—I'm blowed,—I welcome death, an' bid it do its worst!"
Then, like a man whose mind wuz sot on yieldin' to his fate,
He waltzed up to the counter an' demanded whiskey straight,
Wich havin' got outside uv,—both the likker and the door,—
We never seen that stranger in the bloom uv health no more!

But some months later, what the birds had left uv him wuz found
    Associated with a tree, some distance from the ground;
And Husky Sam, the coroner, that set upon him, said
    That two things wuz apparent, namely: first, deceast wuz dead;
And, second, previously had got involved beyond all hope
    In a knotty complication with a yard or two uv rope!

MEDIAEVAL EVENTIDE SONG

Come hither, lyttel childe, and lie upon my breast to-night,
For yonder fares an angell yclad in raimaunt white,
And yonder sings ye angell as onely angells may,
And his songe ben of a garden that bloometh farre awaye.
To them that have no lyttel childe
    Godde sometimes sendeth down
    A lyttel childe that ben a lyttel lambkyn of his owne;
And if so bee they love that childe,
    He willeth it to staye,
    But elsewise, in His mercie He taketh it awaye.
And sometimes, though they love it,
    Godde yearneth for ye childe,
    And sendeth angells singing, whereby it ben beguiled;
They fold their arms about ye lamb that croodleth at his play,
And beare him to ye garden that bloometh farre awaye.
I wolde not lose ye lyttel lamb that Godde hath lent to me;
    If I colde sing that angell songe, how joysome I sholde bee!
For, with mine arms about him, and my musick in his eare,
    What angell songe of paradize soever sholde I feare?
Soe come, my lyttel childe, and lie upon my breast to-night,
For yonder fares an angell yclad in raimaunt white,
    And yonder sings that angell, as onely angells may,
    And his songe ben of a garden that bloometh farre awaye.

MARTHY'S YOUNKIT

The mountain brook sung lonesomelike, and loitered on its way
    Ez if it waited for a child to jine it in its play;
The wild-flowers uv the hillside bent down their heads to hear
    The music uv the little feet that had somehow grown so dear;
The magpies, like winged shadders, wuz a-flutterin' to an' fro
    Among the rocks an' holler stumps in the ragged gulch below;
The pines an' hemlocks tosst their boughs (like they wuz arms) and made
    Soft, sollum music on the slope where he had often played;
But for these lonesome, sollum voices on the mountain-side,
    There wuz no sound the summer day that Marthy's younkit died.
We called him Marthy's younkit, for Marthy wuz the name
    Uv her ez wuz his mar, the wife uv Sorry Tom,—the same
Ez taught the school-house on the hill, way back in '69,
    When she marr'd Sorry Tom, wich owned the Gosh-all-Hemlock mine!
And Marthy's younkit wuz their first, wich, bein' how it meant
    The first on Red Hoss Mountain, wuz truly a' event!
The miners sawed off short on work ez soon ez they got word
    That Dock Devine allowed to Casey what had just occurred;
We loaded up an' whooped around until we all wuz hoarse
    Salutin' the arrival, wich weighed ten pounds, uv course!
Three years, and sech a pretty child!—his mother's counterpart!
    Three years, an' sech a holt ez he had got on every heart!
A peert an' likely little tyke with hair ez red ez gold,
    A-laughin', toddlin' everywhere,— 'nd only three years old!
Up yonder, sometimes, to the store, an' sometimes down the hill
    He kited (boys is boys, you know,— you couldn't keep him still!)

An' there he'd play beside the brook
where purpul wild-flowers grew,
An' the mountain pines an' hemlocks
a kindly shadder threw,
An' sung soft, sollum toons to him,
while in the gulch below
The magpies, like strange sperrits,
went flutterin' to an' fro.
Three years, an' then the fever
come,—it wuzn't right, you know,
With all us old ones in the camp, for
that little child to go;
It's right the old should die, but that
a harmless little child
Should miss the joy uv life an'
love,—that can't be reconciled!
That's what we thought that summer
day, an' that is what we said
Ez we looked upon the piteous face
uv Marthy's younkit dead.
But for his mother's sobbin', the
house wuz very still,
An' Sorry Tom wuz lookin', through
the winder, down the hill,
To the patch beneath the hemlocks
where his darlin' used to play,
An' the mountain brook sung
lonesomelike an' loitered on its way.
A preacher come from Roarin' Crick
to comfort 'em an' pray,
'Nd all the camp wuz present at the
obsequies next day;
A female teacher staged it twenty
miles to sing a hymn,
An' we jined her in the chorus,—
big, husky men an' grim
Sung "Jesus, Lover uv my Soul," an'
then the preacher prayed,
An' preacht a sermon on the death
uv that fair blossom laid
Among them other flowers he
loved,—wich sermon set sech weight
On sinners bein' always heeled
against the future state,
That, though it had been fashionable
to swear a perfec' streak,
There warn't no swearin' in the camp
for pretty nigh a week!
Last thing uv all, four strappin' men
took up the little load
An' bore it tenderly along the
windin', rocky road,
To where the coroner had dug a
grave beside the brook,

In sight uv Marthy's winder, where
the same could set an' look
An' wonder if his cradle in that
green patch, long an' wide,
Wuz ez soothin' ez the cradle that
wuz empty at her side;
An' wonder if the mournful songs
the pines wuz singin' then
Wuz ez tender ez the lullabies she'd
never sing again,
'Nd if the bosom of the earth in wich
he lay at rest
Wuz half ez lovin' 'nd ez warm ez
wuz his mother's breast.
The camp is gone; but Red Hoss
Mountain rears its kindly head,
An' looks down, sort uv tenderly,
upon its cherished dead;
'Nd I reckon that, through all the
years, that little boy wich died
Sleeps sweetly an' contentedly upon
the mountain-side;
That the wild-flowers uv the
summer-time bend down their heads to
hear
The footfall uv a little friend they
know not slumbers near;
That the magpies on the sollum
rocks strange flutterin' shadders make,
An' the pines an' hemlocks wonder
that the sleeper doesn't wake;
That the mountain brook sings
lonesomelike an' loiters on its way
Ez if it waited for a child to jine it in
its play.

IN FLANDERS
Through sleet and fogs to the saline
bogs
Where the herring fish meanders,
An army sped, and then, 't is said,
Swore terribly in Flanders:
"_____!"
"_____!"
A hideous store of oaths they swore,
Did the army over in Flanders!
At this distant day we're unable to
say
What so aroused their danders;
But it's doubtless the case, to their
lasting disgrace,
That the army swore in Flanders:
"_____!"
"_____!"

And many more such oaths they swore,
Did that impious horde in Flanders!
Some folks contend that these oaths without end
Began among the commanders,
That, taking this cue, the subordinates, too,
Swore terribly in Flanders:
Twas "——————!"
"————"

Why, the air was blue with the hullaballoo
Of those wicked men in Flanders!
But some suppose that the trouble arose
With a certain Corporal Sanders,
Who sought to abuse the wooden shoes
That the natives wore in Flanders.
Saying: "————!"
"————"

What marvel then, that the other men
Felt encouraged to swear in Flanders!
At any rate, as I grieve to state,
Since these soldiers vented their danders
Conjectures obtain that for language profane
There is no such place as Flanders.
"————"
"————"

This is the kind of talk you'll find
If ever you go to Flanders.
How wretched is he, wherever he be,
That unto this habit panders!
And how glad am I that my interests lie
In Chicago, and not in Flanders!
"——————!"
"——————!"
Would never go down in this circumspect town
However it might in Flanders.

OUR BIGGEST FISH

When in the halcyon days of old, I was a little tyke,
I used to fish in pickerel ponds for minnows and the like;
And oh, the bitter sadness with which my soul was fraught
When I rambled home at nightfall with the puny string I'd caught!
And, oh, the indignation and the valor I'd display
When I claimed that all the biggest fish I'd caught had got away!
Sometimes it was the rusty hooks, sometimes the fragile lines,
And many times the treacherous reeds would foil my just designs;
But whether hooks or lines or reeds were actually to blame,
I kept right on at losing all the monsters just the same—
I never lost a little fish—yes, I am free to say
It always was the biggest fish I caught that got away.
And so it was, when later on, I felt ambition pass
From callow minnow joys to nobler greed for pike and bass;
I found it quite convenient, when the beauties wouldn't bite
And I returned all bootless from the watery chase at night,
To feign a cheery aspect and recount in accents gay
How the biggest fish that I had caught had somehow got away.
And really, fish look bigger than they are before they are before they're caught—
When the pole is bent into a bow and the slender line is taut,
When a fellow feels his heart rise up like a doughnut in his throat
And he lunges in a frenzy up and down the leaky boat!
Oh, you who've been a-fishing will indorse me when I say
That it always is the biggest fish you catch that gets away!
'T 'is even so in other things—yes, in our greedy eyes
The biggest boon is some elusive, never-captured prize;
We angle for the honors and the sweets of human life—
Like fishermen we brave the seas that roll in endless strife;
And then at last, when all is done and we are spent and gray,
We own the biggest fish we've caught are those that got away.

I would not have it otherwise; 't is
better there should be
Much bigger fish than I have caught
a-swimming in the sea;
For now some worthier one than I
may angle for that game—
May by his arts entice, entrap, and
comprehend the same;
Which, having done, perchance he'll
bless the man who's proud to say
That the biggest fish he ever caught
were those that got away.

THIRTY-NINE

O hapless day! O wretched day!
I hoped you'd pass me by—
Alas, the years have sneaked away
And all is changed but I!
Had I the power, I would remand
You to a gloom condign,
But here you've crept upon me and
I—I am thirty-nine!
Now, were I thirty-five, I could
Assume a flippant guise;
Or, were I forty years, I should
Undoubtedly look wise;
For forty years are said to bring
Sedateness superfine;
But thirty-nine don't mean a thing—
À bas with thirty-nine!
You healthy, hulking girls and
boys,—
What makes you grow so fast?
Oh, I'll survive your lusty noise—
I'm tough and bound to last!
No, no—I'm old and withered too—
I feel my powers decline
(Yet none believes this can be true
Of one at thirty-nine).
And you, dear girl with velvet eyes,
I wonder what you mean
Through all our keen anxieties
By keeping sweet sixteen.
With your dear love to warm my
heart,
Wretch were I to repine;
I was but jesting at the start—
I'm glad I'm thirty-nine!
So, little children, roar and race
As blithely as you can,
And, sweetheart, let your tender
grace
Exalt the Day and Man;
For then these factors (I'll engage)
All subtly shall combine
To make both juvenile and sage
The one who's thirty-nine!
Yes, after all, I'm free to say
I would much rather be
Standing as I do stand to-day,
'Twixt devil and deep sea;
For though my face be dark with
care
Or with a grimace shine,
Each haply falls unto my share,
For I am thirty-nine!
'Tis passing meet to make good
cheer
And lord it like a king,
Since only once we catch the year
That doesn't mean a thing.
O happy day! O gracious day!
I pledge thee in this wine—
Come, let us journey on our way
A year, good Thirty-Nine!
Sept. 2, 1889.

YVYTOT

Where wail the waters in their flaw
A spectre wanders to and fro,
And evermore that ghostly shore
Bemoans the heir of Yvytot.
Sometimes, when, like a fleecy pall,
The mists upon the waters fall,
Across the main float shadows twain
That do not heed the spectre's call.
The king his son of Yvytot
Stood once and saw the waters go
Boiling around with hissing sound
The sullen phantom rocks below.
And suddenly he saw a face
Lift from that black and seething
place—
Lift up and gaze in mute amaze
And tenderly a little space,
A mighty cry of love made he—
No answering word to him gave she,
But looked, and then sunk back
again
Into the dark and depthless sea.
And ever afterward that face,
That he beheld such little space,
Like wraith would rise within his
eyes
And in his heart find biding place.
So oft from castle hall he crept
Where mid the rocks grim shadows
slept,
And where the mist reached down
and kissed

The waters as they wailed and wept.
The king it was of Yvytot
That vaunted, many years ago,
There was no coast his valiant host
Had not subdued with spear and bow.
For once to him the sea-king cried:
"In safety all thy ships shall ride
An thou but swear thy princely heir
Shall take my daughter to his bride.
"And lo, these winds that rove the sea
Unto our pact shall witness be,
And of the oath which binds us both
Shall be the judge 'twixt me and thee!"
Then swore the king of Yvytot
Unto the sea-king years ago,
And with great cheer for many a year
His ships went harrying to and fro.
Unto this mighty king his throne
Was born a prince, and one alone—
Fairer than he in form and blee
And knightly grace was never known.
But once he saw a maiden face
Lift from a haunted ocean place—
Lift up and gaze in mute amaze
And tenderly a little space.
Wroth was the king of Yvytot,
For that his son would never go
Sailing the sea, but liefer be
Where wailed the waters in their flow,
Where winds in clamorous anger swept,
Where to and fro grim shadows crept,
And where the mist reached down and kissed
The waters as they wailed and wept.
So sped the years, till came a day
The haughty king was old and gray,
And in his hold were spoils untold
That he had wrenched from Norroway.
Then once again the sea-king cried:
"Thy ships have harried far and wide;
My part is done—now let thy son
Require my daughter to his bride!"
Loud laughed the king of Yvytot,
And by his soul he bade him no—
"I heed no more what oath I swore,
For I was mad to bargain so!"
Then spake the sea-king in his wrath:
"Thy ships lie broken in my path!
Go now and wring thy hands, false king!
Nor ship nor heir thy kingdom hath!
"And thou shalt wander evermore
All up and down this ghostly shore,
And call in vain upon the twain
That keep what oath a dastard swore!"
The king his son of Yvytot
Stood even then where to and fro
The breakers swelled—and there beheld
A maiden face lift from below.
"Be thou or truth or dream," he cried,
"Or spirit of the restless tide,
It booteth not to me, God wot!
But I would have thee to my bride."
Then spake the maiden: "Come with me
Unto a palace in the sea,
For there my sire in kingly ire
Requires thy king his oath of thee!"
Gayly he fared him down the sands
And took the maiden's outstretched hands;
And so went they upon their way
To do the sea-king his commands.
The winds went riding to and fro
And scourged the waves that crouched below,
And bade them sing to a childless king
The bridal song of Yvytot.
So fell the curse upon that shore,
And hopeless wailing evermore
Was the righteous dole of the craven soul
That heeded not what oath he swore.
An hundred ships went down that day
All off the coast of Norroway,
And the ruthless sea made mighty glee
Over the spoil that drifting lay.
The winds went calling far and wide
To the dead that tossed in the mocking tide:
"Come forth, ye slaves! from your fleeting graves

And drink a health to your prince his bride!"
Where wail the waters in their flow
A spectre wanders to and fro,
But nevermore that ghostly shore
Shall claim the heir of Yvytot.
Sometimes, when, like a fleecy pall,
The mists upon the waters fall,
Across the main flit shadows twain
That do not heed the spectre's call.

LONG AGO

I once knew all the birds that came
And nested in our orchard trees;
For every flower I had a name—
My friends were woodchucks, toads, and bees;
I knew where thrived in yonder glen
What plants would soothe a stone-bruised toe—
  Oh, I was very learned then;
  But that was very long ago!
I knew the spot upon the hill
Where checkerberries could be found,
I knew the rushes near the mill
Where pickerel lay that weighed a pound!
I knew the wood,—the very tree
Where lived the poaching, saucy crow,
And all the woods and crows knew me—
  But that was very long ago.
And pining for the joys of youth,
I tread the old familiar spot
Only to learn this solemn truth:
I have forgotten, am forgot.
Yet here's this youngster at my knee
Knows all the things I used to know;
To think I once was wise as he—
  But that was very long ago.
I know it's folly to complain
Of whatsoe'er the Fates decree;
Yet were not wishes all in vain,
I tell you what my wish should be:
  I'd wish to be a boy again,
  Back with the friends I used to know;
  For I was, oh! so happy then—
  But that was very long ago!

TO A SOUBRETTE

'Tis years, soubrette, since last we met;
And yet—ah, yet, how swift and tender
My thoughts go back in time's dull track
To you, sweet pink of female gender!
I shall not say—though others may—
That time all human joy enhances;
But the same old thrill comes to me still
With memories of your songs and dances.
Soubrettish ways these latter days
Invite my praise, but never get it;
I still am true to yours and you—
My record's made, I'll not upset it!
The pranks they play, the things they say—
I'd blush to put the like on paper,
And I'll avow they don't know how
To dance, so awkwardly they caper!
I used to sit down in the pit
And see you flit like elf or fairy
Across the stage, and I'll engage
No moonbeam sprite was half so airy;
Lo, everywhere about me there
Were rivals reeking with pomatum,
And if, perchance, they caught your glance
In song or dance, how did I hate 'em!
At half-past ten came rapture—then
Of all those men was I most happy,
For bottled beer and royal cheer
And têtes-à-têtes were on the tapis.
Do you forget, my fair soubrette,
Those suppers at the Cafe Rector,—
The cosey nook where we partook
Of sweeter cheer than fabled nectar?
Oh, happy days, when youth's wild ways
Knew every phase of harmless folly!
Oh, blissful nights, whose fierce delights
Defied gaunt-featured Melancholy!
Gone are they all beyond recall,
And I—a shade, a mere reflection—
Am forced to feed my spirit's greed
Upon the husks of retrospection!
And lo! to-night, the phantom light,
That, as a sprite, flits on the fender,
Reveals a face whose girlish grace

Brings back the feeling, warm and tender;
And, all the while, the old-time smile
Plays on my visage, grim and wrinkled,—
As though, soubrette, your footfalls yet
Upon my rusty heart-strings tinkled!

SOME TIME

Last night, my darling, as you slept,
    I thought I heard you sigh,
And to your little crib I crept,
    And watched a space thereby;
And then I stooped and kissed your brow,
    For oh! I love you so—
You are too young to know it now,
    But some time you shall know!

Some time when, in a darkened place
    Where others come to weep,
Your eyes shall look upon a face
    Calm in eternal sleep,
The voiceless lips, the wrinkled brow,
    The patient smile shall show—
You are too young to know it now,
    But some time you may know!

Look backward, then, into the years,
    And see me here to-night—
See, O my darling! how my tears
    Are falling as I write;
And feel once more upon your brow
    The kiss of long ago—
You are too young to know it now,
    But some time you shall know.

Songs and Other Verse

THE SINGING IN GOD'S ACRE

Out yonder in the moonlight,
 wherein God's Acre lies,
Go angels walking to and fro,
 singing their lullabies.
Their radiant wings are folded, and
 their eyes are bended low,
As they sing among the beds
whereon the flowers delight to grow,—
 "Sleep, oh, sleep!
The Shepherd guardeth His sheep.
 Fast speedeth the night away,
 Soon cometh the glorious day;
 Sleep, weary ones, while ye may,
 Sleep, oh, sleep!"
The flowers within God's Acre see
 that fair and wondrous sight,
And hear the angels singing to the
 sleepers through the night;
And, lo! throughout the hours of day
 those gentle flowers prolong
The music of the angels in that
 tender slumber-song,—
 "Sleep, oh, sleep!
The Shepherd loveth His sheep.
He that guardeth His flock the best
Hath folded them to His loving
 breast;
So sleep ye now, and take your
 rest,—
 Sleep, oh, sleep!"
From angel and from flower the
years have learned that soothing song,
 And with its heavenly music speed
 the days and nights along;
So through all time, whose flight the
 Shepherd's vigils glorify,
God's Acre slumbereth in the grace
 of that sweet lullaby,—
 "Sleep, oh, sleep!
The Shepherd loveth His sheep.
 Fast speedeth the night away,
 Soon cometh the glorious day;
 Sleep, weary ones, while ye may,—
 Sleep, oh, sleep!"

THE DREAM-SHIP

When the world is fast asleep,
 Along the midnight skies—
As though it were a wandering
 cloud—
 The ghostly dream-ship flies.
An angel stands at the dream-ship's
 helm,
 An angel stands at the prow,
And an angel stands at the dream-
 ship's side
 With a rue-wreath on her brow.
The other angels, silver-crowned,
 Pilot and helmsman are,
And the angel with the wreath of rue
 Tosseth the dreams afar.
The dreams they fall on rich and
 poor;
 They fall on young and old;
And some are dreams of poverty,
 And some are dreams of gold.
And some are dreams that thrill with
 joy,
 And some that melt to tears;
Some are dreams of the dawn of
 love,
 And some of the old dead years.
On rich and poor alike they fall,
 Alike on young and old,
Bringing to slumbering earth their
 joys
 And sorrows manifold.
The friendless youth in them shall
 do
 The deeds of mighty men,
And drooping age shall feel the
 grace
 Of buoyant youth again.
The king shall be a beggarman—
 The pauper be a king—
In that revenge or recompense
 The dream-ship dreams do bring.
So ever downward float the dreams
 That are for all and me,
And there is never mortal man
 Can solve that mystery.
But ever onward in its course
 Along the haunted skies—
As though it were a cloud astray—
 The ghostly dream-ship flies.
Two angels with their silver crowns
 Pilot and helmsman are,
And an angel with a wreath of rue
 Tosseth the dreams afar.

TO CINNA

Cinna, the great Venusian told
 In songs that will not die

How in Augustan days of old
Your love did glorify
His life and all his being seemed
Thrilled by that rare incense
Till, grudging him the dreams he dreamed,
The gods did call you hence.
Cinna, I've looked into your eyes,
And held your hands in mine,
And seen your cheeks in sweet surprise
Blush red as Massic wine;
Now let the songs in Cinna's praise
Be chanted once again,
For, oh! alone I walk the ways
We walked together then!
Perhaps upon some star to-night,
So far away in space
I cannot see that beacon light
Nor feel its soothing grace—
Perhaps from that far-distant sphere
Her quickened vision seeks
For this poor heart of mine that here
To its lost Cinna speaks.
Then search this heart, beloved eyes,
And find it still as true
As when in all my boyhood skies
My guiding stars were you!
Cinna, you know the mystery
That is denied to men—
Mine is the lot to feel that we
Shall elsewhere love again!

BALLAD OF WOMEN I LOVE

Prudence Mears hath an old blue plate
Hid away in an oaken chest,
And a Franklin platter of ancient date
Beareth Amandy Baker's crest;
What times soever I've been their guest,
Says I to myself in an undertone:
"Of womenfolk, it must be confessed,
These do I love, and these alone."
Well, again, in the Nutmeg State,
Dorothy Pratt is richly blest
With a relic of art and a land effete—
A pitcher of glass that's cut, not pressed.
And a Washington teapot is possessed
Down in Pelham by Marthy Stone—
Think ye now that I say in jest
"These do I love, and these alone?"
Were Hepsy Higgins inclined to mate,
Or Dorcas Eastman prone to invest
In Cupid's bonds, they could find their fate
In the bootless bard of Crockery Quest.
For they've heaps of trumpery—so have the rest
Of those spinsters whose ware I'd like to own;
You can see why I say with such certain zest,
"These do I love, and these alone."

ENVOY

Prince, show me the quickest way and best
To gain the subject of my moan;
We've neither spinsters nor relics out West—
These do I love, and these alone.

SUPPOSE

Suppose, my dear, that you were I
And by your side your sweetheart sate;
Suppose you noticed by and by
The distance 'twixt you were too great;
Now tell me, dear, what would you do?
I know—and so do you.
And when (so comfortably placed)
Suppose you only grew aware
That that dear, dainty little waist
Of hers looked very lonely there;
Pray tell me sooth—what would you do?
I know, and so do you.
When, having done what I just did
With not a frown to check or chill,
Suppose her red lips seemed to bid
Defiance to your lordly will;
Oh, tell me, sweet, what would you do?
I know, and so do you.

MYSTERIOUS DOINGS

As once I rambled in the woods
I chanced to spy amid the brake
A huntsman ride his way beside
A fair and passing tranquil lake;

Though velvet bucks sped here and there,
He let them scamper through the green—
Not one smote he, but lustily
He blew his horn—what could it mean?
As on I strolled beside that lake,
A pretty maid I chanced to see
Fishing away for finny prey,
Yet not a single one caught she;
All round her boat the fishes leapt
And gambolled to their hearts' content,
Yet never a thing did the maid but sing—
I wonder what on earth it meant.
As later yet I roamed my way,
A lovely steed neighed loud and long,
And an empty boat sped all afloat
Where sang a fishermaid her song;
All underneath the prudent shade,
Which yonder kindly willows threw,
Together strayed a youth and maid—
I can't explain it all, can you?

WITH TWO SPOONS FOR TWO SPOONS

How trifling shall these gifts appear
Among the splendid many
That loving friends now send to cheer
Harvey and Ellen Jenney.
And yet these baubles symbolize
A certain fond relation
That well beseems, as I surmise,
This festive celebration.
Sweet friends of mine, be spoons once more,
And with your tender cooing
Renew the keen delights of yore—
The rapturous bliss of wooing.
What though that silver in your hair
Tells of the years aflying?
'T is yours to mock at Time and Care
With love that is undying.
In memory of this Day, dear friends,
Accept the modest token
From one who with the bauble sends
A love that can't be spoken.

MARY SMITH

Away down East where I was reared amongst my Yankee kith,
There used to live a pretty girl whose name was Mary Smith;
And though it's many years since last I saw that pretty girl,
And though I feel I'm sadly worn by Western strife and whirl;
Still, oftentimes, I think about the old familiar place,
Which, someway, seemed the brighter for Miss Mary's pretty face,
And in my heart I feel once more revivified the glow
I used to feel in those old times when I was Mary's beau.
I saw her home from singing school—she warbled like a bird.
A sweeter voice than hers for song or speech I never heard.
She was soprano in the choir, and I a solemn bass,
And when we unisoned our voices filled that holy place;
The tenor and the alto never had the slightest chance,
For Mary's upper register made every heart-string dance;
And, as for me, I shall not brag, and yet I'd have you know
I sung a very likely bass when I was Mary's beau.
On Friday nights I'd drop around to make my weekly call,
And though I came to visit her, I'd have to see 'em all.
With Mary's mother sitting here and Mary's father there,
The conversation never flagged so far as I'm aware;
Sometimes I'd hold her worsted, sometimes we'd play at games,
Sometimes dissect the apples which we'd named each other's names.
Oh how I loathed the shrill-toned clock that told me when to go—
'Twas ten o'clock at half-past eight when I was Mary's beau.
Now there was Luther Baker—because he'd come of age
And thought himself some pumpkins because he drove the stage—
He fancied he could cut me out; but Mary was my friend—

Elsewise I'm sure the issue had had a tragic end.
For Luther Baker was a man I never could abide,
And, when it came to Mary, either he or I had died.
I merely cite this instance incidentally to show
That I was quite in earnest when I was Mary's beau.

How often now those sights, those pleasant sights, recur again:
The little township that was all the world I knew of then—
The meeting-house upon the hill, the tavern just beyond,
Old deacon Packard's general store, the sawmill by the pond,
The village elms I vainly sought to conquer in my quest
Of that surpassing trophy, the golden oriole's nest.
And, last of all those visions that come back from long ago,
The pretty face that thrilled my soul when I was Mary's beau.

Hush, gentle wife, there is no need a pang should vex your heart—
'T is many years since fate ordained that she and I should part;
To each a true, maturer love came in good time, and yet
It brought not with its nobler grace the power to forget.
And would you fain begrudge me now the sentimental joy
That comes of recollections of my sparkings when a boy?
I warrant me that, were your heart put to the rack, 't would show
That it had predilections when I was Mary's beau.

And, Mary, should these lines of mine seek out your biding place,
God grant they bring the old sweet smile back to your pretty face—
God grant they bring you thoughts of me, not as I am to-day,
With faltering step and brimming eyes and aspect grimly gray;
But thoughts that picture me as fair and full of life and glee
As we were in the olden times—as you shall always be.

Think of me ever, Mary, as the boy you used to know
When time was fleet, and life was sweet, and I was Mary's beau.
Dear hills of old New England, look down with tender eyes
Upon one little lonely grave that in your bosom lies;
For in that cradle sleeps a child who was so fair to see
God yearned to have unto Himself the joy she brought to me;
And bid your winds sing soft and low the song of other days,
When, hand in hand and heart to heart, we went our pleasant ways—
Ah me! but could I sing again that song of long ago,
Instead of this poor idle song of being Mary's beau.

JESSIE

When I remark her golden hair Swoon on her glorious shoulders,
I marvel not that sight so rare Doth ravish all beholders;
For summon hence all pretty girls Renowned for beauteous tresses,
And you shall find among their curls There's none so fair as Jessie's.

And Jessie's eyes are, oh, so blue And full of sweet revealings—
They seem to look you through and through And read your inmost feelings;
Nor black emits such ardent fires, Nor brown such truth expresses—
Admit it, all ye gallant squires— There are no eyes like Jessie's.

Her voice (like liquid beams that roll From moonland to the river)
Steals subtly to the raptured soul, Therein to lie and quiver;
Or falls upon the grateful ear With chaste and warm caresses—
Ah, all concede the truth (who hear): There's no such voice as Jessie's.

Of other charms she hath such store All rivalry excelling,
Though I used adjectives galore, They'd fail me in the telling;
But now discretion stays my hand— Adieu, eyes, voice, and tresses.
Of all the husbands in the land There's none so fierce as Jessie's.

TO EMMA ABBOTT

There—let thy hands be folded
Awhile in sleep's repose;
The patient hands that wearied not,
But earnestly and nobly wrought
In charity and faith;
And let thy dear eyes close—
The eyes that looked alway to God,
Nor quailed beneath the chastening rod
Of sorrow;
Fold thou thy hands and eyes
For just a little while,
And with a smile
Dream of the morrow.
And, O white voiceless flower,
The dream which thou shalt dream
Should be a glimpse of heavenly things,
For yonder like a seraph sings
The sweetness of a life
With faith alway its theme;
While speedeth from those realms above
The messenger of that dear love
That healeth sorrow.
So sleep a little while,
For thou shalt wake and sing
Before thy King
When cometh the morrow.

THE GREAT JOURNALIST IN SPAIN

Good editor Dana—God bless him, we say—
Will soon be afloat on the main,
Will be steaming away
Through the mist and the spray
To the sensuous climate of Spain.
Strange sights shall he see in that beautiful land
Which is famed for its soap and its Moor,
For, as we understand,
The scenery is grand
Though the system of railways is poor.
For moonlight of silver and sunlight of gold
Glint the orchards of lemons and mangoes,
And the ladies, we're told,
Are a joy to behold
As they twine in their lissome fandangoes.
What though our friend Dana shall twang a guitar
And murmur a passionate strain;
Oh, fairer by far
Than those ravishments are
The castles abounding in Spain.
These castles are built as the builder may list—
They are sometimes of marble or stone,
But they mostly consist
Of east wind and mist
With an ivy of froth overgrown.
A beautiful castle our Dana shall raise
On a futile foundation of hope,
And its glories shall blaze
In the somnolent haze
Of the mythical lake del y Soap.
The fragrance of sunflowers shall swoon on the air
And the visions of Dreamland obtain,
And the song of "World's Fair"
Shall be heard everywhere
Through that beautiful castle in Spain.

LOVE SONG—HEINE

Many a beauteous flower doth spring
From the tears that flood my eyes,
And the nightingale doth sing
In the burthen of my sighs.
If, O child, thou lovest me,
Take these flowerets fair and frail,
And my soul shall waft to thee
Love songs of the nightingale.

THE STODDARDS

When I am in New York, I like to drop around at night,
To visit with my honest, genial friends, the Stoddards hight;
Their home in Fifteenth street is all so snug, and furnished so,
That, when I once get planted there, I don't know when to go;
A cosy cheerful refuge for the weary homesick guest,
Combining Yankee comforts with the freedom of the west.
The first thing you discover, as you maunder through the hall,

Is a curious little clock upon a bracket on the wall;
'T was made by Stoddard's father, and it's very, very old—
The connoisseurs assure me it is worth its weight in gold;
And I, who've bought all kinds of clocks, 'twixt Denver and the Rhine,
Cast envious eyes upon that clock, and wish that it were mine.
But in the parlor. Oh, the gems on tables, walls, and floor—
Rare first editions, etchings, and old crockery galore.
Why, talk about the Indies and the wealth of Orient things—
They couldn't hold a candle to these quaint and sumptuous things;
In such profusion, too—Ah me! how dearly I recall
How I have sat and watched 'em and wished I had 'em all.
Now, Mr. Stoddard's study is on the second floor,
A wee blind dog barks at me as I enter through the door;
The Cerberus would fain begrudge what sights it cannot see,
The rapture of that visual feast it cannot share with me;
A miniature edition this—this most absurd of hounds—
A genuine unique, I'm sure, and one unknown to Lowndes.
Books—always books—are piled around; some musty, and all old;
Tall, solemn folios such as Lamb declared he loved to hold;
Large paper copies with their virgin margins white and wide,
And presentation volumes with the author's comps. inside;
I break the tenth commandment with a wild impassioned cry:
Oh, how came Stoddard by these things? Why Stoddard, and not I?
From yonder wall looks Thackeray upon his poet friend,
And underneath the genial face appear the lines he penned;
And here, gadzooks, ben honge ye prynte of marvaillous renowne
Yt shameth Chaucers gallaunt knyghtes in Canterbury towne;
And still more books and pictures. I'm dazed, bewildered, vexed;
Since I've broke the tenth commandment, why not break the eighth one next?
And, furthermore, in confidence inviolate be it said
Friend Stoddard owns a lock of hair that grew on Milton's head;
Now I have Gladstone axes and a lot of curious things,
Such as pimply Dresden teacups and old German wedding-rings;
But nothing like that saintly lock have I on wall or shelf,
And, being somewhat short of hair, I should like that lock myself.
But Stoddard has a soothing way, as though he grieved to see
Invidious torments prey upon a nice young chap like me.
He waves me to an easy chair and hands me out a weed
And pumps me full of that advice he seems to know I need;
So sweet the tap of his philosophy and knowledge flows
That I can't help wishing that I knew a half what Stoddard knows.
And so we sit for hours and hours, praising without restraint
The people who are thoroughbreds, and roasting the ones that ain't;
Happy, thrice happy, is the man we happen to admire,
But wretched, oh, how wretched he that hath provoked our ire;
For I speak emphatic English when I once get fairly r'iled,
And Stoddard's wrath's an Ossa upon a Pelion piled.
Out yonder, in the alcove, a lady sits and darns,
And interjects remarks that always serve to spice our yarns;
She's Mrs. Stoddard; there's a dame that's truly to my heart:
A tiny little woman, but so quaint, and good, and smart
That, if you asked me to suggest which one I should prefer
Of all the Stoddard treasures, I should promptly mention her.
O dear old man, how I should like to be with you this night,

Down in your home in Fifteenth street, where all is snug and bright;
Where the shaggy little Cerberus dreams in its cushioned place,
And the books and pictures all around smile in their old friend's face;
Where the dainty little sweetheart, whom you still were proud to woo,
Charms back the tender memories so dear to her and you.

THE THREE TAILORS

I shall tell you in rhyme how, once on a time,
Three tailors tramped up to the inn Ingleheim,
On the Rhine, lovely Rhine;
They were broke, but the worst of it all, they were curst
With that malady common to tailors—a thirst
For wine, lots of wine.
"Sweet host," quoth the three, "we're hard up as can be,
Yet skilled in the practice of cunning are we,
On the Rhine, genial Rhine;
And we pledge you we will impart you that skill
Right quickly and fully, providing you'll fill
Us with wine, cooling wine."
But that host shook his head, and he warily said:
"Though cunning be good, we take money instead,
On the Rhine, thrifty Rhine;
If ye fancy ye may without pelf have your way
You'll find that there's both host and the devil to pay
For your wine, costly wine."
Then the first knavish wight took his needle so bright
And threaded its eye with a wee ray of light
From the Rhine, sunny Rhine;
And, in such a deft way, patched a mirror that day
That where it was mended no expert could say—
Done so fine 't was for wine.
The second thereat spied a poor little gnat
Go toiling along on his nose broad and flat
Towards the Rhine, pleasant Rhine;
"Aha, tiny friend, I should hate to offend,
But your stockings need darning"—which same did he mend,
All for wine, soothing wine.
And next there occurred what you'll deem quite absurd—
His needle a space in the wall thrust the third,
By the Rhine, wondrous Rhine;
And then all so spry, he leapt through the eye
Of that thin cambric needle—nay, think you I'd lie
About wine—not for wine.
The landlord allowed (with a smile) he was proud
To do the fair thing by that talented crowd
On the Rhine, generous Rhine.
So a thimble filled he as full as could be—
"Drink long and drink hearty, my jolly friends three,
Of my wine, filling wine."

THE JAFFA AND JERUSALEM RAILWAY

A tortuous double iron track; a station here, a station there;
A locomotive, tender, tanks; a coach with stiff reclining chair;
Some postal cars, and baggage, too; a vestibule of patent make;
With buffers, duffers, switches, and the soughing automatic brake—
This is the Orient's novel pride, and Syria's gaudiest modern gem:
The railway scheme that is to ply 'twixt Jaffa and Jerusalem.
Beware, O sacred Mooley cow, the engine when you hear its bell;
Beware, O camel, when resounds the whistle's shrill, unholy swell;
And, native of that guileless land, unused to modern travel's snare,
Beware the fiend that peddles books—the awful peanut-boy beware.
Else, trusting in their specious arts, you may have reason to condemn
The traffic which the knavish ply 'twixt Jaffa and Jerusalem.

And when, ah, when the bonds fall
due, how passing wroth will wax the
state
From Nebo's mount to Nazareth will
spread the cry "Repudiate"!
From Hebron to Tiberius, from
Jordan's banks unto the sea,
Will rise profuse anathemas against
"that —— monopoly!"
And F.M.B.A. shepherd-folk, with
Sockless Jerry leading them,
Will swamp that corporation line
'twixt Jaffa and Jerusalem.

HUGO'S "POOL IN THE FOREST"

How calm, how beauteous and how
cool—
How like a sister to the skies,
Appears the broad, transparent pool
That in this quiet forest lies.
The sunshine ripples on its face,
And from the world around, above,
It hath caught down the nameless
grace
Of such reflections as we love.
But deep below its surface crawl
The reptile horrors of the night—
The dragons, lizards, serpents—all
The hideous brood that hate the
light;
Through poison fern and slimy weed
And under ragged, jagged stones
They scuttle, or, in ghoulish greed,
They lap a dead man's bleaching
bones.
And as, O pool, thou dost cajole
With seemings that beguile us well,
So doeth many a human soul
That teemeth with the lusts of hell.

A RHINE-LAND DRINKING SONG

If our own life is the life of a flower
(And that's what some sages are
thinking),
We should moisten the bud with a
health-giving flood
And 'twill bloom all the sweeter—
Yes, life's the completer
For drinking,
and drinking,
and drinking.
If it be that our life is a journey
(As many wise folk are opining),
We should sprinkle the way with the
rain while we may;
Though dusty and dreary,
'Tis made cool and cheery
With wining,
and wining,
and wining.
If this life that we live be a dreaming
(As pessimist people are thinking),
To induce pleasant dreams there is
nothing, meseems,
Like this sweet prescription,
That baffles description—
This drinking,
and drinking,
and drinking.

DER MANN IM KELLER

How cool and fair this cellar where
My throne a dusky cask is;
To do no thing but just to sing
And drown the time my task is.
The cooper he's
Resolved to please,
And, answering to my winking,
He fills me up
Cup after cup
For drinking, drinking, drinking.
Begrudge me not
This cosy spot
In which I am reclining—
Why, who would burst
With envious thirst,
When he can live by wining.
A roseate hue seems to imbue
The world on which I'm blinking;
My fellow-men—I love them when
I'm drinking, drinking, drinking.
And yet I think, the more I drink,
It's more and more I pine for—
Oh, such as I (forever dry)
God made this land of Rhine for;
And there is bliss
In knowing this,
As to the floor I'm sinking:
I've wronged no man
And never can
While drinking, drinking, drinking.

TWO IDYLLS FROM BION THE SMYRNEAN
I

Once a fowler, young and artless,
To the quiet greenwood came;
Full of skill was he and heartless

In pursuit of feathered game.
And betimes he chanced to see
Eros perching in a tree.
"What strange bird is that, I wonder?"
Thought the youth, and spread his snare;
Eros, chuckling at the blunder,
Gayly scampered here and there.
Do his best, the simple clod
Could not snare the agile god!
Blubbering, to his aged master
Went the fowler in dismay,
And confided his disaster
With that curious bird that day;
"Master, hast thou ever heard
Of so ill-disposed a bird?"
"Heard of him? Aha, most truly!"
Quoth the master with a smile;
"And thou too, shall know him duly—
Thou art young, but bide awhile,
And old Eros will not fly
From thy presence by and by!
"For when thou art somewhat older
That same Eros thou didst see,
More familiar grown and bolder,
Shall become acquaint with thee;
And when Eros comes thy way
Mark my word, he comes to stay!"

II

Once came Venus to me, bringing
Eros where my cattle fed—
"Teach this little boy your singing,
Gentle herdsman," Venus said.
I was young—I did not know
Whom it was that Venus led—
That was many years ago!
In a lusty voice but mellow—
Callow pedant! I began
To instruct the little fellow
In the mysteries known to man;
Sung the noble cithern's praise,
And the flute of dear old Pan,
And the lyre that Hermes plays.
But he paid no heed unto me—
Nay, that graceless little boy
Coolly plotted to undo me—
With his songs of tender joy;
And my pedantry o'erthrown,
Eager was I to employ
His sweet ritual for mine own!
Ah, these years of ours are fleeting!
Yet I have not vainly wrought,
Since to-day I am repeating
What dear lessons Eros taught;
Love, and always love, and then—
Counting all things else for naught—
Love and always love again!

THE WOOING OF THE SOUTHLAND
(ALASKAN BALLAD)

The Northland reared his hoary head
And spied the Southland leagues away—
"Fairest of all fair brides," he said,
"Be thou my bride, I pray!"
Whereat the Southland laughed and cried:
"I'll bide beside my native sea,
And I shall never be thy bride
Till thou com'st wooing me!"
The Northland's heart was a heart of ice,
A diamond glacier, mountain high—
Oh, love is sweet at any price,
As well know you and I!
So gayly the Northland took his heart
And cast it in the wailing sea—
"Go, thou, with all thy cunning art,
And woo my bride for me!"
For many a night and for many a day,
And over the leagues that rolled between,
The true-heart messenger sped away
To woo the Southland queen.
But the sea wailed loud, and the sea wailed long,
While ever the Northland cried in glee:
"Oh, thou shalt sing us our bridal song,
When comes my bride, O sea!"
At the foot of the Southland's golden throne
The heart of the Northland ever throbs—
For that true-heart speaks in the waves that moan,
The songs that it sings are sobs.
Ever the Southland spurns the cries
Of the messenger pleading the Northland's part;

The summer shines in the
  Southland's eyes—
The winter bides in her heart!
And ever unto that far-off place
Which love doth render a hallowed
  spot,
The Northland turneth his honest
  face
And wonders she cometh not.
The sea wails loud, and the sea wails
  long,
As the ages of waiting drift slowly
  by,
But the sea shall sing no bridal
  song—
As well know you and I!

HYMN
(FROM THE GERMAN OF MARTIN LUTHER)

O heart of mine! lift up thine eyes
And see who in yon manger lies!
Of perfect form, of face divine—
It is the Christ-child, heart of mine!
O dearest, holiest Christ-child,
  spread
Within this heart of mine thy bed;
Then shall my breast forever be
A chamber consecrate to thee!
Beat high to-day, O heart of mine,
And tell, O lips, what joys are thine;
For with your help shall I prolong
Old Bethlehem's sweetest cradle-
  song.
Glory to God, whom this dear Child
Hath by His coming reconciled,
And whose redeeming love again
Brings peace on earth, good will to
  men!

STAR OF THE EAST

Star of the East, that long ago
Brought wise men on their way
Where, angels singing to and fro,
The Child of Bethlehem lay—
Above that Syrian hill afar
Thou shinest out to-night, O Star!
Star of the East, the night were drear
But for the tender grace
That with thy glory comes to cheer
Earth's loneliest, darkest place;
For by that charity we see
Where there is hope for all and me.
Star of the East! show us the way
In wisdom undefiled
To seek that manger out and lay
Our gifts before the child—
To bring our hearts and offer them

Unto our King in Bethlehem!

TWIN IDOLS

There are two phrases, you must
  know,
So potent (yet so small)
That wheresoe'er a man may go
He needs none else at all;
No servile guide to lead the way
Nor lackey at his heel,
If he be learned enough to say
"Comme bien" and "Wie viel."
The sleek, pomaded Parleyvoo
Will air his sweetest airs
And quote the highest rates when
  you
"Comme bien" for his wares;
And, though the German stolid be,
His so-called heart of steel
Becomes as soft as wax when he
Detects the words "Wie viel."
Go, search the boulevards and rues
From Havre to Marseilles—
You'll find all eloquence you use
Except "Comme bien" fails;
Or in the country auf der Rhine
Essay a business deal
And all your art is good fuhr nein
Beyond the point—"Wie viel."
It matters not what game or prey
Attracts your greedy eyes—
You must pursue the good old way
If you would win the prize;
It is to get a titled mate
All run down at the heel,
If you inquire of stock effete,
"Comme bien" or "Wie viel."
So he is wise who envieth not
A wealth of foreign speech,
Since with two phrases may be got
Whatever's in his reach;
For Europe is a soulless shrine
In which all classes kneel
Before twin idols, deemed divine—
"Comme bien" and "Wie viel."

TWO VALENTINES
I.—TO MISTRESS BARBARA

There were three cavaliers, all
  handsome and true,

On Valentine's day came a maiden to woo,
And quoth to your mother: "Good-morrow, my dear,
We came with some songs for your daughter to hear!"
Your mother replied: "I'll be pleased to convey
To my daughter what things you may sing or may say!"
Then the first cavalier sung: "My pretty red rose,
I'll love you and court you some day, I suppose!"
And the next cavalier sung, with make-believe tears:
"I've loved you! I've loved you these many long years!"
But the third cavalier (with the brown, bushy head
And the pretty blue jacket and necktie of red)
He drew himself up with a resolute air,
And he warbled: "O maiden, surpassingly fair!
I've loved you long years, and I love you to-day,
And, if you will let me, I'll love you for aye!"
I (the third cavalier) sang this ditty to you,
In my necktie of red and my jacket of blue;
I'm sure you'll prefer the song that was mine
And smile your approval on your valentine.

II.—TO A BABY BOY
Who I am I shall not say,
But I send you this bouquet
With this query, baby mine:
"Will you be my valentine?"
See these roses blushing blue,
Very like your eyes of hue;
While these violets are the red
Of your cheeks. It can be said
Ne'er before was babe like you.
And I think it is quite true
No one e'er before to-day
Sent so wondrous a bouquet
As these posies aforesaid—
Roses blue and violets red!
Sweet, repay me sweets for sweets—
'Tis your lover who entreats!
Smile upon me, baby mine—
Be my little valentine!

MOTHER AND SPHINX
(EGYPTIAN FOLK-SONG)
Grim is the face that looks into the night
Over the stretch of sands;
A sullen rock in a sea of white—
A ghostly shadow in ghostly light,
Peering and moaning it stands.
"Oh, is it the king that rides this way—
Oh, is it the king that rides so free?
I have looked for the king this many a day,
But the years that mock me will not say
Why tarrieth he!"
'T is not your king that shall ride to-night,
But a child that is fast asleep;
And the horse he shall ride is the Dream-horse white—
Aha, he shall speed through the ghostly light
Where the ghostly shadows creep!
"My eyes are dull and my face is sere,
Yet unto the word he gave I cling,
For he was a Pharaoh that set me here—
And, lo! I have waited this many a year
For him—my king!"
Oh, past thy face my darling shall ride
Swift as the burning winds that bear
The sand clouds over the desert wide—
Swift to the verdure and palms beside
The wells off there!
"And is it the mighty king I shall see
Come riding into the night?
Oh, is it the king come back to me—
Proudly and fiercely rideth he,
With centuries dight!"
I know no king but my dark-eyed dear
That shall ride the Dream-Horse white;

But see! he wakes at my bosom here,
While the Dream-Horse frettingly lingers near
To speed with my babe to-night!
And out of the desert darkness peers
A ghostly, ghastly, shadowy thing
Like a spirit come out of the mouldering years,
And ever that waiting spectre hears
The coming king!

A SPRING POEM FROM BION

One asketh:
"Tell me, Myrson, tell me true:
What's the season pleaseth you?
Is it summer suits you best,
When from harvest toil we rest?
Is it autumn with its glory
Of all surfeited desires?
Is it winter, when with story
And with song we hug our fires?
Or is spring most fair to you—
Come, good Myrson, tell me true!"
Another answereth:
"What the gods in wisdom send
We should question not, my friend;
Yet, since you entreat of me,
I will answer reverently:
Me the summertime displeases,
For its sun is scorching hot;
Autumn brings such dire diseases
That perforce I like it not;
As for biting winter, oh!
How I hate its ice and snow!
"But, thrice welcome, kindly spring,
With the myriad gifts you bring!
Not too hot nor yet too cold,
Graciously your charms unfold—
Oh, your days are like the dreaming
Of those nights which love beseems,
And your nights have all the seeming
Of those days of golden dreams!
Heaven smiles down on earth, and then
Earth smiles up to heaven again!"

BÉRANGER'S "TO MY OLD COAT."

Still serve me in my age, I pray,
As in my youth, O faithful one;
For years I've brushed thee every day—
Could Socrates have better done?
What though the fates would wreak on thee
The fulness of their evil art?
Use thou philosophy, like me—
And we, old friend, shall never part!
I think—I often think of it—
The day we twain first faced the crowd;
My roistering friends impeached your fit,
But you and I were very proud!
Those jovial friends no more make free
With us (no longer new and smart),
But rather welcome you and me
As loving friends that should not part.
The patch? Oh, yes—one happy night—
"Lisette," says I, "it's time to go"—
She clutched this sleeve to stay my flight,
Shrieking: "What! leave so early? No!"
To mend the ghastly rent she'd made,
Three days she toiled, dear patient heart!
And I—right willingly I staid—
Lisette decreed we should not part!
No incense ever yet profaned
This honest, shiny warp of thine,
Nor hath a courtier's eye disdained
Thy faded hue and quaint design;
Let servile flattery be the price
Of ribbons in the royal mart—
A roadside posie shall suffice
For us two friends that must not part!
Fear not the recklessness of yore
Shall re-occur to vex thee now;
Alas, I am a youth no more—
I'm old and sere, and so art thou!
So bide with me unto the last
And with thy warmth caress this heart
That pleads, by memories of the Past,
That two such friends should never part!

BEN APFELGARTEN

There was a certain gentleman, Ben Apfelgarten called,

Who lived way off in Germany a many years ago,
And he was very fortunate in being very bald
And so was very happy he was so.
He warbled all the day
Such songs as only they
Who are very, very circumspect and very happy may;
The people wondered why,
As the years went gliding by,
They never heard him once complain or even heave a sigh!
The women of the province fell in love with genial Ben,
Till (may be you can fancy it) the dickens was to pay
Among the callow students and the sober-minded men—
With the women-folk a-cuttin' up that way!
Why, they gave him turbans red
To adorn his hairless head,
And knitted jaunty nightcaps to protect him when abed!
In vain the rest demurred—
Not a single chiding word
Those ladies deigned to tolerate— remonstrance was absurd!
Things finally got into such a very dreadful way
That the others (oh, how artful) formed the politic design
To send him to the reichstag; so, one dull November day,
They elected him a member from the Rhine!
Then the other members said: "Gott im Himmel! what a head!"
But they marvelled when his speeches they listened to or read;
And presently they cried:
"There must be heaps inside
Of the smooth and shiny cranium his constituents deride!"
Well, when at last he up 'nd died— long past his ninetieth year—
The strangest and the most lugubrious funeral he had,
For women came in multitudes to weep upon his bier—
The men all wond'ring why on earth the women had gone mad!
And this wonderment increased
Till the sympathetic priest
Inquired of those same ladies: "Why this fuss about deceased?"
Whereupon were they appalled,
For, as one, those women squalled:
"We doted on deceased for being bald—bald—bald!"
He was bald because his genius burnt that shock of hair away
Which, elsewise, clogs one's keenness and activity of mind;
And (barring present company, of course) I'm free to say
That, after all, it's intellect that captures womankind.
At any rate, since then
(With a precedent in Ben),
The women-folk have been in love with us bald-headed men!

A HEINE LOVE SONG
The image of the moon at night
All trembling in the ocean lies,
But she, with calm and steadfast light,
Moves proudly through the radiant skies,
How like the tranquil moon thou art—
Thou fairest flower of womankind!
And, look, within my fluttering heart
Thy image trembling is enshrined!

UHLAND'S "CHAPEL"
Yonder stands the hillside chapel
Mid the evergreens and rocks,
All day long it hears the song
Of the shepherd to his flocks.
Then the chapel bell goes tolling—
Knelling for a soul that's sped;
Silent and sad the shepherd lad
Hears the requiem for the dead.
Shepherd, singers of the valley,
Voiceless now, speed on before;
Soon shall knell that chapel bell
For the songs you'll sing no more.

THE DREAMS
Two dreams came down to earth one night
From the realm of mist and dew;
One was a dream of the old, old days,
And one was a dream of the new.
One was a dream of a shady lane

That led to the pickerel pond
Where the willows and rushes bowed themselves
To the brown old hills beyond.
And the people that peopled the old-time dream
Were pleasant and fair to see,
And the dreamer he walked with them again
As often of old walked he.
Oh, cool was the wind in the shady lane
That tangled his curly hair!
Oh, sweet was the music the robins made
To the springtime everywhere!
Was it the dew the dream had brought
From yonder midnight skies,
Or was it tears from the dear, dead years
That lay in the dreamer's eyes?
The other dream ran fast and free,
As the moon benignly shed
Her golden grace on the smiling face
In the little trundle-bed.
For 't was a dream of times to come—
Of the glorious noon of day—
Of the summer that follows the careless spring
When the child is done with play.
And 't was a dream of the busy world
Where valorous deeds are done;
Of battles fought in the cause of right,
And of victories nobly won.
It breathed no breath of the dear old home
And the quiet joys of youth;
It gave no glimpse of the good old friends
Or the old-time faith and truth.
But 't was a dream of youthful hopes,
And fast and free it ran,
And it told to a little sleeping child
Of a boy become a man!
These were the dreams that came one night
To earth from yonder sky;
These were the dreams two dreamers dreamed—
My little boy and I.

And in our hearts my boy and I
Were glad that it was so;
He loved to dream of days to come,
And I of long ago.
So from our dreams my boy and I
Unwillingly awoke,
But neither of his precious dream
Unto the other spoke.
Yet of the love we bore those dreams
Gave each his tender sign;
For there was triumph in his eyes—
And there were tears in mine!

IN NEW ORLEANS

'Twas in the Crescent City not long ago befell
The tear-compelling incident I now propose to tell;
So come, my sweet collector friends, and listen while I sing
Unto your delectation this brief, pathetic thing—
No lyric pitched in vaunting key, but just a requiem
Of blowing twenty dollars in by nine o'clock a.m.
Let critic folk the poet's use of vulgar slang upbraid,
But, when I'm speaking by the card, I call a spade a spade;
And I, who have been touched of that same mania, myself,
Am well aware that, when it comes to parting with his pelf,
The curio collector is so blindly lost in sin
That he doesn't spend his money— he simply blows it in!
In Royal street (near Conti) there's a lovely curio-shop,
And there, one balmy, fateful morn, it was my chance to stop;
To stop was hesitation—in a moment I was lost—
That kind of hesitation does not hesitate at cost!
I spied a pewter tankard there, and, my! it was a gem—
And the clock in old St. Louis told the hour of eight a.m.!
Three quaint Bohemian bottles, too, of yellow and of green,
Cut in archaic fashion that I ne'er before had seen;

A lovely, hideous platter wreathed
about with pink and rose,
With its curious depression into
which the gravy flows;
Two dainty silver salts—oh, there
was no resisting them—
And I'd blown in twenty dollars by
nine o'clock a.m.
With twenty dollars, one who is a
prudent man, indeed,
Can buy the wealth of useful things
his wife and children need;
Shoes, stockings, knickerbockers,
gloves, bibs, nursing-bottles, caps,
A gown—the gown for which his
spouse too long has pined, perhaps!
These and ten thousand other
spectres harrow and condemn
The man who's blown in twenty by
nine o'clock a.m.
Oh, mean advantage conscience
takes (and one that I abhor!) In asking
one this question: "What did you buy it
for?" Why doesn't conscience ply its
blessed trade beforethe act, Before one's
cussedness becomes a bald,
accomplished fact— Before one's fallen
victim to the Tempter's stratagem And
blown in twenty dollars by nine o'clock
a.m.?
Ah me! now that the deed is done,
how penitent I am!
I was a roaring lion—behold a
bleating lamb!
I've packed and shipped those
precious things to that more precious
wife
Who shares with our sweet babes
the strange vicissitudes of life,
While he who, in his folly, gave up
his store of wealth
Is far away, and means to keep his
distance—for his health!

MY PLAYMATES

The wind comes whispering to me
of the country green and cool—
Of redwing blackbirds chattering
beside a reedy pool;
It brings me soothing fancies of the
homestead on the hill,
And I hear the thrush's evening song
and the robin's morning trill;
So I fall to thinking tenderly of those
I used to know
Where the sassafras and snakeroot
and checkerberries grow.
What has become of Ezra Marsh,
who lived on Baker's hill?
And what's become of Noble Pratt,
whose father kept the mill?
And what's become of Lizzie Crum
and Anastasia Snell,
And of Roxie Root, who 'tended
school in Boston for a spell?
They were the boys and they the
girls who shared my youthful play—
They do not answer to my call! My
playmates—where are they?
What has become of Levi and his
little brother Joe,
Who lived next door to where we
lived some forty years ago?
I'd like to see the Newton boys and
Quincy Adams Brown,
And Hepsy Hall and Ella Cowles,
who spelled the whole school down!
And Gracie Smith, the Cutler boys,
Leander Snow, and all
Who I am sure would answer could
they only hear my call!
I'd like to see Bill Warner and the
Conkey boys again
And talk about the times we used to
wish that we were men!
And one—I shall not name her—
could I see her gentle face
And hear her girlish treble in this
distant, lonely place!
The flowers and hopes of
springtime—they perished long ago,
And the garden where they
blossomed is white with winter snow.
O cottage 'neath the maples, have
you seen those girls and boys
That but a little while ago made, oh!
such pleasant noise?
O trees, and hills, and brooks, and
lanes, and meadows, do you know
Where I shall find my little friends
of forty years ago?
You see I'm old and weary, and I've
traveled long and far;
I am looking for my playmates—I
wonder where they are!

STOVES AND SUNSHINE

Prate, ye who will, of so-called
charms you find across the sea—

The land of stoves and sunshine is
good enough for me!
I've done the grand for fourteen
months in every foreign clime,
And I've learned a heap of learning,
but I've shivered all the time;
And the biggest bit of wisdom I've
acquired—as I can see—
Is that which teaches that this land's
the land of lands for me.
Now, I am of opinion that a person
should get some
Warmth in this present life of ours,
not all in that to come;
So when Boreas blows his blast,
through country and through town,
Or when upon the muddy streets the
stifling fog rolls down,
Go, guzzle in a pub, or plod some
bleak malarious grove,
But let me toast my shrunken shanks
beside some Yankee stove.
The British people say they "don't
believe in stoves, y' know;"
Perchance because we warmed 'em
so completely years ago!
They talk of "drahfts" and
"stuffiness" and "ill effects of heat,"
As they chatter in their barny rooms
or shiver 'round the street;
With sunshine such a rarity, and
stoves esteemed a sin,
What wonder they are wedded to
their fads—catarrh and gin?
In Germany are stoves galore, and
yet you seldom find
A fire within the stoves, for German
stoves are not that kind;
The Germans say that fires make
dirt, and dirt's an odious thing,
But the truth is that the pfennig is
the average Teuton's king,
And since the fire costs pfennigs,
why, the thrifty soul denies
Himself all heat except what comes
with beer and exercise.
The Frenchman builds a fire of
cones, the Irishman of peat;
The frugal Dutchman buys a fire
when he has need of heat—
That is to say, he pays so much each
day to one who brings
The necessary living coals to warm
his soup and things;

In Italy and Spain they have no need
to heat the house—
'Neath balmy skies the native picks
the mandolin and louse.
Now, we've no mouldy catacombs,
no feudal castles grim,
No ruined monasteries, no abbeys
ghostly dim;
Our ancient history is new, our
future's all ahead,
And we've got a tariff bill that's
made all Europe sick abed—
But what is best, though short on
tombs and academic groves,
We double discount Christendom on
sunshine and on stoves.
Dear land of mine! I come to you
from months of chill and storm,
Blessing the honest people whose
hearts and hearths are warm;
A fairer, sweeter song than this I
mean to weave to you
When I've reached my lakeside
'dobe and once get heated through;
But, even then, the burthen of that
fairer song shall be
That the land of stoves and sunshine
is good enough for me.

A DRINKING SONG
Come, brothers, share the fellowship
We celebrate to-night;
There's grace of song on every lip
And every heart is light!
But first, before our mentor chimes
The hour of jubilee,
Let's drink a health to good old
times,
And good times yet to be!
Clink, clink, clink!
Merrily let us drink!
There's store of wealth
And more of health
In every glass, we think.
Clink, clink, clink!
To fellowship we drink!
And from the bowl
No genial soul
In such an hour can shrink.
And you, oh, friends from west and
east
And other foreign parts,
Come share the rapture of our feast,
The love of loyal hearts;
And in the wassail that suspends

All matters burthensome,
We'll drink a health to good old friends
And good friends yet to come.
Clink, clink, clink!
To fellowship we drink!
And from the bowl
No genial soul
In such an hour will shrink.
Clink, clink, clink!
Merrily let us drink!
There's fellowship
In every sip
Of friendship's brew, we think.

THE LIMITATIONS OF YOUTH

I'd like to be a cowboy an' ride a fiery hoss
Way out into the big an' boundless west;
I'd kill the bears an' catamounts an' wolves I come across,
An' I'd pluck the bal' head eagle from his nest!
With my pistols at my side,
I would roam the prarers wide,
An' to scalp the savage Injun in his wigwam would I ride—
If I darst; but I darsen't!
I'd like to go to Afriky an' hunt the lions there,
An' the biggest ollyfunts you ever saw!
I would track the fierce gorilla to his equatorial lair,
An' beard the cannybull that eats folks raw!
I'd chase the pizen snakes
An' the 'pottimus that makes
His nest down at the bottom of unfathomable lakes—
If I darst; but I darsen't!
I would I were a pirut to sail the ocean blue,
With a big black flag aflyin' overhead;
I would scour the billowy main with my gallant pirut crew
An' dye the sea a gouty, gory red!
With my cutlass in my hand
On the quarterdeck I'd stand
And to deeds of heroism I'd incite my pirut band—
If I darst; but I darsen't!
And, if I darst, I'd lick my pa for the times that he's licked me!
I'd lick my brother an' my teacher, too!
I'd lick the fellers that call round on sister after tea,
An' I'd keep on lickin' folks till I got through!
You bet! I'd run away
From my lessons to my play,
An' I'd shoo the hens, an' tease the cat, an' kiss the girls all day—
If I darst; but I darsen't!

THE BOW-LEG BOY

Who should come up the road one day
But the doctor-man in his two-wheel shay!
And he whoaed his horse and he cried "Ahoy!
I have brought you folks a bow-leg boy!
Such a cute little boy!
Such a funny little boy!
Such a dear little bow-leg boy!"
He took out his box and he opened it wide,
And there was the bow-leg boy inside!
And when they saw that cunning little mite,
They cried in a chorus expressive of delight:
"What a cute little boy!
What a funny little boy!
What a dear little bow-leg boy!"
Observing a strict geometrical law,
They cut out his panties with a circular saw;
Which gave such a stress to his oval stride
That the people he met invariably cried:
"What a cute little boy!
What a funny little boy!
What a dear little bow-leg boy!"
They gave him a wheel and away he went
Speeding along to his heart's content;
And he sits so straight and he pedals so strong
That the folks all say as he bowls along:

"What a cute little boy!
What a funny little boy!
What a dear little bow-leg boy!"
With his eyes aflame and his cheeks aglow,
He laughs "aha" and he laughs "oho";
And the world is filled and thrilled with the joy
Of that jolly little human, the bow-leg boy—
The cute little boy!
The funny little boy!
The dear little bow-leg boy!
If ever the doctor-man comes my way
With his wonderful box in his two-wheel shay,
I'll ask for the treasure I'd fain possess—
Now, honest Injun! can't you guess?
Why, a cute little boy—
A funny little boy—
A dear little bow-leg boy!

THE STRAW PARLOR

Way up at the top of a big stack of straw
Was the cunningest parlor that ever you saw!
And there could you lie when aweary of play
And gossip or laze in the coziest way;
No matter how careworn or sorry one's mood
No worldly distraction presumed to intrude.
As a refuge from onerous mundane ado
I think I approve of straw parlors, don't you?
A swallow with jewels aflame on her breast
On that straw parlor's ceiling had builded her nest;
And she flew in and out all the happy day long,
And twittered the soothingest lullaby song.
Now some might suppose that that beautiful bird
Performed for her babies the music they heard;
I reckon she twittered her répertoire through
For the folk in the little straw parlor, don't you?
And down from a rafter a spider had hung
Some swings upon which he incessantly swung.
He cut up such didoes—such antics he played
Way up in the air, and was never afraid!
He never made use of his horrid old sting,
But was just upon earth for the fun of the thing!
I deeply regret to observe that so few
Of these good-natured insects are met with, don't you?
And, down in the strawstack, a wee little mite
Of a cricket went chirping by day and by night;
And further down, still, a cunning blue mouse
In a snug little nook of that strawstack kept house!
When the cricket went "chirp," Miss Mousie would squeak
"Come in," and a blush would enkindle her cheek!
She thought—silly girl! 't was a beau come to woo,
But I guess it was only the cricket, don't you?
So the cricket, the mouse, and the motherly bird
Made as soothingsome music as ever you heard
And, meanwhile, that spider by means of his swings
Achieved most astounding gyrations and things!
No wonder the little folk liked what they saw
And loved what they heard in that parlor of straw!
With the mercury up to 102
In the shade, I opine they just sizzled, don't you?
But once there invaded that Eden of straw
The evilest Feline that ever you saw!

She pounced on that cricket with
rare promptitude
And she tucked him away where
he'd do the most good;
And then, reaching down to the
nethermost house,
She deftly expiscated little Miss
Mouse!
And, as for the Swallow, she
shrieked and withdrew—
I rather admire her discretion, don't
you?
Now listen: That evening a cyclone
obtained,
And the mortgage was all on that
farm that remained!
Barn, strawstack and spider—they
all blew away,
And nobody knows where they're at
to this day!
And, as for the little straw parlor, I
fear
It was wafted clean off this
sublunary sphere!
I really incline to a hearty "boo-hoo"
When I think of this tragical ending,
don't you?

A PITEOUS PLAINT
I cannot eat my porridge,
I weary of my play;
No longer can I sleep at night,
No longer romp by day!
Though forty pounds was once my
weight,
I'm shy of thirty now;
I pine, I wither and I fade
Through love of Martha Clow.
As she rolled by this morning
I heard the nurse girl say:
"She weighs just twenty-seven
pounds
And she's one year old to-day."
I threw a kiss that nestled
In the curls upon her brow,
But she never turned to thank me—
That bouncing Martha Clow!
She ought to know I love her,
For I've told her that I do;
And I've brought her nuts and
apples,
And sometimes candy, too!
I'd drag her in my little cart
If her mother would allow
That delicate attention
To her daughter, Martha Clow.
O Martha! pretty Martha!
Will you always be so cold?
Will you always be as cruel
As you are at one-year-old?
Must your two-year-old admirer
Pine as hopelessly as now
For a fond reciprocation
Of his love for Martha Clow?
You smile on Bernard Rogers
And on little Harry Knott;
You play with them at peek-a-boo
All in the Waller Lot!
Wildly I gnash my new-cut teeth
And beat my throbbing brow,
When I behold the coquetry
Of heartless Martha Clow!
I cannot eat my porridge,
Nor for my play care I;
Upon the floor and porch and lawn
My toys neglected lie;
But on the air of Halsted street
I breathe this solemn vow:
"Though she be false, I will be true
To pretty Martha Clow!"

THE DISCREET COLLECTOR
Down south there is a curio-shop
Unknown to many men;
Thereat do I intend to stop
When I am south again;
The narrow street through which to
go—
Aha! I know it well!
And may be you would like to
know—
But no—I will not tell!
'T is there to find the loveliest plates
(The bluest of the blue!)
At such surprisingly low rates
You'd not believe it true!
And there is one Napoleon vase
Of dainty Sèvres to sell—
I'm sure you'd like to know that
place—
But no—I will not tell!
Then, too, I know another shop
Has old, old beds for sale,
With lovely testers up on top
Carved in ornate detail;
And there are sideboards rich and
rare,
With fronts that proudly swell—
Oh, there are bargains waiting there,
But where I will not tell!

And hark! I know a bottle-man
Smiling and debonair,
And he has promised me I can
Choose of his precious ware!
In age and shape and color, too,
His dainty goods excel—
Aha, my friends, if you but knew—
But no! I will not tell!
A thousand other shops I know
Where bargains can be got—
Where other folk would like to go
Who have what I have not.
I let them hunt; I hold my mouth—
Yes, though I know full well
Where lie the treasures of the south,
I'm not a going to tell!

A VALENTINE
Your gran'ma, in her youth, was quite
As blithe a little maid as you.
And, though her hair is snowy white,
Her eyes still have their maiden blue,
And on her cheeks, as fair as thine,
Methinks a girlish blush would glow
If she recalled the valentine
She got, ah! many years ago.
A valorous youth loved gran'ma then,
And wooed her in that auld lang syne;
And first he told his secret when
He sent the maid that valentine.
No perfumed page nor sheet of gold
Was that first hint of love he sent,
But with the secret gran'pa told—
"I love you"—gran'ma was content.
Go, ask your gran'ma, if you will,
If—though her head be bowed and gray—
If—though her feeble pulse be chill—
True love abideth not for aye;
By that quaint portrait on the wall,
That smiles upon her from above,
Methinks your gran'ma can recall
The sweet divinity of love.
Dear Elsie, here's no page of gold—
No sheet embossed with cunning art—
But here's a solemn pledge of old:
"I love you, love, with all my heart."
And if in what I send you here
You read not all of love expressed,
Go—go to gran'ma, Elsie dear,
And she will tell you all the rest!

THE WIND
(THE TALE)
Cometh the Wind from the garden,
fragrant and full of sweet singing—
Under my tree where I sit cometh
the Wind to confession.
"Out in the garden abides the Queen
of the beautiful Roses—
Her do I love and to-night wooed
her with passionate singing;
Told I my love in those songs, and
answer she gave in her blushes—
She shall be bride of the Wind, and
she is the Queen of the Roses!"
"Wind, there is spice in thy breath;
thy rapture hath fragrance Sabaean!"
"Straight from my wooing I come—
my lips are bedewed with her kisses—
My lips and my song and my heart
are drunk with the rapture of loving!"

(THE SONG)
The Wind he loveth the red, red Rose,
And he wooeth his love to wed:
Sweet is his song
The Summer long
As he kisseth her lips so red;
And he recketh naught of the ruin wrought
When the Summer of love is sped!

(AGAIN THE TALE)
Cometh the Wind from the garden,
bitter with sorrow of winter.
"Wind, is thy love-song forgot?
Wherefore thy dread lamentations?"
Sigheth and moaneth the Wind:
"Out of the desolate garden
Come I from vigils with ghosts over
the grave of the Summer!"
"Thy breath that was fragrant anon
with rapture of music and loving, It
grieveth all things with its sting and the
frost of its wailing displeasure."
The Wind maketh ever more moan
and ever it giveth this answer:
"My heart it is numb with the cold
of the love that was born of the Summer—

I come from the garden all white
with the wrath and the sorrow of
Winter;
I have kissed the low, desolate tomb
where my bride in her loveliness
lieth
And the voice of the ghost in my
heart is the voice that forever
outcrieth!"

(AGAIN THE SONG)

The Wind he waileth the red, red
Rose
When the Summer of love is sped—
He waileth above
His lifeless love
With her shroud of snow
o'erspread—
Crieth such things as a true heart
brings
To the grave of its precious dead.

A PARAPHRASE

Our Father who art in heaven,
hallowed be Thy name;
Thy Kingdom come, Thy will be
done on earth, in Heaven the same;
Give us this day our daily bread, and
may our debts to heaven—
As we our earthly debts forgive—by
Thee be all forgiven;
When tempted or by evil vexed,
restore Thou us again,
And Thine be the Kingdom, the
Power, and the Glory, forever and ever;
amen.

WITH BRUTUS IN ST. JO

Of all the opry-houses then
obtaining in the West
The one which Milton Tootle owned
was, by all odds, the best;
Milt, being rich, was much too
proud to run the thing alone,
So he hired an "acting manager," a
gruff old man named Krone—
A stern, commanding man with
piercing eyes and flowing beard,
And his voice assumed a thunderous
tone when Jack and I appeared;
He said that Julius Caesar had been
billed a week or so,
And would have to have some
armies by the time he reached St. Jo!
O happy days, when Tragedy still
winged an upward flight,
When actors wore tin helmets and
cambric robes at night!
O happy days, when sounded in the
public's rapturous ears
The creak of pasteboard armor and
the clash of wooden spears!
O happy times for Jack and me and
that one other supe
That then and there did constitute
the noblest Roman's troop!
With togas, battle axes, shields, we
made a dazzling show,
When we were Roman soldiers with
Brutus in St. Jo!
We wheeled and filed and double-
quicked wherever Brutus led,
The folks applauding what we did as
much as what he said;
'T was work, indeed; yet Jack and I
were willing to allow
'T was easier following Brutus than
following father's plough;
And at each burst of cheering, our
valor would increase—
We tramped a thousand miles that
night, at fifty cents apiece!
For love of Art—not lust for gold—
consumed us years ago,
When we were Roman soldiers with
Brutus in St. Jo!
To-day, while walking in the
Square, Jack Langrish says to me:
"My friend, the drama nowadays
ain't what it used to be!
These farces and these comedies—
how feebly they compare
With that mantle of the tragic art
which Forrest used to wear!
My soul is warped with bitterness to
think that you and I—
Co-heirs to immortality in seasons
long gone by—
Now draw a paltry stipend from a
Boston comic show,
We, who were Roman soldiers with
Brutus in St. Jo!"
And so we talked and so we mused
upon the whims of Fate
That had degraded Tragedy from its
old, supreme estate;
And duly, at the Morton bar, we
stigmatized the age
As sinfully subversive of the
interests of the Stage!

For Jack and I were actors in the halcyon, palmy days
Long, long before the Hoyt school of farce became the craze;
Yet, as I now recall it, it was twenty years ago
That we were Roman soldiers with Brutus in St. Jo!
We were by birth descended from a race of farmer kings
Who had done eternal battle with grasshoppers and things;
But the Kansas farms grew tedious—we pined for that delight
We read of in the Clipper in the barber's shop by night!
We would be actors—Jack and I—and so we stole away
From our native spot, Wathena, one dull September day,
And started for Missouri—ah, little did we know
We were going to train as soldiers with Brutus in St. Jo!
Our army numbered three in all—Marc Antony's was four;
Our army hankered after fame, but Marc's was after gore!
And when we reached Philippi, at the outset we were met
With an inartistic gusto I can never quite forget.
For Antony's overwhelming force of thumpers seemed to be
Resolved to do "them Kansas jays"—and that meant Jack and me!
My lips were sealed but that it seems quite proper you should know
That Rome was nowhere in it at Philippi in St. Jo!
I've known the slow-consuming grief and ostentatious pain
Accruing from McKean Buchanan's melancholy Dane;
Away out West I've witnessed Bandmann's peerless hardihood,
With Arthur Cambridge have I wrought where walking was not good;
In every phase of horror have I bravely borne my part,
And even on my uppers have I proudly stood for Art!
And, after all my suffering, it were not hard to show
That I got my allopathic dose with Brutus at St. Jo!
That army fell upon me in a most bewildering rage
And scattered me and mine upon that histrionic stage;
My toga rent, my helmet gone and smashed to smithereens,
They picked me up and hove me through whole centuries of scenes!
I sailed through Christian eras and mediæval gloom
And fell from Arden forest into Juliet's painted tomb!
Oh, yes, I travelled far and fast that night, and I can show
The scars of honest wounds I got with Brutus in St. Jo!
Ah me, old Davenport is gone, of fickle fame forgot,
And Barrett sleeps forever in a much neglected spot;
Fred Warde, the papers tell me, in far woolly western lands
Still flaunts the banner of high Tragic Art at one-night stands;
And Jack and I, in Charley Hoyt's Bostonian dramas wreak
Our vengeance on creation at some eensty dolls per week.
By which you see that public taste has fallen mighty low
Since we fought as Roman soldiers with Brutus in St. Jo!

THE TWO LITTLE SKEEZUCKS

There were two little skeezucks who lived in the isle
Of Boo in a southern sea;
They clambered and rollicked in heathenish style
In the boughs of their cocoanut tree.
They didn't fret much about clothing and such
And they recked not a whit of the ills
That sometimes accrue
From having to do
With tailor and laundry bills.
The two little skeezucks once heard of a Fair
Far off from their native isle,
And they asked of King Fan if they mightn't go there

To take in the sights for awhile.
Now old King Fan
Was a good-natured man
(As good-natured monarchs go),
And howbeit he swore that all Fairs were a bore,
He hadn't the heart to say "No."
So the two little skeezucks sailed off to the Fair
In a great big gum canoe,
And I fancy they had a good time there,
For they tarried a year or two.
And old King Fan at last began
To reckon they'd come to grief,
When glory! one day
They sailed into the bay
To the tune of "Hail to the Chief!"
The two little skeezucks fell down on the sand,
Embracing his majesty's toes,
Till his majesty graciously bade them stand
And salute him nose to nose.
And then quoth he:
"Divulge unto me
What happenings have hapt to you;
And how did they dare to indulge in a Fair
So far from the island of Boo?"
The two little skeezucks assured their king
That what he surmised was true;
That the Fair would have been a different thing
Had it only been held in Boo!
"The folk over there in no wise compare
With the folk of the southern seas;
Why, they comb out their heads
And they sleep in beds
Instead of in caverns and trees!"
The two little skeezucks went on to say
That children (so far as they knew)
Had a much harder time in that land far away
Than here in the island of Boo!
They have to wear clo'es
Which (as every one knows)
Are irksome to primitive laddies,
While, with forks and with spoons, they're denied the sweet boons
That accrue from free use of one's paddies!

"And now that you're speaking of things to eat,"
Interrupted the monarch of Boo,
"We beg to inquire if you happened to meet
With a nice missionary or two?"
"No, that we did not; in that curious spot
Where were gathered the fruits of the earth,
Of that special kind
Which Your Nibs has in mind
There appeared a deplorable dearth!"
Then loud laughed that monarch in heathenish mirth
And loud laughed his courtiers, too,
And they cried: "There is elsewhere no land upon earth
So good as our island of Boo!"
And the skeezucks, tho' glad
Of the journey they'd had,
Climbed up in their cocoanut trees,
Where they still may be seen with no shirts to keep clean
Or trousers that bag at the knees.

PAN LIVETH

They told me once that Pan was dead,
And so, in sooth, I thought him;
For vainly where the streamlets led
Through flowery meads I sought him—
Nor in his dewy pasture bed
Nor in the grove I caught him.
"Tell me," 'twas so my clamor ran—
"Tell me, oh, where is Pan?"
But, once, as on my pipe I played
A requiem sad and tender,
Lo, thither came a shepherd-maid—
Full comely she and slender!
I were indeed a churlish blade
With wailings to offend 'er—
For, surely, wooing's sweeter than
A mourning over Pan!
So, presently, whiles I did scan
That shepherd-maiden pretty,
And heard her accents, I began
To pipe a cheerful ditty;
And so, betimes, forgot old Pan
Whose death had waked my pity;
So—so did Love undo the man
Who sought and pined for Pan!

He was not dead! I found him there—
The Pan that I was after!
Caught in that maiden's tangling hair,
Drunk with her song and laughter!
I doubt if there be otherwhere
A merrier god or dafter—
Nay, nor a mortal kindlier than
Is this same dear old Pan!
Beside me, as my pipe I play,
My shepherdess is lying,
While here and there her lambkins stray
As sunny hours go flying;
They look like me—those lambs—they say,
And that I'm not denying!
And for that sturdy, romping clan,
All glory be to Pan!
Pan is not dead, O sweetheart mine!
It is to hear his voices
In every note and every line
Wherein the heart rejoices!
He liveth in that sacred shrine
That Love's first, holiest choice is!
So pipe, my pipe, while still you can,
Sweet songs in praise of Pan!

DR. SAM
TO MISS GRACE KING

Down in the old French quarter,
Just out of Rampart street,
I wend my way
At close of day
Unto the quaint retreat
Where lives the Voodoo Doctor
By some esteemed a sham,
Yet I'll declare there's none elsewhere
So skilled as Doctor Sam
With the claws of a deviled crawfish,
The juice of the prickly prune,
And the quivering dew
From a yarb that grew
In the light of a midnight moon!
I never should have known him
But for the colored folk
That here obtain
And ne'er in vain
That wizard's art invoke;
For when the Eye that's Evil
Would him and his'n damn,
The negro's grief gets quick relief
Of Hoodoo-Doctor Sam.
With the caul of an alligator,
The plume of an unborn loon,
And the poison wrung
From a serpent's tongue
By the light of a midnight moon!
In all neurotic ailments
I hear that he excels,
And he insures
Immediate cures
Of weird, uncanny spells;
The most unruly patient
Gets docile as a lamb
And is freed from ill by the potent skill
Of Hoodoo-Doctor Sam;
Feathers of strangled chickens,
Moss from the dank lagoon,
And plasters wet
With spider sweat
In the light of a midnight moon!
They say when nights are grewsome
And hours are, oh! so late,
Old Sam steals out
And hunts about
For charms that hoodoos hate!
That from the moaning river
And from the haunted glen
He silently brings what eerie things
Give peace to hoodooed men:—
The tongue of a piebald 'possum,
The tooth of a senile 'coon,
The buzzard's breath that smells of death,
And the film that lies
On a lizard's eyes
In the light of a midnight moon!

WINFREDA
(A BALLAD IN THE ANGLO-SAXON TONGUE)

When to the dreary greenwood gloam
Winfreda's husband strode that day,
The fair Winfreda bode at home
To toil the weary time away;
"While thou art gone to hunt," said she,
"I'll brew a goodly sop for thee."
Lo, from a further, gloomy wood,
A hungry wolf all bristling hied
And on the cottage threshold stood
And saw the dame at work inside;
And, as he saw the pleasing sight,

He licked his fangs so sharp and white.
Now when Winfreda saw the beast,
Straight at the grinning wolf she ran,
And, not affrighted in the least,
She hit him with her cooking pan,
And as she thwacked him on the head—
"Scat! scat!" the fair Winfreda said.
The hills gave answer to their din—
The brook in fear beheld the sight.
And all that bloody field within
Wore token of Winfreda's might.
The wolf was very loath to stay—
But, oh! he could not get away.
Winfreda swept him o'er the wold
And choked him till his gums were blue,
And till, beneath her iron hold,
His tongue hung out a yard or two,
And with his hair the riven ground
Was strewn for many leagues around.
They fought a weary time that day,
And seas of purple blood were shed,
Till by Winfreda's cunning lay
That awful wolf all limp and dead;
Winfreda saw him reel and drop—
Then back she went to brewing sop.
So when the husband came at night
From bootless chase, cold, gaunt, and grim,
Great was that Saxon lord's delight
To find the sop dished up for him;
And as he ate, Winfreda told
How she had laid the wolf out cold.
The good Winfreda of those days
Is only "pretty Birdie" now—
Sickly her soul and weak her ways—
And she, to whom we Saxons bow,
Leaps on a bench and screams with fright
If but a mouse creeps into sight.

LYMAN, FREDERICK, AND JIM
(FOR THE FELLOWSHIP CLUB)

Lyman and Frederick and Jim, one day,
Set out in a great big ship—
Steamed to the ocean adown the bay
Out of a New York slip.
"Where are you going and what is your game?"
The people asked those three.
"Darned if we know; but all the same
Happy as larks are we;
And happier still we're going to be!"
Said Lyman
And Frederick
And Jim.
The people laughed "Aha, oho!
Oho, aha!" laughed they;
And while those three went sailing so
Some pirates steered that way.
The pirates they were laughing, too—
The prospect made them glad;
But by the time the job was through
Each of them pirates, bold and bad,
Had been done out of all he had
By Lyman
And Frederick
And Jim.
Days and weeks and months they sped,
Painting that foreign clime
A beautiful, bright vermilion red—
And having a —— of a time!
'T was all so gaudy a lark, it seemed
As if it could not be,
And some folks thought it a dream they dreamed
Of sailing that foreign sea,
But I'll identify you these three—
Lyman
And Frederick
And Jim.
Lyman and Frederick are bankers and sich
And Jim is an editor kind;
The first two named are awfully rich
And Jim ain't far behind!
So keep your eyes open and mind your tricks,
Or you are like to be
In quite as much of a Tartar fix
As the pirates that sailed the sea
And monkeyed with the pardners three,
Lyman
And Frederick
And Jim!

BY MY SWEETHEART

Sweetheart, be my sweetheart
When birds are on the wing,
When bee and bud and babbling flood
Bespeak the birth of spring,
Come, sweetheart, be my sweetheart
And wear this posy-ring!
Sweetheart, be my sweetheart
In the mellow golden glow
Of earth aflush with the gracious blush
Which the ripening fields foreshow;
Dear sweetheart, be my sweetheart,
As into the noon we go!
Sweetheart, be my sweetheart
When falls the bounteous year,
When fruit and wine of tree and vine
Give us their harvest cheer;
Oh, sweetheart, be my sweetheart,
For winter it draweth near.
Sweetheart, be my sweetheart
When the year is white and old,
When the fire of youth is spent, forsooth,
And the hand of age is cold;
Yet, sweetheart, be my sweetheart
Till the year of our love be told!

THE PETER-BIRD

Out of the woods by the creek cometh a calling for Peter,
And from the orchard a voice echoes and echoes it over;
Down in the pasture the sheep hear that strange crying for Peter,
Over the meadows that call is aye and forever repeated.
So let me tell you the tale, when, where, and how it all happened,
And, when the story is told, let us pay heed to the lesson.
Once on a time, long ago, lived in the State of Kentucky
One that was reckoned a witch—full of strange spells and devices;
Nightly she wandered the woods, searching for charms voodooistic—
Scorpions, lizards, and herbs, dormice, chameleons, and plantains!
Serpents and caw-caws and bats, screech-owls and crickets and adders—
These were the guides of that witch through the dank deeps of the forest.
Then, with her roots and her herbs, back to her cave in the morning
Ambled that hussy to brew spells of unspeakable evil;
And, when the people awoke, seeing that hillside and valley
Sweltered in swathes as of mist—
"Look!" they would whisper in terror—
"Look! the old witch is at work brewing her spells of great evil!"
Then would they pray till the sun, darting his rays through the vapor,
Lifted the smoke from the earth and baffled the witch's intentions.
One of the boys at that time was a certain young person named Peter,
Given too little to work, given too largely to dreaming;
Fonder of books than of chores, you can imagine that Peter
Led a sad life on the farm, causing his parents much trouble.
"Peter!" his mother would call, "the cream is a'ready for churning!"
"Peter!" his father would cry, "go grub at the weeds in the garden!"
So it was "Peter!" all day—calling, reminding, and chiding—
Peter neglected his work; therefore that nagging at Peter!
Peter got hold of some books—how, I'm unable to tell you;
Some have suspected the witch—this is no place for suspicions!
It is sufficient to stick close to the thread of the legend.
Nor is it stated or guessed what was the trend of those volumes;
What thing soever it was—done with a pen and a pencil,
Wrought with a brain, not a hoe—surely 't was hostile to farming!
"Fudge on all readin'!" they quoth; or "that's what's the ruin of Peter!"
So, when the mornings were hot, under the beech or the maple,
Cushioned in grass that was blue, breathing the breath of the blossoms,
Lulled by the hum of the bees, the coo of the ring-doves a-mating,
Peter would frivol his time at reading, or lazing, or dreaming.
"Peter!" his mother would call, "the cream is a'ready for churning!"
"Peter!" his father would cry, "go grub at the weeds in the garden!"

"Peter!" and "Peter!" all day—
calling, reminding, and chiding—
Peter neglected his chores; therefore
that outcry for Peter;
Therefore the neighbors allowed evil
would surely befall him—
Yes, on account of these things, ruin
would come upon Peter!
Surely enough, on a time, reading
and lazing and dreaming
Wrought the calamitous ill all had
predicted for Peter;
For, of a morning in spring when lay
the mist in the valleys—
"See," quoth the folk, "how the
witch breweth her evil decoctions!
See how the smoke from her fire
broodeth on woodland and meadow!
Grant that the sun cometh out to
smother the smudge of her caldron!
She hath been forth in the night, full
of her spells and devices,
Roaming the marshes and dells for
heathenish magical nostrums;
Digging in leaves and at stumps for
centipedes, pismires, and spiders,
Grubbing in poisonous pools for hot
salamanders and toadstools;
Charming the bats from the flues,
snaring the lizards by twilight,
Sucking the scorpion's egg and
milking the breast of the adder!"
Peter derided these things held in
such faith by the farmer,
Scouted at magic and charms,
hooted at Jonahs and hoodoos—
Thinking and reading of books must
have unsettled his reason!
"There ain't no witches," he cried; "it
isn't smoky, but foggy!
I will go out in the wet—you all
can't hender me, nuther!"
Surely enough he went out into the
damp of the morning,
Into the smudge that the witch
spread over woodland and meadow,
Into the fleecy gray pall brooding on
hillside and valley.
Laughing and scoffing, he strode
into that hideous vapor;
Just as he said he would do, just as
he bantered and threatened,
Ere they could fasten the door, Peter
had done gone and done it!

Wasting his time over books, you
see, had unsettled his reason—
Soddened his callow young brain
with semi-pubescent paresis,
And his neglect of his chores
hastened this evil condition.
Out of the woods by the creek
cometh a calling for Peter
And from the orchard a voice echoes
and echoes it over;
Down in the pasture the sheep hear
that shrill crying for Peter,
Up from the spring house the wail
stealeth anon like a whisper,
Over the meadows that call is aye
and forever repeated.
Such were the voices that whooped
wildly and vainly for Peter
Decades and decades ago down in
the State of Kentucky—
Such are the voices that cry now
from the woodland and meadow,
"Peter—O Peter!" all day, calling,
reminding, and chiding—
Taking us back to the time when
Peter he done gone and done it!
These are the voices of those left by
the boy in the farmhouse
When, with his laughter and scorn,
hatless and bootless and sockless,
Clothed in his jeans and his pride,
Peter sailed out in the weather,
Broke from the warmth of his home
into that fog of the devil,
Into the smoke of that witch brewing
her damnable porridge!
Lo, when he vanished from sight,
knowing the evil that threatened,
Forth with importunate cries
hastened his father and mother.
"Peter!" they shrieked in alarm,
"Peter!" and evermore "Peter!"—
Ran from the house to the barn, ran
from the barn to the garden,
Ran to the corn-crib anon, then to
the smoke-house proceeded;
Henhouse and woodpile they
passed, calling and wailing and
weeping,
Through the front gate to the road,
braving the hideous vapor—
Sought him in lane and on pike,
called him in orchard and meadow,
Clamoring "Peter!" in vain, vainly
outcrying for Peter.

Joining the search came the rest,
brothers and sisters and cousins,
Venting unspeakable fears in pitiful
wailing for Peter!
And from the neighboring farms
gathered the men and the women,
Who, upon hearing the news,
swelled the loud chorus for Peter.
Farmers and hussifs and maids,
bosses and field-hands and niggers,
Colonels and jedges galore from
cornfields and mint-beds and thickets,
All that had voices to voice, all to
those parts appertaining,
Came to engage in the search,
gathered and bellowed for Peter.
The Taylors, the Dorseys, the
Browns, the Wallers, the Mitchells, the
Logans,
The Yenowines, Crittendens, Dukes,
the Hickmans, the Hobbses, the
Morgans;
The Ormsbys, the Thompsons, the
Hikes, the Williamsons, Murrays, and
Hardins,
The Beynroths, the Sherleys, the
Hokes, the Haldermans, Harneys, and
Slaughters—
All, famed in Kentucky of old for
prowess prodigious at farming,
Now surged from their prosperous
homes to join in that hunt for the
truant,
To ascertain where he was at, to
help out the chorus for Peter.
Still on those prosperous farms
where heirs and assigns of the people
Specified hereinabove and proved
by the records of probate—
Still on those farms shall you hear
(and still on the turnpikes
adjacent)
That pitiful, petulant call, that
pleading, expostulant wailing,
That hopeless, monotonous moan,
that crooning and droning for Peter.
Some say the witch in her wrath
transmogrified all those good people;
That, wakened from slumber that
day by the calling and bawling for
Peter,
She out of her cave in a thrice, and,
waving the foot of a rabbit
(Crossed with the caul of a coon and
smeared with the blood of a chicken),

She changed all those folk into birds
and shrieked with demoniac venom:
"Fly away over the land, moaning
your Peter forever,
Croaking of Peter, the boy who
didn't believe there were hoodoos,
Crooning of Peter, the fool who
scouted at stories of witches,
Crying of Peter for aye, forever
outcalling for Peter!"
This is the story they tell; so in good
sooth saith the legend;
As I have told it to you, so tell the
folk and the legend.
That it is true I believe, for on the
breezes this morning
Come the shrill voices of birds
calling and calling for Peter;
Out of the maple and beech glitter
the eyes of the wailers,
Peeping and peering for him who
formerly lived in these places—
Peter, the heretic lad, lazy and
careless and dreaming,
Sorely afflicted with books and with
pubescent paresis,
Hating the things of the farm, care
of the barn and the garden,
Always neglecting his chores—
given to books and to reading,
Which, as all people allow, turn the
young person to mischief,
Harden his heart against toil, wean
his affections from tillage.
This is the legend of yore told in the
state of Kentucky
When in the springtime the birds
call from the beeches and maples,
Call from the petulant thorn, call
from the acrid persimmon;
When from the woods by the creek
and from the pastures and meadows,
When from the spring house and
lane and from the mint-bed and
orchard,
When from the redbud and gum and
from the redolent lilac,
When from the dirt roads and pikes
cometh that calling for Peter;
Cometh the dolorous cry, cometh
that weird iteration
Of "Peter" and "Peter" for aye, of
"Peter" and "Peter" forever!
This is the legend of old, told in the
tum-titty meter

Which the great poets prefer, being less labor than rhyming
(My first attempt at the same, my last attempt, too, I reckon!);
Nor have I further to say, for the sad story is ended.

SISTER'S CAKE

I'd not complain of Sister Jane, for she was good and kind,
Combining with rare comeliness distinctive gifts of mind;
Nay, I'll admit it were most fit that, worn by social cares,
She'd crave a change from parlor life to that below the stairs,
And that, eschewing needlework and music, she should take
Herself to the substantial art of manufacturing cake.
At breakfast, then, it would befall that Sister Jane would say:
"Mother, if you have got the things, I'll make some cake to-day!"
Poor mother'd cast a timid glance at father, like as not—
For father hinted sister's cooking cost a frightful lot—
But neither she nor he presumed to signify dissent,
Accepting it for gospel truth that what she wanted went!
No matter what the rest of 'em might chance to have in hand,
The whole machinery of the house came to a sudden stand;
The pots were hustled off the stove, the fire built up anew,
With every damper set just so to heat the oven through;
The kitchen-table was relieved of everything, to make
That ample space which Jane required when she compounded cake.
And, oh! the bustling here and there, the flying to and fro;
The click of forks that whipped the eggs to lather white as snow—
And what a wealth of sugar melted swiftly out of sight—
And butter? Mother said such waste would ruin father, quite!
But Sister Jane preserved a mien no pleading could confound
As she utilized the raisins and the citron by the pound.
Oh, hours of chaos, tumult, heat, vexatious din, and whirl!
Of deep humiliation for the sullen hired-girl;
Of grief for mother, hating to see things wasted so,
And of fortune for that little boy who pined to taste that dough!
It looked so sweet and yellow—sure, to taste it were no sin—
But, oh! how sister scolded if he stuck his finger in!
The chances were as ten to one, before the job was through,
That sister'd think of something else she'd great deal rather do!
So, then, she'd softly steal away, as Arabs in the night,
Leaving the girl and ma to finish up as best they might;
These tactics (artful Sister Jane) enabled her to take
Or shift the credit or the blame of that too-treacherous cake!
And yet, unhappy is the man who has no Sister Jane—
For he who has no sister seems to me to live in vain.
I never had a sister—may be that is why today
I'm wizened and dyspeptic, instead of blithe and gay;
A boy who's only forty should be full of romp and mirth,
But I (because I'm sisterless) am the oldest man on earth!
Had I a little sister—oh, how happy I should be!
I'd never let her cast her eyes on any chap but me;
I'd love her and I'd cherish her for better and for worse—
I'd buy her gowns and bonnets, and sing her praise in verse;
And—yes, what's more and vastly more—I tell you what I'd do:
I'd let her make her wondrous cake, and I would eat it, too!
I have a high opinion of the sisters, as you see—
Another fellow's sister is so very dear to me!

I love to work anear her when she's making over frocks,
When she patches little trousers or darns prosaic socks;
But I draw the line at one thing— yes, I don my hat and take
A three hours' walk when she is moved to try her hand at cake!

ABU MIDJAN

When Father Time swings round his scythe,
Intomb me 'neath the bounteous vine,
So that its juices, red and blithe,
May cheer these thirsty bones of mine.
"Elsewise with tears and bated breath
Should I survey the life to be.
But oh! How should I hail the death
That brings that—vinous grace to me!"
So sung the dauntless Saracen,
Whereat the Prophet-Chief ordains
That, curst of Allah, loathed of men,
The faithless one shall die in chains.
But one vile Christian slave that lay
A prisoner near that prisoner saith:
"God willing, I will plant some day
A vine where liest thou in death."
Lo, over Abu Midjan's grave
With purpling fruit a vine-tree grows;
Where rots the martyred Christian slave
Allah, and only Allah, knows!

ED

Ed was a man that played for keeps, 'nd when he tuk the notion,
You cudn't stop him any more'n a dam 'ud stop the ocean;
For when he tackled to a thing 'nd sot his mind plum to it,
You bet yer boots he done that thing though it broke the bank to do it!
So all us boys uz knowed him best allowed he wuzn't jokin'
When on a Sunday he remarked uz how he'd gin up smokin'.
Now this remark, that Ed let fall, fell, ez I say, on Sunday—
Which is the reason we wuz shocked to see him sail in Monday
A-puffin' at a snipe that sizzled like a Chinese cracker
An' smelt fur all the world like rags instead uv like terbacker;
Recoverin' from our first surprise, us fellows fell to pokin'
A heap uv fun at "folks uz said how they had gin up smokin'."
But Ed—sez he: "I found my work cud not be done without it—
Jes' try the scheme yourselves, my friends, ef any uv you doubt it!
It's hard, I know, upon one's health, but there's a certain beauty
In makin' sackerfices to the stern demands uv duty!
So, wholly in a sperrit uv denial 'nd concession,
I mortify the flesh 'nd smoke for the sake uv my perfession!"

JENNIE

Some men affect a liking
For the prim in face and mind,
And some prefer the striking
And the loud in womankind;
Wee Madge is wooed of many,
And buxom Kate, as well,
And Jennie—charming Jennie—
Ah, Jennie doesn't tell!
What eyes so bright as Daisy's,
And who as Maud so fair?
Who does not sing the praises
Of Lucy's golden hair?
There's Sophie—she is witty,
A very sprite is Nell,
And Susie's, oh, so pretty—
But Jennie doesn't tell!
And now for my confession:
Of all the virtues rare,
I argue that discretion
Doth most beseem the fair.
And though I hear the many
Extol each other belle,
I—I pronounce for Jennie,
For Jennie doesn't tell!

CONTENTMENT

Happy the man that, when his day is done,
Lies down to sleep with nothing of regret—
The battle he has fought may not be won—

The fame he sought be just as fleeting yet;
Folding at last his hands upon his breast,
Happy is he, if hoary and forespent,
He sinks into the last, eternal rest,
Breathing these only works: "I am content."
But happier he, that, while his blood is warm,
See hopes and friendships dead about him lie—
Bares his brave breast to envy's bitter storm,
Nor shuns the poison barbs of calumny;
And 'mid it all, stands sturdy and elate,
Girt only in the armor God hath meant
For him who 'neath the buffetings of fate
Can say to God and man: "I am content."

"GUESS"

There is a certain Yankee phrase
I always have revered,
Yet, somehow, in these modern days,
It's almost disappeared;
It was the usage years ago,
But nowadays it's got
To be regarded coarse and low
To answer: "I guess not!"
The height of fashion called the pink
Affects a British craze—
Prefers "I fancy" or "I think"
To that time-honored phrase;
But here's a Yankee, if you please,
That brands the fashion rot,
And to all heresies like these
He answers, "I—guess not!"—
When Chaucer, Wycliff, and the rest
Express their meaning thus,
I guess, if not the very best,
It's good enough for us!
Why! shall the idioms of our speech
Be banished and forgot
For this vain trash which moderns teach?
Well, no, sir; I guess not!
There's meaning in that homely phrase
No other words express—
No substitute therefor conveys
Such unobtrusive stress.
True Anglo-Saxon speech, it goes
Directly to the spot,
And he who hears it always knows
The worth of "I—guess—not!"

NEW-YEAR'S EVE

Good old days—dear old days
When my heart beat high and bold—
When the things of earth seemed full of life,
And the future a haze of gold!
Oh, merry was I that winter night,
And gleeful our little one's din,
And tender the grace of my darling's face
As we watched the new year in.
But a voice—a spectre's, that mocked at love—
Came out of the yonder hall;
"Tick-tock, tick-tock!" 't was the solemn clock
That ruefully croaked to all.
Yet what knew we of the griefs to be
In the year we longed to greet?
Love—love was the theme of the sweet, sweet dream
I fancied might never fleet!
But the spectre stood in that yonder gloom,
And these were the words it spake,
"Tick-tock, tick-tock"—and they seemed to mock
A heart about to break.
'T is new-year's eve, and again I watch
In the old familiar place,
And I'm thinking again of that old time when
I looked on a dear one's face.
Never a little one hugs my knee
And I hear no gleeful shout—
I am sitting alone by the old hearthstone,
Watching the old year out.
But I welcome the voice in yonder gloom
That solemnly calls to me:
"Tick-tock, tick-tock!"—for so the clock
Tells of a life to be;
"Tick-tock, tick-tock!"-'tis so the clock

Tells of eternity.

OLD SPANISH SONG

I'm thinking of the wooing
That won my maiden heart
When he—he came pursuing
A love unused to art.
Into the drowsy river
The moon transported flung
Her soul that seemed to quiver
With the songs my lover sung.
And the stars in rapture twinkled
On the slumbrous world below—
You see that, old and wrinkled,
I'm not forgetful—no!
He still should be repeating
The vows he uttered then—
Alas! the years, though fleeting,
Are truer yet than men!
The summer moonlight glistens
In the favorite trysting spot
Where the river ever listens
For a song it heareth not.
And I, whose head is sprinkled
With time's benumbing snow,
I languish, old and wrinkled,
But not forgetful—no!
What though he elsewhere turneth
To beauty strangely bold?
Still in my bosom burneth
The tender fire of old;
And the words of love he told me
And the songs he sung me then
Come crowding to uphold me,
And I live my youth again!
For when love's feet have tinkled
On the pathway women go,
Though one be old and wrinkled,
She's not forgetful—no!

THE BROKEN RING

To the willows of the brookside
The mill wheel sings to-day—
Sings and weeps,
As the brooklet creeps
Wondering on its way;
And here is the ring she gave me
With love's sweet promise then—
It hath burst apart
Like the trusting heart
That may never be soothed again!
Oh, I would be a minstrel
To wander far and wide,
Weaving in song the merciless
wrong
Done by a perjured bride!
Or I would be a soldier,
To seek in the bloody fray
What gifts of fate can compensate
For the pangs I suffer to-day!
Yet may this aching bosom,
By bitter sorrow crushed,
Be still and cold
In the churchyard mould
Ere thy sweet voice be hushed;
So sing, sing on forever,
O wheel of the brookside mill,
For you mind me again
Of the old time when
I felt love's gracious thrill.

IN PRAISE OF CONTENTMENT
(HORACE'S ODES, III, I)

I hate the common, vulgar herd!
Away they scamper when I "booh"
'em!
But pretty girls and nice young men
Observe a proper silence when
I chose to sing my lyrics to 'em.
The kings of earth, whose fleeting
pow'r
Excites our homage and our wonder,
Are precious small beside old Jove,
The father of us all, who drove
The giants out of sight, by thunder!
This man loves farming, that man
law,
While this one follows pathways
martial—
What moots it whither mortals turn?
Grim fate from her mysterious urn
Doles out the lots with hand
impartial.
Nor sumptuous feasts nor studied
sports
Delight the heart by care tormented;
The mightiest monarch knoweth not
The peace that to the lowly cot
Sleep bringeth to the swain
contented.
On him untouched of discontent
Care sits as lightly as a feather;
He doesn't growl about the crops,
Or worry when the market drops,
Or fret about the changeful weather.
Not so with him who, rich in fact,
Still seeks his fortune to redouble;
Though dig he deep or build he
high,

Those scourges twain shall lurk anigh—
Relentless Care, relentless Trouble!
If neither palaces nor robes
Nor unguents nor expensive toddy
Insure Contentment's soothing bliss,
Why should I build an edifice
Where Envy comes to fret a body?
Nay, I'd not share your sumptuous cheer,
But rather sup my rustic pottage,
While that sweet boon the gods bestow—
The peace your mansions cannot know—
Blesseth my lowly Sabine cottage.

THE BALLAD OF THE TAYLOR PUP

Now lithe and listen, gentles all,
Now lithe ye all and hark
Unto a ballad I shall sing
About Buena Park.
Of all the wonders happening there
The strangest hap befell
Upon a famous Aprile morn,
As I you now shall tell.
It is about the Taylor pup
And of his mistress eke
And of the prankish time they had
That I am fain to speak.

FITTE THE FIRST

The pup was of as noble mien
As e'er you gazed upon;
They called his mother Lady
And his father was a Don.
And both his mother and his sire
Were of the race Bernard—
The family famed in histories
And hymned of every bard.
His form was of exuberant mold,
Long, slim, and loose of joints;
There never yet was pointer-dog
So full as he of points.
His hair was like to yellow fleece,
His eyes were black and kind,
And like a nodding, gilded plume
His tail stuck up behind.
His bark was very, very fierce,
And fierce his appetite,
Yet was it only things to eat
That he was prone to bite.
But in that one particular
He was so passing true
That never did he quit a meal
Until he had got through.
Potatoes, biscuits, mush or hash,
Joint, chop, or chicken limb—
So long as it was edible,
'T was all the same to him!
And frequently when Hunger's pangs
Assailed that callow pup,
He masticated boots and gloves
Or chewed a door-mat up.
So was he much beholden of
The folk that him did keep;
They loved him when he was awake
And better still asleep.

FITTE THE SECOND

Now once his master, lingering o'er
His breakfast coffee-cup,
Observed unto his doting spouse:
"You ought to wash the pup!"
"That shall I do this very day",
His doting spouse replied;
"You will not know the pretty thing
When he is washed and dried.
"But tell me, dear, before you go
Unto your daily work,
Shall I use Ivory soap on him,
Or Colgate, Pears' or Kirk?"
"Odzooks, it matters not a whit—
They all are good to use!
Take Pearline, if it pleases you—
Sapolio, if you choose!
"Take any soap, but take the pup
And also water take,
And mix the three discreetly up
Till they a lather make.
"Then mixing these constituent parts,
Let Nature take her way,"
With which advice that sapient sir
Had nothing more to say.
Then fared he to his daily toil
All in the Board of Trade,
While Mistress Taylor for that bath
Due preparation made.

FITTE THE THIRD

She whistled gayly to the pup
And called him by his name,
And presently the guileless thing
All unsuspecting came.
But when she shut the bath-room door,
And caught him as catch-can,

And hove him in that odious tub,
   His sorrows then began.
How did that callow, yallow thing
   Regret that Aprile morn—
Alas! how bitterly he rued
   The day that he was born!
Twice and again, but all in vain
   He lifted up his wail;
His voice was all the pup could lift,
   For thereby hangs this tale.
'Twas by that tail she held him down,
   And presently she spread
The creamy lather on his back,
   His stomach, and his head.
His ears hung down in sorry wise,
   His eyes were, oh! so sad—
He looked as though he just had lost
   The only friend he had.
And higher yet the water rose,
   The lather still increased,
And sadder still the countenance
   Of that poor martyred beast!
Yet all the time his mistress spoke
   Such artful words of cheer
As "Oh, how nice!" and "Oh, how clean!"
   And "There's a patient dear!"
At last the trial had an end,
   At last the pup was free;
She threw aside the bath-room door—
   "Now get you gone!" quoth she.

FITTE THE FOURTH
Then from that tub and from that room
   He gat with vast ado;
At every hop he gave a shake,
   And—how the water flew!
He paddled down the winding stairs
   And to the parlor hied,
Dispensing pools of foamy suds
   And slop on every side.
Upon the carpet then he rolled
   And brushed against the wall,
And, horror! whisked his lathery sides
   On overcoat and shawl.
Attracted by the dreadful din,
   His mistress came below—
Who, who can speak her wonderment—
   Who, who can paint her woe!

Great smears of soap were here and there—
   Her startled vision met
With blobs of lather everywhere,
   And everything was wet!
Then Mrs. Taylor gave a shriek
   Like one about to die:
"Get out—get out, and don't you dare
   Come in till you are dry!"
With that she opened wide the door
   And waved the critter through;
Out in the circumambient air
   With grateful yelps he flew.

FITTE THE FIFTH
He whisked into the dusty street
   And to the Waller lot,
Where bonnie Annie Evans played
   With charming Sissy Knott.
And with those pretty little dears
   He mixed himself all up—
Oh, fie upon such boisterous play—
   Fie, fie, you naughty pup!
Woe, woe on Annie's India mull,
   And Sissy's blue percale!
One got that pup's belathered flanks,
   And one his soapy tail!
Forth to the rescue of those maids
   Rushed gallant Willie Clow;
His panties they were white and clean—
   Where are those panties now?
Where is the nicely laundered shirt
   That Kendall Evans wore,
And Robbie James' tricot coat
   All buttoned up before?
The leaven, which, as we are told,
   Leavens a monstrous lump,
Hath far less reaching qualities
   Than a wet pup on the jump.
This way and that he swung and swayed,
   He gambolled far and near,
And everywhere he thrust himself
   He left a soapy smear.

FITTE THE SIXTH
That noon a dozen little dears
   Were spanked and put to bed
With naught to stay their appetites
   But cheerless crusts of bread.
That noon a dozen hired girls
   Washed out each gown and shirt
Which that exuberant Taylor pup

Had frescoed o'er with dirt.
That whole day long the Aprile sun
　　Smiled sweetly from above
On clotheslines flaunting to the breeze
　　The emblems mothers love.
That whole day long the Taylor pup
　　This way and that did hie
Upon his mad, erratic course,
　　Intent on getting dry.
That night when Mr. Taylor came
　　His vesper meal to eat,
He uttered things my pious pen
　　Would liefer not repeat.
Yet still that noble Taylor pup
　　Survives to romp and bark
And stumble over folks and things
　　In fair Buena Park.
Good sooth, I wot he should be called
　　Buena's favorite son
Who's sired of such a noble sire
　　And dammed by every one!

AFTER READING TROLLOPE'S HISTORY OF FLORENCE

My books are on their shelves again
And clouds lie low with mist and rain.
　　Afar the Arno murmurs low
The tale of fields of melting snow.
List to the bells of times agone
The while I wait me for the dawn.
Beneath great Giotto's Campanile
　　The gray ghosts throng; their whispers steal
From poets' bosoms long since dust;
　　They ask me now to go. I trust
Their fleeter footsteps where again
They come at night and live as men.
The rain falls on Ghiberti's gates;
The big drops hang on purple dates;
And yet beneath the ilex-shades—
　　Dear trysting-place for boys and maids—
There comes a form from days of old,
　　With Beatrice's hair of gold.
The breath of lands or lilied streams
　　Floats through the fabric of my dreams;
And yonder from the hills of song,
Where psalmists brood and prophets throng,

The lone, majestic Dante leads
His love across the blooming meads.
Along the almond walks I tread
And greet the figures of the dead.
Mirandula walks here with him
Who lived with gods and seraphim;
　　Yet where Colonna's fair feet go
There passes Michael Angelo.
In Rome or Florence, still with her
　　Stands lone and grand her worshipper.
In Leonardo's brain there move
Christ and the children of His love;
And Raphael is touching now,
For the last time, an angel's brow.
　　Angelico is praying yet
Where lives no pang of man's regret,
And, mixing tears and prayers within
　　His palette's wealth, absolved from sin,
He dips his brush in hues divine;
San Marco's angel faces shine.
Within Lorenzo's garden green,
Where olives hide their boughs between,
The lovers, as they read betimes
Their love within Petrarca's lines,
Stand near the marbles found at Rome,
Lost shades that search in vain for home.
　　They pace the paths along the stream,
Dark Vallombrosa in their dream.
　　They sing, amidst the rain-drenched pines,
Of Tuscan gold that ruddier shines
Behind a saint's auroral face
That shows e'en yet the master's trace.
But lo, within the walls of gray,
E're yet there falls a glint of day,
And far without, from hill to vale,
Where honey-hearted nightingale
　　Or meads of pale anemones
Make sweet the coming morning breeze—
I hear a voice, of prophet tone,
A voice of doom, like his alone
That once in Gadara was heard;
The old walls trembled—lo, the bird
Has ceased to sing, and yonder waits
Lorenzo at his palace gates.
　　Some Romola in passing by

Turns toward the ruler, and his sigh
Wanders amidst the myrtle bowers
Or o'er the city's mantled towers,
For she is Florence! "Wilt thou hear
  San Marco's prophet? Doom is
  near."
"Her liberties," he cries, "restore!
This much for Florence—yea, and
  more
To men and God!" The days are
  gone;
And in an hour of perfect dawn
I stand beneath the cypress trees
That shiver still with words like
  these.

A LULLABY

The stars are twinkling in the skies,
The earth is lost in slumbers deep;
So hush, my sweet, and close thine
  eyes,
And let me lull thy soul to sleep.
Compose thy dimpled hands to rest,
  And like a little birdling lie
  Secure within thy cozy nest
Upon my loving mother breast,
  And slumber to my lullaby,
  So hushaby—O hushaby.
The moon is singing to a star
  The little song I sing to you;
The father sun has strayed afar,
  As baby's sire is straying too.
And so the loving mother moon
  Sings to the little star on high;
And as she sings, her gentle tune
Is borne to me, and thus I croon
  For thee, my sweet, that lullaby
  Of hushaby—O hushaby.
  There is a little one asleep
That does not hear his mother's
  song;
But angel watchers—as I weep—
Surround his grave the night-tide
  long.
And as I sing, my sweet, to you,
  Oh, would the lullaby I sing—
  The same sweet lullaby he knew
While slumb'ring on this bosom
  too—
Were borne to him on angel's wing!
  So hushaby—O hushaby.

"THE OLD HOMESTEAD"

JEST as atween the awk'ard lines a
  hand we love has penn'd
Appears a meanin' hid from other
  eyes,
So, in your simple, homespun art,
  old honest Yankee friend,
A power o' tearful, sweet seggestion
  lies.
We see it all—the pictur' that our
  mem'ries hold so dear—
The homestead in New England far
  away,
An' the vision is so nat'ral-like we
  almost seem to hear
The voices that were heshed but
  yesterday.
Ah, who'd ha' thought the music of
  that distant childhood time
  Would sleep through all the
  changeful, bitter years
  To waken into melodies like
  Chris'mas bells a-chime
An' to claim the ready tribute of our
  tears!
Why, the robins in the maples an'
  the blackbirds round the pond,
  The crickets an' the locusts in the
  leaves,
  The brook that chased the trout
adown the hillside just beyond,
  An' the swallers in their nests
  beneath the eaves—
They all come troopin' back with
  you, dear Uncle Josh, to-day,
An' they seem to sing with all the
  joyous zest
Of the days when we were Yankee
  boys an' Yankee girls at play,
With nary thought of "livin' way out
  West"!
God bless ye, Denman Thomps'n,
  for the good y' do our hearts,
With this music an' these memories
  o' youth—
God bless ye for the faculty that tops
  all human arts,
  The good ol' Yankee faculty of
  Truth!

CHRISTMAS HYMN

Sing, Christmas bells!
Say to the earth this is the morn
Whereon our Saviour-King is born;
Sing to all men—the bond, the free,
The rich, the poor, the high, the
  low—
The little child that sports in glee—

The aged folk that tottering go—
Proclaim the morn
That Christ is born,
That saveth them and saveth me!
Sing, angel host!
Sing of the star that God has placed
Above the manger in the east;
Sing of the glories of the night,
The virgin's sweet humility,
The Babe with kingly robes bedight—
Sing to all men where'er they be
This Christmas morn,
For Christ is born,
That saveth them and saveth me!
Sing, sons of earth!
O ransomed seed of Adam, sing!
God liveth, and we have a King!
The curse is gone, the bond are free—
By Bethlehem's star that brightly beamed,
By all the heavenly signs that be,
We know that Israel is redeemed—
That on this morn
The Christ is born
That saveth you and saveth me!
Sing, O my heart!
Sing thou in rapture this dear morn
Whereon the blessed Prince is born!
And as thy songs shall be of love,
So let my deeds be charity—
By the dear Lord that reigns above,
By Him that died upon the tree,
By this fair morn
Whereon is born
The Christ that saveth all and me!

A PARAPHRASE OF HEINE
(LYRIC INTERMEZZO)

There fell a star from realms above—
A glittering, glorious star to see!
Methought it was the star of love,
So sweetly it illumined me.
And from the apple branches fell
Blossoms and leaves that time in June;
The wanton breezes wooed them well
With soft caress and amorous tune.
The white swan proudly sailed along
And vied her beauty with her note—
The river, jealous of her song,
Threw up its arms to clasp her throat.
But now—oh, now the dream is past—
The blossoms and the leaves are dead,
The swan's sweet song is hushed at last,
And not a star burns overhead.

THE CONVALESCENT GRIPSTER

The gods let slip that fiendish grip
Upon me last week Sunday—
No fiercer storm than racked my form
E'er swept the Bay of Fundy;
But now, good-by
To drugs, say I—
Good-by to gnawing sorrow;
I am up to-day,
And, whoop, hooray!
I'm going out to-morrow!
What aches and pain in bones and brain
I had I need not mention;
It seemed to me such pangs must be
Old Satan's own invention;
Albeit I
Was sure I'd die,
The doctor reassured me—
And, true enough,
With his vile stuff,
He ultimately cured me.
As there I lay in bed all day,
How fair outside looked to me!
A smile so mild old Nature smiled
It seemed to warm clean through me.
In chastened mood
The scene I viewed,
Inventing, sadly solus,
Fantastic rhymes
Between the times
I had to take a bolus.
Of quinine slugs and other drugs
I guess I took a million—
Such drugs as serve to set each nerve
To dancing a cotillon;
The doctors say
The only way
To rout the grip instanter
Is to pour in
All kinds of sin—

Similibus curantur!
'Twas hard; and yet I'll soon forget
Those ills and cures distressing;
One's future lies 'neath gorgeous skies
When one is convalescing!
So now, good-by
To drugs say I—
Good-by, thou phantom Sorrow!
I am up to-day,
And, whoop, hooray!
I'm going out to-morrow.

THE SLEEPING CHILD

My baby slept—how calm his rest,
As o'er his handsome face a smile
Like that of angel flitted, while
He lay so still upon my breast!
My baby slept—his baby head
Lay all unkiss'd 'neath pall and shroud:
I did not weep or cry aloud—
I only wished I, too, were dead!
My baby sleeps—a tiny mound,
All covered by the little flowers,
Woos me in all my waking hours,
Down in the quiet burying-ground.
And when I sleep I seem to be
With baby in another land—
I take his little baby hand—
He smiles and sings sweet songs to me.
Sleep on, O baby, while I keep
My vigils till this day be passed!
Then shall I, too, lie down at last,
And with my baby darling sleep.

THE TWO COFFINS

In yonder old cathedral
Two lovely coffins lie;
In one, the head of the state lies dead,
And a singer sleeps hard by.
Once had that King great power
And proudly ruled the land—
His crown e'en now is on his brow
And his sword is in his hand.
How sweetly sleeps the singer
With calmly folded eyes,
And on the breast of the bard at rest
The harp that he sounded lies.
The castle walls are falling
And war distracts the land,
But the sword leaps not from that mildewed spot
There in that dead king's hand.
But with every grace of nature
There seems to float along—
To cheer again the hearts of men
The singer's deathless song.

CLARE MARKET

In the market of Clare, so cheery the glare
Of the shops and the booths of the tradespeople there;
That I take a delight on a Saturday night
In walking that way and in viewing the sight.
For it's here that one sees all the objects that please—
New patterns in silk and old patterns in cheese,
For the girls pretty toys, rude alarums for boys,
And baubles galore while discretion enjoys—
But here I forbear, for I really despair
Of naming the wealth of the market of Clare.
A rich man comes down from the elegant town
And looks at it all with an ominous frown;
He seems to despise the grandiloquent cries
Of the vender proclaiming his puddings and pies;
And sniffing he goes through the lanes that disclose
Much cause for disgust to his sensitive nose;
And free of the crowd, he admits he is proud
That elsewhere in London this thing's not allowed;
He has seen nothing there but filth everywhere,
And he's glad to get out of the market of Clare.
But the child that has come from the gloom of the slum
Is charmed by the magic of dazzle and hum;
He feasts his big eyes on the cakes and the pies,
And they seem to grow green and protrude with surprise

At the goodies they vend and the
toys without end—
And it's oh! if he had but a penny to
spend!
But alas, he must gaze in a hopeless
amaze
At treasures that glitter and torches
that blaze—
What sense of despair in this world
can compare
With that of the waif in the market
of Clare?
So, on Saturday night, when my
custom invites
A stroll in old London for curious
sights,
I am likely to stray by a devious way
Where goodies are spread in a
motley array,
The things which some eyes would
appear to despise
Impress me as pathos in homely
disguise,
And my battered waif-friend shall
have pennies to spend,
So long as I've got 'em (or chums
that will lend);
And the urchin shall share in my joy
and declare
That there's beauty and good in the
market of Clare.

A DREAM OF SUNSHINE

I'm weary of this weather and I
hanker for the ways
Which people read of in the psalms
and preachers paraphrase—
The grassy fields, the leafy woods,
the banks where I can lie
And listen to the music of the brook
that flutters by,
Or, by the pond out yonder, hear the
redwing blackbird's call
Where he makes believe he has a
nest, but hasn't one at all;
And by my side should be a
friend—a trusty, genial friend,
With plenteous store of tales galore
and natural leaf to lend;
Oh, how I pine and hanker for the
gracious boon of spring—
For then I'm going a-fishing with
John Lyle King!
How like to pigmies will appear
creation, as we float
Upon the bosom of the tide in a
three-by-thirteen boat—
Forgotten all vexations and all
vanities shall be,
As we cast our cares to windward
and our anchor to the lee;
Anon the minnow-bucket will emit
batrachian sobs,
And the devil's darning-needles shall
come wooing of our bobs;
The sun shall kiss our noses and the
breezes toss our hair
(This latter metaphoric—we've no
fimbriae to spare!);
And I—transported by the bliss—
shan't do a plaguey thing
But cut the bait and string the fish
for John Lyle King!
Or, if I angle, it will be for bullheads
and the like,
While he shall fish for gamey bass,
for pickerel, and for pike;
I really do not care a rap for all the
fish that swim—
But it's worth the wealth of Indies
just to be along with him
In grassy fields, in leafy woods,
beside the water-brooks,
And hear him tell of things he's seen
or read of in his books—
To hear the sweet philosophy that
trickles in and out
The while he is discoursing of the
things we talk about;
A fountain-head refreshing—a clear,
perennial spring
Is the genial conversation of John
Lyle King!
Should varying winds or shifting
tides redound to our despite—
In other words, should we return all
bootless home at night,
I'd back him up in anything he had a
mind to say
Of mighty bass he'd left behind or
lost upon the way;
I'd nod assent to every yarn
involving piscine game—
I'd cross my heart and make my
affidavit to the same;
For what is friendship but a scheme
to help a fellow out—
And what a paltry fish or two to
make such bones about!

Nay, Sentiment a mantle of sweet charity would fling
O'er perjuries committed for John Lyle King.
At night, when as the camp-fire cast a ruddy, genial flame,
He'd bring his tuneful fiddle out and play upon the same;
No diabolic engine this—no instrument of sin—
No relative at all to that lewd toy, the violin!
But a godly hoosier fiddle—a quaint archaic thing
Full of all the proper melodies our grandmas used to sing;
With "Bonnie Doon," and "Nellie Gray," and "Sitting on the Stile,"
"The Heart Bowed Down," the "White Cockade," and "Charming Annie Lisle"
Our hearts would echo and the sombre empyrean ring
Beneath the wizard sorcery of John Lyle King.
The subsequent proceedings should interest me no more—
Wrapped in a woolen blanket should I calmly dream and snore;
The finny game that swims by day is my supreme delight—
And not the scaly game that flies in darkness of the night!
Let those who are so minded pursue this latter game
But not repine if they should lose a boodle in the same;
For an example to you all one paragon should serve—
He towers a very monument to valor and to nerve;
No bob-tail flush, no nine-spot high, no measly pair can wring
A groan of desperation from John Lyle King!
A truce to badinage—I hope far distant is the day
When from these scenes terrestrial our friend shall pass away!
We like to hear his cheery voice uplifted in the land,
To see his calm, benignant face, to grasp his honest hand;
We like him for his learning, his sincerity, his truth,
His gallantry to woman and his kindliness to youth,
For the lenience of his nature, for the vigor of his mind,
For the fulness of that charity he bears to all mankind—
That's why we folks who know him best so reverently cling
(And that is why I pen these lines) to John Lyle King.
And now adieu, a fond adieu to thee, O muse of rhyme—
I do remand thee to the shades until that happier time
When fields are green, and posies gay are budding everywhere,
And there's a smell of clover bloom upon the vernal air;
When by the pond out yonder the redwing blackbird calls,
And distant hills are wed to Spring in veils of water-falls;
When from his aqueous element the famished pickerel springs
Two hundred feet into the air for butterflies and things—
Then come again, O gracious muse, and teach me how to sing
The glory of a fishing cruise with John Lyle King!

UHLAND'S WHITE STAG.

Into the woods three huntsmen came,
Seeking the white stag for their game.
They laid them under a green fir-tree
And slept, and dreamed strange things to see.

(FIRST HUNTSMAN)
I dreamt I was beating the leafy brush,
When out popped the noble stag—hush, hush!

(SECOND HUNTSMAN)
As ahead of the clamorous pack he sprang,
I pelted him hard in the hide—piff, bang!

(THIRD HUNTSMAN)
And as that stag lay dead I blew
On my horn a lusty tir-ril-la-loo!

So speak the three as there they lay
When lo! the white stag sped that way,

Frisked his heels at those huntsmen three,
Then leagues o'er hill and dale was he—
Hush, hush! Piff, bang! Tir-ril-la-loo!

HOW SALTY WIN OUT

I used to think that luck wuz luck and nuthin' else but luck—
It made no diff'rence how or when or where or why it struck;
But sev'ral years ago I changt my mind, an' now proclaim
That luck's a kind uv science—same as any other game;
It happened out in Denver in the spring uv '80 when
Salty teched a humpback an' win out ten.
Salty wuz a printer in the good ol' Tribune days,
An', natural-like, he fell into the good ol' Tribune ways;
So, every Sunday evenin' he would sit into the game
Which in this crowd uv thoroughbreds I think I need not name;
An' there he'd sit until he rose, an', when he rose, he wore
Invariably less wealth about his person than before.
But once there came a powerful change; one sollum Sunday night
Occurred the tidal wave that put ol' Salty out o' sight.
He win on deuce an' ace an' Jack—he win on king an' queen—
Clif Bell allowed the like uv how he win wuz never seen.
An' how he done it wuz revealed to all us fellers when
He said he teched a humpback to win out ten.
There must be somethin' in it, for he never win afore,
An' when he told the crowd about the humpback, how they swore!
For every sport allows it is a losin' game to luck
Agin the science uv a man who's teched a hump fr luck;
And there is no denyin' luck wuz nowhere in it when
Salty teched a humpback an' win out ten.

I've had queer dreams an' seen queer things, an' allus tried to do
The thing that luck apparently intended fr me to;
Cats, funerils, cripples, beggers have I treated with regard,
An' charity subscriptions have hit me powerful hard;
But what's the use uv talkin'? I say, an' say again:
You've got to tech a humpback to win out ten!
So, though I used to think that luck wuz lucky, I'll allow
That luck, for luck, agin a hump aint nowhere in it now!
An' though I can't explain the whys an' wherefores, I maintain
There must be somethin' in it when the tip's so straight an' plain;
For I wuz there an' seen it, an' got full with Salty when
Salty teched a humpback an' win out ten!

THE END

Second Book of Verse

FATHER'S WAY.

MY father was no pessimist; he loved the things of earth,—
Its cheerfulness and sunshine, its music and its mirth.
He never sighed or moped around whenever things went wrong,—
I warrant me he'd mocked at fate with some defiant song;
But, being he warn't much on tune, when times looked sort o' blue,
He'd whistle softly to himself this only tune he knew,—
Now mother, when she heard that tune which father whistled so,
Would say, "There's something wrong to-day with Ephraim, I know;
He never tries to make believe he's happy that 'ere way
But that I'm certain as can be there's somethin' wrong to pay."
And so betimes, quite natural-like, to us observant youth
There seemed suggestion in that tune of deep, pathetic truth.

When Brother William joined the war, a lot of us went down
To see the gallant soldier boys right gayly out of town.
A-comin' home, poor mother cried as if her heart would break,
And all us children, too,—for hers, and not for William's sake!
But father, trudgin' on ahead, his hands behind him so,
Kept whistlin' to himself, so sort of solemn-like and low.

And when my oldest sister, Sue, was married and went West,
Seemed like it took the tuck right out of mother and the rest.
She was the sunlight in our home,— why, father used to say
It wouldn't seem like home at all if Sue should go away;
But when she went, a-leavin' us all sorrer and all tears,
Poor father whistled lonesome-like—and went to feed the steers.

When crops were bad, and other ills befell our homely lot,
He'd set of nights and try to act as if he minded not;
And when came death and bore away the one he worshipped so,
How vainly did his lips belie the heart benumbed with woe!
You see the telltale whistle told a mood he'd not admit,—
He'd always stopped his whistlin' when he thought we noticed it.

I'd like to see that stooping form and hoary head again,—
To see the honest, hearty smile that cheered his fellow-men.
Oh, could I kiss the kindly lips that spake no creature wrong,
And share the rapture of the heart that overflowed with song!
Oh, could I hear the little tune he whistled long ago,
When he did battle with the griefs he would not have us know!

TO MY MOTHER.

HOW fair you are, my mother!
Ah, though 't is many a year
Since you were here,
Still do I see your beauteous face,
And with the glow
Of your dark eyes cometh a grace
Of long ago.
So gentle, too, my mother!
Just as of old, upon my brow,
Like benedictions now,
Falleth your dear hand's touch;
And still, as then,
A voice that glads me over-much
Cometh again,
My fair and gentle mother!

How you have loved me, mother,
I have not power to tell,
Knowing full well
That even in the rest above
It is your will
To watch and guard me with your love,
Loving me still.

And, as of old, my mother,
I am content to be a child,
By mother's love beguiled
From all these other charms;
So to the last
Within thy dear, protecting arms
Hold thou me fast,
My guardian angel, mother!

KÖRNER'S BATTLE PRAYER.
FATHER, I cry to Thee!
Round me the billows of battle are pouring,
Round me the thunders of battle are roaring;
Father on high, hear Thou my cry,—
Father, oh, lead Thou me!

Father, oh, lead Thou me!
Lead me, o'er Death and its terrors victorious,—
See, I acknowledge Thy will as all-glorious;
Point Thou the way, lead where it may,—
God, I acknowledge Thee!

God, I acknowledge Thee!
As when the dead leaves of autumn whirl round me,
So, when the horrors of war would confound me,
Laugh I at fear, knowing Thee near,—
Father, oh, bless Thou me!

Father, oh, bless Thou me!
Living or dying, waking or sleeping,
Such as I am, I commit to Thy keeping:
Frail though I be, Lord, bless Thou me!
Father, I worship Thee!

Father, I worship Thee!
Not for the love of the riches that perish,
But for the freedom and justice we cherish,
Stand we or fall, blessing Thee, all—
God, I submit to Thee!

God, I submit to Thee!
Yea, though the terrors of Death pass before me,
Yea, with the darkness of Death stealing o'er me,
Lord, unto Thee bend I the knee,—
Father, I cry to Thee!

GOSLING STEW.
IN Oberhausen, on a time,
I fared as might a king;
And now I feel the muse sublime
Inspire me to embalm in rhyme
That succulent and sapid thing
Behight of gentile and of Jew
A gosling stew!

The good Herr Schmitz brought out his best,—
Soup, cutlet, salad, roast,—
And I partook with hearty zest,
And fervently anon I blessed
That generous and benignant host,
When suddenly dawned on my view
A gosling stew!

I sniffed it coming on apace,
And as its odors filled
The curious little dining-place,
I felt a glow suffuse my face,
I felt my very marrow thrilled
With rapture altogether new,—
'Twas gosling stew!

These callow birds had never played
In yonder village pond;
Had never through the gateway strayed,
And plaintive spissant music made
Upon the grassy green beyond:
Cooped up, they simply ate and grew
For gosling stew!

My doctor said I mustn't eat
High food and seasoned game;
But surely gosling is a meat
With tender nourishment replete.
Leastwise I gayly ate this same;
I braved dyspepsy—wouldn't you
For gosling stew?

I've feasted where the possums grow,
Roast turkey have I tried,

The joys of canvasbacks I know,
And frequently I've eaten crow
In bleak and chill Novembertide;
I'd barter all that native crew
For gosling stew!

And when from Rhineland I adjourn
To seek my Yankee shore,
Back shall my memory often turn,
And fiercely shall my palate burn
For sweets I'll taste, alas! no more,—
Oh, that mein kleine frau could brew
A gosling stew!

Vain are these keen regrets of mine,
And vain the song I sing;
Yet would I quaff a stoup of wine
To Oberhausen auf der Rhine,
Where fared I like a very king:
And here's a last and fond adieu
To gosling stew!

CATULLUS TO LESBIA.

COME, my Lesbia, no repining;
Let us love while yet we may!
Suns go on forever shining;
But when we have had our day,
Sleep perpetual shall o'ertake us,
And no morrow's dawn awake us.

Come, in yonder nook reclining,
Where the honeysuckle climbs,
Let us mock at Fate's designing,
Let us kiss a thousand times!
And if they shall prove too few, dear,
When they're kissed we'll start anew, dear!

And should any chance to see us,
Goodness! how they'll agonize!
How they'll wish that they could be us,
Kissing in such liberal wise!
Never mind their envious whining;
Come, my Lesbia, no repining!

JOHN SMITH.

TO-DAY I strayed in Charing Cross, as wretched as could be,
With thinking of my home and friends across the tumbling sea;
There was no water in my eyes, but my spirits were depressed,
And my heart lay like a sodden, soggy doughnut in my breast.
This way and that streamed multitudes, that gayly passed me by;
Not one in all the crowd knew me, and not a one knew I.
"Oh for a touch of home!" I sighed; "oh for a friendly face!
Oh for a hearty hand-clasp in this teeming, desert place!"
And so soliloquizing, as a homesick creature will,
Incontinent, I wandered down the noisy, bustling hill,
And drifted, automatic-like and vaguely, into Lowe's,
Where Fortune had in store a panacea for my woes.
The register was open, and there dawned upon my sight
A name that filled and thrilled me with a cyclone of delight,—
The name that I shall venerate unto my dying day,—
The proud, immortal signature: "John Smith, U. S. A."

Wildly I clutched the register, and brooded on that name;
I knew John Smith, yet could not well identify the same.
I knew him North, I knew him South, I knew him East and West;
I knew him all so well I knew not which I knew the best.
His eyes, I recollect, were gray, and black, and brown, and blue;
And when he was not bald, his hair was of chameleon hue;
Lean, fat, tall, short, rich, poor, grave, gay, a blonde, and a brunette,—
Aha, amid this London fog, John Smith, I see you yet!
I see you yet; and yet the sight is all so blurred I seem
To see you in composite, or as in a waking dream.
Which are you, John? I'd like to know, that I might weave a rhyme
Appropriate to your character, your politics, and clime.
So tell me, were you "raised" or "reared"? your pedigree confess

In some such treacherous ism as "I reckon" or "I guess."
Let fall your telltale dialect, that instantly I may
Identify my countryman, "John Smith, U. S. A."

It's like as not you air the John that lived aspell ago
Deown East, where codfish, beans, 'nd bona-fide schoolma'ams grow;
Where the dear old homestead nestles like among the Hampshire hills,
And where the robin hops about the cherry-boughs 'nd trills;
Where Hubbard squash 'nd huckleberries grow to powerful size,
And everything is orthodox from preachers down to pies;
Where the red-wing blackbirds swing 'nd call beside the pickril pond,
And the crows air cawin' in the pines uv the pasture lot beyond;
Where folks complain uv bein' poor, because their money's lent
Out West on farms 'nd railroads at the rate uv ten per cent;
Where we ust to spark the Baker girls a-comin' home from choir,
Or a-settin' namin' apples round the roarin' kitchen fire;
Where we had to go to meetin' at least three times a week,
And our mothers learnt us good religious Dr. Watts to speak;
And where our grandmas sleep their sleep—God rest their souls, I say;
And God bless yours, ef you're that John, "John Smith, U. S. A."

Or, mebbe, Col. Smith, yo' are the gentleman I know
In the country whar the finest Democrats 'nd hosses grow;
Whar the ladies are all beautiful, an' whar the crap of cawn
Is utilized for Burbon, and true awters are bawn.
You've ren for jedge, and killed yore man, and bet on Proctor Knott;
Yore heart is full of chivalry, yore skin is full of shot;
And I disremember whar I've met with gentlemen so true
As yo' all in Kaintucky, whar blood an' grass are blue,
Whar a niggah with a ballot is the signal fo' a fight,
Whar the yaller dawg pursues the coon throughout the bammy night,
Whar blooms the furtive possum,— pride an' glory of the South!
And anty makes a hoe-cake, sah, that melts within yo' mouth,
Whar all night long the mockin'- birds are warblin' in the trees,
And black-eyed Susans nod and blink at every passing breeze,
Whar in a hallowed soil repose the ashes of our Clay,—
H'yar's lookin' at yo', Col. "John Smith, U. S. A."

Or wuz you that John Smith I knew out yonder in the West,—
That part of our Republic I shall always love the best!
Wuz you him that went prospectin' in the spring of '69
In the Red Hoss Mountain country for the Gosh-all-Hemlock mine?
Oh, how I'd liked to clasped your hand, an' set down by your side,
And talked about the good old days beyond the Big Divide,—
Of the rackaboar, the snaix, the bear, the Rocky Mountain goat,
Of the conversazzhyony, 'nd of Casey's tabble-dote,
And a word of them old pardners that stood by us long ago,—
Three-fingered Hoover, Sorry Tom, and Parson Jim, you know!
Old times, old friends, John Smith, would make our hearts beat high again,
And we'd see the snow-top mountains like we used to see 'em then;
The magpies would go flutterin' like strange sperrits to 'nd fro,
And we'd hear the pines a-singin' in the ragged gulch below;
And the mountain brook would loiter like upon its windin' way,
Ez if it waited for a child to jine it in its play.
You see, John Smith, just which you are I cannot well recall;
And, really, I am pleased to think you somehow must be all!

For when a man sojourns abroad
awhile, as I have done,
He likes to think of all the folks he
left at home as one.
And so they are,—for well you
know there's nothing in a name;
Our Browns, our Joneses, and our
Smiths are happily the same,—
All represent the spirit of the land
across the sea;
All stand for one high purpose in
our country of the free.
Whether John Smith be from the
South, the North, the West, the East,
So long as he's American, it
mattereth not the least;
Whether his crest be badger, bear,
palmetto, sword, or pine,
His is the glory of the stars that with
the stripes combine.
Where'er he be, whate'er his lot, he's
eager to be known,
Not by his mortal name, but by his
country's name alone;
And so, compatriot, I am proud you
wrote your name to-day
Upon the register at Lowe's, "John
Smith, U. S. A."

ST. MARTIN'S LANE.
ST. MARTIN'S LANE winds up the
hill,
And trends a devious way;
I walk therein amid the din
Of busy London day:
I walk where wealth and squalor
meet,
And think upon a time
When others trod this saintly sod,
And heard St. Martin's chime.

But when those solemn bells invoke
The midnight's slumbrous grace,
The ghosts of men come back again
To haunt that curious place:
The ghosts of sages, poets, wits,
Come back in goodly train;
And all night long, with mirth and
song,
They walk St. Martin's Lane.

There's Jerrold paired with
Thackeray,
Maginn and Thomas Moore,
And here and there and everywhere
Fraserians by the score;
And one wee ghost that climbs the
hill
Is welcomed with a shout,—
No king could be revered as he,—
The padre, Father Prout!

They banter up and down the street,
And clamor at the door
Of yonder inn, which once has been
The scene of mirth galore:
'Tis now a lonely, musty shell,
Deserted, like to fall;
And Echo mocks their ghostly
knocks,
And iterates their call.

Come back, thou ghost of ruddy
host,
From Pluto's misty shore;
Renew to-night the keen delight
Of by-gone years once more;
Brew for this merry, motley horde,
And serve the steaming cheer;
And grant that I may lurk hard by,
To see the mirth, and hear.

Ah, me! I dream what things may
seem
To others childish vain,
And yet at night 'tis my delight
To walk St. Martin's Lane;
For, in the light of other days,
I walk with those I love,
And all the time St. Martin's chime
Makes piteous moan above.

THE SINGING IN GOD'S ACRE.
OUT yonder in the moonlight,
wherein God's Acre lies,
Go angels walking to and fro,
singing their lullabies.
Their radiant wings are folded, and
their eyes are bended low,
As they sing among the beds
whereon the flowers delight to grow,—

"Sleep, oh, sleep!
The Shepherd guardeth His sheep.
Fast speedeth the night away,
Soon cometh the glorious day;
Sleep, weary ones, while ye may,—

Sleep, oh, sleep!"

The flowers within God's Acre see
that fair and wondrous sight,
And hear the angels singing to the
sleepers through the night;
And, lo! throughout the hours of day
those gentle flowers prolong
The music of the angels in that
tender slumber-song,—

"Sleep, oh, sleep!
The Shepherd loveth His sheep.
He that guardeth His flock the best
Hath folded them to His loving
breast;
So sleep ye now, and take your
rest,—
Sleep, oh, sleep!"

From angel and from flower the
years have learned that soothing song,
And with its heavenly music speed
the days and nights along;
So through all time, whose flight the
Shepherd's vigils glorify,
God's Acre slumbereth in the grace
of that sweet lullaby,—

"Sleep, oh, sleep!
The Shepherd loveth His sheep.
Fast speedeth the night away,
Soon cometh the glorious day;
Sleep, weary ones, while ye may,—
Sleep, oh, sleep!"

DEAR OLD LONDON.

WHEN I was broke in London in
the fall of '89,
I chanced to spy in Oxford Street
this tantalizing sign,—
"A Splendid Horace cheap for
Cash!" Of course I had to look
Upon the vaunted bargain, and it
was a noble book!
A finer one I've never seen, nor can I
hope to see,—
The first edition, richly bound, and
clean as clean can be;
And, just to think, for three-pounds-
ten I might have had that Pine,
When I was broke in London in the
fall of '89!

Down at Noseda's, in the Strand, I
found, one fateful day,
A portrait that I pined for as only
maniac may,—
A print of Madame Vestris (she
flourished years ago,
Was Bartolozzi's daughter and a
thoroughbred, you know).
A clean and handsome print it was,
and cheap at thirty bob,—
That's what I told the salesman, as I
choked a rising sob;
But I hung around Noseda's as it
were a holy shrine,
When I was broke in London in the
fall of '89.

At Davey's, in Great Russell Street,
were autographs galore,
And Mr. Davey used to let me con
that precious store.
Sometimes I read what warriors
wrote, sometimes a king's command,
But oftener still a poet's verse, writ
in a meagre hand.
Lamb, Byron, Addison, and Burns,
Pope, Johnson, Swift, and Scott,—
It needed but a paltry sum to
comprehend the lot;
Yet, though Friend Davey marked
'em down, what could I but decline?
For I was broke in London in the fall
of '89.

Of antique swords and spears I saw
a vast and dazzling heap
That Curio Fenton offered me at
prices passing cheap;
And, oh, the quaint old bureaus, and
the warming-pans of brass,
And the lovely hideous freaks I
found in pewter and in glass!
And, oh, the sideboards,
candlesticks, the cracked old china
plates,
The clocks and spoons from
Amsterdam that antedate all dates!
Of such superb monstrosities I
found an endless mine
When I was broke in London in the
fall of '89.

O ye that hanker after boons that
others idle by,—

The battered things that please the soul, though they may vex the eye,—
The silver plate and crockery all sanctified with grime,
The oaken stuff that has defied the tooth of envious Time,
The musty tomes, the speckled prints, the mildewed bills of play,
And other costly relics of malodorous decay,—
Ye only can appreciate what agony was mine
When I was broke in London in the fall of '89.

When, in the course of natural things, I go to my reward,
Let no imposing epitaph my martyrdoms record;
Neither in Hebrew, Latin, Greek, nor any classic tongue,
Let my ten thousand triumphs over human griefs be sung;
But in plain Anglo-Saxon—that he may know who seeks
What agonizing pangs I've had while on the hunt for freaks—
Let there be writ upon the slab that marks my grave this line:
"Deceased was broke in London in the fall of '89."

―――――――――

CORSICAN LULLABY.

BAMBINO in his cradle slept;
And by his side his grandam grim
Bent down and smiled upon the child,
And sung this lullaby to him,—
This "ninna and anninia":

"When thou art older, thou shalt mind
To traverse countries far and wide,
And thou shalt go where roses blow
And balmy waters singing glide—
So ninna and anninia!

"And thou shalt wear, trimmed up in points,
A famous jacket edged in red,
And, more than that, a peaked hat,
All decked in gold, upon thy head—
Ah! ninna and anninia!

"Then shalt thou carry gun and knife.
Nor shall the soldiers bully thee;
Perchance, beset by wrong or debt,
A mighty bandit thou shalt be—
So ninna and anninia!

"No woman yet of our proud race
Lived to her fourteenth year unwed;
The brazen churl that eyed a girl
Bought her the ring or paid his head—
So ninna and anninia!

"But once came spies (I know the thieves!)
And brought disaster to our race;
God heard us when our fifteen men
Were hanged within the market-place—
But ninna and anninia!

"Good men they were, my babe, and true,—
Right worthy fellows all, and strong;
Live thou and be for them and me
Avenger of that deadly wrong—
So ninna and anninia!"

―――――――――

THE CLINK OF THE ICE.

NOTABLY fond of music, I dote on a sweeter tone
Than ever the harp has uttered or ever the lute has known.
When I wake at five in the morning with a feeling in my head
Suggestive of mild excesses before I retired to bed;
When a small but fierce volcano vexes me sore inside,
And my throat and mouth are furred with a fur that seemeth a buffalo hide,—
How gracious those dews of solace that over my senses fall
At the clink of the ice in the pitcher the boy brings up the hall!

Oh, is it the gaudy ballet, with features I cannot name,
That kindles in virile bosoms that slow but devouring flame?
Or is it the midnight supper, eaten before we retire,

That presently by combustion setteth us all afire?
Or is it the cheery magnum?—nay, I'll not chide the cup
That makes the meekest mortal anxious to whoop things up:
Yet, what the cause soever, relief comes when we call,—
Relief with that rapturous clinkety-clink that clinketh alike for all.

I've dreamt of the fiery furnace that was one vast bulk of flame,
And that I was Abednego a-wallowing in that same;
And I've dreamt I was a crater, possessed of a mad desire
To vomit molten lava, and to snort big gobs of fire;
I've dreamt I was Roman candles and rockets that fizzed and screamed,—
In short, I have dreamt the cussedest dreams that ever a human dreamed:
But all the red-hot fancies were scattered quick as a wink
When the spirit within that pitcher went clinking its clinkety-clink.

Boy, why so slow in coming with that gracious, saving cup?
Oh, haste thee to the succor of the man who is burning up!
See how the ice bobs up and down, as if it wildly strove
To reach its grace to the wretch who feels like a red-hot kitchen stove!
The piteous clinks it clinks methinks should thrill you through and through:
An erring soul is wanting drink, and he wants it p. d. q.!
And, lo! the honest pitcher, too, falls in so dire a fret
That its pallid form is presently bedewed with a chilly sweat.

May blessings be showered upon the man who first devised this drink
That happens along at five A. M. with its rapturous clinkety-clink!
I never have felt the cooling flood go sizzling down my throat
But what I vowed to hymn a hymn to that clinkety-clink devote;
So now, in the prime of my manhood, I polish this lyric gem
For the uses of all good fellows who are thirsty at five A. M.,
But specially for those fellows who have known the pleasing thrall
Of the clink of the ice in the pitcher the boy brings up the hall.

THE BELLS OF NOTRE DAME.
WHAT though the radiant thoroughfare
Teems with a noisy throng?
What though men bandy everywhere
The ribald jest and song?
Over the din of oaths and cries
Broodeth a wondrous calm,
And mid that solemn stillness rise
The bells of Notre Dame.

"Heed not, dear Lord," they seem to say,
"Thy weak and erring child;
And thou, O gentle Mother, pray
That God be reconciled;
And on mankind, O Christ, our King,
Pour out Thy gracious balm,"—
'Tis thus they plead and thus they sing,
Those bells of Notre Dame.

And so, methinks, God, bending down
To ken the things of earth,
Heeds not the mockery of the town
Or cries of ribald mirth;
For ever soundeth in His ears
A penitential psalm,—
'T is thy angelic voice He hears,
O bells of Notre Dame!

Plead on, O bells, that thy sweet voice
May still forever be
An intercession to rejoice
Benign divinity;
And that thy tuneful grace may fall
Like dew, a quickening balm,
Upon the arid hearts of all,
O bells of Notre Dame!

LOVER'S LANE, SAINT JO.
SAINT JO, Buchanan County,

Is leagues and leagues away;
And I sit in the gloom of this rented room,
And pine to be there to-day.
Yes, with London fog around me
And the bustling to and fro,
I am fretting to be across the sea
In Lover's Lane, Saint Jo.

I would have a brown-eyed maiden
Go driving once again;
And I'd sing the song, as we snailed along,
That I sung to that maiden then:
I purposely say, "as we snailed along,"
For a proper horse goes slow
In those leafy aisles, where Cupid smiles,
In Lover's Lane, Saint Jo.

From her boudoir in the alders
Would peep a lynx-eyed thrush,
And we'd hear her say, in a furtive way,
To the noisy cricket, "Hush!"
To think that the curious creature
Should crane her neck to know
The various things one says and sings
In Lover's Lane, Saint Jo!

But the maples they should shield us
From the gossips of the place;
Nor should the sun, except by pun,
Profane the maiden's face;
And the girl should do the driving,
For a fellow can't, you know,
Unless he's neglectful of what's quite respectful
In Lover's Lane, Saint Jo.

Ah! sweet the hours of springtime,
When the heart inclines to woo,
And it's deemed all right for the callow wight
To do what he wants to do;
But cruel the age of winter,
When the way of the world says no
To the hoary men who would woo again
In Lover's Lane, Saint Jo!

In the Union Bank of London
Are forty pounds or more,
Which I'm like to spend, ere the month shall end,
In an antiquarian store;
But I'd give it all, and gladly,
If for an hour or so
I could feel the grace of a distant place,—
Of Lover's Lane, Saint Jo.

Let us sit awhile, beloved,
And dream of the good old days,—
Of the kindly shade which the maples made
Round the stanch but squeaky chaise;
With your head upon my shoulder,
And my arm about you so,
Though exiles, we shall seem to be
In Lover's Lane, Saint Jo.

CRUMPETS AND TEA.

THERE are happenings in life that are destined to rise
Like dear, hallowed visions before a man's eyes;
And the passage of years shall not dim in the least
The glory and joy of our Sabbath-day feast,—
The Sabbath-day luncheon that's spread for us three,—
My worthy companions, Teresa and Leigh,
And me, all so hungry for crumpets and tea.

There are cynics who say with invidious zest
That a crumpet's a thing that will never digest;
But I happen to know that a crumpet is prime
For digestion, if only you give it its time.
Or if, by a chance, it should not quite agree,
Why, who would begrudge a physician his fee
For plying his trade upon crumpets and tea?

To toast crumpets quite à la mode, I require

A proper long fork and a proper
quick fire;
And when they are browned,
without further ado,
I put on the butter, that soaks
through and through.
And meantime Teresa, directed by
Leigh,
Compounds and pours out a rich
brew for us three;
And so we sit down to our
crumpets—and tea.

A hand-organ grinds in the street a
weird bit,—
Confound those Italians! I wish they
would quit
Interrupting our feast with their
dolorous airs,
Suggestive of climbing the heavenly
stairs.
(It's thoughts of the future, as all will
agree,
That we fain would dismiss from
our bosoms when we
Sit down to discussion of crumpets
and tea!)

The Sabbath-day luncheon whereof
I now speak
Quite answers its purpose the rest of
the week;
Yet with the next Sabbath I wait for
the bell
Announcing the man who has
crumpets to sell;
Then I scuttle downstairs in a frenzy
of glee,
And purchase for sixpence enough
for us three,
Who hunger and hanker for
crumpets and tea.

But soon—ah! too soon—I must bid
a farewell
To joys that succeed to the sound of
that bell,
Must hie me away from the dank,
foggy shore
That's filled me with colic and—
yearnings for more!
Then the cruel, the heartless, the
conscienceless sea
Shall bear me afar from Teresa and
Leigh

And the other twin friendships of
crumpets and tea.

Yet often, ay, ever, before my wan
eyes
That Sabbath-day luncheon of old
shall arise.
My stomach, perhaps, shall improve
by the change,
Since crumpets it seems to prefer at
long range;
But, oh, how my palate will hanker
to be
In London again with Teresa and
Leigh,
Enjoying the rapture of crumpets
and tea!

AN IMITATION OF DR. WATTS.

THROUGH all my life the poor
shall find
In me a constant friend;
And on the meek of every kind
My mercy shall attend.

The dumb shall never call on me
In vain for kindly aid;
And in my hands the blind shall see
A bounteous alms displayed.

In all their walks the lame shall
know
And feel my goodness near;
And on the deaf will I bestow
My gentlest words of cheer.

'Tis by such pious works as these,
Which I delight to do,
That men their fellow-creatures
please,
And please their Maker too.

INTRY-MINTRY.

WILLIE and Bess, Georgie and
May,—
Once as these children were hard at
play,
An old man, hoary and tottering,
came
And watched them playing their
pretty game.

He seemed to wonder, while standing there,
What the meaning thereof could be.
Aha, but the old man yearned to share
Of the little children's innocent glee,
As they circled around with laugh and shout,
And told this rhyme at counting out:
"Intry-mintry, cutrey-corn,
Apple-seed and apple-thorn,
Wire, brier, limber, lock,
Twelve geese in a flock;
Some flew east, some flew west,
Some flew over the cuckoo's nest."

Willie and Bess, Georgie and May,—
Ah, the mirth of that summer day!
'Twas Father Time who had come to share
The innocent joy of those children there.
He learned betimes the game they played,
And into their sport with them went he,—
How could the children have been afraid,
Since little they recked who he might be?
They laughed to hear old Father Time
Mumbling that curious nonsense rhyme
Of intry-mintry, cutrey-corn,
Apple-seed and apple-thorn,
Wire, brier, limber, lock,
Twelve geese in a flock;
Some flew east, some flew west,
Some flew over the cuckoo's nest.

Willie and Bess, Georgie and May,
And joy of summer,—where are they?
The grim old man still standeth near,
Crooning the song of a far-off year;
And into the winter I come alone,
Cheered by that mournful requiem,
Soothed by the dolorous monotone
That shall count me off as it counted them,—
The solemn voice of old Father Time,
Chanting the homely nursery rhyme

He learned of the children a summer morn,
When, with "apple-seed and apple-thorn,"
Life was full of the dulcet cheer
That bringeth the grace of heaven anear:
The sound of the little ones hard at play,—
Willie and Bess, Georgie and May.

MODJESKY AS CAMEEL.

AFORE we went to Denver we had heerd the Tabor Grand,
Allowed by critics ez the finest opry in the land;
And, roundin' up at Denver in the fall of '81,
Well heeled in p'int uv looker 'nd a-pinin' for some fun,
We told Bill Bush that we wuz fixed quite comf'table for wealth,
And hadn't struck that altitood entirely for our health.
You see we knew Bill Bush at Central City years ago;
(An' a whiter man than that same Bill you could not wish to know!)
Bill run the Grand for Tabor, 'nd he gin us two a deal
Ez how we really otter see Modjesky ez Cameel.
Three-Fingered Hoover stated that he'd great deal ruther go
To call on Charley Sampson than frequent a opry show.
"The queen uv tradegy," sez he, "is wot I've never seen,
And I reckon there is more for me in some other kind uv queen."
"Git out!" sez Bill, disgusted-like, "and can't you never find
A pleasure in the things uv life wich ellervates the mind?
You've set around in Casey's restawraw a year or more,
An' heerd ol' Vere de Blaw perform shef doovers by the score,
Only to come down here among us tong an' say you feel
You'd ruther take in faro than a opry like 'Cameel'!"
But it seems it wurn't no opry, but a sort uv foreign play,

116

With a heap uv talk an' dressin' that
wuz both dekollytay.
A young chap sparks a gal, who's
caught a dook that's old an' wealthy,—
She has a cold 'nd faintin' fits, and is
gin'rally onhealthy.
She says she has a record; but the
young chap doesn't mind,
And it looks ez if the feller wuz a
proper likely kind
Until his old man sneaks around 'nd
makes a dirty break,
And the young one plays the sucker
'nd gives the girl the shake.
"Armo! Armo!" she hollers; but he
flings her on the floor,
And says he ainter goin' to have no
truck with her no more.
At that Three-Fingered Hoover says,
"I'll chip into this game,
And see if Red Hoss Mountain
cannot reconstruct the same.
I won't set by an' see the feelin's uv a
lady hurt,—
Gol durn a critter, anyhow, that does
a woman dirt!"
He riz up like a giant in that little
painted pen,
And stepped upon the platform with
the women-folks 'nd men;
Across the trough of gaslights he
bounded like a deer,
An' grabbed Armo an' hove him
through the landscape in the rear;
And then we seen him shed his hat
an' reverently kneel,
An' put his strong arms tenderly
around the gal Cameel.

A-standin' in his stockin' feet, his
height wuz six foot three,
And a huskier man than Hoover wuz
you could not hope to see.
He downed Lafe Dawson wrasslin';
and one night I seen him lick
Three Cornish miners that come into
camp from Roarin' Crick
To clean out Casey's restawraw an'
do the town, they said.
He could whip his weight in
wildcats, an' paint whole townships red,
But good to helpless folks and
weak,—a brave and manly heart
A cyclone couldn't phase, but any
child could rend apart;

Jest like the mountain pine, wich
dares the storm that howls along,
But rocks the winds uv summer-
time, an' sings a soothin' song.

"Cameel," sez he, "your record is
ag'in you, I'll allow,
But, bein' you're a woman, you'll git
justice anyhow;
So, if you say you're sorry, and
intend to travel straight,—
Why, never mind that other chap
with which you meant to mate,—
I'll marry you myself, and take you
back to-morrow night
To the camp on Red Hoss
Mountain, where the boys'll treat you
white,
Where Casey runs a tabble dote, and
folks are brave 'nd true,
Where there ain't no ancient history
to bother me or you,
Where there ain't no law but
honesty, no evidence but facts,
Where between the verdick and the
rope there ain't no onter acts."

I wuz mighty proud of Hoover; but
the folks began to shout
That the feller was intrudin', and
would some one put him out.
"Well, no; I reckon not," says I, or
words to that effect,
Ez I perduced a argument I thought
they might respect,—
A long an' harnsome weepon I'd pre-
empted when I come
Out West (its cartridges wuz big an'
juicy ez a plum),
Wich, when persented properly, wuz
very apt to sway
The popular opinion in a most
persuasive way.
"Well, no; I reckon not," says I; but I
didn't say no more,
Observin' that there wuz a ginral
movement towards the door.

First Dr. Lemen he allowed that he
had got to go
And see a patient he jest heerd wuz
lyin' very low;
An' Charlie Toll riz up an' said he
guessed he'd jine the Dock,

117

An' go to see a client wich wuz waitin' round the block;
John Arkins reckollected he had interviews to write,
And previous engagements hurried Cooper from our sight;
Cal Cole went out to buy a hoss, Fred Skiff and Belford too;
And Stapleton remembered he had heaps uv work to do.
Somehow or other every one wuz full of business then;
Leastwise, they all vamoosed, and didn't bother us again.

I reckollect that Willard Morse an' Bush come runnin' in,
A-hollerin', "Oh, wot two idiots you durned fools have been!"
I reckollect that they allowed we'd made a big mistake,—
They otter knowed us tenderfoots wuz sure to make a break!
An', while Modjesky stated we wuz somewhat off our base,
I half opined she liked it, by the look upon her face.
I reckollect that Hoover regretted he done wrong
In throwin' that there actor through a vista ten miles long.
I reckollect we all shuck hands, and ordered vin frappay,—
And I never shall forget the head I had on me next day!

I haven't seen Modjesky since; I'm hopin' to again.
She's goin' to show in Denver soon; I'll go to see her then.
An' may be I shall speak to her, wich if I do 'twill be
About the old friend restin' by the mighty Western sea,—
A simple man, perhaps, but good ez gold and true ez steel;
He could whip his weight in wildcats, and you never heerd him squeal;
Good to the helpless and the weak; a brave an' manly heart
A cyclone couldn't phase, but any child could rend apart;
So like the mountain pine, that dares the storm wich sweeps along,
But rocks the winds uv summer-time, an' sings a soothin' song.

TELLING THE BEES.

OUT of the house where the slumberer lay
Grandfather came one summer day,
And under the pleasant orchard trees
He spake this wise to the murmuring bees:
"The clover-bloom that kissed her feet
And the posie-bed where she used to play
Have honey store, but none so sweet
As ere our little one went away.
O bees, sing soft, and, bees, sing low;
For she is gone who loved you so."

A wonder fell on the listening bees
Under those pleasant orchard trees,
And in their toil that summer day
Ever their murmuring seemed to say:
"Child, O child, the grass is cool,
And the posies are waking to hear the song
Of the bird that swings by the shaded pool,
Waiting for one that tarrieth long."
'Twas so they called to the little one then,
As if to call her back again.

O gentle bees, I have come to say
That grandfather fell asleep to-day,
And we know by the smile on grandfather's face
He has found his dear one's biding-place.
So, bees, sing soft, and, bees, sing low,
As over the honey-fields you sweep,—
To the trees abloom and the flowers ablow
Sing of grandfather fast asleep;
And ever beneath these orchard trees
Find cheer and shelter, gentle bees.

THE TEA-GOWN.

MY lady has a tea-gown
That is wondrous fair to see,—
It is flounced and ruffed and plaited and puffed,
As a tea-gown ought to be;
And I thought she must be jesting
Last night at supper when
She remarked, by chance, that it came from France,
And had cost but two pounds ten.

Had she told me fifty shillings,
I might (and wouldn't you?)
Have referred to that dress in a way folks express
By an eloquent dash or two;
But the guileful little creature
Knew well her tactics when
She casually said that that dream in red
Had cost but two pounds ten.

Yet our home is all the brighter
For that dainty, sensient thing,
That floats away where it properly may,
And clings where it ought to cling;
And I count myself the luckiest
Of all us married men
That I have a wife whose joy in life
Is a gown at two pounds ten.

It isn't the gown compels me
Condone this venial sin;
It's the pretty face above the lace,
And the gentle heart within.
And with her arms about me
I say, and say again,
"'Twas wondrous cheap,"—and I think a heap
Of that gown at two pounds ten!

DOCTORS.

'Tis quite the thing to say and sing
Gross libels on the doctor,—
To picture him an ogre grim
Or humbug-pill concocter;
Yet it's in quite another light
My friendly pen would show him,
Glad that it may with verse repay
Some part of what I owe him.

When one's all right, he's prone to spite
The doctor's peaceful mission;
But when he's sick, it's loud and quick
He bawls for a physician.
With other things, the doctor brings
Sweet babes, our hearts to soften:
Though I have four, I pine for more,—
Good doctor, pray come often!

What though he sees death and disease
Run riot all around him?
Patient and true, and valorous too,
Such have I always found him.
Where'er he goes, he soothes our woes;
And when skill's unavailing,
And death is near, his words of cheer
Support our courage failing.

In ancient days they used to praise
The godlike art of healing,—
An art that then engaged all men
Possessed of sense and feeling.
Why, Raleigh, he was glad to be
Famed for a quack elixir;
And Digby sold, as we are told,
A charm for folk lovesick, sir.

Napoleon knew a thing or two,
And clearly he was partial
To doctors, for in time of war
He chose one for a marshal.
In our great cause a doctor was
The first to pass death's portal,
And Warren's name at once became
A beacon and immortal.

A heap, indeed, of what we read
By doctors is provided;
For to those groves Apollo loves
Their leaning is decided.
Deny who may that Rabelais
Is first in wit and learning,
And yet all smile and marvel while
His brilliant leaves they're turning.

How Lever's pen has charmed all men!
How touching Rab's short story!
And I will stake my all that Drake
Is still the schoolboy's glory.
A doctor-man it was began

Great Britain's great museum,—
The treasures there are all so rare
It drives me wild to see 'em!

There's Cuvier, Parr, and Rush; they are
Big monuments to learning.
To Mitchell's prose (how smooth it flows!)
We all are fondly turning.
Tomes might be writ of that keen wit
Which Abernethy's famed for;
With bread-crumb pills he cured the ills
Most doctors now get blamed for.

In modern times the noble rhymes
Of Holmes, a great physician,
Have solace brought and wisdom taught
To hearts of all condition.
The sailor, bound for Puget Sound,
Finds pleasure still unfailing,
If he but troll the barcarole
Old Osborne wrote on Whaling.

If there were need, I could proceed
Ad naus. with this prescription,
But, inter nos, a larger dose
Might give you fits conniption;
Yet, ere I end, there's one dear friend
I'd hold before these others,
For he and I in years gone by
Have chummed around like brothers.

Together we have sung in glee
The songs old Horace made for
Our genial craft, together quaffed
What bowls that doctor paid for!
I love the rest, but love him best;
And, were not times so pressing,
I'd buy and send—you smile, old friend?
Well, then, here goes my blessing.

———————

BARBARA.

BLITHE was the youth that summer day,
As he smote at the ribs of earth,
And he plied his pick with a merry click,
And he whistled anon in mirth;
And the constant thought of his dear one's face
Seemed to illumine that ghostly place.

The gaunt earth envied the lover's joy,
And she moved, and closed on his head:
With no one nigh and with never a cry
The beautiful boy lay dead;
And the treasure he sought for his sweetheart fair
Crumbled, and clung to his glorious hair.

Fifty years is a mighty space
In the human toil for bread;
But to Love and to Death 'tis merely a breath,
A dream that is quickly sped,—
Fifty years, and the fair lad lay
Just as he fell that summer day.

At last came others in quest of gold,
And hewed in that mountain place;
And deep in the ground one time they found
The boy with the smiling face:
All uncorrupt by the pitiless air,
He lay, with his crown of golden hair.

They bore him up to the sun again,
And laid him beside the brook,
And the folk came down from the busy town
To wonder and prate and look;
And so, to a world that knew him not,
The boy came back to the old-time spot.

Old Barbara hobbled among the rest,—
Wrinkled and bowed was she,—
And she gave a cry, as she fared anigh,
"At last he is come to me!"
And she kneeled by the side of the dead boy there,
And she kissed his lips, and she stroked his hair.

"Thine eyes are sealed, O dearest one!
And better it is 'tis so,
Else thou mightst see how harsh with me
Dealt Life thou couldst not know:
Kindlier Death has kept thee fair;
The sorrow of Life hath been my share."

Barbara bowed her aged face,
And fell on the breast of her dead;
And the golden hair of her dear one there
Caressed her snow-white head.
Oh, Life is sweet, with its touch of pain;
But sweeter the Death that joined those twain.

THE CAFÉ MOLINEAU.

THE Café Molineau is where
A dainty little minx
Serves God and man as best she can
By serving meats and drinks.
Oh, such an air the creature has,
And such a pretty face!
I took delight that autumn night
In hanging round the place.

I know but very little French
(I have not long been here);
But when she spoke, her meaning broke
Full sweetly on my ear.
Then, too, she seemed to understand
Whatever I'd to say,
Though most I knew was "oony poo,"
"Bong zhoor," and "see voo play."

The female wit is always quick,
And of all womankind
'Tis here in France that you, perchance,
The keenest wits shall find;
And here you'll find that subtle gift,
That rare, distinctive touch,
Combined with grace of form and face,
That glads men overmuch.

"Our girls at home," I mused aloud,
"Lack either that or this;
They don't combine the arts divine
As does the Gallic miss.
Far be it from me to malign
Our belles across the sea,
And yet I'll swear none can compare
With this ideal She."

And then I praised her dainty foot
In very awful French,
And parleyvood in guileful mood
Until the saucy wench
Tossed back her haughty auburn head,
And froze me with disdain:
"There are on me no flies," said she,
"For I come from Bangor, Maine!"

HOLLY AND IVY.

HOLLY standeth in ye house
When that Noel draweth near;
Evermore at ye door
Standeth Ivy, shivering sore
In ye night wind bleak and drear;
And, as weary hours go by,
Doth ye one to other cry.

"Sister Holly," Ivy quoth,
"What is that within you see?
To and fro doth ye glow
Of ye yule-log flickering go;
Would its warmth did cherish me!
Where thou bidest is it warm;
I am shaken of ye storm."

"Sister Ivy," Holly quoth,
"Brightly burns the yule-log here,
And love brings beauteous things,
While a guardian angel sings
To the babes that slumber near;
But, O Ivy! tell me now,
What without there seest thou?"

"Sister Holly," Ivy quoth,
"With fair music comes ye Morn,
And afar burns ye Star
Where ye wondering shepherds are,
And the Shepherd King is born:
'Peace on earth, good-will to men,'
Angels cry, and cry again."

Holly standeth in ye house
When that Noel draweth near;
Clambering o'er yonder door,
Ivy standeth evermore;

And to them that rightly hear
Each one speaketh of ye love
That outpoureth from Above.

THE BOLTONS, 22.

WHEN winter nights are grewsome,
  and the heavy, yellow fog
Gives to Piccadilly semblance of a
  dank, malarious bog;
When a demon, with companion in
  similitude of bell,
Goes round informing people he has
  crumpets for to sell;
When a weird, asthmatic minstrel
haunts your door for hours along,
Until you've paid him tu'pence for
  the thing he calls a song,—
When, in short, the world's against
you, and you'd give that world, and
  more,
To lay your weary heart at rest upon
  your native shore,
There's happily one saving thing for
  you and yours to do:
Go call on Isaac Henderson, The
  Boltons, 22.

The place is all so cheery and so
  warm I love to spend
My evenings in communion with
  the genial host, my friend.
One sees chefs d'œuvre of masters
  in profusion on the walls,
And a monster canine swaggers up
  and down the spacious halls;
There are divers things of beauty to
  astound, instruct, and please,
  And everywhere assurance of
  contentment and of ease:
But best of all the gentle hearts I
  meet with in the place,—
The host's good-fellowship, his
  wife's sincere and modest grace;
Why, if there be cordiality that
  warms you through and through,
It's found at Isaac Henderson's, The
  Boltons, 22.

My favorite room's the study that is
  on the second floor;
And there we sit in judgment on
  men and things galore.
The fire burns briskly in the grate,
  and sheds a genial glare
On me, who most discreetly have
  pre-empted Isaac's chair,—
A big, low chair, with grateful
  springs, and curious device
To keep a fellow's cerebellum
  comf'table and nice,
A shade obscures the functions of
  the stately lamp, in spite
Of Mrs. Henderson's demands for
  somewhat more of light;
But he and I demur, and say a
  mystic gloom will do
For winter-night communion at The
  Boltons, 22.

Sometimes he reads me Browning,
  or from Bryant culls a bit,
And sometimes plucks a gem from
  Hood's philosophy and wit;
And oftentimes I tell him yarns, and
  (what I fear is worse)
Recite him sundry specimens of
  woolly Western verse.
And while his muse and mine
transcend the bright Horatian's stars,
He smokes his modest pipe, and I—
  I smoke his choice cigars!
For best of mild Havanas this
  considerate host supplies,—
The proper brand, the proper shade,
  and quite the proper size;
And so I buckle down and smoke
  and smoke,—and so will you,
If ever you're invited to The
  Boltons, 22.

But, oh! the best of worldly joys is
  as a dream short-lived:
'Tis twelve o'clock, and Robinson
  reports our cab arrived.
A last libation ere we part, and
  hands all round, and then
A cordial invitation to us both to
  come again.
So home through Piccadilly and
  through Oxford Street we jog,
On slippery, noisy pavements and in
  blinding, choking fog,—
The same old route through Circus,
Square, and Quadrant we retrace,
Till we reach the princely mansion
  known as 20 Alfred Place;
And then we seek our feathery beds
  of cotton to renew

In dreams the sweet distractions of
The Boltons, 22.

God bless you, good friend Isaac,
and your lovely, gracious wife;
May health and wealth attend you,
and happiness, through life;
And as you sit of evenings that quiet
room within,
Know that in spirit I shall be your
guest as I have been.
So fill and place beside that chair
that dainty claret-cup;
Methinks that ghostly hands shall
take the tempting offering up,
That ghostly lips shall touch the
bowl and quaff the ruby wine,
Pledging in true affection this toast
to thee and thine:
"May God's best blessings fall as
falls the gentle, gracious dew
Upon the kindly household at The
Boltons, 22!"

DIBDIN'S GHOST.

DEAR wife, last midnight, whilst I
read
The tomes you so despise,
A spectre rose beside the bed,
And spake in this true wise:
"From Canaan's beatific coast
I've come to visit thee,
For I am Frognall Dibdin's ghost,"
Says Dibdin's ghost to me.

I bade him welcome, and we twain
Discussed with buoyant hearts
The various things that appertain
To bibliomaniac arts.
"Since you are fresh from t' other
side,
Pray tell me of that host
That treasured books before they
died,"
Says I to Dibdin's ghost.

"They've entered into perfect rest;
For in the life they've won
There are no auctions to molest,
No creditors to dun.
Their heavenly rapture has no
bounds
Beside that jasper sea;
It is a joy unknown to Lowndes,"
Says Dibdin's ghost to me.

Much I rejoiced to hear him speak
Of biblio-bliss above,
For I am one of those who seek
What bibliomaniacs love.
"But tell me, for I long to hear
What doth concern me most,
Are wives admitted to that sphere?"
Says I to Dibdin's ghost.

"The women folk are few up there;
For 'twere not fair, you know,
That they our heavenly joy should
share
Who vex us here below.
The few are those who have been
kind
To husbands such as we;
They knew our fads, and didn't
mind,"
Says Dibdin's ghost to me.

"But what of those who scold at us
When we would read in bed?
Or, wanting victuals, make a fuss
If we buy books instead?
And what of those who've dusted
not
Our motley pride and boast,—
Shall they profane that sacred spot?"
Says I to Dibdin's ghost.

"Oh, no! they tread that other path,
Which leads where torments roll,
And worms, yes, bookworms, vent
their wrath
Upon the guilty soul.
Untouched of bibliomaniac grace,
That saveth such as we,
They wallow in that dreadful place,"
Says Dibdin's ghost to me.

"To my dear wife will I recite
What things I've heard you say;
She'll let me read the books by night
She's let me buy by day.
For we together by and by
Would join that heavenly host;
She's earned a rest as well as I,"
Says I to Dibdin's ghost.

THE HAWTHORNE CHILDREN.

THE Hawthorne children, seven in all,
Are famous friends of mine;
And with what pleasure I recall
How, years ago, one gloomy fall
I took a tedious railway line,
And journeyed by slow stages down
Unto that soporiferous town
(Albeit one worth seeing)
Where Hildegarde, John, Henry, Fred,
And Beatrix and Gwendolen,
And she that was the baby then,—
These famous seven, as aforesaid,
Lived, moved, and had their being.

The Hawthorne children gave me such
A welcome by the sea
That the eight of us were soon in touch,
And, though their mother marvelled much,
Happy as larks were we.
Egad, I was a boy again
With Henry, John, and Gwendolen;
And oh the funny capers
I cut with Hildegarde and Fred!
And oh the pranks we children played;
And oh the deafening noise we made—
'Twould shock my family if they read
About it in the papers!

The Hawthorne children all were smart:
The girls, as I recall,
Had comprehended every art
Appealing to the head and heart;
The boys were gifted, all.
'Twas Hildegarde who showed me how
To hitch a horse and milk a cow
And cook the best of suppers;
With Beatrix upon the sands
I sprinted daily, and was beat;
'Twas Henry trained me to the feat
Of walking round upon my hands
Instead of on my uppers.

The Hawthorne children liked me best
Of evenings, after tea,
For then, by general request,
I spun them yarns about the West,—
Yarns all involving Me!
I represented how I'd slain
The bison on his native plain;
And divers tales of wonder
I told of how I'd fought and bled
In Indian scrimmages galore,
Till Mrs. Hawthorne quoth, "No more,"
And packed her darlings off to bed,
To dream of blood and thunder.

They must have changed a deal since then;
The misses, tall and fair,
And those three handsome, lusty men,—
Would they be girls and boys again,
Were I to happen there,
Down in that spot beside the sea
Where we made such tumultuous glee
That dull autumnal weather?
Ah, me! the years go swiftly by;
And yet how fondly I recall
The week when we were children all,
Dear Hawthorne children, you and I,
Just eight of us together!

THE BOTTLE AND THE BIRD.

ONCE on a time a friend of mine prevailed on me to go
To see the dazzling splendors of a sinful ballet show;
And after we had revelled in the saltatory sights,
We sought a neighboring café for more tangible delights.
When I demanded of my friend what viands he preferred,
He quoth: "A large cold bottle, and a small hot bird!"

Fool that I was, I did not know what anguish hidden lies
Within the morceau that allures the nostrils and the eyes!
There is a glorious candor in an honest quart of wine,

A certain inspiration which I cannot
  well define!
How it bubbles, how it sparkles,
  how its gurgling seems to say:
"Come! on a tide of rapture let me
  float your soul away!"

But the crispy, steaming mouthful
  that is spread upon your plate,—
How it discounts human sapience
  and satirizes fate!
You wouldn't think a thing so small
  could cause the pains and aches
That certainly accrue to him that of
  that thing partakes;
To me, at least, (a guileless wight!)
  it never once occurred
What horror was encompassed in
  that small hot bird.

Oh, what a head I had on me when I
  awoke next day,
And what a firm conviction of
  intestinal decay!
What seas of mineral water and of
  bromide I applied
To quench those fierce volcanic fires
  that rioted inside!
And oh the thousand solemn, awful
  vows I plighted then
Never to tax my system with a small
  hot bird again!

The doctor seemed to doubt that
  birds could worry people so,
But, bless him! since I ate the bird, I
  guess I ought to know!
The acidous condition of my
  stomach, so he said,
Bespoke a vinous irritant that
  amplified my head,
And, ergo, the causation of the
  thing, as he inferred,
Was the large cold bottle,—not the
  small hot bird.

Of course I know it wasn't, and I'm
  sure you'll say I'm right
If ever it has been your wont to train
  around at night.
How sweet is retrospection when
  one's heart is bathed in wine,
And before its balmy breath how do
  the ills of life decline!

How the gracious juices drown what
  griefs would vex a mortal breast,
And float the flattered soul into the
  port of dreamless rest!

But you, O noxious, pygmy bird!
  whether it be you fly,
Or paddle in the stagnant pools that
  sweltering festering lie,—
I curse you and your evil kind for
  that you do me wrong,
Engendering poisons that corrupt
  my petted muse of song;
Go, get thee hence! and never more
  discomfit me and mine,—
I fain would barter all thy brood for
  one sweet draught of wine!

So hither come, O sportive youth!
  when fades the telltale day,—
Come hither, with your fillets and
  your wreaths of posies gay;
We shall unloose the fragrant seas of
  seething, frothing wine
Which now the cobwebbed glass
  and envious wire and corks confine,
And midst the pleasing revelry the
  praises shall be heard
Of the large cold bottle,—not the
  small hot bird!

AN ECLOGUE FROM VIRGIL.
The exile Melibœus finds Tityrus in
possession of his own farm, restored to
him by the Emperor Augustus, and a
conversation ensues. The poem is in
praise of Augustus, peace, and pastoral
life.

MELIBŒUS.
Tityrus, all in the shade of the wide-
  spreading beech-tree reclining,
Sweet is that music you've made on
  your pipe that is oaten and slender;
Exiles from home, you beguile our
  hearts from their hopeless repining,
As you sing Amaryllis the while in
  pastorals tuneful and tender.

TITYRUS.

A god—yes, a god, I declare—
vouchsafes me these pleasant
conditions,
And often I gayly repair with a
tender white lamb to his altar;
He gives me the leisure to play my
greatly admired compositions,
While my heifers go browsing all
day, unhampered of bell and of halter.

MELIBŒUS.
I do not begrudge you repose; I
simply admit I'm confounded
To find you unscathed of the woes
of pillage and tumult and battle.
To exile and hardship devote, and
by merciless enemies hounded,
I drag at this wretched old goat and
coax on my famishing cattle.
Oh, often the omens presaged the
horrors which now overwhelm me—
But, come, if not elsewise engaged,
who is this good deity, tell me!

TITYRUS (reminiscently).
The city—the city called Rome,
with my head full of herding and
tillage,
I used to compare with my home,
these pastures wherein you now
wander;
But I didn't take long to find out that
the city surpasses the village
As the cypress surpasses the sprout
that thrives in the thicket out yonder.

MELIBŒUS.
Tell me, good gossip, I pray, what
led you to visit the city?

TITYRUS.
Liberty! which on a day regarded
my lot with compassion;
My age and distresses, forsooth,
compelled that proud mistress to pity,
That had snubbed the attentions of
youth in most reprehensible fashion.
Oh, happy, thrice happy, the day
when the cold Galatea forsook me;
And equally happy, I say, the hour
when that other girl took me!

MELIBŒUS (slyly, as if addressing
the damsel).
So now, Amaryllis, the truth of your
ill-disguised grief I discover!
You pined for a favorite youth with
cityfied damsels hobnobbing;
And soon your surroundings partook
of your grief for your recusant lover,—
The pine-trees, the copse and the
brook, for Tityrus ever went sobbing.

TITYRUS.
Melibœus, what else could I do?
Fate doled me no morsel of pity;
My toil was all vain the year
through, no matter how earnest or
clever,
Till, at last, came that god among
men, that king from that wonderful city,
And quoth: "Take your homesteads
again; they are yours and your assigns
forever!"

MELIBŒUS.
Happy, oh, happy old man! rich in
what 's better than money,—
Rich in contentment, you can gather
sweet peace by mere listening;
Bees with soft murmurings go hither
and thither for honey,
Cattle all gratefully low in pastures
where fountains are glistening—
Hark! in the shade of that rock the
pruner with singing rejoices,—
The dove in the elm and the flock of
wood-pigeons hoarsely repining,
The plash of the sacred cascade,—
ah, restful, indeed, are these voices,
Tityrus, all in the shade of your
wide-spreading beech-tree reclining!

TITYRUS.
And he who insures this to me—oh,
craven I were not to love him!
Nay, rather the fish of the sea shall
vacate the water they swim in,
The stag quit his bountiful grove to
graze in the ether above him,
While folk antipodean rove along
with their children and women!

MELIBŒUS (suddenly recalling his own misery).
But we who are exiled must go; and whither—ah, whither—God knoweth!
Some into those regions of snow or of desert where Death reigneth only;
Some off to the country of Crete, where rapid Oaxes down floweth;
And desperate others retreat to Britain, the bleak isle and lonely.
Dear land of my birth! shall I see the horde of invaders oppress thee?
Shall the wealth that outspringeth from thee by the hand of the alien be squandered?
Dear cottage wherein I was born! shall another in conquest possess thee,
Another demolish in scorn the fields and the groves where I've wandered?
My flock! nevermore shall you graze on that furze-covered hillside above me;
Gone, gone are the halcyon days when my reed piped defiance to sorrow!
Nevermore in the vine-covered grot shall I sing of the loved ones that love me,—
Let yesterday's peace be forgot in dread of the stormy to-morrow!

TITYRUS.
But rest you this night with me here; my bed,—we will share it together,
As soon as you've tasted my cheer, my apples and chestnuts and cheeses;
The evening already is nigh,—the shadows creep over the heather,
And the smoke is rocked up to the sky to the lullaby song of the breezes.

PITTYPAT AND TIPPYTOE.

ALL day long they come and go,—
Pittypat and Tippytoe;
Footprints up and down the hall,
Playthings scattered on the floor,
Finger-marks along the wall,
Tell-tale streaks upon the door,—
By these presents you shall know
Pittypat and Tippytoe.

How they riot at their play!
And, a dozen times a day,
In they troop, demanding bread,—
Only buttered bread will do,
And that butter must be spread
Inches thick with sugar too!
Never yet have I said, "No,
Pittypat and Tippytoe!"

Sometimes there are griefs to soothe,
Sometimes ruffled brows to smooth;
For—I much regret to say—
Tippytoe and Pittypat
Sometimes interrupt their play
With an internecine spat;
Fie! oh, fie! to quarrel so,
Pittypat and Tippytoe!

Oh, the thousand worrying things
Every day recurrent brings!
Hands to scrub and hair to brush,
Search for playthings gone amiss,
Many a murmuring to hush,
Many a little bump to kiss;
Life's indeed a fleeting show,
Pittypat and Tippytoe!

And when day is at an end,
There are little duds to mend;
Little frocks are strangely torn,
Little shoes great holes reveal,
Little hose, but one day worn,
Rudely yawn at toe or heel!
Who but you could work such woe,
Pittypat and Tippytoe!

But when comes this thought to me,
"Some there are that childless be,"
Stealing to their little beds,
With a love I cannot speak,
Tenderly I stroke their heads,
Fondly kiss each velvet cheek.
God help those who do not know
A Pittypat or Tippytoe!

On the floor, along the hall,
Rudely traced upon the wall,
There are proofs in every kind
Of the havoc they have wrought;
And upon my heart you'd find
Just such trademarks, if you sought.
Oh, how glad I am 'tis so,
Pittypat and Tippytoe!

ASHES ON THE SLIDE.

WHEN Jim and Bill and I were
boys a many years ago.
How gayly did we use to hail the
coming of the snow!
Our sleds, fresh painted red and with
their runners round and bright,
Seemed to respond right briskly to
our clamor of delight
As we dragged them up the slippery
road that climbed the rugged hill
Where perched the old frame
meetin'-house, so solemn-like and still.

Ah, coasting in those days—those
good old days—was fun indeed!
Sleds at that time I'd have you know
were paragons of speed!
And if the hill got bare in spots, as
hills will do, why then
We'd haul on ice and snow to patch
those bald spots up again;
But, oh! with what sad certainty our
spirits would subside
When Deacon Frisbee sprinkled
ashes where we used to slide!

The deacon he would roll his eyes
and gnash his toothless gums,
And clear his skinny throat, and
twirl his saintly, bony thumbs,
And tell you: "When I wuz a boy,
they taught me to eschew
The godless, ribald vanities which
modern youth pursue!
The pathway that leads down to hell
is slippery, straight, and wide;
And Satan lurks for prey where little
boys are wont to slide!"

Now, he who ever in his life has
been a little boy
Will not reprove me when he hears
the language I employ
To stigmatize as wickedness the
deacon's zealous spite
In interfering with the play wherein
we found delight;
And so I say, with confidence, not
unalloyed of pride:
"Gol durn the man who sprinkles
ashes where the youngsters slide!"

But Deacon Frisbee long ago went
to his lasting rest,
His money well invested in farm
mortgages out West;
Bill, Jim, and I, no longer boys, have
learned through years of strife
That the troubles of the little boy
pursue the man through life;
That here and there along the course
wherein we hoped to glide
Some envious hand has sprinkled
ashes just to spoil our slide!

And that malicious, envious hand is
not the deacon's now.
Grim, ruthless Fate, that evil sprite
none other is than thou!
Riches and honors, peace and care
come at thy beck and go;
The soul, elate with joy to-day, to-
morrow writhes in woe;
And till a man has turned his face
unto the wall and died,
He must expect to get his share of
ashes on his slide!

THE LOST CUPID OF MOSCHUS.

"CUPID!" Venus went a-crying;
"Cupid, whither dost thou stray?
Tell me, people, hither hieing,
Have you seen my runaway?
Speak,—my kiss shall be your pay!
Yes, and sweets more gratifying,
If you bring him back to-day.

"Cupid," Venus went a-calling,
"Is a rosy little youth,
But his beauty is inthralling.
He will speak you fair, in sooth,
Wheedle you with glib untruth,—
Honey-like his words; but galling
Are his deeds, and full of ruth!

"Cupid's hair is curling yellow,
And he hath a saucy face;
With his chubby hands the fellow
Shooteth into farthest space,
Heedless of all time and place;
King and squire and punchinello
He delighteth to abase!

"Nude and winged the prankish
blade is,

And he speedeth everywhere,
Vexing gentlemen and ladies,
Callow youths and damsels fair
Whom he catcheth unaware,—
Venturing even into Hades,
He hath sown his torments there!

"For that bow, that bow and
    quiver,—
Oh, they are a cruel twain!
Thinking of them makes me shiver.
Oft, with all his might and main,
Cupid sends those darts profane
Whizzing through my heart and
    liver,
Setting fire to every vein!

"And the torch he carries blazing,—
Truly 'tis a tiny one;
Yet, that tiny torch upraising,
Cupid scarifies the sun!
Ah, good people, there is none
Knows what mischief most amazing
Cupid's evil torch hath done!

"Show no mercy when you find
    him!
Spite of every specious plea
And of all his whimpering, bind
    him!
Full of flatteries is he;
Armed with treachery, cap-a-pie,
He 'll play 'possum; never mind
    him,—
March him straightway back to me!

"Bow and arrows and sweet kisses
He will offer you, no doubt;
But beware those proffered
    blisses,—
They are venomous throughout!
Seize and bind him fast about;
Mind you,—most important this is:
Bind him, bring him, but—watch
    out!"

CHRISTMAS EVE.
OH, hush thee, little Dear-my-Soul,
The evening shades are falling,—
Hush thee, my dear, dost thou not
    hear
The voice of the Master calling?

Deep lies the snow upon the earth,
But all the sky is ringing
With joyous song, and all night long
The stars shall dance, with singing.

Oh, hush thee, little Dear-my-Soul,
And close thine eyes in dreaming,
And angels fair shall lead thee
    where
The singing stars are beaming.

A shepherd calls his little lambs,
And he longeth to caress them;
He bids them rest upon his breast,
That his tender love may bless them.

So, hush thee, little Dear-my-Soul,
Whilst evening shades are falling,
And above the song of the heavenly
    throng
Thou shalt hear the Master calling.

CARLSBAD.
DEAR Palmer, just a year ago we
    did the Carlsbad cure,
Which, though it be exceeding slow,
    is as exceeding sure;
To corpulency you were prone,
    dyspepsia bothered me,—
You tipped the beam at twenty stone
    and I at ten stone three!
The cure, they told us, works both
    ways: it makes the fat man lean;
The thin man, after many days,
    achieves a portly mien;
And though it 's true you still are fat,
    while I am like a crow,—
All skin and feathers,—what of that?
    The cure takes time, you know.

The Carlsbad scenery is sublime,—
    that's what the guide-books say;
We did not think so at that time, nor
    think I so to-day!
The bluffs that squeeze the panting
    town permit no pleasing views,
But weigh the mortal spirits down
    and give a chap the blues.
With nothing to amuse us then or
    mitigate our spleen,
We rose and went to bed again, with
    three bad meals between;
And constantly we made our
    moan,—ah, none so drear as we,

When you were weighing twenty
stone and I but ten stone three!

We never scaled the mountain-side,
for walking was my bane,
And you were much too big to ride
the mules that there obtain;
And so we loitered in the shade with
Israel out in force,
Or through the Pupp'sche allee
strayed and heard the band discourse.
Sometimes it pleased us to recline
upon the Tepl's brink,
Or watch the bilious human line file
round to get a drink;
Anon the portier's piping tone
embittered you and me,
When you were weighing twenty
stone and I but ten stone three!

And oh! those awful things to eat!
No pudding, cake, or pie,
But just a little dab of meat, and
crusts absurdly dry;
Then, too, that water twice a day,—
one swallow was enough
To take one's appetite away,—the
tepid, awful stuff!
Tortured by hunger's cruel stings, I
'd little else to do
Than feast my eyes upon the things
prescribed and cooked for you.
The goodies went to you alone, the
husks all fell to me,
When you were weighing twenty
stone and I weighed ten stone three.

Yet happy days! and rapturous ills!
and sweetly dismal date!
When, sandwiched in between those
hills, we twain bemoaned our fate.
The little woes we suffered then like
mists have sped away,
And I were glad to share again those
ills with you to-day,—
To flounder in those rains of June
that flood that Austrian vale,
To quaff that tepid Kaiserbrunn and
starve on victuals stale!
And often, leagues and leagues
away from where we suffered then,
With envious yearnings I survey
what cannot be again!

And often in my quiet home,
through dim and misty eyes,
I seem to see that curhaus dome
blink at the radiant skies;
I seem to hear that Wiener band
above the Tepl's roar,—
To feel the pressure of your hand
and hear your voice once more;
And, better yet, my heart is warm
with thoughts of you and yours,
For friendship hath a sweeter charm
than thrice ten thousand cures!
So I am happy to have known that
time across the sea
When you were weighing twenty
stone and I weighed ten stone three.

THE SUGAR-PLUM TREE.

HAVE you ever heard of the Sugar-
Plum Tree?
'Tis a marvel of great renown!
It blooms on the shore of the
Lollipop Sea
In the garden of Shut-Eye Town;
The fruit that it bears is so
wondrously sweet
(As those who have tasted it say)
That good little children have only
to eat
Of that fruit to be happy next day.

When you've got to the tree, you
would have a hard time
To capture the fruit which I sing;
The tree is so tall that no person
could climb
To the boughs where the sugar-
plums swing!
But up in that tree sits a chocolate
cat,
And a gingerbread dog prowls
below;
And this is the way you contrive to
get at
Those sugar-plums tempting you so:

You say but the word to that
gingerbread dog,
And he barks with such terrible zest
That the chocolate cat is at once all
agog,
As her swelling proportions attest.
And the chocolate cat goes
cavorting around

From this leafy limb unto that,
And the sugar-plums tumble, of course, to the ground,—
Hurrah for that chocolate cat!

There are marshmallows, gum-drops, and peppermint canes,
With stripings of scarlet or gold,
And you carry away of the treasure that rains
As much as your apron can hold!
So come, little child, cuddle closer to me
In your dainty white nightcap and gown,
And I'll rock you away to that Sugar-Plum Tree
In the garden of Shut-Eye Town.

───────────

RED.

ANY color, so long as it's red,
Is the color that suits me best,
Though I will allow there is much to be said
For yellow and green and the rest;
But the feeble tints which some affect
In the things they make or buy
Have never—I say it with all respect—
Appealed to my critical eye.

There's that in red that warmeth the blood,
And quickeneth a man within,
And bringeth to speedy and perfect bud
The germs of original sin;
So, though I'm properly born and bred,
I'll own, with a certain zest,
That any color, so long as it's red,
Is the color that suits me best.

For where is a color that can compare
With the blush of a buxom lass;
Or where such warmth as of the hair
Of the genuine white horse class?
And, lo! reflected within this cup
Of cheery Bordeaux I see
What inspiration girdeth me up,—
Yes, red is the color for me!

Through acres and acres of art I've strayed
In Italy, Germany, France;
On many a picture a master has made
I've squandered a passing glance:
Marines I hate, madonnas and
Those Dutch freaks I detest;
But the peerless daubs of my native land,—
They're red, and I like them best.

'Tis little I care how folk deride,—
I'm backed by the West, at least;
And we are free to say that we can't abide
The tastes that obtain down East;
And we're mighty proud to have it said
That here in the versatile West
Most any color, so long as it's red,
Is the color that suits us best.

───────────

JEWISH LULLABY.

MY harp is on the willow-tree,
Else would I sing, O love, to thee
A song of long ago,—
Perchance the song that Miriam sung
Ere yet Judæa's heart was wrung
By centuries of woe.

The shadow of those centuries lies
Deep in thy dark and mournful eyes;
But, hush! and close them now,
And in the dreams that thou shalt dream
The light of other days shall seem
To glorify thy brow.

I ate my crust in tears to-day,
As, scourged, I went upon my way,
And yet my darling smiled,—
Ay, beating at my breast, he laughed;
My anguish curdled not the draught,
'Twas sweet with love, my child.

Our harp is on the willow-tree:
I have no song to sing to thee,
As shadows round us roll;
But, hush! and sleep, and thou shalt hear
Jehovah's voice that speaks to cheer

Judæa's fainting soul.

AT CHEYENNE.

YOUNG Lochinvar came in from
    the west,
With fringe on his trousers and fur
    on his vest;
The width of his hat brim could
    nowhere be beat,
His No. 10 brogans were chock full
    of feet,
His girdle was horrent with pistols
    and things,
And he nourished a handful of aces
    on kings.

The fair Mariana sate watching a
    star,
When who should turn up but the
    young Lochinvar!
Her pulchritude gave him a pectoral
    glow,
And he reined up his hoss with
    stentorian "Whoa!"
Then turned on the maiden a
    rapturous grin,
And modestly asked if he mightn't
    step in.

With presence of mind that was
    marvellous quite,
The fair Mariana replied that he
    might;
So in through the portal rode young
    Lochinvar,
Pre-empted the claim, and cleaned
    out the bar.
Though the justice allowed he wa'n't
    wholly to blame,
He taxed him ten dollars and costs,
    just the same.

THE NAUGHTY DOLL.

MY dolly is a dreadful care,—
    Her name is Miss Amandy;
I dress her up and curl her hair,
    And feed her taffy candy.
Yet, heedless of the pleading voice
    Of her devoted mother,
She will not wed her mother's
    choice,
    But says she'll wed another.

I'd have her wed the china vase,—
    There is no Dresden rarer;
You might go searching every place
    And never find a fairer.
He is a gentle, pinkish youth,—
    Of that there's no denying;
Yet when I speak of him, forsooth!
    Amandy falls to crying.

She loves the drum,—that's very
    plain,—
And scorns the vase so clever,
And, weeping, vows she will remain
    A spinster doll forever!
The protestations of the drum
    I am convinced are hollow;
When once distressing times should
    come
    How soon would ruin follow!

Yet all in vain the Dresden boy
    From yonder mantel woos her;
A mania for that vulgar toy,
    The noisy drum, imbues her.
In vain I wheel her to and fro,
    And reason with her mildly:
Her waxen tears in torrents flow,
    Her sawdust heart beats wildly.

I'm sure that when I'm big and tall,
    And wear long trailing dresses,
I sha'n't encourage beaux at all
    Till mamma acquiesces;
Our choice will be a suitor then
    As pretty as this vase is,—
Oh, how we'll hate the noisy men
    With whiskers on their faces!

THE PNEUMOGASTRIC NERVE.

UPON an average, twice a week,
    When anguish clouds my brow,
My good physician friend I seek
    To know "what ails me now."
He taps me on the back and chest,
    And scans my tongue for bile,
And lays an ear against my breast
    And listens there awhile;
Then is he ready to admit
    That all he can observe
Is something wrong inside, to wit:
    My pneumogastric nerve!

Now, when these Latin names within
Dyspeptic hulks like mine
Go wrong, a fellow should begin
To draw what's called the line.
It seems, however, that this same,
Which in my hulk abounds,
Is not, despite its awful name,
So fatal as it sounds;
Yet of all torments known to me,
I'll say without reserve,
There is no torment like to thee,
Thou pneumogastric nerve!

This subtle, envious nerve appears
To be a patient foe,—
It waited nearly forty years
Its chance to lay me low;
Then, like some blithering blast of hell,
It struck this guileless bard,
And in that evil hour I fell
Prodigious far and hard.
Alas! what things I dearly love—
Pies, puddings, and preserves—
Are sure to rouse the vengeance of
All pneumogastric nerves!

Oh that I could remodel man!
I'd end these cruel pains
By hitting on a different plan
From that which now obtains.
The stomach, greatly amplified,
Anon should occupy
The all of that domain inside
Where heart and lungs now lie.
But, first of all, I should depose
That diabolic curve
And author of my thousand woes,
The pneumogastric nerve!

TEENY-WEENY.

EVERY evening, after tea,
Teeny-Weeny comes to me,
And, astride my willing knee,
Plies his lash and rides away;
Though that palfrey, all too spare,
Finds his burden hard to bear,
Teeny-Weeny doesn't care,—
He commands, and I obey!

First it's trot; and gallop then,—
Now it's back to trot again;
Teeny-Weeny likes it when
He is riding fierce and fast!
Then his dark eyes brighter grow
And his cheeks are all aglow,—
"More!" he cries, and never "Whoa!"
Till the horse breaks down at last!

Oh, the strange and lovely sights
Teeny-Weeny sees of nights,
As he makes those famous flights
On that wondrous horse of his!
Oftentimes, before he knows,
Wearylike his eyelids close,
And, still smiling, off he goes
Where the land of By-low is.

There he sees the folk of fay
Hard at ring-a-rosie play,
And he hears those fairies say,
"Come, let's chase him to and fro!"
But, with a defiant shout,
Teeny puts that host to rout,—
Of this tale I make no doubt,—
Every night he tells it so!

So I feel a tender pride
In my boy who dares to ride
(That fierce horse of his astride)
Off into those misty lands;
And as on my breast he lies,
Dreaming in that wondrous wise,
I caress his folded eyes,—
Pat his little dimpled hands.

On a time he went away,
Just a little while to stay,
And I'm not ashamed to say
I was very lonely then;
Life without him was so sad,
You can fancy I was glad
And made merry when I had
Teeny-Weeny back again!

So of evenings, after tea,
When he toddles up to me
And goes tugging at my knee,
You should hear his palfrey neigh!
You should see him prance and shy,
When, with an exulting cry,
Teeny-Weeny, vaulting high,
Plies his lash and rides away!

TELKA.

THROUGH those golden summer days
Our twin flocks were wont to graze
On the hillside, which the sun
Rested lovingly upon,—
Telka's flock and mine; and we
Sung our songs in rapturous glee,
Idling in the pleasant shade
Which the solemn Yew-tree made,
While the Brook anear us played,
And a white Rose, ghost-like, grew
In the shadow of the Yew.

Telka loved me passing well;
How I loved her none can tell!
How I love her none may know,—
Oh that man love woman so!
When she was not at my side,
Loud my heart in anguish cried,
And my lips, till she replied.
Yet they think to silence me,—
As if love could silenced be!
Fool were I, and fools were they!
Still I wend my lonely way,
"Telka," evermore I cry;
Answer me the woods and sky,
And the weary years go by.

Telka, she was passing fair;
And the glory of her hair
Was such glory as the sun
With his blessing casts upon
Yonder lonely mountain height,
Lifting up to bid good-night
To her sovereign in the west,
Sinking wearily to rest,
Drowsing in that golden sea
Where the realms of Dreamland be.

So our love to fulness grew,
Whilst beneath the solemn Yew
Ghost-like paled the Rose of white,
As it were some fancied sight
Blanched it with a dread affright.

Telka, she was passing fair;
And our peace was perfect there
Till, enchanted by her smile,
Lurked the South Wind there awhile,
Underneath that hillside tree
Where with singing idled we,
And I heard the South Wind say
Flattering words to her that day
Of a city far away.

But the Yew-tree crouched as though
It were like to whisper No
To the words the South Wind said
As he smoothed my Telka's head.
And the Brook, all pleading, cried
To the dear one at my side:
"Linger always where I am;
Stray not thence, O cosset lamb!
Wander not where shadows deep
On the treacherous quicksands sleep,
And the haunted waters leap;
Be thou ware the waves that flow
Toward the prison pool below,
Where, beguiled from yonder sky,
Captive moonbeams shivering lie,
And at dawn of morrow die."
So the Brook to Telka cried,
But my Telka naught replied;
And, as in a strange affright,
Paled the Rose a ghostlier white.

When anon the North Wind came,—
Rudely blustering Telka's name,
And he kissed the leaves that grew
Round about the trembling Yew,—
Kissed and romped till, blushing red,
All one day in terror fled,
And the white Rose hung her head;
Coming to our trysting spot,
Long I called; she answered not.
"Telka!" pleadingly I cried
Up and down the mountain-side
Where we twain were wont to bide.

There were those who thought that I
Could be silenced with a lie,
And they told me Telka's name
Should be spoken now with shame:
"She is lost to us and thee,"—
That is what they said to me.

"Is my Telka lost?" quoth I.
"On this hilltop shall I cry,
So that she may hear and then
Find her way to me again.
The South Wind spoke a lie that day;
All deceived, she lost her way
Yonder where the shadows sleep
'Mongst the haunted waves that leap
Over treacherous quicksands deep,
And where captive moonbeams lie

Doomed at morrow's dawn to die
She is lost, and that is all;
I will search for her, and call."

Summer comes and winter goes,
Buds the Yew and blooms the Rose;
All the others are anear,—
Only Telka is not here!
Gone the peace and love I knew
Sometime 'neath the hillside Yew;
And the Rose, that mocks me so,
I had crushed it long ago
But that Telka loved it then,
And shall soothe its terror when
She comes back to me again.
Call I, seek I everywhere
For my Telka, passing fair.
It is, oh, so many a year
I have called! She does not hear,
Yet nor feared nor worn am I;
For I know that if I cry
She shall sometime hear my call.
She is lost, and that is all,—
She is lost in some far spot;
I have searched, and found it not.
Could she hear me calling, then
Would she come to me again;
For she loved me passing well,—
How I love her none can tell!
That is why these years I've cried
"Telka!" on this mountain-side.
"Telka!" still I, pleading, cry;
Answer me the woods and sky,
And the lonely years go by.

On an evening dark and chill
Came a shadow up the hill,—
Came a spectre, grim and white
As a ghost that walks the night,
Grim and bowed, and with the cry
Of a wretch about to die,—
Came and fell and cried to me:
"It is Telka come!" said she.
So she fell and so she cried
On that lonely mountain-side
Where was Telka wont to bide.

"Who hath bribed those lips to lie?
Telka's face was fair," quoth I;
"Thine is furrowed with despair.
There is winter in thy hair;
But upon her beauteous head
Was there summer glory shed,—
Such a glory as the sun,
When his daily course is run,

Smiles upon this mountain height
As he kisses it good-night.
There was music in her tone,
Misery in thy voice alone.
They have bid thee lie to me.
Let me pass! Thou art not she!
Let my sorrow sacred be
Underneath this trysting tree!"

So in wrath I went my way,
And they came another day,—
Came another day, and said:
"Hush thy cry, for she is dead,
Yonder on the mountain-side
She is buried where she died,
Where you twain were wont to bide,
Where she came and fell and cried
Pardon that thy wrath denied;
And above her bosom grows
As in mockery the Rose:
It was white; but now 'tis red,
And in shame it bows its head
Over sinful Telka dead."

So they thought to silence me,—
As if love could silenced be!
Fool were I, and fools were they!
Scornfully I went my way,
And upon the mountain-side
"Telka!" evermore I cried.
"Telka!" evermore I cry;
Answer me the woods and sky:
So the lonely years go by.

She is lost, and that is all;
Sometime she shall hear my call,
Hear my pleading call, and then
Find her way to me again.

PLAINT OF THE MISSOURI 'COON IN THE BERLIN ZOÖLOGICAL GARDENS.

FRIEND, by the way you hump
yourself you're from the States, I know,
And born in old Mizzoorah, where
the 'coons in plenty grow.
I, too, am native of that clime; but
harsh, relentless fate
Has doomed me to an exile far from
that noble State;
And I, who used to climb around,
and swing from tree to tree,
Now lead a life of ignominious ease,
as you can see.

Have pity, O compatriot mine! and bide a season near,
While I unfurl a dismal tale to catch your friendly ear.

My pedigree is noble: they used my grandsire's skin
To piece a coat for Patterson to warm himself within,—
Tom Patterson, of Denver; no ermine can compare
With the grizzled robe that Democratic statesman loves to wear.
Of such a grandsire I am come; and in the County Cole
All up an ancient cottonwood our family had its hole.
We envied not the liveried pomp nor proud estate of kings,
As we hustled round from day to day in search of bugs and things.

And when the darkness fell around, a mocking-bird was nigh,
Inviting pleasant, soothing dreams with his sweet lullaby;
And sometimes came the yellow dog to brag around all night
That nary 'coon could wallop him in a stand-up barrel fight.
We simply smiled and let him howl, for all Mizzoorians know
That ary 'coon can best a dog, if the coon gets half a show;
But we'd nestle close and shiver when the mellow moon had ris'n,
And the hungry nigger sought our lair in hopes to make us his'n.

Raised as I was, it's hardly strange I pine for those old days;
I cannot get acclimated, or used to German ways.
The victuals that they give me here may all be very fine
For vulgar, common palates, but they will not do for mine.
The 'coon that's been accustomed to stanch democratic cheer
Will not put up with onion tarts and sausage steeped in beer!
No; let the rest, for meat and drink, accede to slavish terms,
But send me back from whence I came, and let me grub for worms!

They come, these gaping Teutons do, on Sunday afternoons,
And wonder what I am,—alas, there are no German 'coons!
For if there were, I still might swing at home from tree to tree,
The symbol of democracy, that's woolly, blithe, and free.
And yet for what my captors are I would not change my lot,
For I have tasted liberty, these others they have not;
So, even caged, the democratic 'coon more glory feels
Than the conscript German puppets with their swords about their heels.

Well, give my love to Crittenden, to Clardy, and O'Neill,
To Jasper Burke and Col. Jones, and tell 'em how I feel;
My compliments to Cockrill, Stephens, Switzler, Francis, Vest,
Bill Nelson, J. West Goodwin, Jedge Broadhead, and the rest.
Bid them be steadfast in the faith, and pay no heed at all
To Joe McCullagh's badinage or Chauncey Filley's gall;
And urge them to retaliate for what I'm suffering here
By cinching all the alien class that wants its Sunday beer.

ARMENIAN LULLABY.

IF thou wilt close thy drowsy eyes,
My mulberry one, my golden son,
The rose shall sing thee lullabies,
My pretty cosset lambkin!
And thou shalt swing in an almond-tree,
With a flood of moonbeams rocking thee,—
A silver boat in a golden sea,—
My velvet love, my nestling dove,
My own pomegranate-blossom!

The stork shall guard thee passing well
All night, my sweet, my dimple-feet,
And bring thee myrrh and asphodel,
My gentle rain-of-springtime;

And for thy slumber-play shall twine
The diamond stars with an emerald vine,
To trail in the waves of ruby wine,
My hyacinth-bloom, my heart's perfume,
My cooing little turtle!

And when the morn wakes up to see
My apple-bright, my soul's delight,
The partridge shall come calling thee,
My jar of milk-and-honey!
Yes, thou shalt know what mystery lies
In the amethyst deep of the curtained skies,
If thou wilt fold thy onyx eyes,
You wakeful one, you naughty son,
You chirping little sparrow!

THE PARTRIDGE.

AS beats the sun from mountain crest,
With "Pretty, pretty,"
Cometh the partridge from her nest.
The flowers threw kisses sweet to her
(For all the flowers that bloomed knew her);
Yet hasteneth she to mine and me,—
Ah, pretty, pretty!
Ah, dear little partridge!

And when I hear the partridge cry
So pretty, pretty,
Upon the house-top breakfast I.
She comes a-chirping far and wide,
And swinging from the mountain-side
I see and hear the dainty dear,—
Ah, pretty, pretty!
Ah, dear little partridge!

Thy nest's inlaid with posies rare,
And pretty, pretty;
Bloom violet, rose, and lily there;
The place is full of balmy dew
(The tears of flowers in love with you!);
And one and all, impassioned, call,
"O pretty, pretty!
O dear little partridge!"

Thy feathers they are soft and sleek,—
So pretty, pretty!
Long is thy neck, and small thy beak,
The color of thy plumage far
More bright than rainbow colors are.
Sweeter than dove is she I love,—
My pretty, pretty!
My dear little partridge!

When comes the partridge from the tree,
So pretty, pretty,
And sings her little hymn to me,
Why, all the world is cheered thereby,
The heart leaps up into the eye,
And Echo then gives back again
Our "Pretty, pretty!"
Our "Dear little partridge!"

Admitting thee most blest of all,
And pretty, pretty,
The birds come with thee at thy call;
In flocks they come, and round thee play,
And this is what they seem to say,—
They say and sing, each feathered thing,
"Ah, pretty, pretty!
Ah, dear little partridge!"

CORINTHIAN HALL.

CORINTHIAN HALL is a tumble-down place,
Which some finical folks have pronounced a disgrace;
But once was a time when Corinthian Hall
Excited the rapture and plaudits of all,
With its carpeted stairs,
And its new yellow chairs,
And its stunning ensemble of citified airs.
Why, the Atchison Champion said 'twas the best
Of Thespian temples extant in the West.

It was new, and was ours,—that was ages ago,

Before opry had spoiled the legitimate show,—
It was new, and was ours! We could toss back the jeers
Our rivals had launched at our city for years.
Corinthian Hall!
Why, it discounted all
Other halls in the Valley, and well I recall
The night of the opening; from near and afar
Came the crowd to see Toodles performed by De Bar.

Oh, those days they were palmy, and never again
Shall earth see such genius as gladdened us then;
For actors were actors, and each one knew how
To whoop up his art in the sweat of his brow.
He'd a tragedy air, and wore copious hair;
And when he ate victuals, he ordered 'em rare.
Dame Fortune ne'er feazed him,—in fact, never could
When liquor was handy and walking was good.

And the shows in those days! Ah, how well I recall
The shows that I saw in Corinthian Hall!
Maggie Mitchell and Lotty were then in their prime;
And as for Jane Coombs, she was simply sublime;
And I'm ready to swear there is none could compare
With Breslau in Borgia, supported by Fair;
While in passionate rôles it was patent to us
That the great John A. Stevens was ne ultra plus.

And was there demand for the tribute of tears,
We had sweet Charlotte Thompson those halcyon years,
And wee Katie Putnam. The savants allow
That the like of Kate Fisher ain't visible now.
What artist to-day have we equal to Rae,
Or to sturdy Jack Langrishe? God rest 'em, I say!
And when died Buchanan, the "St. Joe Gazette"
Opined that the sun of our drama had set.

Corinthian Hall was devoted to song
When the Barnabee concert troupe happened along,
Or Ossian E. Dodge, or the Comical Brown,
Or the Holmans with William H. Crane struck our town;
But the one special card
That hit us all hard
Was Caroline Richings and Peter Bernard;
And the bells of the Bergers still ring in my ears;
And, oh, how I laughed at Sol Russell those years!

The Haverly Minstrels were boss in those days,
And our critics accorded them columns of praise;
They'd handsome mustaches and big cluster rings,
And their shirt fronts were blazing with diamonds and things;
They gave a parade, and sweet music they made
Every evening in front of the house where they played.
'Twixt posters and hand-bills the town was agog
For Primrose and West in their great statue clog.

Many years intervene, yet I'm free to maintain
That I doted on Chanfrau, McWade, and Frank Frayne;
Tom Stivers, the local, declared for a truth
That Mayo as Hamlet was better than Booth:
While in rôles that were thrillin', involving much killin',

Jim Wallick loomed up our ideal of
   a villain;
Mrs. Bowers, Alvin Joslin, Frank
   Aiken,—they all
Earned their titles to fame in
   Corinthian Hall.

But Time, as begrudging the glory
   that fell
On the spot I revere and remember
   so well,
Spent his spite on the timbers, the
   plaster, and paint,
And breathed on them all his
   morbiferous taint;
So the trappings of gold and the gear
   manifold
Got gangrened with rust and
   rheumatic with mould,
And we saw dank decay and
   oblivion fall,
Like vapors of night, on Corinthian
   Hall.

When the gas is ablaze in the opry at
   night,
And the music goes floating on
   billows of light,
Why, I often regret that I'm grown to
   a man,
And I pine to be back where my
   mission began,
And I'm fain to recall
   Reminiscences all
That come with the thought of
   Corinthian Hall,—
To hear and to see what delighted
   me then,
And to revel in raptures of boyhood
   again.

Though Corinthian Hall is a tumble-
   down place,
Which some finical folks have
   pronounced a disgrace,
There is one young old boy, quite as
   worthy as they,
Who, aweary of art as expounded
   to-day,
Would surrender what gold
   He's amassed to behold
A tithe of the wonderful doings of
   old,
A glimpse of the glories that used to
   enthrall
Our crême de la crême in Corinthian
   Hall.

THE RED, RED WEST.
I'VE travelled in heaps of countries,
   and studied all kinds of art,
Till there isn't a critic or connoisseur
   who's properly deemed so smart;
And I'm free to say that the grand
   results of my explorations show
That somehow paint gets redder the
   farther out West I go.

I've sipped the voluptuous sherbet
   that the Orientals serve,
And I've felt the glow of red
   Bordeaux tingling each separate nerve;
I've sampled your classic Massic
   under an arbor green,
And I've reeked with song a whole
   night long over a brown poteen.

The stalwart brew of the land o'
   cakes, the schnapps of the frugal Dutch,
The much-praised wine of the
   distant Rhine, and the beer praised
   overmuch,
The ale of dear old London, and the
   port of Southern climes,—
All, ad infin., have I taken in a
   hundred thousand times.

Yet, as I afore-mentioned, these
   other charms are naught
Compared with the paramount
   gorgeousness with which the West is
   fraught;
For Art and Nature are just the same
   in the land where the porker grows,
And the paint keeps getting redder
   the farther out West one goes.

Our savants have never discovered
   the reason why this is so,
And ninety per cent of the laymen
   care less than the savants know;
It answers every purpose that this is
   manifest:
The paint keeps getting redder the
   farther you go out West.

Give me no home 'neath the pale
   pink dome of European skies,

No cot for me by the salmon sea that
  far to the southward lies;
But away out West I would build
  my nest on top of a carmine hill,
Where I can paint, without restraint,
  creation redder still!

THE THREE KINGS OF COLOGNE.

FROM out Cologne there came
    three kings
To worship Jesus Christ, their King.
To Him they sought fine herbs they
    brought,
And many a beauteous golden thing;
  They brought their gifts to
    Bethlehem town,
And in that manger set them down.

Then spake the first king, and he
    said:
"O Child, most heavenly, bright, and
    fair!
I bring this crown to Bethlehem
    town
For Thee, and only Thee, to wear;
  So give a heavenly crown to me
When I shall come at last to Thee!"

The second, then. "I bring Thee here
This royal robe, O Child!" he cried;
"Of silk 'tis spun, and such an one
There is not in the world beside;
  So in the day of doom requite
Me with a heavenly robe of white!"

The third king gave his gift, and
    quoth:
"Spikenard and myrrh to Thee I
    bring,
And with these twain would I most
    fain
Anoint the body of my King;
  So may their incense sometime rise
To plead for me in yonder skies!"

Thus spake the three kings of
    Cologne,
That gave their gifts, and went their
    way;
And now kneel I in prayer hard by
The cradle of the Child to-day;
  Nor crown, nor robe, nor spice I
    bring
As offering unto Christ, my King.

Yet have I brought a gift the Child
May not despise, however small;
For here I lay my heart to-day,
And it is full of love to all.
  Take Thou the poor but loyal thing,
My only tribute, Christ, my King!

IPSWICH.

IN Ipswich nights are cool and fair,
And the voice that comes from the
    yonder sea
Sings to the quaint old mansions
    there
Of "the time, the time that used to
    be;"
And the quaint old mansions rock
    and groan,
And they seem to say in an
    undertone,
With half a sigh and with half a
    moan:
"It was, but it never again will be."

In Ipswich witches weave at night
Their magic, spells with impish
    glee;
They shriek and laugh in their
    demon flight
From the old Main House to the
    frightened sea.
And ghosts of eld come out to weep
Over the town that is fast asleep;
And they sob and they wail, as on
    they creep:
"It was, but it never again will be."

In Ipswich riseth Heart-Break Hill
Over against the calling sea;
And through the nights so deep and
    chill
Watcheth a maiden constantly,—
Watcheth alone, nor seems to hear
Over the roar of the waves anear
The pitiful cry of a far-off year:
"It was, but it never again will be."

In Ipswich once a witch I knew,—
An artless Saxon witch was she;
By that flaxen hair and those eyes of
    blue,
Sweet was the spell she cast on me.

Alas! but the years have wrought me ill,
And the heart that is old and battered and chill
Seeketh again on Heart-Break Hill
What was, but never again can be.

Dear Anna, I would not conjure down
The ghost that cometh to solace me;
I love to think of old Ipswich town,
Where somewhat better than friends were we;
For with every thought of the dear old place
Cometh again the tender grace
Of a Saxon witch's pretty face,
As it was, and is, and ever shall be.

BILL'S TENOR AND MY BASS.

BILL was short and dapper, while I was thin and tall;
I had flowin' whiskers, but Bill had none at all;
Clothes would never seem to set so nice on me as him,—
Folks used to laugh, and say I was too powerful slim,—
But Bill's clothes fit him like the paper on the wall;
And we were the sparkin'est beaus in all the place
When Bill sung tenor and I sung bass.

Cyrus Baker's oldest girl was member of the choir,—
Eyes as black as Kelsey's cat, and cheeks as red as fire!
She had the best sopranner voice I think I ever heard,—
Sung "Coronation," "Burlington," and "Chiny" like a bird;
Never done better than with Bill a-standin' nigh 'er,
A-holdin' of her hymn-book so she wouldn't lose the place,
When Bill sung tenor and I sung bass.

Then there was Prudence Hubbard, so cosey-like and fat,—
She sung alto, and wore a pee-wee hat;
Beaued her around one winter, and, first thing I knew,
One evenin' on the portico I up and called her "Prue"!
But, sakes alive! she didn't mind a little thing like that;
On all the works of Providence she set a cheerful face
When Bill was singin' tenor and I was singin' bass.

Bill, nevermore we two shall share the fun we used to then,
Nor know the comfort and the peace we had together when
We lived in Massachusetts in the good old courtin' days,
And lifted up our voices in psalms and hymns of praise.
Oh, how I wisht that I could live them happy times again!
For life, as we boys knew it, had a sweet, peculiar grace
When you was singin' tenor and I was singin' bass.

The music folks have nowadays ain't what it used to be,
Because there ain't no singers now on earth like Bill and me.
Why, Lemuel Bangs, who used to go to Springfield twice a year,
Admitted that for singin' Bill and me had not a peer
When Bill went soarin' up to A and I dropped down to D!
The old bull-fiddle Beza Dimmitt played warn't in the race
'Longside of Bill's high tenor and my sonorious bass.

Bill moved to Californy in the spring of '54,
And we folks that used to know him never knew him any more;
Then Cyrus Baker's oldest girl, she kind o' pined a spell,
And, hankerin' after sympathy, it naterally befell
That she married Deacon Pitkin's boy, who kep' the general store;
And so the years, the changeful years, have rattled on apace
Since Bill sung tenor and I sung bass.

As I was settin' by the stove this evenin' after tea,
I noticed wife kep' hitchin' close and closer up to me;
And as she patched the gingham frock our gran'child wore to-day,
I heerd her gin a sigh that seemed to come from fur away.
Couldn't help inquirin' what the trouble might be;
"Was thinkin' of the time," says Prue, a-breshin' at her face,
"When Bill sung tenor and you sung bass."

FIDUCIT.
THREE comrades on the German Rhine,
Defying care and weather,
Together quaffed the mellow wine,
And sung their songs together.
What recked they of the griefs of life,
With wine and song to cheer them?
Though elsewhere trouble might be rife,
It would not come anear them.

Anon one comrade passed away,
And presently another,
And yet unto the tryst each day
Repaired the lonely brother;
And still, as gayly as of old,
That third one, hero-hearted,
Filled to the brim each cup of gold,
And called to the departed,—

"O comrades mine! I see ye not,
Nor hear your kindly greeting,
Yet in this old, familiar spot
Be still our loving meeting!
Here have I filled each bouting-cup
With juices red and cheery;
I pray ye drink the portion up,
And as of old make merry!"

And once before his tear-dimmed eyes,
All in the haunted gloaming,
He saw two ghostly figures rise,
And quaff the beakers foaming;
He heard two spirit voices call,
"Fiducit, jovial brother!"

And so forever from that hall
Went they with one another.

THE "ST. JO GAZETTE."
WHEN I helped 'em run the local on the "St. Jo Gazette,"
I was upon familiar terms with every one I met;
For "items" were my stock in trade in that my callow time,
Before the muses tempted me to try my hand at rhyme,—
Before I found in verses
Those soothing, gracious mercies,
Less practical, but much more glorious than a well-filled purse is.
A votary of Mammon, I hustled round and sweat,
And helped 'em run the local on the "St. Jo Gazette."

The labors of the day began at half-past eight A.M.,
For the farmers came in early, and I had to tackle them;
And many a noble bit of news I managed to acquire
By those discreet attentions which all farmer-folk admire,
With my daily commentary
On affairs of farm and dairy,
The tone of which anon with subtle pufferies I'd vary,—
Oh, many a peck of apples and of peaches did I get
When I helped 'em run the local on the "St. Jo Gazette."

Dramatic news was scarce, but when a minstrel show was due,
Why, Milton Tootle's opera house was then my rendezvous;
Judge Grubb would give me points about the latest legal case,
And Dr. Runcie let me print his sermons when I'd space;
Of fevers, fractures, humors,
Contusions, fits, and tumors,
Would Dr. Hall or Dr. Baines confirm or nail the rumors;
From Colonel Dawes what railroad news there was I used to get,—
When I helped 'em run the local on the "St. Jo Gazette."

For "personals" the old Pacific
House was just the place,—
Pap Abell knew the pedigrees of all
the human race;
And when he'd gin up all he had,
he'd drop a subtle wink,
And lead the way where one might
wet one's whistle with a drink.
Those drinks at the Pacific,
When days were sudorific,
Were what Parisians (pray excuse
my French!) would call "magnifique;"
And frequently an invitation to a
meal I'd get
When I helped 'em run the local on
the "St. Jo Gazette."
And when in rainy weather news
was scarce as well as slow,
To Saxton's bank or Hopkins' store
for items would I go.
The jokes which Colonel Saxton
told were old, but good enough
For local application in lieu of better
stuff;
And when the ducks were flying,
Or the fishing well worth trying—
Gosh! but those "sports" at Hopkins'
store could beat the world at lying!
And I—I printed all their yarns,
though not without regret,
When I helped 'em run the local on
the "St. Jo Gazette."

For squibs political I'd go to Col.
Waller Young,
Or Col. James N. Burnes, the
"statesman with the silver tongue;"
Should some old pioneer take sick
and die, why, then I'd call
On Frank M. Posegate for the "life,"
and Posegate knew 'em all.
Lon Tullar used to pony
Up descriptions that were tony
Of toilets worn at party, ball, or
conversazione;
For the ladies were addicted to the
style called "deckolett"
When I helped 'em run the local on
the "St. Jo Gazette."

So was I wont my daily round of
labor to pursue;
And when came night I found that
there was still more work to do,—
The telegraph to edit, yards and
yards of proof to read,
And reprint to be gathered to supply
the printers' greed.
Oh, but it takes agility,
Combined with versatility,
To run a country daily with
appropriate ability!
There never were a smarter lot of
editors, I'll bet,
Than we who whooped up local on
the "St. Jo Gazette."

Yes, maybe it was irksome; maybe a
discontent
Rebellious rose amid the toil I daily
underwent
If so, I don't remember; this only do
I know,—
My thoughts turn ever fondly to that
time in old St. Jo.
The years that speed so fleetly
Have blotted out completely
All else than that which still remains
to solace me so sweetly;
The friendships of that time,—ah,
me! they are as precious yet
As when I was a local on the "St. Jo
Gazette."

AMSTERDAM.
MEYNHEER Hans Von Der Bloom
has got
A majazin in Kalverstraat,
Where one may buy for sordid gold
Wares quaint and curious, new and
old.
Here are antiquities galore,—
The jewels which Dutch monarchs
wore,
Swords, teacups, helmets, platters,
clocks,
Bright Dresden jars, dull Holland
crocks,
And all those joys I might rehearse
That please the eye, but wreck the
purse.

I most admired an ancient bed,
With ornate carvings at its head,—
A massive frame of dingy oak,
Whose curious size and mould
bespoke
Prodigious age. "How much?" I
cried.

"Ein tousand gildens," Hans replied;
And then the honest Dutchman said
A king once owned that glorious
    bed,—
King Fritz der Foorst, of blessed
    fame,
Had owned and slept within the
    same!

Then long I stood and mutely gazed,
By reminiscent splendors dazed,
And I had bought it right away,
Had I the wherewithal to pay.
But, lacking of the needed pelf,
I thus discoursed within myself:
"O happy Holland! where's the bliss
That can approximate to this
Possession of the rare antique
Which maniacs hanker for and seek?
My native land is full of stuff
That's good, but is not old enough.
Alas! it has no oaken beds
Wherein have slumbered royal
    heads,
No relic on whose face we see
The proof of grand antiquity."

Thus reasoned I a goodly spell
Until, perchance, my vision fell
Upon a trademark at the head
Of Fritz der Foorst's old oaken
    bed,—
A rampant wolverine, and round
This strange device these words I
    found:
"Patent Antique. Birkey & Gay,
Grand Rapids, Michigan, U. S. A."

At present I'm not saying much
About the simple, guileless Dutch;
And as it were a loathsome spot
I keep away from Kalverstraat,
Determined when I want a bed
In which hath slept a royal head
I'll patronize no middleman,
But deal direct with Michigan.

TO THE PASSING SAINT.
AS to-night you came your way,
Bearing earthward heavenly joy,
Tell me, O dear saint, I pray,
Did you see my little boy?

By some fairer voice beguiled,
Once he wandered from my sight;
He is such a little child,
He should have my love this night.

It has been so many a year,—
Oh, so many a year since then!
Yet he was so very dear,
Surely he will come again.

If upon your way you see
One whose beauty is divine,
Will you send him back to me?
He is lost, and he is mine.

Tell him that his little chair
Nestles where the sunbeams meet,
That the shoes he used to wear
Yearn to kiss his dimpled feet.

Tell him of each pretty toy
That was wont to share his glee;
Maybe that will bring my boy
Back to them and back to me.

O dear saint, as on you go
Through the glad and sparkling
    frost,
Bid those bells ring high and low
For a little child that's lost!

O dear saint, that blessest men
With the grace of Christmas joy,
Soothe this heart with love again,—
Give me back my little boy!

THE FISHERMAN'S FEAST.
OF all the gracious gifts of Spring,
Is there another can surpass
This delicate, voluptuous thing,—
This dapple-green, plump-
    shouldered bass?
Upon a damask napkin laid,
What exhalations superfine
Our gustatory nerves pervade,
Provoking quenchless thirsts for
    wine!

The ancients loved this noble fish;
And, coming from the kitchen fire
All piping hot upon a dish,
What raptures did he not inspire?
"Fish should swim twice," they used
    to say,—
Once in their native, vapid brine,

And then again, a better way—
You understand; fetch on the wine!

Ah, dainty monarch of the flood,
How often have I cast for you,
How often sadly seen you scud
Where weeds and water-lilies grew!
How often have you filched my bait,
How often snapped my treacherous line!
Yet here I have you on this plate,—
You shall swim twice, and now in wine.

And, harkee, garçon! let the blood
Of cobwebbed years be spilled for him,—
Ay, in a rich Burgundian flood
This piscatorial pride should swim;
So, were he living, he would say
He gladly died for me and mine,
And, as it were his native spray,
He'd lash the sauce—what, ho! the wine!

I would it were ordained for me
To share your fate, O finny friend!
I surely were not loath to be
Reserved for such a noble end;
For when old Chronos, gaunt and grim,
At last reels in his ruthless line,
What were my ecstasy to swim
In wine, in wine, in glorious wine!

Well, here's a health to you, sweet Spring!
And, prithee, whilst I stick to earth,
Come hither every year and bring
The boons provocative of mirth;
And should your stock of bass run low,
However much I might repine,
I think I might survive the blow,
If plied with wine and still more wine!

NIGHTFALL IN DORDRECHT.
THE mill goes toiling slowly around
With steady and solemn creak,
And my little one hears in the kindly sound
The voice of the old mill speak;
While round and round those big white wings
Grimly and ghostlike creep,
My little one hears that the old mill sings,
"Sleep, little tulip, sleep!"

The sails are reefed and the nets are drawn,
And over his pot of beer
The fisher, against the morrow's dawn,
Lustily maketh cheer;
He mocks at the winds that caper along
From the far-off, clamorous deep,
But we—we love their lullaby-song
Of "Sleep, little tulip, sleep!"

Old dog Fritz, in slumber sound,
Groans of the stony mart;
To-morrow how proudly he'll trot you around,
Hitched to our new milk-cart!
And you shall help me blanket the kine,
And fold the gentle sheep,
And set the herring a-soak in brine,—
But now, little tulip, sleep!

A Dream-One comes to button the eyes
That wearily droop and blink,
While the old mill buffets the frowning skies,
And scolds at the stars that wink;
Over your face the misty wings
Of that beautiful Dream-One sweep,
And, rocking your cradle, she softly sings,
"Sleep, little tulip, sleep!"

THE ONION TART.
OF tarts there be a thousand kinds,
So versatile the art,
And, as we all have different minds,
Each has his favorite tart;
But those which most delight the rest
Methinks should suit me not:
The onion tart doth please me best,—
Ach, Gott! mein lieber Gott!

Where but in Deutschland can be found
This boon of which I sing?
Who but a Teuton could compound
This sui generis thing?
None with the German frau can vie
In arts cuisine, I wot,
Whose summum bonum breeds the sigh,
"Ach, Gott! mein lieber Gott!"

You slice the fruit upon the dough,
And season to the taste,
Then in an oven (not too slow)
The viand should be placed;
And when 'tis done, upon a plate
You serve it piping hot.
Your nostrils and your eyes dilate,—
Ach, Gott! mein lieber Gott!

It sweeps upon the sight and smell
In overwhelming tide,
And then the sense of taste as well
Betimes is gratified:
Three noble senses drowned in bliss!
I prithee tell me, what
Is there beside compares with this?
Ach, Gott! mein lieber Gott!

For if the fruit be proper young,
And if the crust be good,
How shall they melt upon the tongue
Into a savory flood!
How seek the Mecca down below,
And linger round that spot,
Entailing weeks and months of woe,—
Ach, Gott! mein lieber Gott!

If Nature gives men appetites
For things that won't digest,
Why, let them eat whatso delights,
And let her stand the rest;
And though the sin involve the cost
Of Carlsbad, like as not
'Tis better to have loved and lost,—
Ach, Gott! mein lieber Gott!

Beyond the vast, the billowy tide,
Where my compatriots dwell,
All kinds of victuals have I tried,
All kinds of drinks, as well;
But nothing known to Yankee art
Appears to reach the spot
Like this Teutonic onion tart,—
Ach, Gott! mein lieber Gott!

So, though I quaff of Carlsbad's tide
As full as I can hold,
And for complete reform inside
Plank down my horde of gold,
Remorse shall not consume my heart,
Nor sorrow vex my lot,
For I have eaten onion tart,—
Ach, Gott! mein lieber Gott!

GRANDMA'S BOMBAZINE.

IT'S everywhere that women fair
invite and please my eye,
And that on dress I lay much stress I can't and sha'n't deny:
The English dame who's all aflame with divers colors bright,
The Teuton belle, the ma'moiselle,—all give me keen delight;
And yet I'll say, go where I may, I never yet have seen
A dress that's quite as grand a sight as was that bombazine.

Now, you must know 'twas years ago this quaint but noble gown
Flashed in one day, the usual way, upon our solemn town.
'Twas Fisk who sold for sordid gold that gravely scrumptious thing,—
Jim Fisk, the man who drove a span that would have joyed a king,—
And grandma's eye fell with a sigh upon that sombre sheen,
And grandpa's purse looked much the worse for grandma's bombazine.

Though ten years old, I never told the neighbors of the gown;
For grandma said, "This secret, Ned, must not be breathed in town."
The sitting-room for days of gloom was in a dreadful mess
When that quaint dame, Miss Kelsey, came to make the wondrous dress:
To fit and baste and stitch a waist, with whale-bones in between,

146

Is precious slow, as all folks know
who've made a bombazine.

With fortitude dear grandma stood
the trial to the end
(The nerve we find in womankind I
cannot comprehend!);
And when 'twas done resolved that
none should guess at the surprise,
Within the press she hid that dress,
secure from prying eyes;
For grandma knew a thing or two,—
by which remark I mean
That Sundays were the days for her
to wear that bombazine.

I need not state she got there late;
and, sailing up the aisle
With regal grace, on grandma's face
reposed a conscious smile.
It fitted so, above, below, and hung
so well all round,
That there was not one faulty spot a
critic could have found.
How proud I was of her, because
she looked so like a queen!
And that was why, perhaps, that I
admired the bombazine.

But there were those, as you'd
suppose, who scorned that perfect
gown;
For ugly-grained old cats obtained
in that New England town:
The Widow White spat out her spite
in one: "It doesn't fit!"
The Packard girls (they wore false
curls) all giggled like to split;
Sophronia Wade, the sour old maid,
she turned a bilious green,
When she descried that joy and
pride, my grandma's bombazine.

But grandma knew, and I did, too,
that gown was wondrous fine,—
The envious sneers and jaundiced
jeers were a conclusive sign.
Why, grandpa said it went ahead of
all the girls in town,
And, saying this, he snatched a kiss
that like to burst that gown;
But, blushing red, my grandma said,
"Oh, isn't grandpa mean!"
Yet evermore my grandma wore his
favorite bombazine.

And when she died that sombre
pride passed down to heedless heirs,—
Alas, the day 't was hung away
beneath the kitchen stairs!
Thence in due time, with dust and
grime, came foes on foot and wing,
And made their nests and sped their
guests in that once beauteous thing.
'Tis so, forsooth! Time's envious
tooth corrodes each human scene;
And so, at last, to ruin passed my
grandma's bombazine.

Yet to this day, I'm proud to say, it
plays a grateful part,—
The thoughts it brings are of such
things as touch and warm my heart.
This gown, my dear, you show me
here I'll own is passing fair,
Though I'll confess it's no such dress
as grandma used to wear.
Yet wear it, do; perchance when you
and I are off the scene,
Our boy shall sing this comely thing
as I the bombazine.

RARE ROAST BEEF.

WHEN the numerous distempers to
which all flesh is heir
Torment us till our very souls are
reeking with despair;
When that monster fiend, Dyspepsy,
rears its spectral hydra head,
Filling bon vivants and epicures
with certain nameless dread;
When any ill of body or of intellect
abounds,
Be it sickness known to Galen or
disease unknown to Lowndes,—
In such a dire emergency it is my
firm belief
That there is no diet quite so good as
rare roast beef.

And even when the body's in the
very prime of health,
When sweet contentment spreads
upon the cheeks her rosy wealth,
And when a man devours three
meals per day and pines for more,
And growls because instead of three
square meals there are not four,—

Well, even then, though cake and
    pie do service on the side,
And coffee is a luxury that may not
    be denied,
Still of the many viands there is one
    that's hailed as chief,
And that, as you are well aware, is
    rare roast beef.

Some like the sirloin, but I think the
    porterhouse is best,—
'Tis juicier and tenderer and meatier
    than the rest;
Put on this roast a dash of salt, and
    then of water pour
Into the sizzling dripping-pan a
    cupful, and no more;
The oven being hot, the roast will
    cook in half an hour;
Then to the juices in the pan you add
    a little flour,
And so you get a gravy that is called
    the cap sheaf
Of that glorious summum bonum,
    rare roast beef.

Served on a platter that is hot, and
    carved with thin, keen knife,
How does this savory viand enhance
    the worth of life!
Give me no thin and shadowy slice,
    but a thick and steaming slab,—
Who would not choose a generous
    hunk to a bloodless little dab?
Upon a nice hot plate how does the
    juicy morceau steam,
    A symphony in scarlet or a red
        incarnate dream!
Take from me eyes and ears and all,
    O Time, thou ruthless thief!
Except these teeth wherewith to deal
    with rare roast beef.

Most every kind and rôle of modern
    victuals have I tried,
    Including roasted, fricasseed,
broiled, toasted, stewed, and fried,
    Your canvasbacks and papa-bottes
        and muttonchops subese,
    Your patties à la Turkey and your
        doughnuts à la grease;
I've whirled away dyspeptic hours
    with crabs in marble halls,
    And in the lowly cottage I've
        experienced codfish balls;
But I've never found a viand that
    could so allay all grief
And soothe the cockles of the heart
    as rare roast beef.

I honor that sagacious king who, in a
    grateful mood,
Knighted the savory loin that on the
    royal table stood;
And as for me I'd ask no better
    friend than this good roast,
Which is my squeamish stomach's
    fortress (feste Burg) and host;
For with this ally with me I can
    mock Dyspepsy's wrath,
Can I pursue the joy of Wisdom's
    pleasant, peaceful path.
So I do off my vest and let my
    waistband out a reef
When I soever set me down to rare
    roast beef.

GANDERFEATHER'S GIFT.
I WAS just a little thing
When a fairy came and kissed me;
    Floating in upon the light
    Of a haunted summer night,
    Lo! the fairies came to sing
    Pretty slumber songs, and bring
Certain boons that else had missed
    me.
    From a dream I turned to see
    What those strangers brought for
        me,
When that fairy up and kissed me,—
Here, upon this cheek, he kissed me!

    Simmerdew was there, but she
    Did not like me altogether;
    Daisybright and Turtledove,
    Pilfercurds and Honeylove,
    Thistleblow and Amberglee
    On that gleaming, ghostly sea
    Floated from the misty heather,
    And around my trundle-bed
    Frisked and looked and whispering
        said,
    Solemn-like and all together:
    "You shall kiss him,
        Ganderfeather!"

Ganderfeather kissed me then,—
Ganderfeather, quaint and merry!
    No attenuate sprite was he,

But as buxom as could be;
Kissed me twice and once again,
And the others shouted when
On my cheek uprose a berry
Somewhat like a mole, mayhap,
But the kiss-mark of that chap
Ganderfeather, passing merry,—
Humorsome but kindly, very!

I was just a tiny thing
When the prankish Ganderfeather
Brought this curious gift to me
With his fairy kisses three;
Yet with honest pride I sing
That same gift he chose to bring
Out of yonder haunted heather;
Other charms and friendships fly,—
Constant friends this mole and I,
Who have been so long together!
Thank you, little Ganderfeather!

OLD TIMES, OLD FRIENDS, OLD LOVE.
THERE are no days like the good old days,—
The days when we were youthful!
When humankind were pure of mind,
And speech and deeds were truthful;
Before a love for sordid gold
Became man's ruling passion,
And before each dame and maid became
Slave to the tyrant fashion!

There are no girls like the good old girls,—
Against the world I'd stake 'em!
As buxom and smart and clean of heart
As the Lord knew how to make 'em!
They were rich in spirit and common-sense,
And piety all supportin';
They could bake and brew, and had taught school, too,
And they made such likely courtin'!

There are no boys like the good old boys,—
When we were boys together!
When the grass was sweet to the brown bare feet
That dimpled the laughing heather;
When the pewee sung to the summer dawn
Of the bee in the billowy clover,
Or down by the mill the whip-poor-will
Echoed his night song over.

There is no love like the good old love,—
The love that mother gave us!
We are old, old men, yet we pine again
For that precious grace,—God save us!
So we dream and dream of the good old times,
And our hearts grow tenderer, fonder,
As those dear old dreams bring soothing gleams
Of heaven away off yonder.

OUR WHIPPINGS.
COME, Harvey, let us sit awhile and talk about the times
Before you went to selling clothes and I to peddling rhymes,—
The days when we were little boys, as naughty little boys
As ever worried home folks with their everlasting noise!
Egad! and were we so disposed, I'll venture we could show
The scars of wallopings we got some forty years ago;
What wallopings I mean I think I need not specify,—
Mother's whippings didn't hurt; but father's,—oh, my!

The way that we played hookey those many years ago,
We'd rather give 'most anything than have our children know!
The thousand naughty things we did, the thousand fibs we told,—
Why, thinking of them makes my Presbyterian blood run cold!
How often Deacon Sabine Morse remarked if we were his
He'd tan our "pesky little hides until the blisters riz"!
It's many a hearty thrashing to that Deacon Morse we owe,—

Mother's whippings didn't count;
father's did, though!

We used to sneak off swimmin' in
those careless, boyish days,
And come back home of evenings
with our necks and backs ablaze;
How mother used to wonder why
our clothes were full of sand,—
But father, having been a boy,
appeared to understand;
And after tea he'd beckon us to join
him in the shed,
Where he'd proceed to tinge our
backs a deeper, darker red.
Say what we will of mother's, there
is none will controvert
The proposition that our father's
lickings always hurt!

For mother was by nature so
forgiving and so mild
That she inclined to spare the rod
although she spoiled the child;
And when at last in self-defence she
had to whip us, she
Appeared to feel those whippings a
great deal more than we:
But how we bellowed and took on,
as if we'd like to die,—
Poor mother really thought she hurt,
and that's what made her cry!
Then how we youngsters snickered
as out the door we slid,
For mother's whippings never hurt,
though father's always did!

In after years poor father simmered
down to five feet four,
But in our youth he seemed to us in
height eight feet or more!
Oh, how we shivered when he quoth
in cold, suggestive tone:
"I'll see you in the woodshed after
supper all alone!"
Oh, how the legs and arms and dust
and trouser-buttons flew,—
What florid vocalisms marked that
vesper interview!
Yes, after all this lapse of years, I
feelingly assert,
With all respect to mother, it was
father's whippings hurt!

The little boy experiencing that
tingling 'neath his vest
Is often loath to realize that all is for
the best;
Yet, when the boy gets older, he
pictures with delight
The bufferings of childhood,—as we
do here to-night.
The years, the gracious years, have
smoothed and beautified the ways
That to our little feet seemed all too
rugged in the days
Before you went to selling clothes
and I to peddling rhymes,—
So, Harvey, let us sit awhile and
think upon those times.

BION'S SONG OF EROS.
EROS is the god of love;
He and I are hand-in-glove.
All the gentle, gracious Muses
Follow Eros where he leads,
And they bless the bard who
chooses
To proclaim love's famous deeds;
Him they serve in rapturous glee,—
That is why they're good to me.

Sometimes I have gone astray
From love's sunny, flowery way:
How I floundered, how I stuttered!
And, deprived of ways and means,
What egregious rot I uttered,—
Such as suits the magazines!
I was rescued only when
Eros called me back again.

Gods forefend that I should shun
That benignant Mother's son!
Why, the poet who refuses
To emblazon love's delights
Gets the mitten from the Muses,—
Then what balderdash he writes!
I love Love; which being so,
See how smooth my verses flow!

Gentle Eros, lead the way,—
I will follow while I may:
Be thy path by hill or hollow,
I will follow fast and free;
And when I'm too old to follow,
I will sit and sing of thee,—
Potent still in intellect,
Sit, and sing, and retrospect.

MR. BILLINGS OF LOUISVILLE.

THERE are times in one's life which
  one cannot forget;
And the time I remember's the
  evening I met
A haughty young scion of bluegrass
  renown
Who made my acquaintance while
  painting the town:
A handshake, a cocktail, a smoker,
  and then
Mr. Billings of Louisville touched
  me for ten.

There flowed in his veins the blue
  blood of the South,
And a cynical smile curled his
  sensuous mouth;
He quoted from Lanier and Poe by
  the yard,
But his purse had been hit by the
  war, and hit hard:
I felt that he honored and flattered
  me when
Mr. Billings of Louisville touched
  me for ten.

I wonder that never again since that
  night
A vision of Billings has hallowed
  my sight;
I pine for the sound of his voice and
  the thrill
That comes with the touch of a ten-
  dollar bill:
I wonder and pine; for—I say it
  again—
Mr. Billings of Louisville touched
  me for ten.

I've heard what old Whittier sung of
  Miss Maud;
But all such philosophy's nothing
  but fraud;
To one who's a bear in Chicago to-
  day,
With wheat going up, and the devil
  to pay,
These words are the saddest of
  tongue or of pen:
"Mr. Billings of Louisville touched
  me for ten."

POET AND KING.

THOUGH I am king, I have no
  throne
Save this rough wooden siege alone;
I have no empire, yet my sway
Extends a myriad leagues away;
No servile vassal bends his knee
In grovelling reverence to me,
Yet at my word all hearts beat high,
And there is fire in every eye,
And love and gratitude they bring
As tribute unto me, a king.

The folk that throng the busy street
Know not it is a king they meet;
And I am glad there is not seen
The monarch in my face and mien.
I should not choose to be the cause
Of fawning or of coarse applause:
I am content to know the arts
Wherewith to lord it o'er their
  hearts;
For when unto their hearts I sing,
I am a king, I am a king!

My sceptre,—see, it is a pen!
Wherewith I rule these hearts of
  men.
Sometime it pleaseth to beguile
Its monarch fancy with a smile;
Sometime it is athirst for tears:
And so adown the laurelled years
I walk, the noblest lord on earth,
Dispensing sympathy and mirth.
Aha! it is a magic thing
That makes me what I am,—a king!

Let empires crumble as they may,
Proudly I hold imperial sway;
The sunshine and the rain of years
Are human smiles and human tears
That come or vanish at my call,—
I am the monarch of them all!
Mindful alone of this am I:
The songs I sing shall never die;
Not even envious Death can wring
His glory from so great a king.

Come, brother, be a king with me,
And rule mankind eternally;
Lift up the weak, and cheer the
  strong,
Defend the truth, combat the wrong!

You'll find no sceptre like the pen
To hold and sway the hearts of men;
Its edicts flow in blood and tears
That will outwash the flood of years:
So, brother, sing your songs, oh, sing!
And be with me a king, a king!

LYDIA DICK.

WHEN I was a boy at college,
Filling up with classic knowledge,
Frequently I wondered why
Old Professor Demas Bentley
Used to praise so eloquently
"Opera Horatii."

Toiling on a season longer
Till my reasoning powers got stronger,
As my observation grew,
I became convinced that mellow,
Massic-loving poet fellow,
Horace, knew a thing or two.

Yes, we sophomores figured duly
That, if we appraised him truly,
Horace must have been a brick;
And no wonder that with ranting
Rhymes he went a-gallivanting
Round with sprightly Lydia Dick!

For that pink of female gender
Tall and shapely was, and slender,
Plump of neck and bust and arms;
While the raiment that invested
Her so jealously suggested
Certain more potential charms.

Those dark eyes of hers that fired him,
Those sweet accents that inspired him,
And her crown of glorious hair,—
These things baffle my description:
I should have a fit conniption
If I tried; so I forbear.

Maybe Lydia had her betters;
Anyway, this man of letters
Took that charmer as his pick.
Glad—yes, glad I am to know it!
I, a fin de siècle poet,
Sympathize with Lydia Dick!

Often in my arbor shady
I fall thinking of that lady,
And the pranks she used to play;
And I'm cheered,—for all we sages
Joy when from those distant ages
Lydia dances down our way.

Otherwise some folks might wonder,
With good reason, why in thunder
Learned professors, dry and prim,
Find such solace in the giddy
Pranks that Horace played with Liddy
Or that Liddy played on him.

Still this world of ours rejoices
In those ancient singing voices,
And our hearts beat high and quick,
To the cadence of old Tiber
Murmuring praise of roistering Liber
And of charming Lydia Dick.

Still Digentia, downward flowing,
Prattleth to the roses blowing
By the dark, deserted grot.
Still Soracte, looming lonely,
Watcheth for the coming only
Of a ghost that cometh not.

LIZZIE.

I WONDER ef all wimmin air
Like Lizzie is when we go out
To theaters an' concerts where
Is things the papers talk about.
Do other wimmin fret an' stew
Like they wuz bein' crucified,—
Frettin' a show or concert through,
With wonderin' ef the baby cried?

Now Lizzie knows that gran'ma's there
To see that everything is right;
Yet Lizzie thinks that gran'ma's care
Ain't good enuff f'r baby, quite.
Yet what am I to answer when
She kind uv fidgets at my side,
An' asks me every now an' then,
"I wonder ef the baby cried"?

Seems like she seen two little eyes
A-pinin' f'r their mother's smile;

Seems like she heern the pleadin'
  cries
Uv one she thinks uv all the while;
An' so she's sorry that she come.
An' though she allus tries to hide
The truth, she'd ruther stay to hum
Than wonder ef the baby cried.

Yes, wimmin folks is all alike—
By Lizzie you kin jedge the rest;
There never wuz a little tyke,
But that his mother loved him best.
And nex' to bein' what I be—
The husband uv my gentle bride—
I'd wisht I wuz that croodlin' wee,
With Lizzie wonderin' ef I cried.

LITTLE HOMER'S SLATE.

AFTER dear old grandma died,
  Hunting through an oaken chest
In the attic, we espied
  What repaid our childish quest:
'Twas a homely little slate,
Seemingly of ancient date.

On its quaint and battered face
  Was the picture of a cart
Drawn with all that awkward grace
  Which betokens childish art.
But what meant this legend, pray:
"Homer drew this yesterday"?

Mother recollected then
  What the years were fain to hide:
She was but a baby when
  Little Homer lived and died.
Forty years, so mother said,
Little Homer had been dead.

This one secret through those years
  Grandma kept from all apart,
Hallowed by her lonely tears
  And the breaking of her heart;
While each year that sped away
Seemed to her but yesterday.

So the homely little slate
  Grandma's baby's fingers pressed,
To a memory consecrate,
  Lieth in the oaken chest,
Where, unwilling we should know,
Grandma put it years ago.

---

next pg 158

ALWAYS RIGHT.

DON'T take on so, Hiram,
  But do what you're told to do;
It's fair to suppose that yer mother
    knows
  A heap sight more than you.
I'll allow that sometimes her way
  Don't seem the wisest, quite;
    But the easiest way,
    When she's had her say,
Is to reckon yer mother is right.

Courted her ten long winters,
  Saw her to singin'-school;
When she went down one spell to
    town,
  I cried like a durned ol' fool;
Got mad at the boys for callin'
  When I sparked her Sunday night:
    But she said she knew
    A thing or two,—
An' I reckoned yer mother wuz
    right.

I courted till I wuz aging,
  And she wuz past her prime,—
I'd have died, I guess, if she hadn't
    said yes
  When I popped f'r the hundredth
    time.
Said she'd never have took me
  If I hadn't stuck so tight;
    Opined that we
    Could never agree,—
And I reckon yer mother wuz right!

"TROT, MY GOOD STEED, TROT!"

WHERE my true love abideth
  I make my way to-night;
    Lo! waiting, she
    Espieth me,
  And calleth in delight:
"I see his steed anear
Come trotting with my dear,—
Oh, idle not, good steed, but trot,
  Trot thou my lover here!"

Aloose I cast the bridle,
  And ply the whip and spur;
    And gayly I
    Speed this reply,
  While faring on to her:
"Oh, true love, fear thou not!

I seek our trysting spot;
And double feed be yours, my steed,
If you more swiftly trot."

I vault from out the saddle,
And make my good steed fast;
Then to my breast
My love is pressed,—
At last, true heart, at last!
The garden drowsing lies,
The stars fold down their eyes,—
In this dear spot, my steed, neigh not,
Nor stamp in restless wise!

O passing sweet communion
Of young hearts, warm and true!
To thee belongs
The old, old songs
Love finds forever new.
We sing those songs, and then
Cometh the moment when
It's, "Good steed, trot from this dear spot,—
Trot, trot me home again!"

PROVIDENCE AND THE DOG.

WHEN I was young and callow, which was many years ago,
Within me the afflatus went surging to and fro;
And so I wrote a tragedy that fairly reeked with gore,
With every act concluding with the dead piled on the floor,—
A mighty effort, by the gods! and after I had read
The manuscript to Daly, that dramatic censor said:
"The plot is most exciting, and I like the dialogue;
You should take the thing to Providence, and try it on a dog."

McCambridge organized a troupe, including many a name
Unknown alike to guileless me, to riches, and to fame.
A pompous man whose name was Rae was Nestor of this troupe,—
Amphibious, he was quite at home outside or in the soup!
The way McCambridge billed him! Why, such dreams in red and green
Had ne'er before upon the boards of Yankeedom been seen;
And my proud name was heralded,—oh that I'd gone incog.
When we took that play to Providence to try it on a dog!

Shall I forget the awful day we struck that wretched town?
Yet in what melting irony the treacherous sun beamed down!
The sale of seats had not been large; but then McCambridge said
The factory people seldom bought their seats so far ahead,
And Rae indorsed McCambridge. So they partly set at rest
The natural misgivings that perturbed my youthful breast;
For I wondered and lamented that the town was not agog
When I took my play to Providence to try it on a dog.

They never came at all,—aha! I knew it all the time,—
They never came to see and hear my tragedy sublime.
Oh, fateful moment when the curtain rose on act the first!
Oh, moment fateful to the soul for wealth and fame athirst!
But lucky factory girls and boys to stay away that night,
When the author's fervid soul was touched by disappointment's blight,—
When desolation settled down on me like some dense fog
For having tempted Providence, and tried it on a dog!

Those actors didn't know their parts; they maundered to and fro,
Ejaculating platitudes that were quite mal à propos;
And when I sought to reprimand the graceless scamps, the lot
Turned fiercely on me, and denounced my charming play as rot.
I might have stood their bitter taunts without a passing grunt,
If I'd had a word of solace from the people out in front;
But that chilly corporal's guard sat round like bumps upon a log

When I played that play at
Providence with designs upon the dog.

We went with lots of baggage, but
we didn't bring it back,—
For who would be so hampered as
he walks a railway track?
"Oh, ruthless muse of tragedy! what
prodigies of shame,
What marvels of injustice are
committed in thy name!"
Thus groaned I in the spirit, as I
strode what stretch of ties
'Twixt Providence, Rhode Island,
and my native Gotham lies;
But Rae, McCambridge, and the rest
kept up a steady jog,—
'Twas not the first time they had
plied their arts upon the dog.

So much for my first battle with the
fickle goddess, Fame,—
And I hear that some folks
nowadays are faring just the same.
Oh, hapless he that on the graceless
Yankee dog relies!
The dog fares stout and hearty, and
the play it is that dies.
So ye with tragedies to try, I beg of
you, beware!
Put not your trust in Providence, that
most delusive snare;
Cast, if you will, your pearls of
thought before the Western hog,
But never go to Providence to try it
on a dog.

GETTIN' ON.
WHEN I wuz somewhat younger,
I wuz reckoned purty gay;
I had my fling at everything
In a rollickin', coltish way.
But times have strangely altered
Since sixty years ago—
This age of steam an' things don't
seem
Like the age I used to know.
Your modern innovations
Don't suit me, I confess,
As did the ways of the good ol'
days,—
But I'm gettin' on, I guess.

I set on the piazza,
An' hitch round with the sun;
Sometimes, mayhap, I take a nap,
Waitin' till school is done.
An' then I tell the children
The things I done in youth,—
An' near as I can, as a vener'ble man,
I stick to the honest truth,—
But the looks of them 'at listen
Seem sometimes to express
The remote idee that I'm gone—you
see?—
An' I am gettin' on, I guess.

I get up in the mornin',
An', nothin' else to do,
Before the rest are up an' dressed,
I read the papers through.
I hang round with the women
All day an' hear 'em talk;
An' while they sew or knit I show
The baby how to walk.
An', somehow, I feel sorry
When they put away his dress
An' cut his curls ('cause they're like
a girl's!)—
I'm gettin' on, I guess.

Sometimes, with twilight round me,
I see, or seem to see,
A distant shore where friends of
yore
Linger an' watch for me.
Sometimes I've heered 'em callin'
So tender-like 'nd low
That it almost seemed like a dream I
dreamed,
Or an echo of long ago;
An' sometimes on my forehead
There falls a soft caress,
Or the touch of a hand,—you
understand,—
I'm gettin' on, I guess.

THE SCHNELLEST ZUG.
FROM Hanover to Leipzig is but a
little way,
Yet the journey by the so-called
schnellest zug consumes a day;
You start at half-past ten or so, and
not till nearly night
Do the double towers of Magdeburg
loom up before your sight;

From thence to Leipzig's quick enough,—of that I'll not complain,—
But from Hanover to Magdeburg—confound that schnellest train!

The Germans say that "schnell" means fast, and "schnellest" faster yet,—
In all my life no grimmer bit of humor have I met!
Why, thirteen miles an hour's the greatest speed they ever go,
While on the engine piston-rods do moss and lichens grow;
And yet the average Teuton will presumptuously maintain
That one can't know what swiftness is till he's tried das schnellest train!

Fool that I was! I should have walked,—I had no time to waste;
The little journey I had planned I had to do in haste,—
The quaint old town of Leipzig with its literary mart,
And Dresden with its crockery-shops and wondrous wealth of art,
The Saxon Alps, the Carlsbad cure for all dyspeptic pain,—
These were the ends I had in view when I took that schnellest train.

The natives dozed around me, yet none too deep to hear
The guard's sporadic shout of "funf minuten" (meaning beer);
I counted forty times at least that voice announce the stops
Required of those fat natives to glut their greed for hops,
Whilst I crouched in a corner, a monument to woe,
And thought unholy, awful things, and felt my whiskers grow!
And then, the wretched sights one sees while travelling by that train,—
The women doing men-folks' work at harvesting the grain,
Or sometimes grubbing in the soil, or hitched to heavy carts
Beside the family cow or dog, doing their slavish parts!
The husbands strut in soldier garb,—indeed they were too vain
To let creation see them work from that creeping schnellest train!

I found the German language all too feeble to convey
The sentiments that surged through my dyspeptic hulk that day;
I had recourse to English, and exploded without stint
Such virile Anglo-Saxon as would never do in print,
But which assuaged my rising gorge and cooled my seething brain
While snailing on to Magdeburg upon that schnellest train.

The typical New England freight that maunders to and fro,
The upper Mississippi boats, the bumptious B. & O.,
The creeping Southern railroads with their other creeping things,
The Philadelphy cable that is run out West for rings,
The Piccadilly 'buses with their constant roll and shake,—
All have I tried, and yet I'd give the "schnellest zug" the cake!
My countrymen, if ever you should seek the German clime,
Put not your trust in Baedeker if you are pressed for time;
From Hanover to Magdeburg is many a weary mile
By "schnellest zug," but done afoot it seems a tiny while;
Walk, swim, or skate, and then the task will not appear in vain,
But you'll break the third commandment if you take the schnellest train!

BETHLEHEM-TOWN.

AS I was going to Bethlehem-town,
Upon the earth I cast me down
All underneath a little tree
That whispered in this wise to me:
"Oh, I shall stand on Calvary
And bear what burthen saveth thee!"

As up I fared to Bethlehem-town,
I met a shepherd coming down,
And thus he quoth: "A wondrous sight

Hath spread before mine eyes this night,—
An angel host most fair to see,
That sung full sweetly of a tree
That shall uplift on Calvary
What burthen saveth you and me!"

And as I gat to Bethlehem-town,
Lo! wise men came that bore a crown.
"Is there," cried I, "in Bethlehem
A King shall wear this diadem?"
"Good sooth," they quoth, "and it is He
That shall be lifted on the tree
And freely shed on Calvary
What blood redeemeth us and thee!"

Unto a Child in Bethlehem-town
The wise men came and brought the crown;
And while the infant smiling slept,
Upon their knees they fell and wept;
But, with her babe upon her knee,
Naught recked that Mother of the tree,
That should uplift on Calvary
What burthen saveth all and me.

Again I walk in Bethlehem-town
And think on Him that wears the crown.
I may not kiss His feet again,
Nor worship Him as did I then;
My King hath died upon the tree,
And hath outpoured on Calvary
What blood redeemeth you and me!

THE PEACE OF CHRISTMAS-TIME.

DEAREST, how hard it is to say
That all is for the best,
Since, sometimes, in a grievous way
God's will is manifest.

See with what hearty, noisy glee
Our little ones to-night
Dance round and round our Christmas-tree
With pretty toys bedight.

Dearest, one voice they may not hear,
One face they may not see,—

Ah, what of all this Christmas cheer
Cometh to you and me?

Cometh before our misty eyes
That other little face;
And we clasp, in tender, reverent wise,
That love in the old embrace.

Dearest, the Christ-Child walks to-night,
Bringing His peace to men;
And He bringeth to you and to me the light
Of the old, old years again:

Bringeth the peace of long ago
When a wee one clasped your knee
And lisped of the morrow,—dear one, you know,—
And here come back is he!

Dearest, 'tis sometimes hard to say
That all is for the best,
For, often in a grievous way,
God's will is manifest.

But in the grace of this holy night
That bringeth us back our child,
Let us see that the ways of God are right,
And so be reconciled.

THE DOINGS OF DELSARTE.

IN former times my numerous rhymes excited general mirth,
And I was then of all good men the merriest man on earth;
And my career
From year to year
Was full of cheer
And things,
Despite a few regrets, perdieu! which grim dyspepsia brings;
But now how strange and harsh a change has come upon the scene!
Horrors appall the life where all was formerly so serene:
Yes, wasting care hath cast its snare about my honest heart,
Because, alas! it hath come to pass my daughter's learned Delsarte.
In flesh and joint and every point the counterpart of me,

She grew so fast she grew at last a marvellous thing to see,—
Long, gaunt, and slim, each gangling limb played stumbling-block to t'other,
The which excess of awkwardness quite mortified her mother.
Now, as for me, I like to see the carriages uncouth
Which certify to all the shy, unconscious age of youth.
If maidenkind be pure of mind, industrious, tidy, smart,
What need that they should fool away their youth upon Delsarte?

In good old times my numerous rhymes occasioned general mirth,
But now you see
Revealed in me
The gloomiest bard on earth.
I sing no more of the joys of yore that marked my happy life,
But rather those depressing woes with which the present's rife.
Unreconciled to that gaunt child, who's now a fashion-plate,
One song I raise in Art's dispraise, and so do I fight with Fate:
This gangling bard has found it hard to see his counterpart
Long, loose, and slim, divorced from him by that hectic dude, Delsarte.

Where'er she goes,
She loves to pose,
In classic attitudes,
And droop her eyes in languid wise, and feign abstracted moods;
And she, my child,
Who all so wild,
So helpless and so sweet,
That once she knew not what to do with those great big hands and feet,
Now comes and goes with such repose, so calmly sits or stands,
Is so discreet with both her feet, so deft with both her hands.
Why, when I see that satire on me, I give an angry start,
And I utter one word—it is commonly heard—derogatory to Delsarte.

In years gone by 't was said that I was quite a scrumptious man;
Conceit galore had I before this Delsarte craze began;
But now these wise
Folks criticise
My figure and my face,
And I opine they even incline to sneer at my musical bass.
Why, sometimes they presume to say this wart upon my cheek
Is not refined, and remarks unkind they pass on that antique,—
With lusty bass and charms of face and figure will I part
Ere they extort this grand old wart to placat their Delsarte.

Oh, wretched day! as all shall say who've known my Muse before,
When by this rhyme you see that I'm not in it any more.
Good-by the mirth that over earth diffused such keen delight;
The old-time bard
Of pork and lard
Is plainly out of sight.
All withered now about his brow the laurel fillets droop,
While Lachesis brews
For the poor old Muse
A portion of scalding soup.
Engrave this line, O friends of mine! over my broken heart:
"He hustled and strove, and fancied he throve, till his daughter learned Delsarte."

BUTTERCUP, POPPY, FORGET-ME-NOT.

Buttercup, Poppy, Forget-me-not,—
These three bloomed in a garden spot;
And once, all merry with song and play,
A little one heard three voices say:
"Shine or shadow, summer or spring,
O thou child with the tangled hair
And laughing eyes, we three shall bring
Each an offering, passing fair!"
The little one did not understand;

But they bent and kissed the
dimpled hand.

Buttercup gambolled all day long,
Sharing the little one's mirth and
song;
Then, stealing along on misty
gleams,
Poppy came, bringing the sweetest
dreams,
Playing and dreaming, that was all,
Till once the sleeper would not
awake;
Kissing the little face under the pall,
We thought of the words the third
flower spake,
And we found, betimes, in a
hallowed spot,
The solace and peace of Forget-me-
not.

Buttercup shareth the joy of day,
Glinting with gold the hours of play;
Bringeth the Poppy sweet repose,
When the hands would fold and the
eyes would close.
And after it all,—the play and the
sleep
Of a little life,—what cometh then?
To the hearts that ache and the eyes
that weep,
A wee flower bringeth God's peace
again:
Each one serveth its tender lot,—
Buttercup, Poppy, Forget-me-not.

Hoosier Lyrics

HOOSIER LYRICS PARAPHRASED.

We've come from Indiany, five hundred miles or more,
Supposin' we wuz goin' to get the nominashin, shore;
For Col. New assured us (in that noospaper o' his)
That we cud hev the airth, if we'd only tend to biz.
But here we've been a-slavin' more like bosses than like men
To diskiver that the people do not hanker arter Ben;
It is fur Jeems G. Blaine an' not for Harrison they shout—
And the gobble-uns 'el git us
    Ef we
    Don't
    Watch
    Out!

When I think of the fate that is waiting for Ben,
I pine for the peace of my childhood again;
I wish in my sorrow I could strip to the soul
And hop off once more in the old swimmin' hole!

The world is full of roses, and the roses full of dew
(Which is another word for soup) that drips for me and you.

"Little Benjy! Little Benjy!" chirps the robin in the tree;
"Little Benjy!" sighs the clover, "Little Benjy!" moans the bee;
"Little Benjy! Little Benjy!" murmurs John C. New,
A-stroking down the whiskers which the winds have whistled through.

Looks jest like his grampa, who's dead these many years—
He wears the hat his grampa wore, pulled down below his ears;
We'd like to have him four years more, but if he cannot stay—
Nothin' to say, good people; nothin' at all to say!

There, little Ben, don't cry!
They have busted your boom, I know;
And the second term
For which you squirm
Has gone where good niggers go!
But Blaine is safe, and the goose hangs high—
There, little Ben, don't cry!

Mabbe we'll git even for this unexpected shock,
When the frost is on the pumpkin and the fodder's in the shock!

Oh, the newspaper man! He works for paw;
He's the liveliest critter 'at ever you saw;
With whiskers 'at reach f'om his eyes to his throat.
He knows how to wheedle and rivet a vote;
He wunst wuz a consul 'way over the sea—
But never again a consul he'll be!
He come back f'om Lon'on one mornin' in May—
He come back for bizness, an' here he will stay—
Ain't he a awful slick newspaper man?
A newspaper, newspaper, newspaper man!

You kin talk about yer cities where the politicians meet—
You kin talk about yer cities where a decent man gits beat;
With the general run o' human kind I beg to disagree—
The little town of Tailholt is good enough f'r me!

Chicago was a pleasant town in eighteen-eighty-eight,
And I have lived in Washington long time in splendid state;

160

But all the present prospects are that after ninety-three
The little town o' Tailholt 'll be good enough f'r me!

———————

"I wunst lived in Indiany," said a consul, gaunt and grim,
As most of us Blaine delegates wuz kind o' guyin' him;
"I wunst lived in Indiany, and my views wuz widely read,
Fur I run a daily paper w'ich 'Lije Halford edited;
But since I've been away f'm home, my paper (seems to me)
Ain't nearly such a inflooence ez wot it used to be;
So, havin' done with consulin', I'm goin' to make a break
Towards making of a paper like the one I used to make."

———————

Think, if you kin, of his term mos' through,
An' that ol' man wantin' a secon' term, too;
Picture him bendin' over the form
Of his consul-gineril, stanch an' grim,
Who has stood the brunt of that jimblain storm—
An' that ol' man jest wrapt up in him!
An' the consul-gineril, with eyes all bleared
An' a haunted look in his ashen beard,
Kind o' gaspin' a feeble way—
But soothed to hear the ol' man say
In a meaning tone (as one well may
When words are handy and ———'s to pay):
"Good-by, John; take care of yo'self!"

———————

GETTIN' ON.

When I wuz somewhat younger,
  I wuz reckoned purty gay—
I had my fling at everything
  In a rollickin', coltish way,
But times have strangely altered
  Since sixty years ago—
This age of steam an' things don't seem
  Like the age I used to know,
Your modern innovations
  Don't suit me, I confess,
As did the ways of the good ol' days—
  But I'm gettin' on, I guess.

I set on the piazza
  An' hitch around with the sun—
Sometimes, mayhap, I take a nap,
  Waitin' till school is done,
An' then I tell the children
  The things I done in youth,
An' near as I can (as a venerable man)
  I stick to the honest truth!
But the looks of them 'at listen
  Seems sometimes to express
The remote idee that I'm gone—you see!
  An' I am gettin' on, I guess.

I get up in the mornin',
  An' nothin' else to do,
Before the rest are up and dressed
  I read the papers through;
I hang 'round with the women
  All day an' hear 'em talk,
An' while they sew or knit I show
  The baby how to walk;
An' somehow, I feel sorry
  When they put away his dress
An' cut his curls ('cause they're like a girl's)—
  I'm gettin' on, I guess!

Sometimes, with twilight round me,
  I see (or seem to see)
A distant shore where friends of yore
  Linger and watch for me;
Sometimes I've heered 'em callin'
  So tenderlike 'nd low
That it almost seemed like a dream I dreamed,
  Or an echo of long ago;
An' sometimes on my forehead
  There falls a soft caress,
Or the touch of a hand—you understand—
  I'm gettin' on, I guess.

MINNIE LEE.

Writing from an Indiana town a
young woman asks: "Is the enclosed
poem worth anything?"
We find that the poem is as follows:
    She has left us, our own darling—
      And we never more shall see
    Here on earth our dearly loved
        one—
      God has taken Minnie Lee.

    Her heart was full of goodness
      And her face was fair to see
    And her life was full of beauty—
      How we miss our Minnie Lee!

    But her work on earth is over
      And her spirit now is free
    She has gone to live in heaven—
      Shall we weep for Minnie Lee?

    Would we call our angel darling
      Back again across the sea?
    No! but sometime up in heaven
      We will meet loved Minnie Lee.
To the question as to whether this
poem is worth anything we chose to
answer in verse as follows:
    Sweet poetess, your poetry
      Is bad as bad can be,
    And yet we heartily deplore
      The death of Minnie Lee.

    It would have pleased us better
      If, in His wisdom, He
    Had taken you, sweet poetess,
      Instead of Minnie Lee.

    Your turn will come, however,
      And swift and sure 'twill be
    If you continue sending
      Your rhymes on Minnie Lee.

    From this we hope you will gather
      A dim surmise that we
    Don't take much stock in poems
      Concerning Minnie Lee.

LIZZIE.

    I wonder ef all wimmin air
    Like Lizzie is when we go out
    To theaters an' concerts where
    Is things the papers talk about.
    Do other wimmin fret and stew
    Like they wuz bein' crucified—
  Frettin' a show or a concert through,
    With wonderin' ef the baby cried?

    Now Lizzie knows that gran'ma's
      there
    To see that everything is right,
  Yet Lizzie thinks that gran'ma's care
    Ain't good enuf f'r baby, quite;
    Yet what am I to answer when
    She kind uv fidgets at my side,
      An' every now and then;
    "I wonder ef the baby cried?"

  Seems like she seen two little eyes
    A-pinin' f'r their mother's smile—
    Seems like she heern the pleadin'
      cries
  Uv one she thinks uv all the while;
    An' she's sorry that she come,
    'An' though she allus tries to hide
    The truth, she'd ruther stay to hum
    Than wonder ef the baby cried.

    Yes, wimmin folks is all alike—
    By Lizzie you kin jedge the rest.
    There never was a little tyke,
  But that his mother loved him best,
    And nex' to bein' what I be—
    The husband of my gentle bride—
  I'd wisht I wuz that croodlin' wee,
    With Lizzie wonderin' ef I cried.

OUR LADY OF THE MINE.

    The Blue Horizon wuz a mine us
      fellers all thought well uv,
  And there befell the episode I now
      perpose to tell uv;
    'Twuz in the year of sixty-nine—
      somewhere along in summer—
    There hove in sight one afternoon a
      new and curious comer;
    His name wuz Silas Pettibone—an
      artist by perfession,
    With a kit of tools and a big
mustache and a pipe in his possession;
    He told us, by our leave, he'd kind
      uv like to make some sketches
    Uv the snowy peaks, 'nd the foamin'
crick, 'nd the distant mountain stretches;

"You're welkim, sir," sez we,
although this scenery dodge seemed to us
A waste uv time where scenery wuz
already sooper-floo-us.

All through the summer Pettibone
kep' busy at his sketchin'—
At daybreak, off for Eagle Pass, and
home at nightfall, fetchin'
That everlastin' book uv his with
spider lines all through it—
Three-Fingered Hoover used to say
there warn't no meanin' to it—
"God durn a man," sez he to him,
"whose shif'less hand is sot at
A-drawin' hills that's full of quartz
that's pinin' to be got at!"
"Go on," sez Pettibone, "go on, if
joshin' gratifies ye,
But one uv these fine times, I'll
show ye sumthin' will surprise ye!"
The which remark led us to think—
although he didn't say it—
That Pettibone wuz owin' us a
gredge 'nd meant to pay it.

One evenin' as we sat around the
restauraw de Casey,
A-singin' songs 'nd tellin' yarns the
which wuz sumwhat racy,
In come that feller Pettibone 'nd sez:
"With your permission
I'd like to put a picture I have made
on exhibition."
He sot the picture on the bar 'nd
drew aside its curtain,
Sayin': "I recken you'll allow as how
that's art, f'r certain!"
And then we looked, with jaws
agape, but nary word wuz spoken,
And f'r a likely spell the charm uv
silence wuz unbroken—
Till presently, as in a dream,
remarked Three-Fingered Hoover:
"Onless I am mistaken, this is
Pettibone's shef doover!"
It wuz a face, a human face—a
woman's, fair 'nd tender,
Sot gracefully upon a neck white as
a swan's, and slender;
The hair wuz kind of sunny, 'nd the
eyes wuz sort uv dreamy,
The mouth wuz half a-smilin', 'nd
the cheeks wuz soft 'nd creamy;

It seemed like she wuz lookin' off
into the west out yonder,
And seemed like, while she looked,
we saw her eyes grow softer, fonder—
Like, lookin' off into the west where
mountain mists wuz fallin',
She saw the face she longed to see
and heerd his voice a-callin';
"Hooray!" we cried; "a woman in
the camp uv Blue Horizon—
Step right up, Colonel Pettibone, 'nd
nominate your pizen!"

A curious situation—one deservin'
uv your pity—
No human, livin' female thing this
side of Denver City!
But jest a lot uv husky men that
lived on sand 'nd bitters—
Do you wonder that that woman's
face consoled the lonesome critters?
And not a one but what it served in
some way to remind him
Of a mother or a sister or a
sweetheart left behind him—
And some looked back on happier
days and saw the old-time faces
And heerd the dear familiar sounds
in old familiar places—
A gracious touch of home—"Look
here," sez Hoover, "ever'body
Quit thinkin' 'nd perceed at oncet to
name his favorite toddy!"

It wuzn't long afore the news had
spread the country over,
And miners come a-flockin' in like
honey bees to clover;
It kind uv did 'em good they said, to
feast their hungry eyes on
That picture uv Our Lady in the
camp uv Blue Horizon.
But one mean cuss from Nigger
Crick passed criticisms on 'er—
Leastwise we overheerd him call her
Pettibone's madonner,
The which we did not take to be
respectful to a lady—
So we hung him in a quiet spot that
wuz cool 'nd dry 'nd shady;
Which same might not have been
good law, but it wuz the right maneuver
To give the critics due respect for
Pettibone's shef doover.

Gone is the camp—yes, years ago,
the Blue Horizon busted,
And every mother's son uv us got up
one day 'nd dusted,
While Pettibone perceeded east with
wealth in his possession
And went to Yurrup, as I heerd, to
study his perfession;
So, like as not, you'll find him now
a-paintin' heads 'nd faces
At Venus, Billy Florence and the
like I-talyun places—
But no such face he'll paint again as
at old Blue Horizon,
For I'll allow no sweeter face no
human soul sot eyes on;
And when the critics talk so grand
uv Paris 'nd the loover,
I say: "Oh, but you orter seen the
Pettibone shef doover!"

PENN-YAN BILL.

I.

In gallus old Kentucky, where the
grass is very blue,
Where the liquor is the smoothest
and the girls are fair and true,
Where the crop of he-gawd
gentlemen is full of heart and sand,
And the stock of four-time winners
is the finest in the land;
Where the democratic party in
bourbon hardihood
For more than half a century
unterrified has stood,
Where nod the black-eyed Susans to
the prattle of the rill—
There—there befell the wooing of
Penn-Yan Bill.

II.

Down yonder in the cottage that is
nestling in the shade
Of the walnut trees that seem to love
that quiet little glade
Abides a pretty maiden of the bonny
name of Sue—
As pretty as the black-eyed flow'rs
and quite as modest, too;
And lovers came there by the score,
of every age and kind,
But not a one (the story goes) was
quite to Susie's mind.
Their sighs, their protestations, and
their pleadings made her ill—
Till at once upon the scene hove
Penn-Yan Bill.

III.

He came from old Montana and he
rode a broncho mare,
He had a rather howd'y'do and
rough-and-tumble air;
His trousers were of buckskin and
his coat of furry stuff—
His hat was drab of color and its
brim was wide enough;
Upon each leg a stalwart boot
reached just above the knee,
And in the belt about his waist his
weepons carried he;
A rather strapping lover for our little
Susie—still,
She was his choice and he was hers,
was Penn-Yan Bill.

IV.

We wonder that the ivy seeks out
the oaken tree,
And twines her tendrils round him,
though scarred and gnarled he be;
We wonder that a gentle girl, unused
to worldly cares,
Should choose a man whose life has
been a constant scrap with bears;
Ah, 'tis the nature of the vine, and of
the maiden, too—
So when the bold Montana boy
came from his lair to woo,
The fair Kentucky blossom felt all
her heartstrings thrill
Responsive to the purring of Penn-
Yan Bill.

V.

He told her of his cabin in the
mountains far away,
Of the catamount that howls by
night, the wolf that yawps by day;
He told her of the grizzly with the
automatic jaw,
He told her of the Injun who
devours his victims raw;
Of the jayhawk with his tawdry crest
and whiskers in his throat,
Of the great gosh-awful sarpent and
the Rocky mountain goat.

A book as big as Shakespeare's or as Webster's you could fill
With the yarns that emanated from Penn-Yan Bill!

VI.

Lo, as these mighty prodigies the westerner relates,
Her pretty mouth falls wide agape— her eyes get big as plates;
And when he speaks of varmints that in the Rockies grow
She shudders and she clings to him and timidly cries "Oh!"
And then says he: "Dear Susie, I'll tell you what to do—
You be my wife, and none of these 'ere things dare pester you!"
And she? She answers, clinging close and trembling yet: "I will."
And then he gives her one big kiss, does Penn-Yan Bill.

VII.

Avaunt, ye poet lovers, with your wishywashy lays!
Avaunt, ye solemn pedants, with your musty, bookish ways!
Avaunt, ye smurking dandies who air your etiquette
Upon the gold your fathers worked so long and hard to get!
How empty is your nothingness beside the sturdy tales
Which mountaineers delight to tell of border hills and vales—
Of snaix that crawl, of beasts that yowl, of birds that flap and trill
In the wild egregious altitude of Penn-Yan Bill.

VIII.

Why, over all these mountain peaks his honest feet have trod—
So high above the rest of us he seemed to walk with God;
He's breathed the breath of heaven, as it floated, pure and free,
From the everlasting snow-caps to the mighty western sea;
And he's heard that awful silence which thunders in the ear:
"There is a great Jehovah, and His biding place is here!"
These—these solemn voices and these the sights that thrill
In the far-away Montana of Penn-Yan Bill.

IX.

Of course she had to love him, for it was her nature to;
And she'll wed him in the summer, if all we hear be true.
The blue grass will be waving in that cool Kentucky glade
Where the black-eyed Susans cluster in the pleasant walnut shade—
Where the doves make mournful music and the locust trills a song
To the brook that through the pasture scampers merrily along;
And speechless pride and rapture ineffable shall fill
The beatific bosom of Penn-Yan Bill!

ED.

Ed was a man that played for keeps, 'nd when he tuk the notion,
You cudn't stop him any more'n a dam 'ud stop the ocean;
For when he tackled to a thing 'nd sot his mind plum to it,
You bet yer boots he done that thing though it broke the bank to do it!
So all us boys uz knowed him best allowed he wusn't jokin'
When on a Sunday he remarked uz how he'd gin up smokin'.
Now this remark, that Ed let fall, fell, ez I say, on Sunday—
Which is the reason we wuz shocked to see him sail in Monday
A-puffin' at a snipe that sizzled like a Chinese cracker
An' smelt fur all the world like rags instead uv like terbacker;
Recoverin' from our first surprise, us fellows fell to pokin'
A heap uv fun at "folks uz said how they had gin up smokin'."
But Ed—sez he: "I found my work cud not be done without it—
Jes' try the scheme yourself, my friends, ef any uv you doubt it!

It's hard, I know, upon one's health,
but there's a certain beauty
In makin' sackerfices to the stern
demand uv duty!
So, wholly in a sperrit uv denial 'nd
concession
I mortify the flesh 'nd fur the sake
uv my perfession!"

HOW SALTY WIN OUT.

Used to think that luck wuz luck and
nuthin' else but luck—
It made no diff'rence how or when
or where or why it struck;
But sev'ral years ago I changt my
mind and now proclaim
That luck's a kind uv science—same
as any other game;
It happened out in Denver in the
spring uv '80, when
Salty teched a humpback an' win out
ten.

Salty wuz a printer in the good ol'
Tribune days,
An', natural-like, he fell in love with
the good ol' Tribune ways;
So, every Sunday evenin' he would
sit into the game
Which in this crowd uv
thoroughbreds I think I need not name;
An' there he'd sit until he rose, an',
when he rose he wore
Invariably less wealth about his
person than before.

But once there come a powerful
change; one sollum Sunday night
Occurred the tidle wave what put ol'
Salty out o' sight!
He win on deuce an' ace an' jack—
he win on king an' queen—
Cliff Bill allowed the like uv how he
win wuz never seen!
An' how he done it wuz revealed to
all us fellers when
He said he teched a humpback to
win out ten.

There must be somethin' in it for he
never win afore,
An' when he tole the crowd about
the humpback, how they swore!
For every sport allows it is a losin'
game to buck
Agin the science of a man who's
teched a hump f'r luck;
An' there is no denyin' luck was
nowhere in it when
Salty teched a humpback an' win out
ten.

I've had queer dreams an' seen queer
things, an' allus tried to do
The thing that luck apparently
intended f'r me to;
Cats, funerils, cripples, beggars have
I treated with regard,
An' charity subscriptions have hit
me powerful hard;
But what's the use uv talkin'? I say,
an' say again;
You've got to tech a humpback to
win out ten!

So, though I used to think that luck
wuz lucky, I'll allow
That luck, for luck, agin a hump
ain't nowhere in it now!
An' though I can't explain the whys
an' wherefores, I maintain
There must be somethin' in it when
the tip's so straight an' plain;
For I wuz there an' seen it, an' got
full with Salty when
Salty teched a humpback and win
out ten!

HIS QUEEN.

Our gifted and genial friend, Mr. William J. Florence, the comedian, takes to verses as naturally as a canvas-back duck takes to celery sauce. As a balladist he has few equals and no superiors, and when it comes to weaving compliments to the gentler sex he is without a peer. We find in the New York Mirror the latest verses from Mr. Florence's pen; they are entitled "Pasadene," and the first stanza flows in this wise:
I've journeyed East, I've journeyed
West,
And fair Italia's fields I've seen;
But I declare
None can compare

166

With thee, my rose-crowned Pasadene.
Following this introduction come five stanzas heaping even more glowing compliments upon this Miss Pasadene—whoever she may be—we know her not. They are handsome compliments, beautifully phrased, yet they give us the heartache, for we know Mrs. Florence, and it grieves us to see her husband dribbling away his superb intellect in penning verses to other women. Yet we think we understand it all; these poets have a pretty way of hymning the virtues of their wives under divers aliases. So, catching the afflatus of the genial actor-poet's muse, we would answer:

Come, now, who is this Pasadene
That such a whirl of praises warrant?
And is a rose
Her only clo'es?
Oh, fie upon you, Billy Florence!

Ah, no; that's your poetic way
Of turning loose your rhythmic torrents—
This Pasadene
Is not your queen—
We know you know we know it, Florence!

So sing your songs of women folks—
We'll read without the least abhorrence,
Because we know
Through weal and woe
Your queen is Mrs. Billy Florence!

ALASKAN BALLADRY.—III.
(Skans in Love.)

I am like the wretched seal
Wounded by a barbed device—
Helpless fellow! how I bellow,
Floundering on the jagged ice!

Sitka's beauty is the steel
That hath wrought this piteous woe:
Yet would I rather die
Than recover from the blow!

Still I'd rather live than die,
Grievous though my torment be;
Smite away, but, I pray,
Smite no victim else than me!

THE BIGGEST FISH.

When, in the halcyon days of old, I was a little tyke,
I used to fish in pickerel ponds for minnows and the like;
And, oh, the bitter sadness with which my soul was fraught
When I rambled home at nightfall with the puny string I'd caught!
And, oh, the indignation and the valor I'd display
When I claimed that all the biggest fish I'd caught had got away!

Sometimes it was the rusty hooks, sometimes the fragile lines,
And many times the treacherous reeds were actually to blame.
I kept right on at losing all the monsters just the same—
I never lost a little fish—yes, I am free to say
It always was the biggest fish I caught that got away.
And so it was, when, later on, I felt ambition pass
From callow minnow joys to nobler greed for pike and bass;
I found it quite convenient, when the beauties wouldn't bite
And I returned all bootless from the watery chase at night,
To feign a cheery aspect and recount in accents gay
How the biggest fish that I had caught had somehow got away.

And, really, fish look bigger than they are before they're caught—
When the pole is bent into a bow and the slender line is taut,
When a fellow feels his heart rise up like a doughnut in his throat
And he lunges in a frenzy up and down the leaky boat!
Oh, you who've been a-fishing will indorse me when I say

That it always is the biggest fish you catch that gets away!

'Tis even so in other things—yes, in our greedy eyes
The biggest boon is some elusive, never-captured prize;
We angle for the honors and the sweets of human life—
Like fishermen we brave the seas that roll in endless strife;
And then at last, when all is done and we are spent and gray,
We own the biggest fish we've caught are those that get away.

I would not have it otherwise; 'tis better there should be
Much bigger fish than I have caught a-swimming in the sea;
For now some worthier one than I may angle for that game—
May by his arts entice, entrap, and comprehend the same;
Which, having done, perchance he'll bless the man who's proud to say
That the biggest fish he ever caught were those that got away.

BONNIE JIM CAMPBELL: A LEGISLATIVE MEMORY.

Bonnie Jim Campbell rode up the glen,
But it wasn't to meet the butterine men;
It wasn't Phil Armour he wanted to see,
Nor Haines nor Crafts—though their friend was he.
Jim Campbell was guileless as man could be—
No fraud in his heart had he;
'Twas all on account of his character's sake
That he sought that distant Wisconsin lake.
* * * * * *
Bonnie Jim Campbell came riding home,
And now he sits in the rural gloom;
A tear steals furtively down his nose
As salt as the river that yonder flows;
To the setting sun and the rising moon
He plaintively warbles the good old tune:

"Of all the drinks that ever were made—
From sherbet to circus lemonade—
Not one's so healthy and sweet, I vow,
As the rich, thick cream of the Elgin cow!
Oh, that she were here to enliven the scene,
Right merry would be our hearts, I ween;
Then, then again, Bob Wilbanks and I
Would take it by turns and milk her dry!
We would stuff her paunch with the best of hay
And milk her a hundred times a day!"

'Tis thus that Bonnie Jim Campbell sings—
A young he-angel with sprouting wings;
He sings and he prays that Fate'll allow
Him one more whack at the Elgin cow!

LYMAN, FREDERICK AND JIM.

Lyman and Frederick and Jim, one day,
Set out in a great big ship—
Steamed to the ocean down to the bay
Out of a New York slip.
"Where are you going and what is your game?"
The people asked to those three.
"Darned, if we know; but all the same
Happy as larks are we;
And happier still we're going to be!"
Said Lyman
And Frederick
And Jim.

The people laughed "Aha, oho!
Oho, aha!" laughed they;
And while those three went sailing
so
Some pirates steered that way.
The pirates they were laughing,
too—
The prospect made them glad;
But by the time the job was through
Each of them pirates bold and bad,
Had been done out of all he had
By Lyman
And Frederick
And Jim.

Days and weeks and months they
sped,
Painting that foreign clime
A beautiful, bright vermillion red—
And having a — of a time!
'Twas all so gaudy a lark, it seemed,
As if it could not be,
And some folks thought it a dream
they dreamed
Of sailing that foreign sea,
But I'll identify you these three—
Lyman
And Frederick
And Jim.

Lyman and Frederick are bankers
and sich
And Jim is an editor kind;
The first two named are awfully rich
And Jim ain't far behind!
So keep your eyes open and mind
your tricks,
Or you are like to be
In quite as much of a Tartar fix
As the pirates that sailed the sea
And monkeyed with the pardners
three,
Lyman
And Frederick
And Jim.

A WAIL.

My name is Col. Johncey New,
And by a hoosier's grace
I have congenial work to do
At 12 St. Helen's place.
I was as happy as a clam
A-floating with the tide,
Till one day came a cablegram
To me from t'other side.

It was a Macedonian cry
From Benjy o'er the sea;
"Come hither, Johncey, instantly,
And whoop things up for me!"
I could not turn a callous ear
Unto that piteous cry;
I packed my grip, and for the pier
Directly started I.

Alas! things are not half so fair
As four short years ago—
The clouds are gathering
everywhere
And boisterous breezes blow;
My wilted whiskers indicate
The depth of my disgrace—
Would I were back, enthroned in
state,
At 12 St. Helen's place!

The saddest words, as I'll allow,
That drop from tongue or pen,
Are these sad words I utter now:
"They can't, shan't, won't have Ben!"
So, with my whiskers in my hands,
My journey I'll retrace,
To wreak revenge on foreign lands
At 12 St. Helen's place.

CLENDENIN'S LAMENT.

While bridal knots are being tied
And bridal meats are being basted,
I shiver in the cold outside
And pine for joys I've never tasted.

Oh, what's a nomination worth,
When you have labored months to
get it
If, all at once, with heartless mirth,
The cruel senator's upset it?

Fate weaves me such a toilsome
way,
My modest wisdom may not ken
it—
But, all the same, a plague I say
Upon that stingy, hostile senate!

ON THE WEDDING OF G. C.

(June 2, 1886.)

Oh, hand me down my spike tail coat
And reef my waistband in,
And tie this necktie round my throat
And fix my bosom pin;
I feel so weak and flustered like,
I don't know what I say—
For I am to be wedded to-day, Dan'l,
I'm to be wedded to-day!

Put double sentries at the doors
And pull the curtains down,
And tell the democratic bores
That I am out of town;
It's funny folks haint decency
Enough to stay away,
When I'm to be wedded to-day, Dan'l,
I'm to be wedded to-day!

The bride, you say, is calm and cool
In satin robes of white—
Well, I am stolid, as a rule,
But now I'm flustered quite;
Upon a surging sea of bliss
My soul is borne away,
For I'm to be wedded to-day, Dan'l,
I'm to be wedded to-day!

TO G. C.
(July 12, 1886.)

They say our president has stuck
Above his good wife's door
The sign provocative of luck—
A horseshoe—nothing more.

Be hushed, O party hates, the while
That emblem lingers there,
And thou, dear fates, propitious smile
Upon the wedded pair.

I've tried the horseshoe's weird intent
And felt its potent joy—
God bless you, Mr. President,
And may it be a boy.

TO DR. F. W. R.

If I were rich enough to buy
A case of wine (though I abhor it),
I'd send a quart of extra dry
And willingly get trusted for it.
But, lackaday! You know that I'm
As poor as Job's historic turkey—
In lieu of Mumm, accept this rhyme,
An honest gift though somewhat jerky.

This is your silver wedding day—
You didn't mean to let me know it!
And yet your smiles and raiments gay
Beyond all peradventure show it!
By all you say and do it's clear
A birdling in your heart is singing,
And everywhere you go you hear
The old-time bridal bells a-ringing.

Ah, well, God grant that these dear chimes
May mind you of the sweetness only
Of those far distant, callow times
When you were Benedick and lonely—
And when an angel blessed your lot—
For angel is your helpmeet, truly—
And when, to share the joy she brought,
Came other little angels, duly.

So here's a health to you and wife—
Long may you mock the Reaper's warning,
And may the evening of your life
In rising sons renew the morning;
May happiness and peace and love
Come with each morrow to caress ye,
And when you're done with earth, above—
God bless ye, dear old friend—God bless ye!

HORACE'S ODE TO "LYDIA" ROCHE.

No longer the boys,
With their music and noise,
Demand your election as mayor;
Such a milk-wagon hack
Has no place on the track

When his rival's a thoroughbred
stayer.

With your coarse, shallow wit
Every rational cit
At last is completely disgusted;
The tool of the rings,
Trusts, barons, and things,
What wonder, I wonder, you're
busted!

As soon as that Yerkes
Finds out you can't work his
Intrigues for the popular nickel,
With a tear to deceive you
He'll drop you and leave you
In your normal condition—a pickle.

Go, dodderer, go
Where the whisker winds blow
And spasms of penitence trouble;
Or flounder and whoop
In an ocean of soup
Where the pills of adversity bubble.

A PARAPHRASE, CIRCA 1715.

Since Chloe is so monstrous fair,
With such an eye and such an air,
What wonder that the world
complains
When she each am'rous suit
disdains?

Close to her mother's side she clings
And mocks the death her folly
brings
To gentle swains that feel the smarts
Her eyes inflict upon their hearts.

Whilst thus the years of youth go by,
Shall Colin languish, Strephon die?
Nay, cruel nymph! come, choose a
mate,
And choose him ere it be too late!

A PARAPHRASE,
OSTENSIBLY BY DR. I. W.

Why, Mistress Chloe, do you bother
With prattlings and with vain ado
Your worthy and industrious
mother,
Eschewing them that come to woo?

Oh, that the awful truth might
quicken
This stern conviction to your breast:
You are no longer now a chicken
Too young to quit the parent nest.

So put aside your froward carriage
And fix your thoughts, whilst yet
there's time,
Upon the righteousness of marriage
With some such godly man as I'm.

HORACE I, 27.

In maudlin spite let Thracians fight
Above their bowls of liquor,
But such as we, when on a spree,
Should never bawl and bicker!

These angry words and clashing
swords
Are quite de trop, I'm thinking;
Brace up, my boys, and hush your
noise,
And drown your wrath in drinking.

Aha, 'tis fine—this mellow wine
With which our host would dope us!
Now let us hear what pretty dear
Entangles him of Opus.

I see you blush—nay, comrades,
hush!
Come, friend, though they despise
you,
Tell me the name of that fair
dame—
Perchance I may advise you.

O wretched youth! and is it truth
You love that fickle lady?
I, doting dunce, courted her once,
And she is reckoned shady!

HEINE'S "WIDOW OR
DAUGHTER."

Shall I woo the one or the other?
Both attract me—more's the pity!
Pretty is the widowed mother,
And the daughter, too, is pretty.

When I see that maiden shrinking,
By the gods, I swear I'll get 'er!
But, anon, I fall to thinking
That the mother'll suit me better!

So, like any idiot ass—
Hungry for the fragrant fodder,
Placed between two bales of grass,
Lo, I doubt, delay, and dodder!

HORACE II, 20.

Maecenas, I propose to fly
To realms beyond these human portals;
No common things shall be my wings,
But such as sprout upon immortals.

Of lowly birth, once shed of earth,
Your Horace, precious (so you've told him),
Shall soar away—no tomb of clay
Nor Stygian prison house shall hold him.

Upon my skin feathers begin
To warn the songster of his fleeting;
But never mind—I leave behind
Songs all the world shall keep repeating.

Lo, Boston girls with corkscrew curls,
And husky westerns, wild and woolly,
And southern climes shall vaunt my rhymes—
And all profess to know me fully.

Methinks the west shall know me best
And therefore hold my memory dearer,
For by that lake a bard shall make
My subtle, hidden meanings clearer.

So cherished, I shall never die—
Pray, therefore, spare your dolesome praises,
Your elegies and plaintive cries,
For I shall fertilize no daisies!

HORACE'S SPRING POEM.
(Odes I, 4.)

The western breeze is springing up,
the ships are in the bay,
And Spring has brought a happy
change as Winter melts away;
No more in stall or fire the herd or
plowman finds delight,
No longer with the biting frosts the
open fields are white.

Our Lady of Lythera now prepares
to lead the dance,
While from above the ruddy moon
bestows a friendly glance;
The nymphs and comely Graces join
with Venus and the choir,
And Vulcan's glowing fancy lightly
turns to thoughts of fire.

Now is the time with myrtle green to
crown the shining pate,
And with the early blossoms of the
spring to decorate;
To sacrifice to Faunus—on whose
favor we rely—
A sprightly lamb, mayhap a kid, as
he may specify.

Impartially the feet of Death at huts
and castles strike—
The influenza carries off the rich
and poor alike;
O Sestius! though blest you are
beyond the common run,
Life is too short to cherish e'en a
distant hope begun.

The Shades and Pluto's mansion
follow hard upon la grippe—
Once there you cannot throw at dice
or taste the wine you sip,
Nor look on Lycidas, whose beauty
you commend,
To whom the girls will presently
their courtesies extend.

HORACE TO LIGURINE.
(Odes IV, 10.)

O cruel fair,
Whose flowing hair

172

The envy and the pride of all is,
As onward roll
The years, that poll
Will get as bald as a billiard ball is;
Then shall your skin, now pink and dimply,
Be tanned to parchment, sear and pimply!

When you behold
Yourself grown old
These words shall speak your spirits moody:
"Unhappy one!
What heaps of fun
I've missed by being goody-goody!
Oh! that I might have felt the hunger
Of loveless age when I was younger!"

HORACE ON HIS MUSCLE.
(Epode VI.)

You (blatant coward that you are!)
Upon the helpless vent your spite;
Suppose you ply your trade on me—
Come, monkey with this bard and see
How I'll repay your bark with bite!

Ay, snarl just once at me, you brute!
And I shall hound you far and wide,
As fiercely as through drifted snow
The shepherd dog pursues what foe
Skulks on the Spartan mountain side!

The chip is on my shoulder, see?
But touch it and I'll raise your fur;
I'm full of business; so beware,
For, though I'm loaded up for bear,
I'm quite as likely to kill a cur!

HORACE TO MAECENAS.
(Odes III, 29.)

Dear noble friend! a virgin cask
Of wine solicits attention—
And roses fair, to deck your hair,
And things too numerous to mention,
So tear yourself awhile away
From urban turmoil, pride and splendor
And deign to share what humble fare
And sumptuous fellowship I tender;
The sweet content retirement brings
Smoothes out the ruffled front of kings.

The evil planets have combined
To make the weather hot and hotter—
By parboiled streams the shepherd dreams
Vainly of ice-cream soda-water;
And meanwhile you, defying heat,
With patriotic ardor ponder
On what old Rome essays at home
And what her heathen do out yonder.
Maecenas, no such vain alarm
Disturbs the quiet of this farm!

God in his providence observes
The goal beyond this vale of sorrow,
And smiles at men in pity when
They seek to penetrate the morrow.
With faith that all is for the best,
Let's bear what burdens are presented,
That we shall say, let come what may,
"We die, as we have lived, contented!
Ours is to-day; God's is the rest—
He doth ordain who knoweth best!"

Dame Fortune plays me many a prank—
When she is kind, oh! how I go it!
But if, again, she's harsh, why, then
I am a very proper poet!
When favoring gales bring in my ships,
I hie to Rome and live in clover—
Elsewise, I steer my skiff out here,
And anchor till the storm blows over.
Compulsory virtue is the charm
Of life upon the Sabine farm!

HORACE IN LOVE AGAIN.
(Epode XI.)

Dear Pettius, once I reeled off rhyme
Satiric, sad and tender,
But now my quill
Has lost its skill
And I am dying in my prime
Through love of female gender!
Nay, do not laugh
Nor deign to chaff
Your friend with taunts of Lyde
And other dames
Who've been my flames—
This time it's bona-fide!

I maunder sadly to and fro—
I who was once so jolly!
My old time chums
Gyrate their thumbs
And taunt me, as I sighing go,
With what they term my folly.
I told you once,
Lake a garrulous dunce,
Of my all consuming passion,
And I rolled my eyes
In tragedy wise
And raved in lovesick fashion.

And when I'd aired my woes profound
You volunteered this warning:
"Horace, go light
On the bowl to-night—
Ten hours of sleep will bring you round
All right to-morrow morning!"
Now ten hours sleep
May do a heap
For callow hearts a-patter,
But I tell you, sir,
This affair du coeur
Of mine is a serious matter!

"GOOD-BY—GOD BLESS YOU!"

I like the Anglo-Saxon speech
With its direct revealings—
It takes a hold and seems to reach
Way down into your feelings;
That some folk deem it rude, I know,
And therefore they abuse it;
But I have never found it so—
Before all else I choose it.
I don't object that men should air
The Gallic they have paid for—
With "au revoir," "adieu, ma chere"—
For that's what French was made for—
But when a crony takes your hand
At parting to address you,
He drops all foreign lingo and
He says: "Good-by—God bless you!"

This seems to me a sacred phrase
With reverence impassioned—
A thing come down from righteous days,
Quaintly but nobly fashioned;
It well becomes an honest face—
A voice that's round and cheerful;
It stays the sturdy in his place
And soothes the weak and fearful.
Into the porches of the ears
It steals with subtle unction
And in your heart of hearts appears
To work its gracious function;
And all day long with pleasing song
It lingers to caress you—
I'm sure no human heart goes wrong
That's told "Good-by—God bless you!"

I love the words—perhaps because,
When I was leaving mother,
Standing at last in solemn pause
We looked at one another,
And—I saw in mother's eyes
The love she could not tell me—
A love eternal as the skies,
Whatever fate befell me;
She put her arms about my neck
And soothed the pain of leaving,
And, though her heart was like to break,
She spoke no word of grieving;
She let no tear bedim her eye,
For fear that might distress me,
But, kissing me, she said good-by
And asked her God to bless me.

HORACE.
(Epode XIV.)

You ask me, friend,
Why I don't send

The long since due-and-paid-for
numbers—
Why, songless, I
As drunken lie
Abandoned to Lethæan slumbers.

Long time ago
(As well you know)
I started in upon that carmen;
My work was vain—
But why complain?
When gods forbid, how helpless are
men!

Some ages back,
The sage Anack
Courted a frisky Samian body,
Singing her praise
In metered phrase
As flowing as his bowls of toddy.

'Till I was hoarse
Might I discourse
Upon the cruelties of Venus—
'Twere waste of time
As well of rhyme,
For you've been there yourself,
Maecenas!

Perfect your bliss,
If some fair miss
Love you yourself and not your
minæ;
I, fortune's sport,
All vainly court
The beauteous, polyandrous Phryne!

HORACE I, 23.

Chloe, you shun me like a hind
That, seeking vainly for her mother,
Hears danger in each breath of wind
And wildly darts this way and
t'other.

Whether the breezes sway the wood
Or lizards scuttle through the
brambles,
She starts, and off, as though
pursued,
The foolish, frightened creature
scrambles.

But, Chloe, you're no infant thing
That should esteem a man an ogre—
Let go your mother's apron-string
And pin your faith upon a toga!

A PARAPHRASE.

How happens it, my cruel miss,
You're always giving me the mitten?
You seem to have forgotten this:
That you no longer are a kitten!

A woman that has reached the years
Of that which people call discretion
Should put aside all childish fears
And see in courtship no
transgression.

A mother's solace may be sweet,
But Hymen's tenderness is sweeter,
And though all virile love be meet,
You'll find the poet's love is metre.

A PARAPHRASE BY CHAUCER.

Syn that you, Chloe, to your moder
sticken,
Maketh all ye yonge bacheloures
full sicken;
Like as a lyttel deere you been y-
hiding
Whenas come lovers with theyre
pityse chiding,
Sothly it ben faire to give up your
moder
For to beare swete company with
some oder;
Your moder ben well enow so farre
shee goeth,
But that ben not farre enow, God
knoweth;
Wherefore it ben sayed that foolysh
ladyes
That marrye not shall leade an aype
in Hayde;
But all that do with gode men wed
full quicklye
When that they be on dead go to ye
seints full sickerly.

HORACE I, 5.

What perfumed, posie-dizened
sirrah,
With smiles for diet,
Clasps you, O fair but faithless
Pyrrha,
On the quiet?
For whom do you bind up your
tresses,
As spun-gold yellow—
Meshes that go with your caresses,
To snare a fellow?

How will he rail at fate capricious,
And curse you duly;
Yet now he deems your wiles
delicious—
You perfect truly!
Pyrrha, your love's a treacherous
ocean—
He'll soon fall in there!
Then shall I gloat on his commotion,
For I have been there!

HORACE I, 20.

Than you, O valued friend of mine!
A better patron non est—
Come, quaff my home-made Sabine
wine—
You'll find it poor but honest.

I put it up that famous day
You patronized the ballet
And the public cheered you such a
way
As shook your native valley.

Cæcuban and the Calean brand
May elsewhere claim attention,
But I have none of these on hand—
For reasons I'll not mention.

ENVOY.

So come! though favors I bestow
Can not be called extensive,
Who better than my friend should
know
That they're, at least, expensive!

HORACE II, 7.

Pompey, what fortune gives you
back
To the friends and the gods who
love you—
Once more you stand in your native
land,
With your native sky above you!
Ah, side by side, in years agone,
We've faced tempestuous weather,
And often quaffed
The genial draft
From an amphora together!

When honor at Phillippi fell
A pray to brutal passion,
I regret to say that my feet ran away
In swift Iambic fashion;
You were no poet-soldier born,
You staid, nor did you wince then—
Mercury came
To my help, which same
Has frequently saved me since then.

But now you're back, let's celebrate
In the good old way and classic—
Come, let us lard our skins with nard
And bedew our souls with Massic!
With fillets of green parsley leaves
Our foreheads shall be done up,
And with song shall we
Protract our spree
Until the morrow's sun-up.

HORACE I, 11.

Seek not, Lucome, to know how
long you're going to live yet—
What boons the gods will yet
withhold, or what they're going to give
yet;
For Jupiter will have his way,
despite how much we worry—
Some will hang on for many a day
and some die in a hurry,
The wisest thing for you to do is to
embark this diem
Upon a merry escapade with some
such bard as I am;
And while we sport, I'll reel you off
such odes as shall surprise ye—
To-morrow, when the headache
comes—well, then I'll satirize ye!

HORACE I, 13.

When, Lydia, you (once fond and true,
    But now grown cold and supercilious)
Praise Telly's charms of neck and arms—
    Well, by the dog! it makes me bilious!

Then, with despite, my cheeks wax white,
    My doddering brain gets weak and giddy,
My eyes o'erflow with tears which show
    That passion melts my vitals, Liddy!

Deny, false jade, your escapade,
    And, lo! your wounded shoulders show it!
No manly spark left such a mark—
    (Leastwise he surely was no poet!)

With savage buss did Telephus
    Abraid your lips, so plump and mellow—
As you would save what Venus gave,
    I charge you shun that awkward fellow!

And now I say thrice happy they
    That call on Hymen to requite 'em;
For, though love cools, the wedded fools
    Must cleave 'till death doth disunite 'em!

HORACE IV, 1.

O Mother Venus, quit, I pray,
    Your violent assailing;
The arts, forsooth, that fired my youth
    At last are unavailing—
My blood runs cold—I'm getting old
    And all my powers are failing!

Speed thou upon thy white swan's wings
    And elsewhere deign to mellow
With my soft arts the anguished hearts
    Of swain that writhe and bellow;
And right away, seek out, I pray,
    Young Paullus—he's your fellow.

You'll find young Paullus passing fate,
    Modest, refined, and toney—
Go, now, incite the favored wight!
    With Venus for a crony.
He'll outshine all at feast and ball
    And conversazione!

Then shall that godlike nose of thine
    With perfumes be requited,
And then shall prance in Salian dance
    The girls and boys delighted,
And, while the lute blends with the flute,
    Shall tender loves be blighted.

But as for me—as you can see—
    I'm getting old and spiteful;
I have no mind to female kind
    That once I deemed delightful—
No more brim up the festive cup
    That sent me home at night full.

Why do I falter in my speech,
    O cruel Ligurine?
Why do I chase from place to place
    In weather wet and shiny?
Why down my nose forever flows
    The tear that's cold and briny?

HORACE TO HIS PATRON.

Mæcenas, you're of noble line—
    (Of which the proof convincing
Is that you buy me all my wine
    Without so much as wincing.)

To different men of different minds
    Come different kinds of pleasure;
There's Marshall Field—what joy he finds
    In shears and cloth-yard measure!

With joy Prof. Swing is filled
    While preaching godly sermons;
With bliss is Hobart Taylor thrilled
    When he is leading germans.

While Uncle Joe Medill prefers
To run a daily paper,
To Walter Gresham it occurs
That law's the proper caper.

With comedy a winning card,
How blithe is Richard Hooley;
Per contra, making soap and lard,
Rejoices Fairbank duly.

While Armour in the sugar ham
His summum bonum reaches,
MacVeagh's as happy as a clam
In canning pears and peaches.

Let Farwell glory in the fray
Which party hate increases—
His son-in-law delights to play
Gavottes and such like pieces.

So each betakes him to his task—
So each his hobby nurses—
While I—well, all the boon I ask
Is leave to write my verses.

Give, give that precious boon to me
And I shall envy no man;
If not the noblest I shall be
At least the happiest Roman!

THE "ARS POETICA" OF HORACE—XVIII.
(Lines 323-333.)

The Greeks had genius—'twas a gift
The Muse vouchsafed in glorious
measure;
The boon of Fame they made their
aim
And prized above all worldly
treasure.

But we—how do we train our
youth?
Not in the arts that are immortal,
But in the greed for gains that speed
From him who stands at Death's
dark portal.

Ah, when this slavish love of gold
Once binds the soul in greasy fetters,
How prostrate lies—how droops and
dies
The great, the noble cause of letters!

HORACE I, 34.

I have not worshiped God, my
King—
Folly has led my heart astray;
Backward I turn my course to learn
The wisdom of a wiser way.

How marvelous is God, the King!
How do His lightnings cleave the
sky—
His thundering car spreads fear afar,
And even hell is quaked thereby!

Omnipotent is God, our King!
There is no thought He hath not
read,
And many a crown His hand plucks
down
To place it on a worthier head!

HORACE I, 33.

Not to lament that rival flame
Wherewith the heartless Glycera
scorns you,
Nor waste your time in maudlin
rhyme,
How many a modern instance warns
you.

Fair-browed Lycoris pines away
Because her Cyrus loves another;
The ruthless churl informs the girl
He loves her only as a brother.

For he, in turn, courts Pholoe—
A maid unscotched of love's fierce
virus—
Why, goats will mate with wolves
they hate
Ere Pholoe will mate with Cyrus!

Ah, weak and hapless human
hearts—
By cruel Mother Venus fated
To spend this life in hopeless strife,
Because incongruously mated!

Such torture, Albius, is my lot;

For, though a better mistress wooed me,
My Myrtale has captured me
And with her cruelties subdued me!

THE "ARS POETICA" OF HORACE—I.
(Lines 1-23.)

Should painters attach to a fair human head
The thick, turgid neck of a stallion,
Or depict a spruce lass with the tail of a bass—
I am sure you would guy the rapscallion!

Believe me, dear Pisos, that such a freak
Is the crude and preposterous poem
Which merely abounds in a torrent of sounds
With no depth of reason below 'em.

'Tis all very well to give license to art—
The wisdom of license defend I;
But the line should be drawn at the fripperish sprawn
Of a mere cacoethes scribendi.

It is too much the fashion to strain at effects—
Yes, that's what's the matter with Hannah!
Our popular taste by the tyros debased
Paints each barnyard a grove of Diana!

Should a patron require you to paint a marine,
Would you work in some trees with their barks on?
When his strict orders are for a Japanese jar,
Would you give him a pitcher like Clarkson?

Now this is my moral: Compose what you may,
And fame will be ever far distant,
Unless you combine with a simple design
A treatment in toto consistent.

THE GREAT JOURNALIST IN SPAIN.

Good Editor Dana—God bless him, we say!
Will soon be afloat on the main,
Will be steaming away
Through the mist and the spray
To the sensuous climate of Spain.

Strange sights shall he see in that beautiful land
Which is famed for its soap and Moor,
For, as we understand,
The scenery is grand,
Though the system of railway is poor.

For moonlight of silver and sunlight of gold
Glint the orchards of lemons and mangoes,
And the ladies, we're told,
Are a joy to behold
As they twine in their lissome fandangoes.

What though our friend Dana shall twang a guitar
And murmur a passionate strain—
Oh, fairer by far
Than these ravishments are
The castles abounding in Spain!

These castles are built as the builder may list—
They are sometimes of marble or stone,
But they mostly consist
Of east wind and mist
With an ivy of froth overgrown.

A beautiful castle our Dana shall raise
On a futile foundation of hope,
And its glories shall blaze
In the somnolent haze
Of the mythical lake del y Soap.

The fragrance of sunflowers shall swoon on the air,

And the visions of dreamland obtain,
And the song of "World's Fair"
Shall be heard everywhere
Through that beautiful castle in Spain.

REID, THE CANDIDATE.

I saw a brave compositor
Go hustling o'er the mead,
Who bore a banner with these words:
"Hurrah for Whitelaw Reid!"

"Where go you, brother slug," I asked,
"With such unusual speed?"
He quoth: "I go to dump my vote
For gallant Whitelaw Reid!"

"But what has Whitelaw done," I asked,
"That now he should succeed?"
Said he: "The stanchest, truest friend
We have is Whitelaw Reid!

"There are no terms we can suggest
That he will not concede;
He is converted to our faith,
Is gallant Whitelaw Reid!

"The union it must be preserved—
That is this convert's creed,
And that is why we're whooping up
The cause of Whitelaw Reid!"

"If what you say of him be sooth,
You have a friend indeed,
So go on your winding way," quoth I,
"And whoop for Whitelaw Reid!"

So on unto the polls I saw
That printer straight proceed
While other printers swarmed in swarms
To vote for Whitelaw Reid.

A VALENTINE.

Four little sisters standing in a row—
Which of them I love best I really do not know.
Sometimes it is the sister dressed out so fine in blue,
And sometimes she who flaunts the beauteous robe of emerald hue;
Sometimes for her who wears the brown my tender heart has bled,
And then again I am consumed of love for her in red.
So now I think I'll send this valentine unto the four—
I love them all so very much—how could a man do more?

KISSING-TIME.

'Tis when the lark goes soaring,
And the bee is at the bud,
When lightly dancing zephyrs
Sing over field and flood;
When all sweet things in Nature
Seem joyfully a-chime—
'Tis then I wake my darling,
For it is kissing-time!

Go, pretty lark, a-soaring,
And suck your sweets, O bee;
Sing, O ye winds of summer,
Your songs to mine and me.
For with your song and rapture
Cometh the moment when
It is half-past kissing-time
And time to kiss again!

So—so the days go fleeting
Like golden fancies free,
And every day that cometh
Is full of sweets for me;
And sweetest are those moments
My darling comes to climb
Into my lap to mind me
That it is kissing-time.

Sometimes, may be, he wanders
A heedless, aimless way—
Sometimes, may be, he loiters
In pretty, prattling play;
But presently bethinks him
And hastens to me then,
For it's half-past kissing time
And time to kiss again!

THE FIFTH OF JULY.

The sun climbs up, but still the tyrant Sleep
Holds fast our baby boy in his embrace;
The slumb'rer sighs, anon athwart his face
Faint, half-suggested frowns like shadows creep,
One little hand lies listless on his breast,
One little thumb sticks up with mute appeal,
While motley burns and powder marks reveal
The fruits of boyhood's patriotic zest.

Our baby's faithful poodle crouches near—
He, too, is weary of the din and play
That come with glorious Independence Day,
But which, thank God! come only once a year!
And Fido, too, has suffered in this cause,
Which once a year right noisily obtains,
For Fido's tail—or what thereof remains—
Is not so fair a sight as once it was.

PICNIC-TIME.

It's June agin, an' in my soul I feel the fillin' joy
That's sure to come this time o' year to every little boy;
For, every June, the Sunday schools at picnics may be seen,
Where "fields beyont the swellin' floods stand dressed in livin' green."
Where little girls are skeered to death with spiders, bugs an' ants,
An' little boys get grass-stains on their go-to-meetin' pants.
It's June agin, an' with it all what happiness is mine—
There's goin' to be a picnic an' I'm goin' to jine!

One year I jined the Baptists, an' goodness! how it rained!
(But grampa says that that's the way "Baptizo" is explained.)
And once I jined the 'piscopils an' had a heap o' fun—
But the boss of all the picnics was the Presbyterium!
They had so many puddin's, sallids, sandwidges an' pies,
That a feller wisht his stummick was as hungry as his eyes!
Oh, yes, the eatin' Presbyteriums give yer is so fine
That when they have a picnic, you bet I'm goin' to jine!

But at this time the Methodists have special claims on me,
For they're goin' to give a picnic on the 21st, D. V.;
Why should a liberal Universalist like me object
To share the joys of fellowship with every friendly sect?
However het'rodox their articles of faith elsewise may be,
Their doctrine of fried chick'n is a savin' grace to me!
So on the 21st of June, the weather bein' fine,
They're goin' to give a picnic, and I'm goin' to jine!

THE ROMANCE OF A WATCH.

One day his father said to John:
"Come here and see what I hev bought—
A Waterbury watch, my son—
It is the boon you long hev sought!"

The boy could scarcely believe his eyes—
The watch was shiny, smooth an' slick—
He snatched the nickel-plated prize
An' wound away to hear it tick.

He wound an' wound, an' wound an' wound,
An' kept a windin' fit to kill—

The weeks an' months an' years
rolled round,
But John he kep' a windin', still!

As autumns came an' winters went
An' summers follered arter spring,
John didn't mind—he was intent
On windin' up that darned ol' thing.

He got to be a poor ol' man—
He's bald an' deaf an' blind an' lame,
But, like he did when he began,
He keeps on windin', jest the same!

OUR BABY.

'Tis very strange, but quite as true,
That when our Baby smiles
Our club gets walloped black and
blue
In all the latest styles;
But when our Baby's hopping mad
It's quite the other way—
Chicago beats the Yankees bad
When Baby doesn't play.

When baby stands upon his base,
Just after having kicked,
Upon his Scandinavian face
Appears the legend, "Licked";
But when he orders out a sub,
We well may hip-hooray—
Chicago has the winning club
When Baby doesn't play.

But, if our Baby's getting old,
And stiff, and cross, and vain,
And if his days are nearly told,
Oh, let us not complain.
Let's rather think of what he was
And how he's made it pay
To hire the kids that win because
Our Baby doesn't play.

THE COLOR THAT SUITS ME BEST.

Any color—so long as it's red—
Is the color that suits me best,
Though I will allow there is much to
be said
For yellow and green and the rest;
But the feeble tints, which some
affect
In the things they make or buy,
Have never (I say it with all respect)
Appealed to my critical eye.

There's that in red that warmeth the
blood
And quickeneth a man within,
And bringeth to speedy and perfect
bud
The germs of original sin;
So, though I am properly born and
bred,
I'll own, with a certain zest,
That any color—so long as it's red—
Is the color that suits me best!

For where is a color that can be
compared
With the blush of a buxom lass—
Or where such warmth as of the hair
Of the genuine white horse class?
And, lo, reflected in this cup
Of cherry Bordeaux I see
What inspiration girdeth me up—
Yes, red is the color for me!

Through acres and acres of art I've
strayed
In Italy, Germany, France;
On many a picture a master has
made
I've squandered a passing glance;
Marines I hate, madonnas and
Those Dutch freaks I detest!
But the peerless daubs of my native
land—
They're red, and I like them best!

'Tis little I care how folks deride—
I'm backed by the west, at least,
And we are free to say that we can't
abide
The tastes that obtain down east;
And we are mighty proud to have it
said
That here in the critical west,
Most any color—so long as it's
red—
Is the color that suits us best!

HOW TO "FILL."

It is understood that our esteemed Col. Franc B. Wilkie is going to formulate a reply to Mrs. Ella Wheeler Wilcox's latest poem, which begins as follows:
"I hold it as a changeless law
From which no soul can sway or swerve,
We have that in us which will draw
Whate'er we need or most deserve."
We fancy the genial colonel will start off with some such quatrain as this:
"I fain would have your recipe,
If you'll but give the snap away;
Now when four clubs are dealt to me,
How may I draw another, pray?"

POLITICS IN 1888.

The Cleveland Leader must be getting ready for the campaign of 1888. We find upon its editorial page quite a pretentious poem, entitled "Alpha and Omega," and here is a sample stanza:
"Whose name will stand for coming time
As hypocrites in prose and rhyme,
And be despised in every clime?
The Mugwumps."
Well, may be so, but may we be permitted to add a stanza which seems to us to be very pertinent just now?
And who next year, we'd like to know,
Will feed the Cleveland Leader crow,
Just as they did three years ago?
The Mugwumps.

THE BASEBALL SCORE.

A boy came racing down the street
In a most tumultuous way,
And he hollered at all he chanced to meet:
"Hooray, hooray, hooray!"
His eyes and his breath were hot with joy
And his cheeks were all aflame—
'Twas a rare event with the little boy
When the champions won a game!

"Twenty to 6" and "10 to 2"
Were rather dismal scores,
And they wreathed in a somewhat somber hue
These classic western shores;
We shuddered and winced at the cruel sport
And our heads were bowed in shame
'Till Somewhere sent us the glad report
That the champions won the game!

Our Baby says it'll be all right
For the champions by and by,
And the twin emotions of Hope and Fright
Gleam in his cod fish eye;
And Spalding says (in his modest way)
That we'll get there all the same;
So let us holler, "Hooray, hooray,"
When the champions win the game.

CHICAGO NEWSPAPER LIFE.

It pleases us to observe that the shocking habit of hurling opprobrious epithets at each other has been abandoned by the venerable editor of the Journal and the venerable editor of the Tribune. At this moment we are reminded of the inspired lines of the eminent but now, alas! neglected Watts:
"Birds in their nests agree,
And 'tis a shocking sight
When folks, who should harmonious be,
Fall out and chide and fight.

"The tones of Andy and of Joe
Should join in friendly games—
Not be debased to vice so low
As that of calling names.

"Bad names and naughty names require
To be chastized at school,
But he's in danger of hell-fire
Who talks of 'crank' and 'fool.'

"Oh 'tis a dreadful thing to see
The old folks smite and jaw,

But pleasant it is to agree
On the election law.

"Let Joe and Andy leave their wrongs
For sinners to contest;
So shall they some time swell the songs
Of Israel's ransomed blest."

THE MIGHTY WEST.

Oh, where abides the fond kazoo,
The barrel-organ fair,
And where is heard the tra-la-loo
Of fish horns on the air?
And where are found the fife and drum
Discoursed with goodliest zest?
And where do fiddles liveliest hum?
The west—the mighty west!

Sonatas, fugues, and all o' that
Are rightly judged effete,
While largos written in B-flat
Are clearly out of date;
Some like the cold pianny-forty,
But whistling suits us best—
And op'ry, if it isn't naughty,
Will not catch on out west.

From skinning hogs or canning beef
Or diving into stocks,
Could we expect to find relief
In Haydns or in Bachs?
Ah, no; from pork and wheat and lard
We turn aside with zest
To sing some opus of some bard
Whose home is in the west.

So get ye gone, ye weakling crew!
Your tunes are stale and flat,
And cannot hold a candle to
The works of Silas Pratt!
His opuses are in demand
And are the final test
By which all others fall or stand
In this the mighty west!

APRIL.

Now April with sweet showers of freshening rain
Has roused last summer's vigorous breath once more;
'Tis in the air, the house, the street, the lane—
Puffs through the walls and oozes through the floor.

The rau-cous-throated frog ayont the sty
Sends forth, as erst, his amerous vermal croak,
Each hungry mooly casts her swivel eye
For pots and pails in which her nose to poke.

With gurgling glee the gutter gushes by,
Fraught all with filth, unknown and nameless dirt—
A dead green goose, an o'er-ripe rat I spy;
Head of a cat, tail of a flannel shirt.

The querulous cry of every gabbling goose
From thousand-scented mudholes echoes o'er;
The dogs and yawling cats have gotten loose
And mock the hideous howls of hell once more.

By yon scrub oak, where roots the sallow sow,
In where John Murphy's wife outpours her slop;
Right there you'll find there's almost stench now
To cause the world its nostrils to estop.

And yonder dauntless goat that bank adown,
That wreathes his old fantastic horns so high,
Gnaws sadly on the bustle of Miss Brown,
Which she discarded in the months gone by.

So in Goose Island cometh April round;

Full eagerly we watch the month's
approach—
The season of sweet sight and
pleasant sound,
The season of the bedbug and the
roach.

REPORT OF THE BASEBALL GAME.

It was a very pleasant game,
And there was naught of grumbling
Until the baleful tidings came
That Williamson was "fumbling."
Then all at once a hideous gloom
Fell o'er all manly features,
And Clayton's cozy, quiet room
Was full of frantic creatures.

"Click, click," the tiny ticker went,
The tape began to rattle,
And pallid, eager faces bent
To read the news from battle;
Down, down, ten million feet or
more,
Chicago's hope went tumbling,
When came the word that Burns and
Gore
And Pfeffer, too, were "fumbling."

No diagram was needed then
To point the Browns to glory—
The simple fact that these four men
Were "fumbling" told the story.
There is not a club in all the land—
No odds how weak or humble—
That beats us when our short-stop
and
Our second baseman "fumble."

There was some talk of hippodrome
'Mid frequent calls for liquor,
Then each Chicago man went home
Much wiser, poorer, sicker;
And many a giant intellect
Seemed slowly, surely crumbling
Beneath the dolorous effect
Of that St. Louis "fumbling."

Ah, well, the struggle's but just
begun,
So what is the use of fretting
If by a little harmless fun
Our boys can bull the betting?

When comes the tug of war there'll
be
No accidental stumbling,
And then, you bet your boots, you'll
see
No mention made of "fumbling."

THE ROSE.

Since the days of old Adam the
welkin has rung
With the praises of sweet scented
posies,
And poets in rapturous phrases have
sung
The paramount beauties of roses.

Wheresoever she bides, whether
nestling in lanes
Or gracing the proud urban bowers,
The red, royal rose her distinction
maintains
As the one regnant queen among
flowers.

How joyous are we of the west
when we find
That Fate, with her gifts ever chary,
Has decreed that the Rose, who is
queen of her kind
Shall bloom on our wild western
prairie.

Let us laugh at the east as an
impotent thing
With envy and jealously crazy,
While grateful Chicago is happy to
sing
In the praise of the rose—she's a
daisy.

KANSAS CITY VS. DETROIT.

A rooster flapped his wings and
crowed
A merrysome cockadoodledoo,
As out of the west a cowboy rode
To the land where the peach and the
clapboard grew,
Humming a gentle tralalaloo.

"O insect with the gilded wing,"
The cowboy cried, "Pray tell me true

Why do you crane your neck and sing
That wearisome cockadoodledoo?
Would you like to learn the tralalaloo?"

Now the rooster squawked an impudent word
Whereat the angered cowboy threw
His lariat at the haughty bird
And choked him until his gills were blue
And his eyes hung out an inch or two.

"Now hear me sing," the cowboy cried;
"It ain't no cockadoodledoo—
It's a song we sing on the prairies wide—
The simple song of tralalaloo,
Which is cowboy slang for 12 to 2."

ME AND BILKAMMLE.

I will, if you choose,
Impart you some news
That will greatly astound you, I know;
You would never suspect
My ambition was wreck'd
'Till you heard my confession of woe.
'Tis not that my boom
Has ascended the flume—
In other words, gone up the spout—
I could smile a sweet smile
This tempestuous while,
But me and Bilkammle are out!

Being timid and shrinkin',
He did all the thinkin',
When I did the talkin' worth mention;
'Twas my constant ambition
To soar to position
So I gave it exclusive attention;
And supposin' that he
Would of course be for me,
I rambled and prattled about
'Till I found to my horror,
Vexation, and sorror,
That me and Bilkammle were out.

As I tore my red hair
In a fit of despair
I heard my Achates complain
That the gent with the coffer
Had nothing to offer
In the way of relieving his pain!
* * * * * *
If there's mortal to blame
For this villainous game
Which has snuffed a great man beyond doubt.
It's that treacherous mammal
Entitled Bilkammle—
Which accounts for us two bein' out!

TO THE DETROIT BASEBALL CLUB.

You've scooped the vealy city crowd
Of glory and of purse—
Why shouldn't Pegasus be proud
To trot you out in a verse?
Chicago hoped to wallop you
By a tremendous score,
But bit off more than it could chew,
As witness: "5 to 4."

Well done, you 'Ganders! here's a hand
To every one of you;
These record-breakers of the land
Now break themselves in two.
Well get their pennant—it shall float
Upon our distant shore,
So let each patriotic throat
Hurrah for "5 to 4."

A BALLAD OF ANCIENT OATHS.

Ther ben a knyght, Sir Hoten hight,
That on a time did swere
In mighty store othes mickle sore,
Whiche grieved his wiffe to here.

Soth, whenne she scoft, his wiffe did oft
Swere as a lady may;
"I'faith," "I'sooth," or "lawk" in truth
Ben alle that wiffe wold say.

186

Soe whenne her good man waxed him wood
She mervailed much to here
The hejeous sound of othes full round
The which her lord did swere.

"Now, pray thee, speke and tell me eke
What thing hath vexed thee soe?"
The wiffe she cried; but he replied
By swereing moe and moe.

Her sweren zounds which be Gog's wounds,
By bricht Marie and Gis,
By sweit Sanct Ann and holie Tan
And by Bryde's bell, ywis.

By holie grails, by 'slids and 'snails,
By old Sanct Dunstan bauld,
The virgin faire that him did beare,
By him that Judas sauld;

By Arthure's sword, by Paynim horde,
By holie modyr's teir,
By Cokis breath, by Zooks and 's death,
And by Sanct Swithen deir;

By divells alle, both greate and smalle,
And in hell there be,
By bread and salt, and by Gog's malt,
And by the blody tree;

By Him that worn the crown of thorn
And by the sun and mone,
By deir Sanct Blanc and Sanct Fillane,
And three kings of Cologne;

By the gude Lord and His sweit word,
By him that herryit hell,
By blessed Jude, by holie rude,
And eke be Gad himsell!

He sweren soe (and mickle moe)
It made man's flesch to creepen,
The air ben blue with his ado
And sore his wiffe ben wepen.

Giff you wold know why sweren soe
The goodman high Sir Hoten,
He ben full wroth, because, in soth,
He leesed his coler boten.

AN OLD SONG REVISED.

John Hamilton, my Jo John,
When first we were acquaint
You were as lavish as could be
With your vermillion paint;
But now the head that once was red
Seems veiled in sable woe,
And clouds of gloom obscure your boom,
John Hamilton, my Jo.

Oh, was it Campbell's hatchet wrought
The ruin we deplore?
Or was it Abnor Taylor's thirst
For your abundant gore?
Or was it Hank's ambitious pranks
That laid our idol low?
Come, let us know how came you so,
John Hamilton, my Joe!

We pine to know the awful truth.
So, pray, be pleased to tell
The story—full of tragic fire—
How one great statesman fell;
How dives' hand stalked in the land
And dealt a crushing blow
At one proud name—which you're the same,
John Hamilton, my Jo!

THE GRATEFUL PATIENT.

The doctor leaned tenderly over the bed
And looked at the patient's complexion,
And felt of the pulse and the feverish head,
Then stood for a time in reflection.
"A strange complication!
My recommendation

Is morphia by hypodermic
injection."

The patient looked up with a leer in
his eye
And winked in the doctor's
direction—
"Well, Doc," he remarked, "since
you say I must die,
I'm grateful to you for protection—
I'm now in position
To ask the commission
T' excuse me from serving as judge
of election."

───────────

THE BEGINNING AND THE END.

Death
In my breath,
Cried I then:
"Men
Burn and blight!
Nourish crime!
Scale the height!
Climb, men, climb!
Climb and fight!
Win by might!
Wrong or right!
Blood!"

Well
In a cell
Here I am—
D——n!
From my flight
So sublime
I alight
Ere my time,
And in fright
Here I grope
Through the night
Without hope.
What a plight!
Ah, the rope!
Thud!

───────────

CLARE MARKET.

In the market of Clare, so cheery the
glare
Of the shops and the booths of the
tradespeople there,
That I take a delight, on a Saturday
night,
In walking that way and viewing the
sight;
For it's here that one sees all the
objects that please—
New patterns in silk and old patterns
in cheese,
For the girls pretty toys, rude
alarums for boys,
And baubles galore which discretion
enjoys—
But here I forbear, for I really
despair
Of naming the wealth of the market
of Clare!

The rich man comes down from the
elegant town,
And looks at it all with an ominous
frown;
He seems to despise the
grandiloquent cries
Of the vender proclaiming his
puddings and pies;
And sniffing he goes through the
lanes that disclose
Much cause for disgust to his
sensitive nose;
Once free from the crowd, he admits
that he is proud
That elsewhere in London this
thing's not allowed—
He has seen nothing there but filth
everywhere,
And he's glad to get out of the
market of Clare.

But the child that has come from the
neighboring slum
Is charmed by the magic of dazzle
and hum;
He feasts his big eyes on the cakes
and pies
And they seem to grow green and
protrude with surprise
At the goodies they vend and the
toys without end—
And it's oh if he had but a penny to
spend!
But alas! he must gaze in a hopeless
amaze
At treasures that glitter and torches
that blaze—

What sense of despair in this world
    can compare
With that of the waif in the market
    of Clare?

So, on Saturday nights, when my
    custom invites
A stroll in old London for curious
    sights,
I am likely to stray by a devious way
    Where goodies are spread in a
        motley array,
The things which some eyes would
    appear to despise
Impress me as pathos in homely
    disguise,
And my tattered waif friend shall
    have pennies to spend,
As long as I've got 'em (or friends
    that will lend);
And the urchin shall share in my joy
    and declare
That there's beauty and good in that
    marketplace there!

UNCLE EPHRAIM.

My Uncle Ephraim was a man who
    did not live in vain,
And yet, why he succeeded so I
    never could explain;
By nature he was not endowed with
    wit to a degree,
But folks allowed there nowhere
    lived a better man than he;
He started poor but soon got rich; he
    went to congress then,
And held that post of honor long
    against much brainier men;
He never made a famous speech or
    did a thing of note,
And yet the praise of Uncle Eph
    welled up from every throat.

I recollect I never heard him say a
    bitter word;
He never carried to and fro
    unpleasant things he heard;
He always doffed his hat and spoke
    to every one he knew,
He tipped to poor and rich alike a
    genial "how-dy'-do";
He kissed the babies, praised their
looks, and said: "That child will grow
    To be a Daniel Webster or our
        president, I know!"
His voice was so mellifluous, his
    smile so full of mirth,
That folks declared he was the best
    and smartest man on earth!

Now, father was a smarter man, and
    yet he never won
Such wealth and fame as Uncle Eph,
    "the deestrick's favorite son";
He had "convictions" and he was not
    loath to speak his mind—
He went his way and said his say as
    he might be inclined;
Yes, he was brainy; yet his life was
    hardly a success—
He was too honest and too smart for
    this vain world, I guess!
At any rate, I wondered he was
    unsuccessful when
My Uncle Eph, a duller man, was so
    revered of men!

When Uncle Eph was dying he
    called me to his bed,
And in a tone of confidence
    inviolate he said:
"Dear Willyum, ere I seek repose in
    yonder blissful sphere
I fain would breathe a secret in your
    adolescent ear;
Strive not to hew your way through
    life—it really doesn't pay;
Be sure the salve of flattery soaps all
    you do and say!
Herein the only royal road to fame
    and fortune lies;
Put not your trust in vinegar—
    molasses catches flies!"

THIRTY-NINE.

O hapless day! O wretched day!
    I hoped you'd pass me by—
Alas, the years have sneaked away
    And all is changed but I!
Had I the power, I would remand
    You to a gloom condign,
But here you've crept upon me and
    I—I am thirty-nine!

Now, were I thirty-five, I could
    Assume a flippant guise,

Or, were I forty years, I should
Undoubtedly look wise;
For forty years are said to bring
Sedateness superfine,
But thirty-nine don't mean a thing—
A bas with thirty-nine!

You healthy, hulking girls and boys—
What makes you grow so fast?
Oh, I'll survive your lusty noise—
I'm tough and bound to last!
No, no—I'm old and withered, too—
I feel my powers decline.
(Yet none believes this can be true
Of one at thirty-nine.)

And you, dear girl with velvet eyes,
I wonder what you mean
Through all our keen anxieties
By keeping sweet sixteen.
With your dear love to warm my heart,
Wretch were I to repine—
I was but jesting at the start—
I'm glad I'm thirty-nine!

So, little children, roar and race
As blithely as you can
And, sweetheart, let your tender grace
Exalt the Day and Man;
For then these factors (I'll engage)
All subtly shall combine
To make both juvenile and sage
The one who's thirty-nine!

Yes, after all, I'm free to say
That I rejoice to be
Standing as I do stand to-day
'Twixt devil and deep sea;
For, though my face be dark with care
Or with a grimace shine,
Each haply falls unto my share;
Since I am thirty-nine!

'Tis passing meet to make good cheer
And lord it like a king,
Since only once we catch the year
That doesn't mean a thing.
O happy day! O gracious day!
I pledge thee in this wine—
Come let us journey on our way
A year, good Thirty-Nine!

HORACE I, 18.

O Varus mine
Plant thou the vine
Within this kindly soil of Tibur;
Nor temporal woes
Nor spiritual knows
The man who's a discreet imbiber.
For who doth croak
Of being broke
Or who of warfare, after drinking?
With bowl atween us,
Of smiling Venus
And Bacchus shall we sing, I'm thinking.

Of symptoms fell
Which brawls impel
Historic data give us warning;
The wretch who fights
When full of nights
Is bound to have a head next morning.
I do not scorn
A friendly horn,
But noisy toots—I can't abide 'em!
Your howling bat
Is stale and flat
To one who knows, because he's tried 'em!

The secrets of
The life of love
(Companionship with girls and toddy)
I would not drag
With drunken brag
Into the ken of everybody,
But in the shade
Let some coy maid
With smilax wreathe my flagon's nozzle—
Then, all day long,
With mirth and song,
Shall I enjoy a quiet sozzle!

THREE RHINELAND DRINKING SONGS.

I.

If our life is the life of a flower
(And that's what some sages are thinking),
We should moisten the bud with a health-giving flood
And 'twill bloom all the sweeter—
Yes, life's the completer
For drinking,
and drinking,
and drinking!

If it be that our life is a journey
(As many wise folks are opining),
We should sprinkle the way with the rain while we may;
Though dusty and dreary,
'Tis made cool and cheery
With wining,
and wining,
and wining!

If this life that we live be a dreaming
(As pessimist people are thinking),
To induce pleasant dreams there is nothing, me seems,
Like this sweet prescription,
That baffles description—
This drinking,
and drinking,
and drinking!

II.
("Fiducit.")
Three comrades on the German Rhine—
Defying care and weather—
Together quaffed the mellow wine
And sung their songs together,
What recked they of the griefs of life
With wine and song to cheer them?
Though elsewhere trouble might be rife,
It would not come anear them!

Anon one comrade passed away,
And presently another—
And yet unto the tryst each day
Repaired the lonely brother,
And still, as gayly as of old,
That third one, hero-hearted,
Filled to the brim each cup of gold
And called to the departed:

"O comrades mine, I see you not,
Nor hear your kindly greeting;
Yet in this old familiar spot
Be still our loving meeting!
Here have I filled each bouting cup
With juices red and cherry—
I pray ye drink the portion up,
And, as of old, make merry!"

And once before his tear-dimmed eyes,
All in the haunted gloaming,
He saw two ghostly figures rise
And quaff the beakers foaming;
He heard two spirit voices call:
"Fiducit, jovial brother!"
And so forever from that hall
Went they with one another.

III.
(Der Mann im Keller.)
How cool and fair this cellar where
My throne a dusky cask is!
To do no thing but just to sing
And drown the time my task is!
The cooper, he's
Resolved to please,
And, answering to my winking,
He fills me up
Cup after cup
For drinking, drinking, drinking.

Begrudge me not this cozy spot
In which I am reclining—
Why, who would burst with envious thirst
When he can live by wining?
A roseate hue seems to imbue
The world on which I'm blinking;
My fellow men—I love them when
I'm drinking, drinking, drinking.

And yet, I think, the more I drink,
It's more and more I pine for—
Oh such as I (forever dry!)
God made this land of Rhine for!
And there is bliss
In knowing this,
As to the floor I'm sinking;
I've wronged no man,
And never can,
While drinking, drinking, drinking!

THE THREE TAILORS.
(From the German of C. Herlossohn.)

I shall tell you in rhyme how, once on a time,
Three tailors tramped up to the Inn Ingleheim
On the Rhine—lovely Rhine;
They were broke, but, the worst of it all, they were curst
With that malady common to tailors—a thirst
For wine—lots of wine!

"Sweet host," quoth the three, "we're as hard up as can be,
Yet skilled in the practice of cunning are we
On the Rhine—genial Rhine;
And we pledge you we will impart you that skill
Right quickly and fully, providing you'll fill
Us with wine—cooling wine!"

But that host shook his head, and warily said:
"Though cunning be good, we take money instead,
On the Rhine—thrifty Rhine;
If ye fancy ye may without pelf have your way
You'll find there's both host and the devil to pay
For your wine—costly wine!"

Then the first knavish wight took his needle so bright
And threaded its eye with a wee ray of light
From the Rhine—sunny Rhine;
And in such a deft way patched a mirror that day
That where it was mended no expert could say—
Done so fine—'twas for wine!

The second thereat spied a poor little gnat
Go toiling along on his nose broad and flat
Toward the Rhine—pleasant Rhine;
"Aha, tiny friend, I should hate to offend,
But your stockings need darning," which same did he mend,
All for wine—soothing wine!

And next there occurred what you'll deem quite absurd—
His needle a space in the wall thrust the third,
By the Rhine—wondrous Rhine;
And then, all so spry, he leapt through the eye
Of that thin cambric needle; nay, think you I'd lie
About wine? Not for wine!

The landlord allowed (with a smile) he was proud
To do the fair thing by that talented crowd
On the Rhine—generous Rhine!
So a thimble filled he as full as could be;
"Drink long and drink hearty, my jolly guests three,
Of my wine—filling wine!"

MORNING HYMN.

I'd dearly love to tear my hair
And romp around a bit,
For I am mad enough to swear
Since Brother Chauncy quit.

I am so vilely prone to sin—
Vain ribald that I am—
I'd take a hideous pleasure in
Just one prodigious "damn."

But shall I yield to Satan's wiles
And let my passions swell?
Nay, I will wreath my face in smiles,
And mock the powers of hell.

And howsoever pride may roll
Its billows through my frame,
I'll not condemn my precious soul
Unto the quenchless flame!

But rather will I humbly pray
Divinity to wash
From out my mouth such words away
As "Jiminy" and "Gosh."

DOCTORS.

'Tis quite the thing to say and sing
    Gross libels on the doctor—
To picture him an ogre grim
    Or humbug-pill concocter;
Yet it's in quite another light
    My friendly pen would show him—
Glad that it might with verse repay
    Some part of what I owe him!

When one's all right he's prone to spite
    The doctor's peaceful mission;
But, when he's sick, it's loud and quick
    He bawls for a physician!
With other things the doctor brings
    Sweet babes our hearts to soften;
Though I have four, I pine for more—
    Good doctor, pray, come often!

What though he sees death and disease
    Run riot all around him,
Patient and true, and valorous, too—
    Such have I always found him!
Where'er he goes he soothes our woes,
    And, when skill's unavailing
And death is near, his words of cheer
    Support our courage failing.

In ancient days they used to praise
    The godlike art of healing;
An art that then engaged all men
    Possessed of sense and feeling;
Why, Raleigh—he was glad to be
    Famed for a quack elixir,
And Digby sold (as we are told)
    A charm for folk love-sick, sir!

Napoleon knew a thing or two,
    And clearly he was partial
To doctors, for, in time of war,
    He chose one for marshal,
In our great cause a doctor was
    The first to pass death's portal,
And Warren's name at once became
    A beacon and immortal!

A heap, indeed, of what we read
    By doctors is provided,
For to those groves Apollo loves
    Their leaning is decided;
Deny who may that Rabelais
    Is first in wit and learning—
And yet all smile and marvel while
    His brilliant leaves they're turning.

How Lever's pen has charmed all men—
    How touching Rab's short story!
And I will stake my all that Drake
    Is still the schoolboy's glory!
A doctor-man it was began
    Great Britain's great museum;
The treasures there are all so rare,
    It drives me wild to see 'em!

There's Cuvier, Parr and Rush—they are
    Big monuments to learning;
To Mitchell's prose (how smooth it flows!)
    We all are fondly turning;
Tomes might be writ of that keen wit
    Which Abernethy's famed for—
With bread-crumb pills he cured the ills
    Most doctors get blamed for!

In modern times the noble rhymes
    Of Holmes (a great physician!)
Have solace brought and wisdom taught
    To hearts of all conditions.
The sailor bound for Puget sound
    Finds pleasure still unfailing,
If he but troll the barcarole
    Old Osborne wrote on Whaling!

If there were need I could proceed
    Ad naus, with this prescription,
But, inter nos, a larger dose
    Might give you fits conniption;
Yet, ere I end, there's one dear friend
    I'd hold before these others,
For he and I in years gone by,
    Have chummed around like brothers.

Together we have sung in glee
    The songs old Horace made for
Our genial craft—together quaffed
    What bowls that doctor paid for!
I love the rest, but love him best,
    And, were not times so pressing,

I'd buy and send—you smile, old friend?
Well, then, here goes my blessing.

BEN APFELGARTEN.

There was a certain gentleman, Ben Apfelgarten called,
Who lived way off in Germany a many years ago,
And he was very fortunate in being very bald,
And so was very happy he was so.
He warbled all the day
Such songs as only they
Who are very, very circumspect and very happy may;
The people wondered why,
As the years went grinding by,
They never heard him once complain or even heave a sigh!

The women of the province fell in love with genial Ben,
Till (maybe you can fancy it) the dickens was to pay
Among the callow students and the sober-minded men—
With the women folk a-cuttin' up that way!
Why, they gave him turbans red
To adorn his hairless head,
And knitted jaunty nightcaps to protect him when abed!
In vain the rest demurred—
Not a single chiding word
Those ladies deigned to tolerate—remonstrance was absurd!

Things finally got into such a very dreadful way
That the others (oh, how artful!) formed the politic design
To send him to the reichstag; so, one dull November day
They elected him a member from the Rhine!
Then the other members said:
"Gott in Himmel; what a head!"
But they marveled when his speeches they listened to or read;
And presently they cried:
"There must be heaps inside
Of the smooth and shiny cranium his constituents deride!"

Well, when at last he up 'nd died—long past his ninetieth year—
The strangest and the most luguberous funeral he had,
For women came in multitudes to weep upon his bier—
The men all wond'ring why on earth the women had gone mad!
And this wonderment increased,
Till the sympathetic priest
Inquired of those same ladies: "Why this fuss about deceased?"
Whereupon they were appalled,
For, as one, those women squalled:
"We doted on deceased for being bald—bald—bald!"

He was bald because his genius burnt that shock of hair away,
Which, elsewise, clogs one's keenness and activity of mind,
And (barring present company, of course,) I'm free to say
That, after all, it's intellect that captures woman-kind.
At any rate, since then
(With a precedent in Ben),
The women-folk have been in love with us bald-headed men!

IN HOLLAND.

Our course lay up a smooth canal
Through tracks of velvet green,
And through the shade that windmills made,
And pasture lands between.
The kine had canvas on their backs
To temper Autumn's spite,
And everywhere there was an air
Of comfort and delight.

My wife, dear philosophic soul!
Saw here whereof to prate:
"Vain fools are we across the sea
To boast our nobler state!
Go north or south or east or west,
Or wheresoever you please,
You shall not find what's here combined—
Equality and ease!

"How tidy are these honest homes
In every part and nook—
The men folk wear a prosperous air,
The women happy look.
Seeing the peace that smiles around,
I would our land was such—
Think as you may, I'm free to say
I would we were the Dutch!"

Just then we overtook a boat
(The Golden Tulip hight)—
Big with the weight of motley
freight,
It was a goodly sight!
Meynheer van Blarcom sat on deck,
With pipe in lordly pose,
And with his son of twenty-one
He played at dominoes.

Then quoth my wife: "How fair to
see
This sturdy, honest man
Beguile all pain and lust of gain
With whatso joys he can;
Methinks his spouse is down below
Beading a kerchief gay—
A babe, mayhap, lolls in her lap
In the good old Milky way.

"Where in the land from whence we
came
Is there content like this—
Where such disdain of sordid gain,
Such sweet domestic bliss?
A homespun woman I, this land
Delights me overmuch—
Think as you will and argue still,
I like the honest Dutch."

And then my wife made end of
speech—
Her voice stuck in her throat,
For, swinging around the turn, we
found
What motor moved the boat;
Hitched up in tow-path harness there
Was neither horse nor cow,
But the buxom frame of a
Hollandische dame—
Meynheer van Blarcom's frau.

———————

Christmas Tales and Christmas Verse

Sing, O my heart! Sing thou in rapture this dear morn Whereon the blessed Prince is born!

Sing, Christmas bells!
Say to the earth this is the morn
Whereon our Savior-King is born;
Sing to all men,—the bond, the free,
The rich, the poor, the high, the low,
The little child that sports in glee,
The aged folk that tottering go,
—Proclaim the morn
That Christ is born,
That saveth them and saveth me!
Sing, angel host!
Sing of the star that God has placed
Above the manger in the East;
Sing of the glories of the night,
The virgin's sweet humility,
The Babe with kingly robes bedight,
—Sing to all men where'er they be
This Christmas morn; For Christ is born,
That saveth them and saveth me!
Sing, sons of earth!
O ransomed seed of Adam, sing!
God liveth, and we have a king!
The curse is gone, the bond are free
—By Bethlehem's star that brightly beamed,
By all the heavenly signs that be,
We know that Israel is redeemed;
That on this morn
The Christ is born
That saveth you and saveth me!
Sing, O my heart!
Sing thou in rapture this dear morn
Whereon the blessed Prince is born!
And as thy songs shall be of love,
So let my deeds be charity
By the dear Lord that reigns above,
By Him that died upon the tree,
By this fair morn
Whereon is born
The Christ that saveth all and me!

THE SYMBOL AND THE SAINT

Once upon a time a young man made ready for a voyage. His name was Norss; broad were his shoulders, his cheeks were ruddy, his hair was fair and long, his body betokened strength, and good-nature shone from his blue eyes and lurked about the corners of his mouth.

"Where are you going?" asked his neighbor Jans, the forge-master.

"I am going sailing for a wife," said Norss.

"For a wife, indeed!" cried Jans. "And why go you to seek her in foreign lands? Are not our maidens good enough and fair enough, that you must need search for a wife elsewhere? For shame, Norss! for shame!"

But Norss said: "A spirit came to me in my dreams last night and said, 'Launch the boat and set sail to-morrow. Have no fear; for I will guide you to the bride that awaits you.' Then, standing there, all white and beautiful, the spirit held forth a symbol—such as I had never before seen—in the figure of a cross, and the spirit said: 'By this symbol shall she be known to you.'"

"If this be so, you must need go," said Jans. "But are you well victualled? Come to my cabin, and let me give you venison and bear's meat."

Norss shook his head. "The spirit will provide," said he. "I have no fear, and I shall take no care, trusting in the spirit."

So Norss pushed his boat down the beach into the sea, and leaped into the boat, and unfurled the sail to the wind. Jans stood wondering on the beach, and watched the boat speed out of sight.

On, on, many days on sailed Norss—so many leagues that he thought he must have compassed the earth. In all this time he knew no hunger nor thirst; it was as the spirit had told him in his dream—no cares nor dangers beset him. By day the dolphins and the other creatures of the sea gambolled about his boat; by night a beauteous Star seemed to direct his course; and when he slept and dreamed, he saw ever the spirit clad in white, and holding forth to him the symbol in the similitude of a cross.

At last he came to a strange country—a country so very different from his own that he could scarcely trust his senses. Instead of the rugged mountains of the North, he saw a gentle landscape of velvety green; the trees were not pines and firs, but cypresses, cedars, and palms; instead of the cold, crisp air of his native land, he scented the perfumed zephyrs of the Orient; and the wind that filled the sail of his boat and smote his tanned cheeks was heavy and hot with the odor of cinnamon and spices. The waters were calm and blue—very different from the white and angry waves of Norss's native fiord.

As if guided by an unseen hand, the boat pointed straight for the beach of this strangely beautiful land; and ere its prow cleaved the shallower waters, Norss saw a maiden standing on the shore, shading her eyes with her right hand, and gazing intently at him. She was the most beautiful maiden he had ever looked upon. As Norss was fair, so was this maiden dark; her black hair fell loosely about her shoulders in charming contrast with the white raiment in which her slender, graceful form was clad. Around her neck she wore a golden chain, and therefrom was suspended a small symbol, which Norss did not immediately recognize.

"Hast thou come sailing out of the North into the East?" asked the maiden.

"Yes," said Norss.

"And thou art Norss?" she asked.

"I am Norss; and I come seeking my bride," he answered.

"I am she," said the maiden. "My name is Faia. An angel came to me in my dreams last night, and the angel said: 'Stand upon the beach to-day, and Norss shall come out of the North to bear thee home a bride.' So, coming here, I found thee sailing to our shore."

Remembering then the spirit's words, Norss said: "What symbol have you, Faia, that I may know how truly you have spoken?"

"No symbol have I but this," said Faia, holding out the symbol that was attached to the golden chain about her neck. Norss looked upon it, and lo! it was the symbol of his dreams,—a tiny wooden cross.

Then Norss clasped Faia in his arms and kissed her, and entering into the boat they sailed away into the North. In all their voyage neither care nor danger beset them; for as it had been told to them in their dreams, so it came to pass.

By day the dolphins and the other creatures of the sea gambolled about them; by night the winds and the waves sang them to sleep; and, strangely enough, the Star which before had led Norss into the East, now shone bright and beautiful in the Northern sky!

When Norss and his bride reached their home, Jans, the forge-master, and the other neighbors made great joy, and all said that Faia was more beautiful than any other maiden in the land. So merry was Jans that he built a huge fire in his forge, and the flames thereof filled the whole Northern sky with rays of light that danced up, up, up to the Star, singing glad songs the while. So Norss and Faia were wed, and they went to live in the cabin in the fir grove.

To these two was born in good time a son, whom they named Claus. On the night that he was born wondrous things came to pass. To the cabin in the fir grove came all the quaint, weird spirits,—the fairies, the elves, the trolls, the pixies, the fadas, the crions, the goblins, the kobolds, the moss-people, the gnomes, the dwarfs, the water-sprites, the courils, the bogles, the brownies, the nixies, the trows, the stille-volk,—all came to the cabin in the fir grove, and capered about and sang the strange, beautiful songs of the Mist-Land. And the flames of old Jans's forge leaped up higher than ever into the Northern sky, carrying the joyous tidings to the Star, and full of music was that happy night.

Even in infancy Claus did marvellous things. With his baby hands he wrought into pretty figures the willows that were given him to play with. As he grew older, he fashioned, with the knife old Jans had made for him, many curious toys,—carts, horses, dogs, lambs, houses, trees, cats, and birds, all of wood and very like to nature. His mother taught him how to make dolls too,—dolls of every kind, condition, temper, and color; proud dolls, homely dolls, boy dolls, lady dolls, wax dolls, rubber dolls, paper dolls, worsted dolls, rag dolls,—dolls of every description and without end. So Claus became at once quite as popular with the little girls as with the little boys of his native village; for he was so generous that he gave away all these pretty things as fast as he made them.

Claus seemed to know by instinct every language. As he grew older he would ramble off into the woods and talk with the trees, the rocks, and the beasts of the greenwood; or he would sit on the cliffs overlooking the fiord, and listen to the stories that the waves of the sea loved to tell him; then, too, he knew the haunts of the elves and the stille-volk, and many a pretty tale he learned from these little people. When night came, old Jans told him the quaint legends of the North, and his mother sang to him the lullabies she had heard when a little child herself in the far-distant East. And every night his mother held out to him the symbol in the similitude of the cross, and bade him kiss it ere he went to sleep.

So Claus grew to manhood, increasing each day in knowledge and in wisdom. His works increased too; and his liberality dispensed everywhere the beauteous things which his fancy conceived and his skill executed. Jans, being now a very old man, and having no son of his own, gave to Claus his forge and workshop, and taught him those secret arts which he in youth had learned from cunning masters. Right joyous now was Claus; and many, many times the Northern sky glowed with the flames that danced singing from the forge while Claus moulded his pretty toys. Every color of the rainbow were these flames; for they reflected the bright colors of the beauteous things strewn round that wonderful workshop. Just as of old he had dispensed to all children alike the homelier toys of his youth, so now he gave to all children alike these more beautiful and more curious gifts. So little children everywhere loved Claus, because he gave them pretty toys, and their parents loved him because he made their little ones so happy.

But now Norss and Faia were come to old age. After long years of love and happiness, they knew that death could not be far distant. And one day Faia said to Norss: "Neither you nor I, dear love, fear death; but if we could choose, would we not choose to live always in this our son Claus, who has been so sweet a joy to us?"

"Ay, ay," said Norss; "but how is that possible?"

"We shall see," said Faia.

That night Norss dreamed that a spirit came to him, and that the spirit said to him: "Norss, thou shalt surely live forever in thy son Claus, if thou wilt but acknowledge the symbol."

Then when the morning was come Norss told his dream to Faia, his wife; and Faia said:

"The same dream had I,—an angel appearing to me and speaking these very words."

"But what of the symbol?" cried Norss.

"I have it here, about my neck," said Faia.

So saying, Faia drew from her bosom the symbol of wood,—a tiny cross suspended about her neck by the golden chain. And as she stood there holding the symbol out to Norss, he—he thought of the time when first he saw her on the far-distant Orient shore, standing beneath the Star in all her maidenly glory, shading her beauteous eyes with one hand, and with the other clasping the cross,—the holy talisman of her faith.

"Faia, Faia!" cried Norss, "it is the same,—the same you wore when I fetched you a bride from the East!"

"It is the same," said Faia, "yet see how my kisses and my prayers have worn it away; for many, many times in these years, dear Norss, have I pressed it to my lips and breathed your name upon it. See now—see what a beauteous light its shadow makes upon your aged face!"

The sunbeams, indeed, streaming through the window at that moment, cast the shadow of the symbol on old Norss's brow. Norss felt a glorious warmth suffuse him, his heart leaped with joy, and he stretched out his arms and fell about Faia's neck, and kissed the symbol and acknowledged it. Then likewise did Faia; and suddenly the place was filled with a wondrous brightness and with strange music, and never thereafter were Norss and Faia beholden of men.

Until late that night Claus toiled at his forge; for it was a busy season with him, and he had many, many curious and beauteous things to make for the little children in the country round about. The colored flames leaped singing from his forge, so that the Northern sky seemed to be lighted by a thousand rainbows; but above all this voiceful glory beamed the Star, bright, beautiful, serene.

Coming late to the cabin in the fir grove, Claus wondered that no sign of his father or of his mother was to be seen. "Father—mother!" he cried, but he received no answer. Just then the Star cast its golden gleam through the latticed window, and this strange, holy light fell and rested upon the symbol of the cross that lay upon the floor. Seeing it, Claus stooped and picked it up, and kissing it reverently, he cried: "Dear talisman, be thou my inspiration evermore; and wheresoever thy blessed influence is felt, there also let my works be known henceforth forever!"

No sooner had he said these words than Claus felt the gift of immortality bestowed upon him; and in that moment, too, there came to him a knowledge that his parents' prayer had been answered, and that Norss and Faia would live in him through all time.

And lo! to that place and in that hour came all the people of Mist-Land and of Dream-Land to declare allegiance to him: yes, the elves, the fairies, the pixies,—all came to Claus, prepared to do his bidding. Joyously they capered about him, and merrily they sang.

"Now haste ye all," cried Claus,—"haste ye all to your homes and bring to my workshop the best ye have. Search, little hill-people, deep in the bowels of the earth for finest gold and choicest jewels; fetch me, O mermaids, from the bottom of the sea the treasures hidden there,—the shells of rainbow tints, the smooth, bright pebbles, and the strange ocean flowers; go, pixies, and other water-sprites, to your secret lakes, and bring me pearls! Speed! speed you all! for many pretty things have we to make for the little ones of earth we love!"

But to the kobolds and the brownies Claus said: "Fly to every house on earth where the cross is known; loiter unseen in the corners, and watch and hear the children through the day. Keep a strict account of good and bad, and every night bring back to me the names of good and bad that I may know them."

The kobolds and the brownies laughed gleefully, and sped away on noiseless wings; and so, too, did the other fairies and elves.

There came also to Claus the beasts of the forest and the birds of the air, and bade him be their master. And up danced the Four Winds, and they said: "May we not serve you, too?"

The Snow King came stealing along in his feathery chariot. "Oho!" he cried, "I shall speed over all the world and tell them you are coming. In town and country, on the mountain-tops and in the valleys,—wheresoever the cross is raised,—there will I herald your approach, and thither will I strew you a pathway of feathery white. Oho! oho!" So, singing softly, the Snow King stole upon his way.

But of all the beasts that begged to do him service, Claus liked the reindeer best. "You shall go with me in my travels; for henceforth I shall bear my treasures not only to the children of the North, but to the children in every land whither the Star points me and where the cross is lifted up!" So said Claus to the reindeer, and the reindeer neighed joyously and stamped their hoofs impatiently, as though they longed to start immediately.

Oh, many, many times has Claus whirled away from his far Northern home in his sledge drawn by the reindeer, and thousands upon thousands of beautiful gifts—all of his own making—has he borne to the children of every land; for he loves them all alike, and they all alike love him, I trow. So truly do they love him that they call him Santa Claus, and I am sure that he must be a saint; for he has lived these many hundred years, and we, who know that he was born of Faith and Love, believe that he will live forever.

CHRISTMAS EVE

Oh, hush thee, little Dear-my-Soul,
The evening shades are falling,
—Hush thee, my dear, dost thou not hear
The voice of the Master calling?
Deep lies the snow upon the earth,
But all the sky is ringing
With joyous song, and all night long
The stars shall dance, with singing.
Oh, hush thee, little Dear-my-Soul,
And close thine eyes in dreaming,
And angels fair shall lead thee where
The singing stars are beaming.
A shepherd calls his little lambs,
And he longeth to caress them;
He bids them rest upon his breast,
That his tender love may bless them.
So, hush thee, little Dear-my-Soul,
Whilst evening shades are falling,
And above the song of the heavenly throng
Thou shalt hear the Master calling.

JOEL'S TALK WITH SANTA CLAUS

One Christmas eve Joel Baker was in a most unhappy mood. He was lonesome and miserable; the chimes making merry Christmas music outside disturbed rather than soothed him, the jingle of the sleigh-bells fretted him, and the shrill whistling of the wind around the corners of the house and up and down the chimney seemed to grate harshly on his ears.

"Humph," said Joel, wearily, "Christmas is nothin' to me; there was a time when it meant a great deal, but that was long ago—fifty years is a long stretch to look back over. There is nothin' in Christmas now, nothin' for me at least; it is so long since Santa Claus remembered me that I venture to say he has forgotten that there ever was such a person as Joel Baker in all the world. It used to be different; Santa Claus used to think a great deal of me when I was a boy. Ah! Christmas nowadays ain't what it was in the good old time—no, not what it used to be."

As Joel was absorbed in his distressing thoughts he became aware very suddenly that somebody was entering or trying to enter the room. First came a draught of cold air, then a scraping, grating sound, then a strange shuffling, and then,—yes, then, all at once, Joel saw a pair of fat legs and a still fatter body dangle down the chimney, followed presently by a long white beard, above which appeared a jolly red nose and two bright twinkling eyes, while over the head and forehead was drawn a fur cap, white with snowflakes.

"Ha, ha," chuckled the fat, jolly stranger, emerging from the chimney and standing well to one side of the hearth-stone; "ha, ha, they don't have the big, wide chimneys they used to build, but they can't keep Santa Claus out—no, they can't keep Santa Claus out! Ha, ha, ha. Though the chimney were no bigger than a gas pipe, Santa Claus would slide down it!"

It didn't require a second glance to assure Joel that the new-comer was indeed Santa Claus. Joel knew the good old saint—oh, yes—and he had seen him once before, and, although that was when Joel was a little boy, he had never forgotten how Santa Claus looked.

Nor had Santa Claus forgotten Joel, although Joel thought he had; for now Santa Claus looked kindly at Joel and smiled and said: "Merry Christmas to you, Joel!"

"Thank you, old Santa Claus," replied Joel, "but I don't believe it's going to be a very merry Christmas. It's been so long since I've had a merry Christmas that I don't believe I'd know how to act if I had one."

"Let's see," said Santa Claus, "it must be going on fifty years since I saw you last—yes, you were eight years old the last time I slipped down the chimney of the old homestead and filled your stocking. Do you remember it?"

"I remember it well," answered Joel. "I had made up my mind to lie awake and see Santa Claus; I had heard tell of you, but I'd never seen you, and Brother Otis and I concluded we'd lie awake and watch for you to come."

Santa Claus shook his head reproachfully.

"That was very wrong," said he, "for I'm so scarey that if I'd known you boys were awake I'd never have come down the chimney at all, and then you'd have had no presents."

"But Otis couldn't keep awake," explained Joel. "We talked about everythin' we could think of, till father called out to us that if we didn't stop talking he'd have to send one of us up into the attic to sleep with the hired man. So in less than five minutes Otis was sound asleep and no pinching could wake him up. But I was bound to see Santa Claus and I don't believe anything would've put me to sleep. I heard the big clock in the sitting-room strike eleven, and I had begun wonderin' if you never were going to come, when all of a sudden I heard the tinkle of the bells around your reindeers' necks. Then I heard the reindeers prancin' on the roof and the sound of your sleigh-runners cuttin' through the crust and slippin' over the shingles. I was kind o' scared and I covered my head up with the sheet and quilts—only I left a little hole so I could peek out and see what was goin' on. As soon as I saw you I got over bein' scared—for you were jolly and smilin' like, and you chuckled as you went around to each stockin' and filled it up."

"Yes, I can remember the night," said Santa Claus. "I brought you a sled, didn't I?"

"Yes, and you brought Otis one, too," replied Joel. "Mine was red and had 'Yankee Doodle' painted in black letters on the side; Otis's was black and had 'Snow Queen' in gilt letters."

"I remember those sleds distinctly," said Santa Claus, "for I made them specially for you boys."

"You set the sleds up against the wall," continued Joel, "and then you filled the stockin's."

"There were six of 'em, as I recollect?" said Santa Claus.

"Let me see," queried Joel. "There was mine, and Otis's, and Elvira's, and Thankful's, and Susan Prickett's—Susan was our help, you know. No, there were only five, and, as I remember, they were the biggest we could beg or borrer of Aunt Dorcas, who weighed nigh unto two hundred pounds. Otis and I didn't like Susan Prickett, and we were hopin' you'd put a cold potato in her stockin'."

"But Susan was a good girl," remonstrated Santa Claus. "You know I put cold potatoes only in the stockin's of boys and girls who are bad and don't believe in Santa Claus."

"At any rate," said Joel, "you filled all the stockin's with candy and pop-corn and nuts and raisins, and I can remember you said you were afraid you'd run out of pop-corn balls before you got around. Then you left each of us a book. Elvira got the best one, which was 'The Garland of Frien'ship,' and had poems in it about the bleeding of hearts, and so forth. Father wasn't expectin' anything, but you left him a new pair of mittens, and mother got a new fur boa to wear to meetin'."

"Of course," said Santa Claus, "I never forgot father and mother."

"Well, it was as much as I could do to lay still," continued Joel, "for I'd been longin' for a sled, an' the sight of that red sled with 'Yankee Doodle' painted on it jest made me wild. But, somehow or other, I began to get powerful sleepy all at once, and I couldn't keep my eyes open. The next thing I knew Otis was nudgin' me in the ribs. 'Git up, Joel,' says he; 'it's Chris'mas an' Santa Claus has been here.' 'Merry Chris'mas! Merry Chris'mas!' we cried as we tumbled out o' bed. Then Elvira an' Thankful came in, not more 'n half dressed, and Susan came in, too, an' we just made Rome howl with 'Merry Chris'mas! Merry Chris'mas!' to each other. 'Ef you children don't make less noise in there,' cried father, 'I'll hev to send you all back to bed.' The idea of askin' boys an' girls to keep quiet on Chris'mas mornin' when they've got new sleds an' 'Garlands of Frien'ship'!"

Santa Claus chuckled; his rosy cheeks fairly beamed joy.

"Otis an' I didn't want any breakfast," said Joel. "We made up our minds that a stockin'ful of candy and pop-corn and raisins would stay us for a while. I do believe there wasn't buckwheat cakes enough in the township to keep us indoors that mornin'; buckwheat cakes don't size up much 'longside of a red sled with 'Yankee Doodle' painted onto it and a black sled named 'Snow Queen.' We didn't care how cold it was—so much the better for slidin' downhill! All the boys had new sleds—Lafe Dawson, Bill Holbrook, Gum Adams, Rube Playford, Leander Merrick, Ezra Purple—all on 'em had new sleds excep' Martin Peavey, and he said he calculated Santa Claus had skipped him this year 'cause his father had broke his leg haulin' logs from the Pelham woods and had been kep' indoors six weeks. But Martin had his ol' sled, and he didn't hev to ask any odds of any of us, neither."

"I brought Martin a sled the next Christmas," said Santa Claus.

"Like as not—but did you ever slide downhill, Santa Claus? I don't mean such hills as they hev out here in this new country, but one of them old-fashioned New England hills that was made 'specially for boys to slide down, full of bumpers an' thank-ye-marms, and about ten times longer comin' up than it is goin' down! The wind blew in our faces and almos' took our breath away. 'Merry Chris'mas to ye, little boys!' it seemed to say, and it untied our mufflers an' whirled the snow in our faces, jist as if it was a boy, too, an' wanted to play with us. An ol' crow came flappin' over us from the cornfield beyond the meadow. He said: 'Caw, caw,' when he saw my new sled—I s'pose he'd never seen a red one before. Otis had a hard time with his sled—the black one—an' he wondered why it wouldn't go as fast as mine would. 'Hev you scraped the paint off'n the runners?' asked Wralsey Goodnow. 'Course I hev,' said Otis; 'broke my own knife an' Lute Ingraham's a-doin' it, but it don't seem to make no dif'rence—the darned ol' thing won't go!' Then, what did Simon Buzzell say but that, like's not, it was because Otis's sled's name was 'Snow Queen.' 'Never did see a girl sled that was worth a cent, anyway,' sez Simon. Well, now, that jest about broke Otis up in business. 'It ain't a girl sled,' sez he, 'and its name ain't "Snow Queen"! I'm a-goin' to call it "Dan'l Webster," or "Ol'ver Optic," or "Sheriff Robbins," or after some other big man!' An' the boys plagued him so much about that pesky girl sled that he scratched off the name, an', as I remember, it did go better after that!

"About the only thing," continued Joel, "that marred the harmony of the occasion, as the editor of the Hampshire County Phoenix used to say, was the ashes that Deacon Morris Frisbie sprinkled out in front of his house. He said he wasn't going to have folks breakin' their necks jest on account of a lot of frivolous boys that was goin' to the gallows as fas' as they could! Oh, how we hated him! and we'd have snowballed him, too, if we hadn't been afraid of the constable that lived next door. But the ashes didn't bother us much, and every time we slid side-saddle we'd give the ashes a kick, and that sort of scattered 'em."

The bare thought of this made Santa Claus laugh.

"Goin' on about nine o'clock," said Joel, "the girls come along—Sister Elvira an' Thankful, Prudence Tucker, Belle Yocum, Sophrone Holbrook, Sis

Hubbard, an' Marthy Sawyer. Marthy's brother Increase wanted her to ride on his sled, but Marthy allowed that a red sled was her choice every time. 'I don't see how I'm goin' to hold on,' said Marthy. 'Seems as if I would hev my hands full keepin' my things from blowin' away.' 'Don't worry about yourself, Marthy,' sez I, 'for if you'll look after your things, I kind o' calc'late I'll manage not to lose you on the way.' Dear Marthy—seems as if I could see you now, with your tangled hair a-blowin' in the wind, your eyes all bright and sparklin', an' your cheeks as red as apples. Seems, too, as if I could hear you laughin' and callin', jist as you did as I toiled up the old New England hill that Chris'mas mornin'—a-callin': 'Joel, Joel, Joel—ain't ye ever comin', Joel?' But the hill is long and steep, Marthy, an' Joel ain't the boy he used to be; he's old, an' gray, an' feeble, but there's love an' faith in his heart, an' they kind o' keep him totterin' tow'rd the voice he hears a-callin': 'Joel, Joel, Joel!'"

"I know—I see it all," murmured Santa Claus very softly.

"Oh, that was so long ago," sighed Joel; "so very long ago! And I've had no Chris'mas since—only once, when our little one—Marthy's an' mine—you remember him, Santa Claus?"

"Yes," said Santa Claus, "a toddling little boy with blue eyes—"

"Like his mother," interrupted Joel; "an' he was like her, too—so gentle an' lovin', only we called him Joel, for that was my father's name and it kind o' run in the fam'ly. He wa'n't more'n three years old when you came with your Chris'mas presents for him, Santa Claus. We had told him about you, and he used to go to the chimney every night and make a little prayer about what he wanted you to bring him. And you brought 'em, too—a stick-horse, an' a picture-book, an' some blocks, an' a drum—they're on the shelf in the closet there, and his little Chris'mas stockin' with 'em—I've saved 'em all, an' I've taken 'em down an' held 'em in my hands, oh, so many times!"

"But when I came again," said Santa Claus—

"His little bed was empty, an' I was alone. It killed his mother—Marthy was so tender-hearted; she kind o' drooped an' pined after that. So now they've been asleep side by side in the buryin'-ground these thirty years.

"That's why I'm so sad-like whenever Chris'mas comes," said Joel, after a pause. "The thinkin' of long ago makes me bitter almost. It's so different now from what it used to be."

"No, Joel, oh, no," said Santa Claus. "'Tis the same world, and human nature is the same and always will be. But Christmas is for the little folks, and you, who are old and grizzled now, must know it and love it only through the gladness it brings the little ones."

"True," groaned Joel; "but how may I know and feel this gladness when I have no little stocking hanging in my chimney corner—no child to please me with his prattle? See, I am alone."

"No, you're not alone, Joel," said Santa Claus. "There are children in this great city who would love and bless you for your goodness if you but touched their hearts. Make them happy, Joel; send by me this night some gift to the little boy in the old house yonder—he is poor and sick; a simple toy will fill his Christmas with gladness."

"His little sister, too—take her some presents," said Joel; "make them happy for me, Santa Claus—you are right—make them happy for me."

How sweetly Joel slept! When he awoke, the sunlight streamed in through the window and seemed to bid him a merry Christmas. How contented and happy Joel felt! It must have been the talk with Santa Claus that did it all; he had never known a sweeter sense of peace. A little girl came out of the house over the way. She had a new doll in her arms, and she sang a merry little song and she laughed with joy as she skipped along the street. Ay, and at the window sat the little sick boy, and the toy Santa Claus left him seemed to have brought him strength and health, for his eyes sparkled and his cheeks glowed, and it was plain to see his heart was full of happiness.

And, oh! how the chimes did ring out, and how joyfully they sang their Christmas carol that morning! They sang of Bethlehem and the manger and the Babe; they sang of love and charity, till all the Christmas air seemed full of angel voices.

Carol of the Christmas morn—Carol of the Christ-child born—Carol to the list'ning skyTill it echoes back again"Glory be to God on high,Peace on earth, good will tow'rd men!"

So all this music—the carol of the chimes, the sound of children's voices, the smile of the poor little boy over the way—all this sweet music crept into Joel's heart that Christmas morning; yes, and with these sweet, holy influences came others so subtile and divine that in its silent communion with them, Joel's heart cried out amen and amen to the glory of the Christmas time.

THE THREE KINGS OF COLOGNE

From out Cologne there came three kingsTo worship Jesus Christ, their King.To Him they sought fine herbs they brought,And many a beauteous golden thing;They brought their gifts to Bethlehem town,And in that manger set them down.

Then spake the first king, and he said:"O Child, most heavenly, bright, and fair!I bring this crown to Bethlehem townFor Thee, and only Thee, to wear;So give a heavenly crown to meWhen I shall come at last to Thee!"

The second, then. "I bring Thee hereThis royal robe, O Child!" he cried;"Of silk 'tis spun, and such an oneThere is not in the world beside;So in the day of doom requiteMe with a heavenly robe of white!"

The third king gave his gift, and quoth:"Spikenard and myrrh to Thee I bring,And with these twain would I most fainAnoint the body of my King;So may their incense sometime riseTo plead for me in yonder skies!"

Thus spake the three kings of Cologne,That gave their gifts, and went their way;And now kneel I in prayer hard byThe cradle of the Child to-day;Nor crown, nor robe, nor spice I bringAs offering unto Christ, my King.

Yet have I brought a gift the ChildMay not despise, however small;For here I lay my heart to-day,And it is full of love to all.Take Thou the poor but loyal thing,My only tribute, Christ, my King!

THE COMING OF THE PRINCE
I

"Whirr-r-r! whirr-r-r! whirr-r-r!" said the wind, and it tore through the streets of the city that Christmas eve, turning umbrellas inside out, driving the snow in fitful gusts before it, creaking the rusty signs and shutters, and playing every kind of rude prank it could think of.

"How cold your breath is to-night!" said Barbara, with a shiver, as she drew her tattered little shawl the closer around her benumbed body.

"Whirr-r-r! whirr-r-r! whirr-r-r!" answered the wind; "but why are you out in this storm? You should be at home by the warm fire."

"I have no home," said Barbara; and then she sighed bitterly, and something like a tiny pearl came in the corner of one of her sad blue eyes.

But the wind did not hear her answer, for it had hurried up the street to throw a handful of snow in the face of an old man who was struggling along with a huge basket of good things on each arm.

"Why are you not at the cathedral?" asked a snowflake, as it alighted on Barbara's shoulder. "I heard grand music, and saw beautiful lights there as I floated down from the sky a moment ago."

"What are they doing at the cathedral?" inquired Barbara.

"Why, haven't you heard?" exclaimed the snowflake. "I supposed everybody knew that the prince was coming to-morrow."

204

"Surely enough; this is Christmas eve," said Barbara, "and the prince will come to-morrow."

Barbara remembered that her mother had told her about the prince, how beautiful and good and kind and gentle he was, and how he loved the little children; but her mother was dead now, and there was none to tell Barbara of the prince and his coming,—none but the little snowflake.

"I should like to see the prince," said Barbara, "for I have heard he was very beautiful and good."

"That he is," said the snowflake. "I have never seen him, but I heard the pines and the firs singing about him as I floated over the forest to-night."

"Whirr-r-r! whirr-r-r!" cried the wind, returning boisterously to where Barbara stood. "I've been looking for you everywhere, little snowflake! So come with me."

And without any further ado, the wind seized upon the snowflake and hurried it along the street and led it a merry dance through the icy air of the winter night.

Barbara trudged on through the snow and looked in at the bright things in the shop windows. The glitter of the lights and the sparkle of the vast array of beautiful Christmas toys quite dazzled her. A strange mingling of admiration, regret, and envy filled the poor little creature's heart.

"Much as I may yearn to have them, it cannot be," she said to herself, "yet I may feast my eyes upon them."

"Go away from here!" said a harsh voice. "How can the rich people see all my fine things if you stand before the window? Be off with you, you miserable little beggar!"

It was the shopkeeper, and he gave Barbara a savage box on the ear that sent her reeling into the deeper snowdrifts of the gutter.

Presently she came to a large house where there seemed to be much mirth and festivity. The shutters were thrown open, and through the windows Barbara could see a beautiful Christmas-tree in the centre of a spacious room—a beautiful Christmas-tree ablaze with red and green lights, and heavy with toys and stars and glass balls and other beautiful things that children love. There was a merry throng around the tree, and the children were smiling and gleeful, and all in that house seemed content and happy. Barbara heard them singing, and their song was about the prince who was to come on the morrow.

"This must be the house where the prince will stop," thought Barbara. "How I would like to see his face and hear his voice!—yet what would he care for me, a 'miserable little beggar'?"

So Barbara crept on through the storm, shivering and disconsolate, yet thinking of the prince.

"Where are you going?" she asked of the wind as it overtook her.

"To the cathedral," laughed the wind. "The great people are flocking there, and I will have a merry time amongst them, ha, ha, ha!"

And with laughter the wind whirled away and chased the snow toward the cathedral.

"It is there, then, that the prince will come," thought Barbara. "It is a beautiful place, and the people will pay him homage there. Perhaps I shall see him if I go there."

So she went to the cathedral. Many folk were there in their richest apparel, and the organ rolled out its grand music, and the people sang wondrous songs, and the priests made eloquent prayers; and the music, and the songs, and the prayers were all about the prince and his expected coming. The throng that swept in and out of the great edifice talked always of the prince, the prince, the prince, until Barbara really loved him very much, for all the gentle words she heard the people say of him.

"Please, can I go and sit inside?" inquired Barbara of the sexton.

"No!" said the sexton gruffly, for this was an important occasion with the sexton, and he had no idea of wasting words on a beggar child.

"But I will be very good and quiet," pleaded Barbara. "Please may I not see the prince?"

"I have said no, and I mean it," retorted the sexton. "What have you for the prince, or what cares the prince for you? Out with you, and don't be blocking up the door-way!" So the sexton gave Barbara an angry push, and the child fell half-way down the icy steps of the cathedral. She began to cry. Some great people were entering the cathedral at the time, and they laughed to see her falling.

"Have you seen the prince?" inquired a snowflake, alighting on Barbara's cheek. It was the same little snowflake that had clung to her shawl an hour ago, when the wind came galloping along on his boisterous search.

"Ah, no!" sighed Barbara in tears; "but what cares the prince for me?"

"Do not speak so bitterly," said the little snowflake. "Go to the forest and you shall see him, for the prince always comes through the forest to the city."

Despite the cold, and her bruises, and her tears, Barbara smiled. In the forest she could behold the prince coming on his way; and he would not see her, for she would hide among the trees and vines.

"Whirr-r-r, whirr-r-r!" It was the mischievous, romping wind once more; and it fluttered Barbara's tattered shawl, and set her hair to streaming in every direction, and swept the snowflake from her cheek and sent it spinning through the air.

Barbara trudged toward the forest. When she came to the city gate the watchman stopped her, and held his big lantern in her face, and asked her who she was and where she was going.

"I am Barbara, and I am going into the forest," said she boldly.

"Into the forest?" cried the watchman, "and in this storm? No, child; you will perish!"

"But I am going to see the prince," said Barbara. "They will not let me watch for him in the church, nor in any of their pleasant homes, so I am going into the forest."

The watchman smiled sadly. He was a kindly man; he thought of his own little girl at home.

"No, you must not go to the forest," said he, "for you would perish with the cold."

But Barbara would not stay. She avoided the watchman's grasp and ran as fast as ever she could through the city gate.

"Come back, come back!" cried the watchman; "you will perish in the forest!"

But Barbara would not heed his cry. The falling snow did not stay her, nor did the cutting blast. She thought only of the prince, and she ran straightway to the forest.

II

"What do you see up there, O pine-tree?" asked a little vine in the forest. "You lift your head among the clouds to-night, and you tremble strangely as if you saw wondrous sights."

"I see only the distant hill-tops and the dark clouds," answered the pine-tree. "And the wind sings of the snow-king to-night; to all my questionings he says, 'Snow, snow, snow,' till I am wearied with his refrain."

"But the prince will surely come to-morrow?" inquired the tiny snowdrop that nestled close to the vine.

"Oh, yes," said the vine. "I heard the country folks talking about it as they went through the forest to-day, and they said that the prince would surely come on the morrow."

"What are you little folks down there talking about?" asked the pine-tree.

"We are talking about the prince," said the vine.

"Yes, he is to come on the morrow," said the pine-tree, "but not until the day dawns, and it is still all dark in the east."

"Yes," said the fir-tree, "the east is black, and only the wind and the snow issue from it."

"Keep your head out of my way!" cried the pine-tree to the fir; "with your constant bobbing around I can hardly see at all."

"Take that for your bad manners," retorted the fir, slapping the pine-tree savagely with one of her longest branches.

The pine-tree would put up with no such treatment, so he hurled his largest cone at the fir; and for a moment or two it looked as if there were going to be a serious commotion in the forest.

"Hush!" cried the vine in a startled tone; "there is some one coming through the forest."

The pine-tree and the fir stopped quarrelling, and the snowdrop nestled closer to the vine, while the vine hugged the pine-tree very tightly. All were greatly alarmed.

"Nonsense!" said the pine-tree, in a tone of assumed bravery. "No one would venture into the forest at such an hour."

"Indeed! and why not?" cried a child's voice. "Will you not let me watch with you for the coming of the prince?"

"Will you not chop me down?" inquired the pine-tree gruffly.

"Will you not tear me from my tree?" asked the vine.

"Will you not pluck my blossoms?" plaintively piped the snowdrop.

"No, of course not," said Barbara; "I have come only to watch with you for the prince."

Then Barbara told them who she was, and how cruelly she had been treated in the city, and how she longed to see the prince, who was to come on the morrow. And as she talked, the forest and all therein felt a great compassion for her.

"Lie at my feet," said the pine-tree, "and I will protect you."

"Nestle close to me, and I will chafe your temples and body and limbs till they are warm," said the vine.

"Let me rest upon your cheek, and I will sing you my little songs," said the snowdrop.

And Barbara felt very grateful for all these homely kindnesses. She rested in the velvety snow at the foot of the pine-tree, and the vine chafed her body and limbs, and the little flower sang sweet songs to her.

"Whirr-r-r, whirr-r-r!" There was that noisy wind again, but this time it was gentler than it had been in the city.

"Here you are, my little Barbara," said the wind, in kindly tones. "I have brought you the little snowflake. I am glad you came away from the city, for the people are proud and haughty there; oh, but I will have my fun with them!"

Then, having dropped the little snowflake on Barbara's cheek, the wind whisked off to the city again. And we can imagine that it played rare pranks with the proud, haughty folk on its return; for the wind, as you know, is no respecter of persons.

"Dear Barbara," said the snowflake, "I will watch with thee for the coming of the prince."

And Barbara was glad, for she loved the little snowflake, that was so pure and innocent and gentle.

"Tell us, O pine-tree," cried the vine, "what do you see in the east? Has the prince yet entered the forest?"

"The east is full of black clouds," said the pine-tree, "and the winds that hurry to the hill-tops sing of the snow."

"But the city is full of brightness," said the fir. "I can see the lights in the cathedral, and I can hear wondrous music about the prince and his coming."

"Yes, they are singing of the prince in the cathedral," said Barbara sadly.

"But we shall see him first," whispered the vine reassuringly.

"Yes, the prince will come through the forest," said the little snowdrop gleefully.

"Fear not, dear Barbara, we shall behold the prince in all his glory," cried the snowflake.

Then all at once there was a strange hub-bub in the forest; for it was midnight, and the spirits came from their hiding-places to prowl about and to disport themselves. Barbara beheld them all in great wonder and trepidation, for she had never before seen the spirits of the forest, although she had often heard of them. It was a marvellous sight.

"Fear nothing," whispered the vine to Barbara,—"fear nothing, for they dare not touch you."

The antics of the wood-spirits continued but an hour; for then a cock crowed, and immediately thereat, with a wondrous scurrying, the elves and the gnomes and the other grotesque spirits sought their abiding-places in the caves and in the hollow trunks and under the loose bark of the trees. And then it was very quiet once more in the forest.

"It is very cold," said Barbara. "My hands and feet are like ice."

Then the pine-tree and the fir shook down the snow from their broad boughs, and the snow fell upon Barbara and covered her like a white mantle.

"You will be warm now," said the vine, kissing Barbara's forehead. And Barbara smiled.

Then the snowdrop sang a lullaby about the moss that loved the violet. And Barbara said, "I am going to sleep; will you wake me when the prince comes through the forest?"

And they said they would. So Barbara fell asleep.

III

"The bells in the city are ringing merrily," said the fir, "and the music in the cathedral is louder and more beautiful than before. Can it be that the prince has already come into the city?"

"No," cried the pine-tree, "look to the east and see the Christmas day a-dawning! The prince is coming, and his pathway is through the forest!"

The storm had ceased. Snow lay upon all the earth. The hills, the forest, the city, and the meadows were white with the robe the storm-king had thrown over them. Content with his wondrous work, the storm-king himself had fled to his far Northern home before the dawn of the Christmas day. Everything was bright and sparkling and beautiful. And most beautiful was the great hymn of praise the forest sang that Christmas morning,—the pine-trees and the firs and the vines and the snow-flowers that sang of the prince and of his promised coming.

"Wake up, little one," cried the vine, "for the prince is coming!"

But Barbara slept; she did not hear the vine's soft calling nor the lofty music of the forest.

A little snow-bird flew down from the fir-tree's bough and perched upon the vine, and carolled in Barbara's ear of the Christmas morning and of the coming of the prince. But Barbara slept; she did not hear the carol of the bird.

"Alas!" sighed the vine, "Barbara will not awaken, and the prince is coming."

Then the vine and the snowdrop wept, and the pine-tree and the fir were very sad.

The prince came through the forest clad in royal raiment and wearing a golden crown. Angels came with him, and the forest sang a great hymn unto the prince, such a hymn as had never before been heard on earth. The prince came to the sleeping child and smiled upon her and called her by name.

"Barbara, my little one," said the prince, "awaken, and come with me."

Then Barbara opened her eyes and beheld the prince. And it seemed as if a new life had come to her, for there was warmth in her body and a flush upon her cheeks and a light in her eyes that were divine. And she was clothed no longer in rags, but in white flowing raiment; and upon the soft brown hair there was a crown like those which angels wear. And as Barbara arose and went to the prince, the little snowflake fell from her cheek upon her bosom, and forthwith became a pearl more precious than all other jewels upon earth.

And the prince took Barbara in his arms and blessed her, and turning round about, returned with the little child unto his home, while the forest and the sky and the angels sang a wondrous song.

The city waited for the prince, but he did not come. None knew of the glory of the forest that Christmas morning, nor of the new life that came to little Barbara.

Come thou, dear Prince, oh, come to us this holy Christmas time! Come to the busy marts of earth, the quiet homes, the noisy streets, the humble lanes; come to us all, and with thy love touch every human heart, that we may know that love, and in its blessed peace bear charity to all mankind!

CHRYSTMASSE OF OLDE

God rest you, Chrysten gentil men, Wherever you may be,—God rest you all in fielde or hall, Or on ye stormy sea; For on this morn oure Chryst is born That saveth you and me.

Last night ye shepherds in ye east Saw many a wondrous thing; Ye sky last night flamed passing bright Whiles that ye stars did sing, And angels came to bless ye name Of Jesus Chryst, oure Kyng.

God rest you, Chrysten gentil men, Faring where'er you may; In noblesse court do thou no sport, In tournament no playe, In paynim lands hold thou thy hands From bloudy works this daye.

But thinking on ye gentil Lord That died upon ye tree, Let troublings cease and deeds of peace Abound in Chrystantie; For on this morn ye Chryst is born That saveth you and me.

———————————

The mouse and the moonbeam

Whilst you were sleeping, little Dear-my-Soul, strange things happened; but that I saw and heard them, I should never have believed them. The clock stood, of course, in the corner, a moonbeam floated idly on the floor, and a little mauve mouse came from the hole in the chimney corner and frisked and scampered in the light of the moonbeam upon the floor. The little mauve mouse was particularly merry; sometimes she danced upon two legs and sometimes upon four legs, but always very daintily and always very merrily.

"Ah, me!" sighed the old clock, "how different mice are nowadays from the mice we used to have in the good old times! Now there was your grandma, Mistress Velvetpaw, and there was your grandpa, Master Sniffwhisker,—how grave and dignified they were! Many a night have I seen them dancing upon the carpet below me, but always the stately minuet and never that crazy frisking which you are executing now, to my surprise—yes, and to my horror, too."

"But why shouldn't I be merry?" asked the little mauve mouse. "Tomorrow is Christmas, and this is Christmas eve."

"So it is," said the old clock. "I had really forgotten all about it. But tell me, what is Christmas to you, little Miss Mauve Mouse?"

"A great deal to me!" cried the little mauve mouse. "I have been very good a very long time: I have not used any bad words, nor have I gnawed any holes, nor have I stolen any canary seed, nor have I worried my mother by running behind the flour-barrel where that horrid trap is set. In fact, I have been so good that I'm very sure Santa Claus will bring me something very pretty."

This seemed to amuse the old clock mightily; in fact, the old clock fell to laughing so heartily that in an unguarded moment she struck twelve instead of ten, which was exceedingly careless and therefore to be reprehended.

"Why, you silly little mauve mouse," said the old clock, "you don't believe in Santa Claus, do you?"

"Of course I do," answered the little mauve mouse. "Believe in Santa Claus? Why shouldn't I? Didn't Santa Claus bring me a beautiful butter-cracker last Christmas, and a lovely gingersnap, and a delicious rind of cheese, and—and—lots of things? I should be very ungrateful if I did not believe in Santa Claus, and I certainly shall not disbelieve in him at the very moment when I am expecting him to arrive with a bundle of goodies for me.

"I once had a little sister," continued the little mauve mouse, "who did not believe in Santa Claus, and the very thought of the fate that befell her makes my blood run cold and my whiskers stand on end. She died before I was born, but my mother has told me all about her. Perhaps you never saw her; her name was Squeaknibble, and she was in stature oneof those long, low, rangy mice that are seldom found in well-stocked pantries. Mother says that Squeaknibble took after our ancestors who came from New England, where the malignant ingenuity of the people and the ferocity of the cats rendered life precarious indeed. Squeaknibble seemed to inherit many ancestral traits, the most conspicuous of which was a disposition to sneer at some of the most respected dogmas in mousedom. From her very infancy she doubted, for example, the widely accepted theory that the moon was composed of green cheese; and this heresy was the first intimation her parents had of the sceptical turn of her mind. Of course, her parents were vastly annoyed, for their maturer natures saw that this youthful scepticism portended serious, if not fatal, consequences. Yet all in vain did the sagacious couple reason and plead with their headstrong and heretical child.

"For a long time Squeaknibble would not believe that there was any such archfiend as a cat; but she came to be convinced to the contrary one memorable night, on which occasion she lost two inches of her beautiful tail, and received so terrible a fright that for fully an hour afterward her little heart beat so violently as to lift her off her feet and bump her head against the top of our domestic hole. The cat that deprived my sister of so large a percentage of her vertebral colophon was the same brindled ogress that nowadays steals ever and anon into this room, crouches treacherously behind the sofa, and feigns to be asleep, hoping, forsooth, that some of us, heedless of her hated presence, will venture within reach of her diabolical claws. So enraged was this ferocious monster at the escape of my sister that she ground her fangs viciously together, and vowed to take no pleasure in life until she held in her devouring jaws the innocent little mouse which belonged to the mangled bit of tail she even then clutched in her remorseless claws."

"Yes," said the old clock, "now that you recall the incident, I recollect it well. I was here then, in this very corner, and I remember that I laughed at the cat and chided her for her awkwardness. My reproaches irritated her; she told me that a clock's duty was to run itself down,not to be depreciating the merits of others! Yes, I recall the time; that cat's tongue is fully as sharp as her claws."

"Be that as it may," said the little mauve mouse, "it is a matter of history, and therefore beyond dispute, that from that very moment the cat pined for Squeaknibble's life; it seemed as if that one little two-inch taste of Squeaknibble's tail had filled the cat with a consuming passion, or appetite, for the rest of Squeaknibble. So the cat waited and watched and hunted and schemed and devised and did everything possible for a cat—a cruel cat—to do in order to gain her murderous ends. One night—one fatal Christmas eve—our mother had undressed the children for bed, and was urging upon them to go to sleep earlier than usual, since she fully expected that Santa Claus would bring each of them something very palatable and nice before morning. Thereupon the little dears whisked their cunning tails, pricked up their beautiful ears, and began telling one another what they hoped Santa Claus would bring. One asked for a slice of Roquefort, another for Neufchatel, another for Sap Sago, and a fourth for Edam; one expressed a preference for de Brie, while another hoped to get Parmesan; one clamored for imperial blue Stilton, and another craved the fragrant boon of Caprera. There were fourteen little ones then, and consequently there were diverse opinions as to the kind of gift which Santa Claus should best bring; still, there was, as you can readily understand, an enthusiastic unanimity upon this point, namely, that the gift should be cheese of some brand or other.

"'My dears,' said our mother, 'what matters it whether the boon which Santa Claus brings be royal English cheddar or fromage de Bricquebec, Vermont sage, or Herkimer County skim-milk? We should be content with whatsoever Santa Claus bestows, so long as it be cheese, disjoined from all traps whatsoever, unmixed with Paris green, and free from glass, strychnine, and other harmful ingredients. As for myself, I shall be satisfied with a cut of nice, fresh Western reserve; for truly I recognize in no other viand or edible half the fragrance or half the gustfulness to be met with in one of these pale but aromatic domestic products. So run away to your dreams now, that Santa Claus may find you sleeping.'

"The children obeyed,—all but Squeaknibble. 'Let the others think what they please,' said she, 'but I don't believe in Santa Claus. I'm not going to bed, either. I'm going to creep out of this dark hole and have a quiet romp, all by myself, in the moonlight.' Oh, what a vain, foolish, wicked little mouse was Squeaknibble! But I will not reproach the dead; her punishment came all too swiftly. Now listen: who do you suppose overheard her talking so disrespectfully of Santa Claus?"

"Why, Santa Claus himself," said the old clock.

"Oh, no," answered the little mauve mouse. "It was that wicked, murderous cat! Just as Satan lurks and lies in wait for bad children, so does the cruel cat lurk and lie in wait for naughty little mice. And you can depend upon it that, when that awful cat heard Squeaknibble speak so disrespectfully of Santa Claus, her wicked eyes glowed with joy, her sharp teeth watered, and her bristling fur emitted electric sparks as big as marrowfat peas. Then what did that blood-thirsty monster do but scuttle as fast as she could into Dear-my-Soul's room, leap up into Dear-my-Soul's crib, and walk off with the pretty little white muff which Dear-my-Soul used to wear when she went for a visit to the little girl in the next block! What upon earth did the horrid old cat want with Dear-my-Soul's pretty little white muff? Ah, the duplicity, the diabolical ingenuity of that cat! Listen.

"In the first place," resumed the little mauve mouse, after a pause that testified eloquently to the depth of her emotion,—"in the first place, that wretched cat dressed herself up in that pretty little white muff, by which you are to understand that she crawled through the muff just so far as to leave her four cruel legs at liberty."

"Yes, I understand," said the old clock.

"Then she put on the boy doll's fur cap," said the little mauve mouse, "and when she was arrayed in the boy doll's fur cap and Dear-my-Soul's pretty little white muff, of course she didn't look like a cruel cat at all. But whom did she look like?"

"Like the boy doll," suggested the old clock.

"No, no!" cried the little mauve mouse.

"Like Dear-my-Soul?" asked the old clock.

"How stupid you are!" exclaimed the little mauve mouse. "Why, she looked like Santa Claus, of course!"

"Oh, yes; I see," said the old clock. "Now I begin to be interested; go on."

"Alas!" sighed the little mauve mouse, "not much remains to be told; but there is more of my story left than there was of Squeaknibble when that horrid cat crawled out of that miserable disguise. You are to understand that, contrary to her sagacious mother's injunction, and in notorious derision of the mooted coming of Santa Claus, Squeaknibble issued from the friendly hole in the chimney corner, and gambolled about over this very carpet, and, I dare say, in this very moonlight."

"I do not know," said the moonbeam faintly. "I am so very old, and I have seen so many things—I do not know."

"Right merrily was Squeaknibble gambolling," continued the little mauve mouse, "and she had just turned a double back somersault without the use of what remained of her tail, when, all of a sudden, she beheld, looming up like a monster ghost, a figure all in white fur! Oh, how frightened she was, and how her little heart did beat! 'Purr, purr-r-r,' said the ghost in white fur. 'Oh, please don't hurt me!' pleaded Squeaknibble. 'No; I'll not hurt you,' said the ghost in white fur; 'I'm Santa Claus, and I've brought you a beautiful piece of savory old cheese, you dear little mousie, you.' Poor Squeaknibble was deceived; a sceptic all her life, she was at last befooled by the most palpable and most fatal of frauds. 'How good of you!' said Squeaknibble. 'I didn't believe there was a Santa Claus, and—' but before she could say more she was seized by two sharp, cruel claws that conveyed her crushed body to the murderous mouth of mousedom's most malignant foe. I can dwell no longer upon this harrowing scene. Suffice it to say that ere the morrow's sun rose like a big yellow Herkimer County cheese upon the spot where that tragedy had been enacted, poor Squeaknibble passed to that bourn whence two inches of her beautiful tail had preceded her by the space of three weeks to a day. As for Santa Claus, when he came that Christmas eve, bringing morceaux de Brie and of

212

Stilton for the other little mice, he heard with sorrow of Squeaknibble's fate; and ere he departed he said that in all his experience he had never known of a mouse or of a child that had prospered after once saying that he didn't believe in Santa Claus."

"Well, that is a remarkable story," said the old clock. "But if you believe in Santa Claus, why aren't you in bed?"

"That's where I shall be presently," answered the little mauve mouse, "but I must have my scamper, you know. It is very pleasant, I assure you, to frolic in the light of the moon; only I cannot understand why you are always so cold and so solemn and so still, you pale, pretty little moonbeam."

"Indeed, I do not know that I am so," said the moonbeam. "But I am very old, and I have travelled many, many leagues, and I have seen wondrous things. Sometimes I toss upon the ocean, sometimes I fall upon a slumbering flower, sometimes I rest upon a dead child's face. I see the fairies at their play, and I hear mothers singing lullabies. Last night I swept across the frozen bosom of a river. A woman's face looked up at me; it was the picture of eternal rest. 'She is sleeping,' said the frozen river. 'I rock her to and fro, and sing to her. Pass gently by, O moonbeam; pass gently by, lest you awaken her.'"

"How strangely you talk," said the old clock. "Now, I'll warrant me that, if you wanted to, you could tell many a pretty and wonderful story. You must know many a Christmas tale; pray, tell us one to wear away this night of Christmas watching."

"I know but one," said the moonbeam. "I have told it over and over again, in every land and in every home; yet I do not weary of it. It is very simple. Should you like to hear it?"

"Indeed we should," said the old clock; "but before you begin, let me strike twelve; for I shouldn't want to interrupt you."

When the old clock had performed this duty with somewhat more than usual alacrity, the moonbeam began its story:

"Upon a time—so long ago that I can't tell how long ago it was—I fell upon a hill-side. It was in a far distant country; this I know, because, although it was the Christmas time, it was not in that country as it is wont to be in countries to the north. Hither the snow-king never came; flowers bloomed all the year, and at all times the lambs found pleasant pasturage on the hill-sides. The night wind was balmy, and there was a fragrance of cedar in its breath. There were violets on the hill-side, and I fell amongst them and lay there. I kissed them, and they awakened. 'Ah, is it you, little moonbeam?' they said, and they nestled in the grass which the lambs had left uncropped.

"A shepherd lay upon a broad stone on the hill-side; above him spread an olive-tree, old, ragged, and gloomy; but now it swayed its rusty branches majestically in the shifting air of night. The shepherd's name was Benoni. Wearied with long watching, he had fallen asleep; his crook had slipped from his hand. Upon the hill-side, too, slept the shepherd's flock. I had counted them again and again; I had stolen across their gentle faces and brought them pleasant dreams of green pastures and of cool water-brooks. I had kissed old Benoni, too, as he lay slumbering there; and in his dreams he seemed to see Israel's King come upon earth, and in his dreams he murmured the promised Messiah's name.

"'Ah, is it you, little moonbeam?' quoth the violets. 'You have come in good time. Nestle here with us, and see wonderful things come to pass.'

"'What are these wonderful things of which you speak?' I asked.

"'We heard the old olive-tree telling of them to-night,' said the violets. 'Do not go to sleep, little violets,' said the old olive-tree, 'for this is Christmas night, and the Master shall walk upon the hill-side in the glory of the midnight hour.' So we waited and watched; one by one the lambs fell asleep; one by one the stars peeped out; the shepherd nodded and crooned, and crooned and nodded, and at last he, too, went fast

213

asleep, and his crook slipped from his keeping. Then we called to the old olive-tree yonder, asking how soon the midnight hour would come; but all the old olive-tree answered was 'Presently, presently,' and finally we, too, fell asleep, wearied by our long watching, and lulled by the rocking and swaying of the old olive-tree in the breezes of the night.

"'But who is this Master?' I asked.

"'A child, a little child,' they answered. 'He is called the little Master by the others. He comes here often, and plays among the flowers of the hill-side. Sometimes the lambs, gambolling too carelessly, have crushed and bruised us so that we lie bleeding and are like to die; but the little Master heals our wounds and refreshes us once again.'

"I marvelled much to hear these things. 'The midnight hour is at hand,' said I, 'and I will abide with you to see this little Master of whom you speak.' So we nestled among the verdure of the hill-side, and sang songs one to another.

"'Come away!' called the night wind; 'I know a beauteous sea not far hence, upon whose bosom you shall float, float, float away out into the mists and clouds, if you will come with me.'

"But I hid under the violets and amid the tall grass, that the night wind might not woo me with its pleading. 'Ho, there, old olive-tree!' cried the violets; 'do you see the little Master coming? Is not the midnight hour at hand?'

"'I can see the town yonder,' said the old olive-tree. 'A star beams bright over Bethlehem, the iron gates swing open, and the little Master comes.'

"Two children came to the hill-side. The one, older than his comrade, was Dimas, the son of Benoni. He was rugged and sinewy, and over his brown shoulders was flung a goatskin; a leathern cap did not confine his long, dark curly hair. The other child was he whom they called the little Master; about his slender form clung raiment white as snow, and around his face of heavenly innocence fell curls of golden yellow. So beautiful a child I had not seen before, nor have I ever since seen such as he. And as they came together to the hill-side, there seemed to glow about the little Master's head a soft white light, as if the moon had sent its tenderest, fairest beams to kiss those golden curls.

"'What sound was that?' cried Dimas, for he was exceeding fearful.

"'Have no fear, Dimas,' said the little Master. 'Give me thy hand, and I will lead thee.'

"Presently they came to the rock whereon Benoni, the shepherd, lay; and they stood under the old olive-tree, and the old olive-tree swayed no longer in the night wind, but bent its branches reverently in the presence of the little Master. It seemed as if the wind, too, stayed in its shifting course just then; for suddenly there was a solemn hush, and you could hear no noise, except that in his dreams Benoni spoke the Messiah's name.

"'Thy father sleeps,' said the little Master, 'and it is well that it is so; for that I love thee Dimas, and that thou shalt walk with me in my Father's kingdom, I would show thee the glories of my birthright.'

"Then all at once sweet music filled the air, and light, greater than the light of day, illumined the sky and fell upon all that hill-side. The heavens opened, and angels, singing joyous songs, walked to the earth. More wondrous still, the stars, falling from their places in the sky, clustered upon the old olive-tree, and swung hither and thither like colored lanterns. The flowers of the hill-side all awakened, and they, too, danced and sang. The angels, coming hither, hung gold and silver and jewels and precious stones upon the old olive, where swung the stars; so that the glory of that sight, though I might live forever, I shall never see again. When Dimas heard and saw these things he fell upon his knees, and catching the hem of the little Master's garment, he kissed it.

"'Greater joy than this shall be thine, Dimas,' said the little Master; 'but first must all things be fulfilled.'

"All through that Christmas night did the angels come and go with their sweet anthems; all through that Christmas night did the stars dance and sing; and when it came my time to steal away, the hill-side was still beautiful with the glory and the music of heaven."

"Well, is that all?" asked the old clock.

"No," said the moonbeam; "but I am nearly done. The years went on. Sometimes I tossed upon the ocean's bosom, sometimes I scampered o'er a battle-field, sometimes I lay upon a dead child's face. I heard the voices of Darkness and mothers' lullabies and sick men's prayers—and so the years went on.

"I fell one night upon a hard and furrowed face. It was of ghostly pallor. A thief was dying on the cross, and this was his wretched face. About the cross stood men with staves and swords and spears, but none paid heed unto the thief. Somewhat beyond this cross another was lifted up, and upon it was stretched a human body my light fell not upon. But I heard a voice that somewhere I had heard before,—though where I did not know,—and this voice blessed those that railed and jeered and shamefully entreated. And suddenly the voice called 'Dimas, Dimas!' and the thief upon whose hardened face I rested made answer.

"Then I saw that it was Dimas; yet to this wicked criminal there remained but little of the shepherd child whom I had seen in all his innocence upon the hill-side. Long years of sinful life had seared their marks into his face; yet now, at the sound of that familiar voice, somewhat of the old-time boyish look came back, and in the yearning of the anguished eyes I seemed to see the shepherd's son again.

"'The Master!' cried Dimas, and he stretched forth his neck that he might see him that spake.

"'O Dimas, how art thou changed!' cried the Master, yet there was in his voice no tone of rebuke save that which cometh of love.

"Then Dimas wept, and in that hour he forgot his pain. And the Master's consoling voice and the Master's presence there wrought in the dying criminal such a new spirit, that when at last his head fell upon his bosom, and the men about the cross said that he was dead, it seemed as if I shined not upon a felon's face, but upon the face of the gentle shepherd lad, the son of Benoni.

"And shining on that dead and peaceful face, I bethought me of the little Master's words that he had spoken under the old olive-tree upon the hill-side: 'Your eyes behold the promised glory now, O Dimas,' I whispered, 'for with the Master you walk in Paradise.'"

Ah, little Dear-my-Soul, you know—you know whereof the moonbeam spake. The shepherd's bones are dust, the flocks are scattered, the old olive-tree is gone, the flowers of the hill-side are withered, and none knoweth where the grave of Dimas is made. But last night, again, there shined a star over Bethlehem, and the angels descended from the sky to earth, and the stars sang together in glory. And the bells,—hear them, little Dear-my-Soul, how sweetly they are ringing,—the bells bear us the good tidings of great joy this Christmas morning, that our Christ is born, and that with him he bringeth peace on earth and good-will toward men.

CHRISTMAS MORNING
The angel host that sped last night,
Bearing the wondrous news afar,
Came in their ever-glorious flight
Unto a slumbering little star.
"Awake and sing, O star!" they cried."
Awake and glorify the morn!
Herald the tidings far and wide
—He that shall lead His flock is born!"
The little star awoke and sung
As only stars in rapture may,
And presently where church bells hung
The joyous tidings found their way.
"Awake, O bells! 'tis Christmas morn
—Awake and let thy music tell

To all mankind that now is born
What Shepherd loves His lambkins
well!"
Then rang the bells as fled the night
O'er dreaming land and drowsing
deep,
And coming with the morning light,
They called, my child, to you asleep.
Sweetly and tenderly they spoke
,And lingering round your little bed,
Their music pleaded till you woke,
And this is what their music said:
"Awake and sing! 't is Christmas
morn,
Whereon all earth salutes her King!
In Bethlehem is the Shepherd born.
Awake, O little lamb, and sing!"
So, dear my child, kneel at my feet,
And with those voices from above
Share thou this holy time with me,
The universal hymn of love.
December 25, 1890.

MISTRESS MERCILESS

This is to tell of our little Mistress Merciless, who for a season abided with us, but is now and forever gone from us unto the far-off land of Ever-Plaisance.

The tale is soon told; for it were not seemly to speak all the things that are in one's heart when one hath to say of a much-beloved child, whose life here hath been shortened so that, in God's wisdom and kindness, her life shall be longer in that garden that bloometh far away.

You shall know that all did call her Mistress Merciless; but her mercilessness was of a sweet, persuasive kind: for with the beauty of her face and the music of her voice and the exceeding sweetness of her virtues was she wont to slay all hearts; and this she did unwittingly, for she was a little child. And so it was in love that we did call her Mistress Merciless, just as it was in love that she did lord it over all our hearts.

Upon a time walked she in a full fair garden, and there went with her an handmaiden that we did call in merry wise the Queen of Sheba; for this handmaiden was in sooth no queen at all, but a sorry and ill-favored wench; but she was assotted upon our little Mistress Merciless and served her diligently, and for that good reason was vastly beholden of us all. Yet, in a jest, we called her the Queen of Sheba; and I make a venture that she looked exceeding fair in the eyes of our little Mistress Merciless: for the eyes of children look not upon the faces but into the hearts and souls of others.

Whilst these two walked in the full fair garden at that time they came presently unto an arbor wherein there was a rustic seat, which was called the Siege of Restfulness; and hereupon sate a little sick boy that, from his birth, had been lame, so that he could not play and make merry with other children, but was wont to come every day into this full fair garden and content himself with the companionship of the flowers. And, though he was a little lame boy, he never trod upon those flowers; and even had he done so, methinks the pressure of those crippled feet had been a caress, for the little lame boy was filled with the spirit of love and tenderness. As the tiniest, whitest, shrinking flower exhaleth the most precious perfume, so in and from this little lame boy's life there came a grace that was hallowing in its beauty.

Since they never before had seen him, they asked him his name; and he answered them that of those at home he was called Master Sweetheart, a name he could not understand: for surely, being a cripple, he must be a very sorry sweetheart; yet, that he was a sweetheart unto his mother at least he had no doubt, for she did love to hold him in her lap and call him by that name; and many times when she did so he saw that tears were in her eyes,—a proof, she told him when he asked, that Master Sweetheart was her sweetheart before all others upon earth.

It befell that our little Mistress Merciless and Master Sweetheart became fast friends, and the Queen of Sheba was handmaiden to them both; for the simple, loyal creature had not a mind above the artless prattle of childhood, and the strange allegory of the lame boy's speech filled her with awe, even as the innocent lisping of our little Mistress Merciless delighted her heart and came within the comprehension of her limited understanding. So each day, when it was fair, these three came into the full fair garden, and rambled there together; and when they were weary they entered into the arbor and sate together upon the Siege of Restfulness. Wit ye well there was not a flower or a tree or a shrub or a bird in all that full fair garden which they did not know and love, and in very sooth every flower and tree and shrub and bird therein did know and love them.

When they entered into the arbor, and sate together upon the Siege of Restfulness, it was Master Sweetheart's wont to tell them of the land of Ever-Plaisance, for it was a conceit of his that he journeyed each day nearer and nearer to that land, and that his journey thitherward was nearly done. How came he to know of that land I cannot say, for I do not know; but I am fain to believe that, as he said, the exceeding fair angels told him thereof when by night, as he lay sleeping, they came singing and with caresses to his bedside.

I speak now of a holy thing, therefore I speak truth when I say that while little children lie sleeping in their beds at night it pleaseth God to send His exceeding fair angels with singing and caresses to bear messages of His love unto those little sleeping children. And I have seen those exceeding fair angels bend with folded wings over the little cradles and the little beds, and kiss those little sleeping children and whisper God's messages of love to them, and I knew that those messages were full of sweet tidings; for, even though they slept, the little children smiled. This have I seen, and there is none who loveth little children that will deny the truth of this thing which I have now solemnly declared.

Of that land of Ever-Plaisance was our little Mistress Merciless ever fain to hear tell. But when she beset the rest of us to speak thereof we knew not what to say other than to confirm such reports as Master Sweetheart had already made. For when it cometh to knowing of that far-off land,—ah me, who knoweth more than the veriest little child? And oftentimes within the bosom of a little, helpless, fading one there bloometh a wisdom which sages cannot comprehend. So when she asked us we were wont to bid her go to Master Sweetheart, for he knew the truth and spake it.

It is now to tell of an adventure which on a time befell in that full fair garden of which you have heard me speak. In this garden lived many birds of surpassing beauty and most rapturous song, and among them was one that they called Joyous, for that he did ever carol forth so joyously, it mattered not what the day soever might be. This bird Joyous had his home in the top of an exceeding high tree, hard by the pleasant arbor, and here did he use to sit at such times as the little people came into that arbor, and then would he sing to them such songs as befitted that quiet spot, and them that came thereto. But there was a full evil cat that dwelt near by, and this cruel beast found no pleasure in the music that Joyous did make continually; nay, that music filled this full evil cat with a wicked thirst for the blood of that singing innocent, and she had no peace for the malice that was within her seeking to devise a means whereby she might comprehend the bird Joyous to her murderous intent. Now you must know that it was the wont of our little Mistress Merciless and of Master Sweetheart to feed the birds in that fair garden with such crumbs as they were suffered to bring with them into the arbor, and at such times would those birds fly down with grateful twitterings and eat of those crumbs upon the greensward round about the arbor. Wit ye well, it was a merry sight to see those twittering birds making feast upon the good things which those children brought, and our little Mistress Merciless and little Master Sweetheart had sweet satisfaction therein. But, on a day, whilst thus those twittering birds made great feasting, lo! on a sudden did that full evil cat whereof I have spoken steal softly from a thicket, and with one hideous bound make her way into the very midst of those birds and seize upon that bird Joyous, that was wont to sing so merrily from the tree hard by the arbor. Oh, there was a mighty din and a fearful fluttering, and the rest flew swiftly away, but Joyous could not do so, because the full evil cat held him in her cruel fangs and claws. And I make no doubt that Joyous would speedily have met his death, but that with a wrathful cry did our little Mistress Merciless hasten to his rescue. And our little Mistress belabored that full evil cat with Master Sweetheart's crutch, until that cruel beast let loose her hold upon the fluttering bird and was full glad to escape with her aching bones into the thicket again. So it was that Joyous was recovered from death; but even then might it have fared ill with him, had they not taken him up and dressed his wounds and cared for him until duly he was well again. And then they released him to do his plaisance, and he returned to his home in the tree hard by the arbor and there he sung unto those children more sweetly than ever before; for his heart was full of gratitude to our little Mistress Merciless and Master Sweetheart.

Now, of the dolls that she had in goodly number, that one which was named Beautiful did our little Mistress Merciless love best. Know well that the doll Beautiful had come not from oversea, and was neither of wax nor of china; but she was right ingeniously constructed of a bed-key that was made of wood, and unto the top of this bed-key had the Queen of Sheba superadded a head with a fair face, and upon the body and the arms of the key had she hung passing noble raiment. Unto this doll Beautiful was our little Mistress Merciless vastly beholden, and she did use to have the doll Beautiful lie by her side at night whilst she slept, and whithersoever during the day she went, there also would she take the doll Beautiful, too. Much sorrow and lamentation, therefore, made our little Mistress Merciless when on an evil day the doll Beautiful by chance fell into the fish-pond, and was not rescued therefrom until one of her beauteous eyes had been devoured of the envious water; so that ever thereafter the doll Beautiful had but one eye, and that, forsooth, was grievously faded. And on another evil day came a monster ribald dog pup and seized upon the doll Beautiful whilst she reposed in the arbor, and bore her away, and romped boisterously with her upon the sward, and tore off her black-thread hair, and sought to destroy her wholly, which surely he would have done but for the Queen of Sheba, who made haste to rescue the doll Beautiful, and chastise that monster ribald dog pup.

Therefore, as you can understand, the time was right busily spent. The full fair garden, with its flowers and the singing birds and the gracious arbor and the Siege of Restfulness, found favor with those children, and amid these joyous scenes did Master Sweetheart have to tell each day of that far-off land of Ever-Plaisance, whither he said he was going. And one day, when the sun shone very bright, and the full fair garden joyed in the music of those birds, Master Sweetheart did not come, and they missed the little lame boy and wondered where he was. And as he never came again they thought at last that of a surety he had departed into that country whereof he loved to tell. Which thing filled our little Mistress Merciless with wonder and inquiry; and I think she was lonely ever after that,—lonely for Master Sweetheart.

I am thinking now of her and of him; for this is the Christmas season,— the time when it is most meet to think of the children and other sweet and holy things. There is snow everywhere, snow and cold. The garden is desolate and voiceless: the flowers are gone, the trees are ghosts, the birds have departed. It is winter out there, and it is winter, too, in this heart of mine. Yet in this Christmas season I think of them, and it pleaseth me—God forbid that I offend with much speaking—it pleaseth me to tell of the little things they did and loved. And you shall understand it all if, perchance, this sacred Christmas time a little Mistress Merciless of your own, or a little Master Sweetheart, clingeth to your knee and sanctifieth your hearth-stone.

When of an evening all the joy of day was done, would our little Mistress Merciless fall aweary; and then her eyelids would grow exceeding heavy and her little tired hands were fain to fold. At such a time it was my wont to beguile her weariness with little tales of faery, or with the gentle play that sleepy children like. Much was her fancy taken with what I told her of the train that every night whirleth away to Shut-Eye Town, bearing unto that beauteous country sleepy little girls and boys. Nor would she be content until I told her thereof,—yes, every night whilst I robed her in her cap and gown would she demand of me that tale of Shut-Eye Town, and the wonderful train that was to bear her thither. Then would I say in this wise:

At Bedtime-ville there is a train of cars that waiteth for you, my sweet,—for you and for other little ones that would go to quiet, slumbrous Shut-Eye Town.

But make no haste; there is room for all. Each hath a tiny car that is snug and warm, and when the train starteth each car swingeth soothingly this way and that way, this way and that way, through all the journey of the night.

Your little gown is white and soft; your little cap will hold those pretty curls so fast that they cannot get away. Here is a curl that peepeth out to see what is going to happen. Hush, little curl! make no noise; we will let you peep out at the wonderful sights, but you must not tell the others about it; let them sleep, snuggled close together.

The locomotive is ready to start. Can you not hear it?

"Shug-chug! Shug-chug! Shug-chug!" That is what the locomotive is saying, all to itself. It knoweth how pleasant a journey it is about to make.

"Shug-chug! Shug-chug! Shug-chug!"

Oh, many a time hath it proudly swept over prairie and hill, over river and plain, through sleeping gardens and drowsy cities, swiftly and quietly, bearing the little ones to the far, pleasant valley where lieth Shut-Eye Town.

"Shug-chug! Shug-chug! Shug-chug!"

So sayeth the locomotive to itself at the station in Bedtime-ville; for it knoweth how fair and far a journey is before it.

Then a bell soundeth. Surely my little one heareth the bell!

"Ting-long! Ting-a-long! Ting-long!"

So soundeth the bell, and it seemeth to invite you to sleep and dreams.

"Ting-long! Ting-a-long! Ting-long!"

How sweetly ringeth and calleth that bell.

"To sleep—to dreams, O little lambs!" it seemeth to call. "Nestle down close, fold your hands, and shut your dear eyes! We are off and away to Shut-Eye Town! Ting-long! Ting-a-long! Ting-long! To sleep—to dreams, O little cosset lambs!"

And now the conductor calleth out in turn. "All aboard!" he calleth. "All aboard for Shut-Eye Town!" he calleth in a kindly tone.

But, hark ye, dear-my-soul, make thou no haste; there is room for all. Here is a cosey little car for you. How like your cradle it is, for it is snug and warm, and it rocketh this way and that way, this way and that way, all night long, and its pillows caress you tenderly. So step into the pretty nest, and in it speed to Shut-Eye Town.

"Toot! Toot!"

That is the whistle. It soundeth twice, but it must sound again before the train can start. Now you have nestled down, and your dear hands are folded; let your two eyes be folded, too, my sweet; for in a moment you shall be rocked away, and away, away into the golden mists of Balow!

"Ting-long! Ting-a-long! Ting-long!"

"All aboard!"

"Toot! Toot! Toot!"

And so my little golden apple is off and away for Shut-Eye Town!

Slowly moveth the train, yet faster by degrees. Your hands are folded, my beloved, and your dear eyes they are closed; and yet you see the beauteous sights that skirt the journey through the mists of Balow. And it is rockaway, rockaway, rockaway, that your speeding cradle goes,—rockaway, rockaway, rockaway, through the golden glories that lie in the path that leadeth to Shut-Eye Town.

"Toot! Toot!"

So crieth the whistle, and it is "down-brakes," for here we are at Ginkville, and every little one knoweth that pleasant waking-place, where mother with her gentle hands holdeth the gracious cup to her sleepy darling's lips.

"Ting-long! Ting-a-long! Ting-long!" and off is the train again. And swifter and swifter it speedeth,—oh, I am sure no other train speedeth half so swiftly! The sights my dear one sees! I cannot tell of them—one must see those beauteous sights to know how wonderful they are!

"Shug-chug! Shug-chug! Shug-chug!"

On and on and on the locomotive proudly whirleth the train.

"Ting-long! Ting-a-long! Ting-long!"

The bell calleth anon, but fainter and evermore fainter; and fainter and fainter groweth that other calling—"Toot! Toot! Toot!"—till finally I know that in that Shut-Eye Town afar my dear one dreameth the dreams of Balow.

This was the bedtime tale which I was wont to tell our little Mistress Merciless, and at its end I looked upon her face to see it calm and beautiful in sleep.

Then was I wont to kneel beside her little bed and fold my two hands,—thus,—and let my heart call to the host invisible: "O guardian angels of this little child, hold her in thy keeping from all the perils of darkness and the night! O sovereign Shepherd, cherish Thy little lamb and mine, and, Holy Mother, fold her to thy bosom and thy love! But give her back to me,—when morning cometh, restore ye unto me my little one!"

But once she came not back. She had spoken much of Master Sweetheart and of that land of Ever-Plaisance whither he had gone. And she was not afeard to make the journey alone; so once upon a time when our little Mistress Merciless bade us good-by, and went away forever, we knew that it were better so; for she was lonely here, and without her that far-distant country whither she journeyed were not content. Though our hearts were like to break for love of her, we knew that it were better so.

The tale is told, for it were not seemly to speak all the things that are in one's heart when one hath to say of a much-beloved child whose life here hath been shortened so that, in God's wisdom and kindness, her life shall be longer in that garden that bloometh far away.

About me are scattered the toys she loved, and the doll Beautiful hath come down all-battered and grim,—yet, oh! so very precious to me, from those distant years; yonder fareth the Queen of Sheba in her service as handmaiden unto me and mine,—gaunt and doleful-eyed, yet stanch and sturdy as of old. The garden lieth under the Christmas snow,—the garden where ghosts of trees wave their arms and moan over the graves of flowers; the once gracious arbor is crippled now with the infirmities of age, the Siege of Restfulness fast sinketh into decay, and long, oh! long ago did that bird Joyous carol forth his last sweet song in the garden that was once so passing fair.

And amid it all,—this heartache and the loneliness which the years have brought,—cometh my Christmas gift to-day: the solace of a vision of that country whither she—our little Mistress Merciless—hath gone; a glimpse of that far-off land of Ever-Plaisance.

———————

BETHLEHEM-TOWN

As I was going to Bethlehem-town,

Upon the earth I cast me down
All underneath a little tree
That whispered in this wise to
me:"Oh, I shall stand on Calvary
And bear what burthen saveth thee!"
As up I fared to Bethlehem-town,
I met a shepherd coming down,
And thus he quoth: "A wondrous
sight
Hath spread before mine eyes this
night,
—An angel host most fair to see,
That sung full sweetly of a treeThat
shall uplift on Calvary
What burthen saveth you and me!"
And as I gat to Bethlehem-town,
Lo! wise men came that bore a
crown."Is there," cried I, "in Bethlehem
A King shall wear this
diadem?""Good sooth," they quoth,
"and it is
HeThat shall be lifted on the tree
And freely shed on Calvary
What blood redeemeth us and thee!"
Unto a Child in Bethlehem-town
The wise men came and brought the
crown;
And while the infant smiling slept,
Upon their knees they fell and wept;
But, with her babe upon her knee,
Naught recked that Mother of the
tree,
That should uplift on Calvary
What burthen saveth all and me.
Again I walk in Bethlehem-town
And think on Him that wears the
crown.
I may not kiss His feet again,
Nor worship Him as did I then;
My King hath died upon the tree,
And hath outpoured on Calvary
What blood redeemeth you and me!

THE FIRST CHRISTMAS TREE

Once upon a time the forest was in a great commotion. Early in the evening the wise old cedars had shaken their heads ominously and predicted strange things. They had lived in the forest many, many years; but never had they seen such marvellous sights as were to be seen now in the sky, and upon the hills, and in the distant village.

"Pray tell us what you see," pleaded a little vine; "we who are not as tall as you can behold none of these wonderful things. Describe them to us, that we may enjoy them with you."

"I am filled with such amazement," said one of the cedars, "that I can hardly speak. The whole sky seems to be aflame, and the stars appear to be dancing among the clouds; angels walk down from heaven to the earth, and enter the village or talk with the shepherds upon the hills."

The vine listened in mute astonishment. Such things never before had happened. The vine trembled with excitement. Its nearest neighbor was a tiny tree, so small it scarcely ever was noticed; yet it was a very beautiful little tree, and the vines and ferns and mosses and other humble residents of the forest loved it dearly.

"How I should like to see the angels!" sighed the little tree, "and how I should like to see the stars dancing among the clouds! It must be very beautiful."

As the vine and the little tree talked of these things, the cedars watched with increasing interest the wonderful scenes over and beyond the confines of the forest. Presently they thought they heard music, and they were not mistaken, for soon the whole air was full of the sweetest harmonies ever heard upon earth.

"What beautiful music!" cried the little tree. "I wonder whence it comes."

"The angels are singing," said a cedar; "for none but angels could make such sweet music."

"But the stars are singing, too," said another cedar; "yes, and the shepherds on the hills join in the song, and what a strangely glorious song it is!"

The trees listened to the singing, but they did not understand its meaning: it seemed to be an anthem, and it was of a Child that had been born; but further than this they did not understand. The strange and glorious song continued all the night; and all that night the angels walked to and fro, and the shepherd-folk talked with the angels, and the stars danced and carolled in high heaven.

And it was nearly morning when the cedars cried out, "They are coming to the forest! the angels are coming to the forest!" And, surely enough, this was true. The vine and the little tree were very terrified, and they begged their older and stronger neighbors to protect them from harm. But the cedars were too busy with their own fears to pay any heed to the faint pleadings of the humble vine and the little tree. The angels came into the forest, singing the same glorious anthem about the Child, and the stars sang in chorus with them, until every part of the woods rang with echoes of that wondrous song. There was nothing in the appearance of this angel host to inspire fear; they were clad all in white, and there were crowns upon their fair heads, and golden harps in their hands; love, hope, charity, compassion, and joy beamed from their beautiful faces, and their presence seemed to fill the forest with a divine peace. The angels came through the forest to where the little tree stood, and gathering around it, they touched it with their hands, and kissed its little branches, and sang even more sweetly than before. And their song was about the Child, the Child, the Child that had been born. Then the stars came down from the skies and danced and hung upon the branches of the tree, and they, too, sang that song,—the song of the Child. And all the other trees and the vines and the ferns and the mosses beheld in wonder; nor could they understand why all these things were being done, and why this exceeding honor should be shown the little tree.

When the morning came the angels left the forest,—all but one angel, who remained behind and lingered near the little tree. Then a cedar asked: "Why do you tarry with us, holy angel?" And the angel answered: "I stay to guard this little tree, for it is sacred, and no harm shall come to it."

The little tree felt quite relieved by this assurance, and it held up its head more confidently than ever before. And how it thrived and grew, and waxed in strength and beauty! The cedars said they never had seen the like. The sun seemed to lavish its choicest rays upon the little tree, heaven dropped its sweetest dew upon it, and the winds never came to the forest that they did not forget their rude manners and linger to kiss the little tree and sing it their prettiest songs. No danger ever menaced it, no harm threatened; for the angel never slept,—through the day and through the night the angel watched the little tree and protected it from all evil.

Oftentimes the trees talked with the angel; but of course they understood little of what he said, for he spoke always of the Child who was to become the Master; and always when thus he talked, he caressed the little tree, and stroked its branches and leaves, and moistened them with his tears. It all was so very strange that none in the forest could understand.

So the years passed, the angel watching his blooming charge. Sometimes the beasts strayed toward the little tree and threatened to devour its tender foliage; sometimes the woodman came with his axe, intent upon hewing down the straight and comely thing; sometimes the hot, consuming breath of drought swept from the south, and sought to blight the forest and all its verdure: the angel kept them from the little tree. Serene and beautiful it grew, until now it was no longer a little tree, but the pride and glory of the forest.

One day the tree heard some one coming through the forest. Hitherto the angel had hastened to its side when men approached; but now the angel strode away and stood under the cedars yonder.

"Dear angel," cried the tree, "can you not hear the footsteps of some one approaching? Why do you leave me?"

"Have no fear," said the angel; "for He who comes is the Master."

The Master came to the tree and beheld it. He placed His hands upon its smooth trunk and branches, and the tree was thrilled with a strange and glorious delight. Then He stooped and kissed the tree, and then He turned and went away.

Many times after that the Master came to the forest, and when He came it always was to where the tree stood. Many times He rested beneath the tree and enjoyed the shade of its foliage, and listened to the music of the wind as it swept through the rustling leaves. Manytimes He slept there, and the tree watched over Him, and the forest was still, and all its voices were hushed. And the angel hovered near like a faithful sentinel.

Ever and anon men came with the Master to the forest, and sat with Him in the shade of the tree, and talked with Him of matters which the tree never could understand; only it heard that the talk was of love and charity and gentleness, and it saw that the Master was beloved and venerated by the others. It heard them tell of the Master's goodness and humility,—how He had healed the sick and raised the dead and bestowed inestimable blessings wherever He walked. And the tree loved the Master for His beauty and His goodness; and when He came to the forest it was full of joy, but when He came not it was sad. And the other trees of the forest joined in its happiness and its sorrow, for they, too, loved the Master. And the angel always hovered near.

The Master came one night alone into the forest, and His face was pale with anguish and wet with tears, and He fell upon His knees and prayed. The tree heard Him, and all the forest was still, as if it were standing in the presence of death. And when the morning came, lo! the angel had gone.

Then there was a great confusion in the forest. There was a sound of rude voices, and a clashing of swords and staves. Strange men appeared, uttering loud oaths and cruel threats, and the tree was filled with terror. It called aloud for the angel, but the angel came not.

"Alas," cried the vine, "they have come to destroy the tree, the pride and glory of the forest!"

The forest was sorely agitated, but it was in vain. The strange men plied their axes with cruel vigor, and the tree was hewn to the ground. Its beautiful branches were cut away and cast aside, and its soft, thick foliage was strewn to the tenderer mercies of the winds.

"They are killing me!" cried the tree; "why is not the angel here to protect me?"

But no one heard the piteous cry,— none but the other trees of the forest; and they wept, and the little vine wept too.

Then the cruel men dragged the despoiled and hewn tree from the forest, and the forest saw that beauteous thing no more.

But the night wind that swept down from the City of the Great King that night to ruffle the bosom of distant Galilee, tarried in the forest awhile to say that it had seen that day a cross upraised on Calvary,—the tree on which was stretched the body of the dying Master.

STAR OF THE EAST

Star of the East, that long ago
Brought wise men on their way
Where, angels singing to and fro,
The Child of Bethlehem lay
—Above that Syrian hill afar
Thou shinest out to-night, O Star!
Star of the East, the night were drear
But for the tender grace
That with thy glory comes to cheer
Earth's loneliest, darkest place;
For by that charity we see
Where there is hope for all and me.
Star of the East! show us the way
In wisdom undefiled
To seek that manger out and lay
Our gifts before the child
—To bring our hearts and offer them
Unto our King in Bethlehem!

Printed in Great Britain
by Amazon